THE ROOTS
OF
CHRISTIAN
MYSTICISM

Olivier Clément

THE ROOTS
OF
CHRISTIAN
MYSTICISM

Texts from the Patristic Era
with Commentary

New City Press
Hyde Park, New York

Published in the United States by New City Press
202 Comforter Blvd., Hyde Park, NY 12538
©1993 English Translation New City, London

Translated by Theodore Berkeley, O.C.S.O. and Jeremy
Hummerstone from the original French edition *Sources*
©1982 Éditions Stock, Paris

Cover picture: La résurrection by ARCABAS
Eglise de Saint Hugues de Chartreuse, France

Library of Congress Cataloging-in-Publication Data:

Clément, Olivier.
    [Sources. English]
    The roots of Christian mysticism : text and commentary / Olivier
Clément.

    Includes bibliographical references and index.
    ISBN 1-56548-029-5
    1. Mysticism—History—Early church, ca. 30-600. 2. Fathers of
the church. I. Title.
    BV5075.C5713   1995
    248.2'2'09015—dc 20   94-32957

1st U.S. printing: November 1995
10th printing: November 2011

Printed in the United States of America

CONTENTS

PART THREE: Approaches to Contemplation

PREFACE

Christianity is in the first place an Oriental religion, and it is a mystical religion. These assertions sound strange today, in an age when it is generally assumed that to be a Christian means to lead a good life. As for prayer, what does that amount to but a set of exercises which are both pointless and tedious? Nevertheless, whilst our consumer society has lost all feeling for mysticism, on the fringes there are thousands of people thirsting for it. When we see the shallow syncretism, the sentimental fascination with anything Eastern, and the bogus 'gurus' crowding round for the pickings, it is easy to sneer. But instead of laughing the Churches ought to be examining their consciences. Whose fault is it that so many have to resort to Tao or Zen in order to rediscover truths which were actually part of the Christian heritage right from the beginning? Who has hidden from them the fact that of all Oriental religions Christianity is the best and most complete; that mysticism is as necessary to humanity as science, if not more so? Intellectual research may be exciting, but it will not lead us to the secret of life. Nor will the truth be found through consumerism, though of course we must eat. Nor will it be found through action, although action is inevitable if we are to restrain our tendency to exploit one another. The researcher, the consumer, the politician are merely the avatars of a much deeper human nature. Intellectual knowledge, possession, action, all express a desire which transcends them. The human being is a craftsman - *faber* - and rational - *sapiens* - qualities which we share with the higher animals (the difference between us being one of degree and not of kind), but more importantly than that, we are mystical. In other words our roots are in fact religious and artistic, and therefore non-rational, or rather supra-rational. As soon as our material needs are satisfied, deeper needs assert themselves. It is now twenty centuries since Jesus declared that 'man does not

live by bread alone', and we know today that not even the most
effective psychoanalytical treatment can cure us of a deep sense of
disquiet within us. There is not a superman or revolutionary who
is not beset by unappeased desires. The Fathers of the Christian
Church, for whom prayer was as natural as breathing, discovered
this truth before we did, saying, 'Birds fly, fishes swim and man
prays'. Islamic spiritual writers would later express the same idea,
saying that the first cry of the new-born babe and the last breath of
the dying person together make up and proclaim the divine name.

This anthology of the first Christian mystics therefore meets an
urgent need, that of rediscovering the mystical sources of Christianity.
It is not so much an anthology as a selection of passages with
an extended and lively commentary. The authors represented here
do not appear in chronological or alphabetical order. The extracts
are arranged according to a theological plan, since the book deals
specifically with 'Christian' mystics, those whose spirituality bears
the deep marks of the revelation received from God. Most of these
texts are hard to find, and many have been out of print for a
long time. Some of them will seem astonishingly modern, others
more obscure, but all should prove interesting. For mysticism is an
existential attitude, a way of living at a greater depth. It is not the
possession of any one religion or of any one Church; even atheists can
be mystics. But perhaps Christianity with its fresh vitality was able to
reconcile negation and affirmation in a new way. Perhaps it was able
to unite together the divine and the human whilst neither confusing
nor separating them. That vitality is still possible today; indeed the
very future of the human race depends upon it. It is my hope that
Olivier Clément's fine work will convince the reader of this truth.

Jean-Claude Barreau

INTRODUCTION

This book is intended not so much to popularize its subject as to make it known in the first place. Not only is Christianity something strange to people today, but it cannot even attract by its strangeness, because people are familiar with the distortions and caricatures of it which are constantly being hawked about. Therefore, in response to many requests, I have tried to allow the chief witnesses of the undivided Church to speak for themselves, to make audible the voice of Tradition, from which all the Churches spring and which alone enables them to share in an 'ecumenism in time', by recalling the experience in which they had their common origin.

Tradition is not a written text with which we can choose to agree or disagree; it is not material suitable for dissection by scholars. It is the expression of the Spirit *juvenescens*, as Irenæus of Lyons says, 'in its youthfulness'. It is of course our foundation history, but it is also a living force, a tremendous 'passover', a passing over from the God-man to God-humanity and to the universe, to quote the Russian religious philosophers, whose disciple I gladly acknowledge myself to be.

There can be no doubt that since the fourth or seventh century our spiritual awareness has changed profoundly. We live in the aftermath of Auschwitz, Hiroshima and the Gulag. Christendom, the society in which Christianity was, to the great detriment of freedom, the dominant ideology, has finally collapsed, and we can no longer talk about matters of faith in the way that we used to do. The living God is no longer the Emperor of the World but crucified Love. Remember that many of the witnesses whose voices we are about to hear lived in times of persecution, when society veered between scepticism on the one hand and various forms of *gnosis* on the other. Others lived during the emergence of the monastic movement, which, in the face of the blandishments of the 'establishment', sternly and

recklessly asserted the irreducible nonconformity of the person who
is 'drunk with God', the one who, 'after God, regards his brother
as God'. Newman compared the early history of the Church to the
opening chords of a symphony, when the subjects which will later be
brought out one by one are introduced all together in a concentrated
burst of creativity. It was in 553, after all, that the Fifth Ecumenical
Council reaffirmed that God 'suffered death in the flesh'. In making
my selection I have been guided by Tradition, continuing into our
own time, which is a time of darkness worthy of a vision of
Dostoyevsky, teeming with expectations and intuitions, while seeds
of fire multiply in the earth beneath.

The witnesses whose words I have gathered are known as 'the
Fathers'. Some of these first mystics were martyrs, others were monks
in the mountains and deserts. Others were great minds illuminated
by the Spirit, which penetrated even through their foolishness (which
Tradition has been able to balance against the *consensus* of other
Fathers). Many were bishops, elected by their people to be pastors of
local churches, secure and independent at the heart of their spiritual
communities, where they preached the only 'good news' which can
possibly reach us today in our state of hopeless nihilism: the 'descent'
of the God-made-man into death and hell so that he might triumph
over death and hell in whatever shape they appear.

In those days mysticism was not analysed in terms of religious
psychology as it is in the West today. The whole of life, the whole
universe was interpreted in the light of Christ's death and resurrection, which was the key to understanding all significant processes
of change. A few individuals, to be sure, shone out like candles
or torches. But 'the light and the fire' which was concentrated in
them is offered to all in the dazzling flesh of the Bible and the
sacraments, through the Church which is the 'mystery' of Him
who was crucified and is risen, who restores us to life and brings
about in himself the transfiguration of the cosmos. The state of
'ecclesial being', to adopt the expression of a modern Greek theologian, was a fact of experience for the person in communion, for whom
humanity and the universe were of their very nature 'resurrectional'
and paschal. This understanding far transcends our endless debates
about the Church as an 'institution'.

This book first approaches the subject doctrinally, reflecting *in* the
mystery rather than *on* it, because we must not only love God, but
must love him, as the Gospel says, 'with all our mind'. Then we deal
with the path of *ascesis*, that 'spiritual combat, harder than the battles
of men', the objective of which, however, is to let go. Finally we come

to contemplation, which is expressed most clearly in a capacity for loving, with a love that is creative, because it is an activity shared with the incarnate and crucified God. This book will also, we hope, make it possible to judge more precisely where Christianity stands in relation to other world religions and to the various forms of atheism. Indeed, as we consider the basic themes of the Three-in-One and the Divine humanity, the universal and traditional experience of the divine may come to appear no less clear and compelling than the modern Western experience of the human.

The following pages therefore contain:

1. Texts, translated so as to appeal as directly as possible to non-specialists. Slight transpositions or adaptations have been made here and there the better to convey the spirit of the original.

2. An accompanying commentary which goes some way to compensate for the necessarily fragmentary and disjointed selection of texts, and which in itself forms a kind of essay.

3. Notes at the end of the book in alphabetical order of authors quoted, referring to the works from which the texts have been taken. These notes provide the indispensable historical element, describing briefly the characters and lives of the writers, and helping us to distinguish the ephemeral from the lasting, or, in the communion of saints, from the eternal. Finally, I have added notes on Arianism, Early Monasticism and Monophysitism.

Olivier Clément

ABBREVIATIONS

Bickell I   G. Bickell, *Ausgewählte Gedichte der Syrischen Kirchenväter*, Kempten, 1872.

Bickell II   G. Bickell, *Ausgewählte Schriften der Syrischen Kirchenväter*, Kempten, 1874.

CSCO   *Corpus Scriptorum Christianorum Orientalium*, Louvain.

CSEL   *Corpus Scriptorum Ecclesiasticorum Latinorum*, Louvain.

GCS   *Griechische Christliche Schriftsteller*, Berlin.

Ichthys   *Collection Ichthys, Littératures Chrétiennes*, A. Hamman, Paris, later Grasset, later Centurion.

Philokalia   *Philocalie des Pères neptiques*, Astir, Athens.

PL   *Patrologia Latina*, Migne.

PG   *Patrologia Græca*, Migne.

PO   *Patrologia Orientalis*, Paris.

SC   *Sources Chrétiennes*, Cerf, Paris.

SO   *Spiritualité Orientale*, Bellefontaine Abbey.

PART ONE

Understanding the Mystery

1

Quest, Encounter, and Decision

Human beings are mere scraps of life, here only for an instant. We live a 'dead life', according to Gregory of Nyssa, in a world permeated by death, in which everything gravitates continually towards nothingness. And this is the root of all our ill. For unlike the animals, we know we are going to die.

But our very anguish is a source of grace, for it betrays a longing for being and unity, a yearning to know the Being and the One. The anguish and the grace are a constant theme of Augustine of Hippo, the Western Church Father. We may find him somewhat schematic, but his cry from the heart demands to be heard.

> Brethren, do our years last? They slip away day by day. Those which were, no longer are; those to come are not yet here. The former are past, the latter will come, only to pass away in their turn. Today exists only in the moment in which we speak. Its first hours have passed, the remainder do not yet exist; they will come, but only to fall into nothingness ... Nothing contains constancy in itself. The body does not possess being: it has no permanence. It changes with age, it changes with time and place, it changes with illness and accident. The stars have as little constancy; they change in hidden ways, they go whirling through space ... they are not steady, they do not possess being.
>
> Nor is the human heart any more constant. How many thoughts disturb it, how many ambitions! How many pleasures draw it this way and that, tearing it apart! The human spirit itself, although endowed with reason, changes; it does not possess being. It wills and does not will; it knows and does not know; it remembers and forgets. No one has in himself the unity of being ... After so many sufferings, diseases, troubles and pains, let us return

humbly to that One Being. Let us enter into that city whose inhabitants share in Being itself.

AUGUSTINE OF HIPPO *Commentary on Psalm 121, 6* (PL 36,1623)

It is true that human beings have been eager 'to achieve unity by themselves, to be their own masters and to depend only on themselves' (ibid.). But that is an adventure like Lucifer's which leaves us in pure nihilism. That is why *metanoia*, the great 'turning round' of the mind and heart, and of our whole grasp of reality,

is the daughter of hope. It is the renunciation of despair.

JOHN CLIMACUS *The Ladder of Divine Ascent*, 5th step, 2
(Astir, Athens 1970, p. 51)

This is a matter not of mere speculation, but of life or death, of life stronger than death:

for communion with God is life, and separation from God is death.

IRENÆUS OF LYONS *Against Heresies*, V,27,2 (SC 153, p. 342)

A life without eternity is unworthy of the name of life. Only eternal life is true.

AUGUSTINE OF HIPPO *Sermon 346,1* (PL 38,1522)

That is still true, even though turning to God is generally considered madness these days, even more than it was in the Roman Empire at the peak of its glory. There is a sort of sleep of the soul and people hope to escape death by sleep-walking, or by losing themselves in frantic activity.

Abbot Anthony says, 'A time is coming when people will go mad, and when they meet someone who is not mad, they will turn to him and say, "You are out of your mind," just because he is not like them.'

Sayings of the Desert Fathers Anthony, 25 (PG 65,84)

Anguish and despair are not the only starting point. There is also our sense of wonder, and the riddle which we perceive in the order and beauty of the world on the one hand, and all the events of history on the other.

Through intelligent and beautiful forms of creation the invisible gives structure and balance to the visible, but the means employed are gravity, death, disintegration. Humanity likewise, consciously or not, draws from the invisible not only the very idea of justice but also the high demands of knowledge and art and the possibility of those laws that set a limit to violence and protect friendship.

> Who gave you the ability to contemplate the beauty of the skies, the course of the sun, the round moon, the millions of stars, the harmony and rhythm that issue from the world as from a lyre, the return of the seasons, the alternation of the months, the demarcation of day and night, the fruits of the earth, the vastness of the air, the ceaseless motion of the waves, the sound of the wind? Who gave you the rain, the soil to cultivate, food to eat, arts, houses, laws, a republic, cultivated manners, friendship with your fellows?
>
> GREGORY NAZIANZEN *On love for the poor*, 23 (PG 35,273)

Through anguish and wonder humanity has some inkling of the great depth of divine wisdom. But no full understanding is possible; only a holy fear, a trembling in the face of the immeasurable.

> 'Such knowledge is too wonderful for me' (Psalm 139.6). 'I praise thee, for thou art fearful and wonderful' (ibid. v. 14) . . . There are many things at which we marvel without fear, for example the beauty of architecture, the masterpieces of painting, or the glory of the human form. We also marvel at the vastness and infinite depth of the sea, but to be above that depth is also terrifying. In the same way the sacred writer as he leaned out over the infinite abyss of God's wisdom was seized with giddiness. Filled with wonder he drew back trembling, and said, 'I praise thee, for thou art fearful and wonderful. Wonderful are thy works.' And again: 'Such knowledge is too wonderful for me; it is high, I cannot attain it.'
>
> JOHN CHRYSOSTOM *On the incomprehensibility of God*, I (PG 48, 705)

We can see the whole process displayed in the life of a certain Hilary of Poitiers, a fourth century Roman-French citizen remarkable for his relevance to ourselves. The élite of the declining Roman

Empire lived in an intellectual climate very like our own; materialism
and scepticism, together with dabblings in syncretist beliefs, were
resulting in a mixture very different from the ancient religions, which
had long ago been rendered obsolete by rationalism and the discovery
of the individual. In short, what was then true of restricted urban
groups is now true of everybody.

Hilary quickly took the measure of a society bent upon instant
gratification, and, driven on by his horror at the prospect of purpose-
lessness and nothingness, set out on the search for the meaning of life.
Passing rapidly through stupid materialism and decaying paganism
and pseudo-scientific occultism, he discovered in the biblical teaching
of the Jews the living God who transcends all things yet is present
in them, outside everything yet inside, the ex-centric centre, the
'author of beauty' disclosed in the beauty of the world. But only
the Gospel of the Word-made-flesh, the Gospel of the resurrection
of the flesh, could assure him that he would not be 'reduced to
non-being': that he, Hilary, was an irreplaceable person and would
be wholly loved and saved, body and soul, by the combination
of grace and his own freedom.

> I began the search for the meaning of life. At first I was attracted by
> riches and leisure . . . But most people discover that human nature
> wants something better to do than just gormandize and kill time.
> They have been given life in order to achieve something worth
> while, to make use of their talents. It could not have been given
> them without some benefit in eternity. How otherwise could one
> regard as a gift from God a life so eaten away by anguish, so riddled
> with vexation, which left to itself would simply wear out, from the
> prattle of the cradle to the drivel of senility? Look at people who
> have practised patience, chastity and forgiveness. The good life for
> them meant good deeds and good thoughts. Could the immortal
> God have given us life with no other horizon but death? Could
> he have inspired us with such a desire to live, if the only outcome
> would be the horror of death? . . .
>
> Then I sought to know God better . . . Some religions teach
> that there are different families of deities. They imagine male gods
> and female ones and can trace the lineage of these gods born
> from one another. Other religions teach that there are greater
> and lesser deities, with different attributes. Some claim that there
> is no God at all and worship nature, which, according to them,
> came about purely by chance. Most, however, admit that God
> exists, but hold him to be indifferent to human beings . . . I

was reflecting on these problems when I discovered the books which the Jewish religion says were composed by Moses and the prophets. There I discovered that God bears witness to himself in these terms: 'I am who I am,' and: 'Say this to the people of Israel, "I AM has sent me to you"' (Exodus 3.14). I was filled with wonder at this perfect definition which translates into intelligible words the incomprehensible knowledge of God. Nothing better suggests God than Being. 'He who is' can have neither end nor beginning ... And since God's eternity cannot contradict itself, in order to assert his unapproachable eternity, God needed only to assert solemnly that he is.

But it was necessary also to recognize God's work ...

'Who has measured the waters in the hollow of his hand and marked off the heavens with a span?' (Isaiah 40.12).

and later:

'Heaven is my throne and the earth is my footstool ... All these things my hand has made' (Isaiah 66.1-2).

The whole heavens are held in God's hand, the whole earth in the hollow of his hand ... The heaven is also his throne and the earth his footstool. We should certainly avoid too human an image of God, as someone sitting on a throne with his feet on a footstool. His throne and footstool are his infinite omnipotence, which embraces everything in the hollow of his hand. The imagery borrowed from created things signifies that God exists in them and outside them, that he both transcends and pervades them, that he surpasses all creatures and yet dwells in them. The hollow of his hand symbolizes the power of his divinity revealing itself. The throne and the footstool show he controls external objects because he is within them, but at the same time he envelops them and encloses them within himself. He is inside and outside everything ... Nothing is beyond the reach of the one who is infinite ... What came to light as a result of my search was well expressed by the prophet:

'Whither shall I go from thy Spirit?

Or whither shall I flee from thy presence?

If I ascend to heaven, thou art there!

If I make my bed in Sheol, thou art there!

If I take the wings of the morning and dwell in the uttermost parts of the sea,

even there thy hand shall lead me, and thy right hand shall hold me' (Psalm 139.7-10).

There is no place without God; place does not exist except in
God . . .

I was happy contemplating the mystery of his wisdom and his
unapproachableness. I worshipped the eternity and immeasurable
greatness of my Father and Creator. But I longed also to behold
the beauty of my Lord . . . My ardour, deceived by the weakness
of my mind, was trapped in its own search, when I discovered in
the words of the prophet this magnificent thought about God:

'For from the greatness and beauty of created things comes a
corresponding perception of their Creator' (Wisdom 13.5).

The sky and the air are beautiful, the earth and the sea are
beautiful. By divine grace the universe was called by the Greeks
'cosmos', meaning 'ornament' . . . Surely the author of all created
beauty must himself be the beauty in all beauty? . . . But if we are
blessed with an intuition of God, what shall we gain from it if death
does away with all feeling and puts an irrevocable end to a weary existence? . . . My mind was bewildered, trembling for itself and for its
body. It was troubled at its fate and that of the body in which it was
dwelling when, following on from the Law and the Prophets, I made
the acquaintance of the teaching of the Gospel and of the apostles:

'In the beginning was the Word, and the Word was with God,
and the Word was God. He was in the beginning with God; all
things were made through him, and without him was not anything
made that was made. In him was life, and life was the light of men.
The light shines in darkness, and the darkness has not overcome
it . . . The true light that enlightens every man was coming into
the world. He was in the world, and the world was made through
him, yet the world knew him not . . . But to all who received him,
who believed in his name, he gave power to become children of
God . . . And the Word became flesh and dwelt among us, full of
grace and truth; we have beheld his glory, glory as of the only Son
from the Father' (John 1.1-14).

My intellect overstepped its limits at that point and I learnt
more about God than I had expected. I understood that my Creator
was God born of God. I learnt that the Word was God and was
with him from the beginning. I came to know the light of the world
. . . I understood that the Word was made flesh and dwelt among
us . . . Those who welcomed him became children of God, by a
birth not in the flesh but in faith. . . . This gift of God is offered
to everyone . . . We can receive it because of our freedom which
was given us expressly for this purpose. But this very power given
to each person to be a child of God was bogged down in weak and

hesitant faith. Our own difficulties make hope painful, our desire becomes infuriating and our faith grows weak. That is why the Word was made flesh: by means of the Word-made-flesh the flesh was enabled to raise itself up to the Word . . . Without surrendering his divinity God was made of our flesh . . . My soul joyfully received the revelation of this mystery. By means of my flesh I was drawing near to God, by means of my faith I was called to a new birth. I was able to receive this new birth from on high . . . I was assured that I could not be reduced to non-being.

HILARY OF POITIERS *The Trinity,* 1,1-13 (PL 10,25-35)

God is absolute beauty because he is absolute personal existence. As such, he awakens our desire, sets it free and draws it to himself. He sets beings within their limits but he calls them into communion with one another without confusing them. Being himself beyond movement or rest, he gives to each creature an identity that is exact and distinct, but is nevertheless capable of development when brought to life by the dynamic power of love.

[God is Beauty.] This Beauty is the source of all friendship and all mutual understanding. It is this Beauty . . . which moves all living things and preserves them whilst filling them with love and desire for their own particular sort of beauty. For each one, therefore, Beauty is both its limit and the object of its love, since it is its goal . . . and its model (for it is by its likeness to this Beauty that everything is defined). Thus true Beauty and Goodness are mixed together because, whatever the force may be that moves living things, it tends always towards Beauty-and-Goodness, and there is nothing that does not have a share in Beauty-and-Goodness . . . By virtue of this reality all creatures subsist, united and separate, identical and opposite, alike and unlike; contraries are united and the united elements are not confused . . . By virtue of Beauty-and-Goodness everything is in communion with everything else, each in its own way; creatures love one another without losing themselves in one another; everything is in harmony, parts fit snugly into the whole . . . one generation succeeds another; spirits, souls and bodies remain at the same time steady and mobile; because for all of them Beauty-and-Goodness is at once repose and movement, being itself beyond both.

DIONYSIUS THE AREOPAGITE *Divine Names,* IV,7 (PG 3,701)

The language of souls is their desire.
GREGORY THE GREAT *Commentary on the Book of Job*, 2,7,11 (SC 32, vol.2 p. 189)

God is Love. He is the ecstasy of Love, overflowing outside himself, enabling creatures to share in his life. Through his life they share the same overflowing force, which we see already displayed in *eros*, the love of man and woman, and which is designed to be perfected in holiness, in conscious fellowship with him who is the fullness of Beauty and Goodness. Amidst horror and death there is something greater, the secret of love: the story of creation is a magnificent 'Song of Songs'. Desire is in the first place God's desire for us, to which all human (or to be exact divine-human) eros is seeking to respond. The inspired poet of *eros* is Dionysius the Areopagite. And Maximus the Confessor, commenting on him, does not hesitate to equate *eros* with *agape* (Latin *caritas*: disinterested love, considerateness and service, which participates in the love of God for his creatures). Eros expresses chiefly a natural impulse, *agape* a meeting between persons that is full of tenderness. One might say that *eros* is meant to become the subject of agape.

> In God, the '*eros* desire' is outgoing, ecstatic. Because of it lovers no longer belong to themselves but to those whom they love. God also goes out of himself ... when he captivates all creatures by the spell of his love and his desire ... In a word, we might say that Beauty-and-Goodness is the object of the eros desire and is the *eros* desire itself ...
> DIONYSIUS THE AREOPAGITE *Divine Names*, IV,13 (PG 3,712)

> God is the producer and generator of tenderness and *eros*. He has set outside himself what was within himself, namely, creatures. Which is why it is said of him: God is Love. The Song of Songs calls him *agape*, or 'sensual pleasure', and 'desire', which means *eros*. In so far as the *eros* desire originates from him, he can be said to be the moving force of it, since he generated it. But in so far as he is himself the true object of the love, he is the moving force in others who look to him and possess according to their own nature the capacity for desire.
> MAXIMUS THE CONFESSOR *On the Divine Names*, IV,4 (PG 4,296)

Hence the conclusion of Climacus:

Blessed is the person whose desire for God has become like the lover's passion for the beloved.

JOHN CLIMACUS *The Ladder of Divine Ascent*, 30th step, 5 (11)[1], p. 168.

Even more than hunger, thirst, which can so torment someone in the desert, expresses the desire for God.
And what thirst there is today!

Hunger makes itself felt only gradually and vaguely, but the raging of intense thirst is unmistakable and intolerable. No wonder the person who longs for God cries, 'My soul thirsts for God, for the living God' (Psalm 42.2).

JOHN CLIMACUS *The Ladder of Divine Ascent*, 30th step, 9 (15), p. 168.

That is the mysterious dialectic of faith, hope and charity, God never ceasing to 'empty out souls' in order to fill them up better.

Desire for vision: Faith.
Desire for possession: Hope.
Desire for love: Charity.
By expectation, God increases desire.
By desire, he empties out souls.
In emptying them out, he makes them more capable of receiving him.

AUGUSTINE OF HIPPO *Commentary on the First Epistle of St John*, 4,6 (SC 75, p. 230)

Within the person the 'inward thirst' is awoken, the 'inward eye' is opened.

Hasten to the springs, draw from the wells.
In God is the wellspring of life,
A spring that can never fail.
In his light is found a light
That nothing can darken.
Desire that light which your eyes know not!
Your inward eye is preparing to see the light.
Your inward thirst burns to be quenched at the spring.

AUGUSTINE OF HIPPO *Commentary on Psalm* 41,2 (PL 36,465)

---

[1]Numbering of sentences in SO 24 is given in brackets

So then God offers himself, wishes to disclose himself, but he does not force us. His power is the power of love, and love wants the freedom of the beloved. God speaks, and at the same time keeps silence; he knocks at the door and waits. Everything is dependent upon the royal freedom of faith. Everything hangs upon our decision.

Here [in the spiritual realm] birth is not the result of intervention from outside, as happens with bodily creatures who reproduce in an external way. Spiritual birth is the result of free choice and we are thus, in a sense, our own parents, creating ourselves as we want to be, freely fashioning ourselves according to the pattern of our choice.

GREGORY OF NYSSA *Life of Moses*, (PG 44,328C)

This is the wonderful call to conversion, a conversion attested by deeds. The father of Western monasticism, St Benedict, throws out the challenge:

Then let us arise! Scripture invites us in the words, 'It is full time now for you to wake from sleep' (Romans 13.11). With our eyes open to the light that transfigures, our ears filled with the thunder of his voice, let us listen to the powerful voice of God, urging us day by day, 'Oh, that today you would hearken to his voice! Harden not your hearts' (Psalm 95.8). And again: 'He who has an ear, let him hear what the Spirit says to the churches' (Revelation 2.7). And what does he say? 'Come, O children, listen to me, I will teach you the fear of the Lord' (Psalm 34.11). 'Walk while you have the light, lest the darkness overtake you' (John 12.35). Moreover the Lord, in seeking among the crowd for someone to work for him, says, 'Who is there who desires life?' (Psalm 34.12). If you hear him and answer, 'I do', God says to you, 'Do you desire true life, eternal life?' then: 'Keep your tongue from evil, and your lips from speaking deceit. Depart from evil, and do good; seek peace, and pursue it' (Psalm 34.13-14). And when you have done this I will set my eyes upon you, I will give ear to your prayers, and 'Before they call, I will answer' (Isaiah 65.24).

BENEDICT OF NURSIA *Rule*, Prologue 8-18 (XV Centenary edition, Desclée & Brouwer, Paris 1980, pp. 2 & 4)

The Lord waits for us to respond day by day to his holy counsels by our actions. In fact the days of this life are given us as a respite to correct our errors, as the Apostle Paul says: 'Do you not know that God's kindness is meant to lead you to repentance?' (Romans 2.4). And in his loving-kindness the Lord says, 'Have I any pleasure in the death of the wicked ... and not rather that he should turn from his way and live?' (Ezekiel 18.23)

BENEDICT OF NURSIA *Rule*, Prologue, 35-38 (XV Centenary edition p. 6)

2

God, Hidden and Universal

History, including the history of Christianity, is littered with caricatures of God, like so many mental idols which have led people either
to cruelty or to atheism. But how, in modern times, after the growth
of liberty and the critical spirit, could people have accepted a God
who seemed to them worse than themselves, or at least inferior to the
highest demands of a conscience secretly nourished by the Gospel?

People never cease to project on to God their individual and
collective obsessions, so that they can appropriate and make use of
him. But they ought to understand that God cannot be apprehended
from without, as if he were an object, for with him there is no outside;
nor can the Creator be set side by side with the creature. 'In him we
live and move and have our being' (Acts 17.28), as St Paul said to the
Athenians. But, enclosed as we are within ourselves and also enclosed
'in his hand', we can know him only if he freely establishes with us a
relationship in which distance and nearness are made the setting for
a Word, of Someone speaking to someone.

> Most people are enclosed in their mortal bodies like a snail in its
> shell, curled up in their obsessions after the manner of hedgehogs.
> They form their notion of God's blessedness taking themselves for
> a model.
>
> CLEMENT OF ALEXANDRIA *Miscellanies*, V,11 (PG 9,103)

> Seeds in a pomegranate cannot see objects outside its rind, because
> they are inside. Similarly human beings who are enclosed with all
> creation in the hand of God cannot see God . . .
>
> Friend, it is through him that you are speaking, it is he whom
> you breathe, and you do not know it! For your eye is blind, your

heart hardened. But, if you wish, you can be cured. Entrust yourself
to the doctor, and he will open the eyes of your soul and your heart.
Who is the doctor? God, using his word and his wisdom . . .
THEOPHILUS OF ANTIOCH *First Book to Autolycus*, 5 & 7 (SC 20,
pp. 66 & 72)

Nor is God an object of knowledge. Concepts, which never come
without a secret wish to classify and to possess, are powerless to grasp
the one by whom we ought to let ourselves be grasped. 'Grasped'
in two senses: of being opened to receive him, as he freely reveals
himself, and of being seized with wonder.

Every concept formed by the intellect in an attempt to comprehend
and circumscribe the divine nature can succeed only in fashioning
an idol, not in making God known.
GREGORY OF NYSSA *Life of Moses*, (PG 44,377)

Only wonder can comprehend his incomprehensible power.
MAXIMUS THE CONFESSOR *On the Divine Names*, 1 (PG 4,192)

Thus the Bride in the Song of Songs, according to the commentary of Gregory of Nyssa, never ceases to seek the Bridegroom, who
attracts her from a distance to which he constantly withdraws.

The Bride speaks: 'Upon my bed by night I sought him whom
my soul loves . . . but found him not. I called him, but he
gave no answer.' How indeed could she reach with a name the
one who is above every name?
GREGORY OF NYSSA *Homilies on the Song of Songs*, 6 (PG 44,893)

The true way to approach the mystery is in the first place celebration, celebration by the whole cosmos. According to the Fathers,
the fall impaired the capacity of creatures to see the divine light, but
did not destroy it. The universal aspiration towards God has, it is true,
become a 'groaning', a 'sigh of creation', but it is still prayer, which is
the essential activity of all created things: 'Everything that exists prays
to thee'. The inexhaustible nature of transcendence is expressed in
the profusion of creatures. The universe is the first Bible. Each being
manifests the creative word which gives it its identity and attracts it.
Each being manifests a dynamic idea, something willed by God. Ultimately each thing is a created name of him who cannot be named.

O thou who art beyond all,
How canst thou be called by another name?
What hymn can sing of thee?
No name describes thee.
What mind can grasp thee?
No intellect conceives thee.
Thou only art inexpressible;
All that is spoken comes forth from thee.
Thou only art unknowable;
All that is thought comes forth from thee.
All creatures praise thee,
Those that speak and those that are dumb.
All creatures bow down before thee,
Those that can think and those that have no power of thought.
The universal longing, the groaning of creation tends towards
    thee.
Everything that exists prays to thee
And to thee every creature that can read thy universe
Sends up a hymn of silence.
In thee alone all things dwell.
With a single impulse all things find their goal in thee.
Thou art the purpose of every creature.
Thou art unique.
Thou art each one and art not any.
Thou art not a single creature nor art thou the sum of creatures;
All names are thine; how shall I address thee,
Who alone cannot be named? . . .
Have mercy, O thou, the Beyond All;
How canst thou be called by any other name?

GREGORY NAZIANZEN *Dogmatic Poems*, (PG 37,507-8)

From all eternity God lives and reigns in glory. Each ray of that
glory is a divine Name and these Names are innumerable. Dionysius
the Areopagite, who wrote an admirable treatise, the *Divine Names*,
lists some of them taken from the Bible and the Gospels. The Fathers
also identify them with the 'powers' or the 'energies' that spring from
the unapproachable nature of God. At the moment of creation it
is this glory, the *chabod* of the Bible, which completes the things
created, giving them at once their density and their transparency.
The energies then become so many modes of the divine presence.
The 'Word', the *logos*, that establishes each creature, enables it to
share these energies, or, in the case of human beings, invites them

to share them. Thus every creature names, or ought to name, in its own peculiar fashion, the divine Names. In spite of sin, which means exile from the glory, the world is still the vast theophany honoured by the religions of antiquity.

> Taught thus, theologians praise the divine Origin for having no name and yet possessing all names.
>
> For not having any name because, as they recall, the deity himself, in one of the mystical visions in which he is symbolically revealed, reproved the man who asked, 'Tell, I pray, your name' (Genesis 32.29), and to avert him from any knowledge that could be expressed in a name, said, 'Why do you ask my name, seeing it is wonderful?' (Judges 13.18). And is it not indeed wonderful, this name which surpasses every name, this nameless name, that is 'above every name that is named, not only in this age but also in that which is to come' (Ephesians 1.21)?
>
> And they praise him for having many names, when they see that he says of himself, 'I am who I am' (Exodus 3.14), or again Life, Light, God, Truth, and when those who know God honour the universal Cause with various names inspired by his effects, such as Goodness, Beauty, Wisdom, ... Giver of life, Intelligence, ... Ancient of Days, Eternal Youth, Salvation, Justice, Sanctification, Liberation, as surpassing all grandeur, and manifesting himself to humanity in a gentle breeze. They declare, moreover, that this divine Origin ... is simultaneously at the heart of the universe and far beyond the sky, sun, stars, fire, water, wind, dew, cloud, rock, stone, and in a word all that is and nothing that is.
>
> So this cause of everything which surpasses everything is at the same time namelessness which befits him and all the names of all the creatures ... He contains in himself from the beginning all creatures ... in such a way that he can be honoured and named in terms of every creature.
>
> DIONYSIUS THE AREOPAGITE *Divine Names*, I,1,6 (PG 3,596)

However, the world masks the mystery as much as it expresses it. A negative approach is therefore indispensable, one which sweeps away the idols of the mind, the systems, the intellectual concepts, along with the images of sense experience. In the first place, the mystery of Being cannot be confounded with *a* being, even though it might be at the summit of the hierarchy of beings. The one Being is the cause of being, and so cannot be *a* being. That philosophical idol, the 'Good Lord' of a certain type of Christianity, or the 'supreme being' of spiritualism, has brought about simultaneously the 'death of God' and the loss of the mystery of Being.

The Living One, however, is no more the unlimited Being, the *theotes*, or divinity, of the gnostics than he is the supreme being of a closed monotheism. The life of the Living One that is expressed in the profusion of divine names and theophanies originates in the inexhaustible depths of personal Love. So the abyss is neither undifferentiated nor indifferent. From it we derive freedom and love, crucified and divinizing love. It is this supreme revelation – that of Christ – which we must understand from expressions suggesting both an unfathomable plenitude exceeding even our idea of God and our absorption in Being. And perhaps contemporary atheism, to the extent that it is not stupidity but a purifying revolt, could be understood in a new way, as the path of 'unknowing' that is not an intellectual path (for negation is denied just as much as affirmation) but is pure adoration.

> To celebrate the negations . . . in order to attain unveiled knowledge of this unknowing, that is hidden in every being by the knowledge that can be had of it, in order to see in this way that superessential obscurity, that is hidden by all the light that is contained in beings.
>
> DIONYSIUS THE AREOPAGITE *Mystical Theology*, II (PG 3,1025)

> If it happens that in seeing God one understands what is seen, that means it is not God himself who is seen but one of those knowable things that owe their being to him. For in himself he transcends all intelligence and all essence. He exists in a superessential mode and is known beyond all understanding only in so far as he is utterly unknown and does not exist at all. And it is that perfect unknowing, taken in the best sense of the word, that constitutes the true knowing of him who transcends all knowing.
>
> DIONYSIUS THE AREOPAGITE *Letter I to Gaius* (PG 3,1065)

> The infinite is without doubt something of God, but not God himself, who is infinitely beyond even that.
>
> MAXIMUS THE CONFESSOR *Ambigua* (PG 91,1224)

> We therefore say that the universal Cause, which is situated beyond the whole universe, is neither matter . . . nor body; that it has neither figure nor form, nor quality nor mass; that it is not in any

place, that it defies all apprehension by the senses . . . Rising higher, we now say that this Cause is neither soul nor intelligence . . . that it can be neither expressed nor conceived, that it has neither number nor order, nor greatness, nor littleness, nor equality, nor inequality, nor likeness, nor unlikeness; it neither remains stationary nor moves . . . that it is neither power nor light; that it neither lives nor is life; that it is neither essence nor perpetuity, nor time; that it cannot be grasped by the intellect; that it is neither science nor truth, nor sovereignty, nor wisdom, nor singularity, nor unity, nor divinity, nor goodness; neither spirit nor sonship nor fatherhood in any sense that we can understand them; that it is not anything accessible to our knowledge or to the knowledge of any being; it has nothing to do with non-being, but no more has it anything to do with being; that no one knows its nature . . . that it eludes all reasoning, all nomenclature, all knowing; that it is neither darkness nor light, neither error nor truth; that absolutely nothing can be asserted of it and absolutely nothing denied; that when we formulate affirmations or negations applying to realities that are inferior to it, we are not affirming or denying anything about the Cause itself: because all affirmation remains on this side of the transcendence of him who is divested of everything and stands beyond everything.

DIONYSIUS THE AREOPAGITE *Mystical Theology*, IV & V (PG 3, 1047-8)

The mystery that is beyond God himself,
the Ineffable,
that gives its name to everything,
is complete affirmation, complete negation,
beyond all affirmation and all negation.

DIONYSIUS THE AREOPAGITE *Divine Names*, II,4 (PG 3,641)

This simultaneous negation of affirmation *and negation* means that God's transcendence eludes our very idea of transcendence. God transcends his own transcendence, so that he may not be lost in abstract nothingness, but may give himself. The simultaneous overcoming of affirmation and negation already outlines the antinomy of personal existence: the more it is hidden the more it is given; the more it is given the more hidden it is. That is why the Fathers also speak of God as inaccessible, of God beyond God, in terms of a springing forth, a creative and redemptive leap outside his essence, following the eternal movement of the divine energies, but also in order to communicate these to creatures by personal actions, because the living God is a God who acts. He is not being but he contains it, and by his actions enables creatures to share in it.

> When God, who is absolute fullness, brought creatures into exist-
> ence, it was not done to fulfil any need, but so that his creatures
> should be happy to share his likeness, and so that he himself might
> rejoice in the joy of his creatures as they draw inexhaustibly upon
> the Inexhaustible.
>
> MAXIMUS THE CONFESSOR *Centuries on Charity*, III, 46 (PG 90,
> 434)

> He is called God because he has built everything on its own
> foundations, and because he makes a leap:[1] leaping means giving
> life to the world ... He is almighty, he contains everything: the
> heights of heaven, the depths of the abyss, the bounds of the earth
> are in his hand.
>
> THEOPHILUS OF ANTIOCH *First Book to Autolycus*, 4 (SC 20, p. 64)

> God has always existed and he always will exist: or to put
> it better, God always exists. In fact 'past' and 'future' express the
> fragments of duration as we know it, gliding naturally along. But
> he, God, is 'eternal Existence' and this is the name that he gives
> himself when he reveals the future to Moses on the mountain. He
> actually contains in himself all being, that which had no being
> and will have no end, what I would call an ocean of being without
> limit and without end, beyond any notions of duration and nature
> that our intellect could form for itself. The intellect can evoke him
> only obscurely ... not with any knowledge of his true nature, but
> by looking at what surrounds it. By assembling and interpreting
> the images in our mind we can begin to reconstruct something
> approaching an idea of the Truth ... He enlightens the higher part
> of our being, provided it has been purified, just as a sudden flash of
> lightning strikes our eyes; and that, in my opinion, is so that he
> may draw us to himself in proportion to the understanding we
> have of him ... and that in so far as we fail to understand him he
> may excite our curiosity; this will awake in our soul the longing to
> know him further; this longing will lay bare our soul; this nakedness

[1] The word *theos* (God) is here derived from the verbs *theirai* (to found) and
theein (to leap) – beyond every limit!

will make us like God. When we have reached this state, God will converse with us as friends. If I may dare say so, God will be united with gods, and revealing himself to them, and will be known to the same extent as he is known.

GREGORY NAZIANZEN *Oration 45*, For Easter, 3 (PG 36,847)

These words are charged with the negative approach to God, with his silence. Referring to the Ineffable, they speak of the presence and the action of the One of whom a 19th century saint declared that 'he is a fire that inflames our entrails'. These affirmations perfected by negations state that God is Spirit, Fire, Light, Life, Love. Here one recognizes the very words and attitudes of Jesus.

God is Breath, for the breath of the wind is shared by all, goes everywhere; nothing shuts it in, nothing holds it prisoner.

MAXIMUS THE CONFESSOR *On the Divine Names*, I, 4 (PG 4,208)

The sacred theologians often describe the superessential essence in terms of fire . . . the fire can be experienced everywhere, so to speak; it illumines everything whilst remaining distinct from everything . . . It shines with a total brilliance and at the same time its presence is secret, being unknown outside of the material that is making it visible. It is not possible to bear its brightness nor to behold it face to face, but its power extends everywhere, and wherever it appears it attracts everything . . . By means of this transmutation it gives itself to anyone who approaches it, however distantly: it restores creatures to life with its quickening warmth, it enlightens them, but in itself it remains pure and unabsorbed . . . It is active, powerful, everywhere present and invisible. Neglected, it seems as if it did not exist. But as a result of the friction which is a kind of prayer it suddenly appears, leaps up and spreads all round. One could find more than one other property of fire that would be applicable, as a visual image, to the operations of the divine Principle.

DIONYSIUS THE AREOPAGITE *Celestial Hierarchy*, XV, 2 (PG 3, 328-9)

Just as light which enables us to see each object does not need any other light to be visible itself, so God who enables us to see everything does not need a light by which we might be able to see him, because he is light by his very essence.

EVAGRIUS OF PONTUS *Centuries*, I, 35 (Frankenberg p. 79)

We must now praise that perpetual Life from which all life proceeds and by means of which every living thing according to its own particular capacity receives life ... Whether you are speaking of the life of the spirit or of reason or of the senses, and what feeds it and makes it grow, or of any other kind of life that can possibly be, it is thanks to the Life that trancends all life that it lives and communicates life ... Indeed, it is not enough to say that this Life is alive. It is the very principle of life, and its sole source. It is that which perfects and differentiates all life, and its praises should be sung by all life ... Bestower of life and more than life, it deserves to be honoured with every name that human beings can apply to this inexpressible Life.

DIONYSIUS THE AREOPAGITE *Divine Names*, VI, 1 & 3 (PG 3,856-7)

God is Love. Whoever sought to define him would be like a blind person trying to count the grains of sand on the sea shore.

JOHN CLIMACUS *The Ladder of Divine Ascent*, 30th step, 2(6), p. 167.

3

The God-Man

One of the most beautiful liturgies of the ancient Church, largely the work of St Basil of Cæsarea, recalls the history of salvation thus:

> Thou hast visited [humanity] in many ways, in the loving-kindness of thy heart: thou hast sent the prophets, thou hast worked mighty wonders through the saints who, from generation to generation, were close to thee ... Thou hast given us the help of the Law. Thou hast charged angels to watch over us. And when the fullness of time was come, thou didst speak to us by thine own Son ...

There is no culture or religion that has not received and does not express a 'visitation of the Word'. Maximus the Confessor distinguishes three degrees in the 'embodiment' of the Word. In the first place, the very existence of the cosmos, understood as a theophany; this symbolism is the foundation of the ancient religions, which see in it the means to the deepest spiritual understanding. Secondly, the revelation of the personal God, who engendered history, and the embodying of the Word in the Law, in a sacred Scripture; Judaism and Islam are obvious examples. Finally, the personal incarnation of the Word who gives full meaning to his cosmic and scriptural embodiments, freeing the former from the temptation to absorb the divine 'Self' in an impersonal divine essence, and the latter from the temptation to separate God and humanity, leaving no possibility of communion between them. For in Christ, to quote the Fourth Ecumenical Council, God and man are united 'without confusion or change', but also 'without division or separation'. And the divine energies, reflected by creatures and objects, do not lead to anonymous divinity but to the face of the transfigured Christ.

The Word is concentrated and takes bodily form.

That can be first understood in this sense ... that by coming in the flesh he deigned to concentrate himself in order to assume a body and teach us in our human tongue, and by means of parables, the knowledge of holy and hidden things, which surpasses all language ...

It can also be understood to mean that for love of us he hides himself mysteriously in the spiritual essences of created beings, as if in so many individual letters [of the alphabet], present totally in each one in all his fullness ... In all the variety is hidden the one who is eternally the same, in composite things the one who is simple and without parts, in those things which had to begin on a certain day the one who has no beginning, in the visible the one who is invisible, in the tangible the one who cannot be touched ...

It can finally be understood to mean that for love of us who are slow to comprehend, he has deigned to use these letters to express the syllables and sounds of Scripture, in order to draw us after him and unite us in spirit.

MAXIMUS THE CONFESSOR *Ambigua* (PG 91,1285-8)

Jesus reveals in its fullness the mystery of the living God.

There is only one God,
revealed by Jesus Christ his Son
who is his Word sprung from the silence ...

IGNATIUS OF ANTIOCH *Letter to the Magnesians*, 8,2 (SC 10, p. 102)

God, in Christ, comes to seek for humankind, the 'lost sheep' of the parable in the Gospel, even in the 'depths of the earth', which denotes a finiteness that has become impenetrable and recalcitrant, buried in nothingness.

The Lord has given us a sign 'as deep as Sheol and as high as heaven', such as we should not have dared to hope for. How could we have expected to see a virgin with child, and to see in this Child a 'God with us' (Isaiah 7.11 & 14) who would descend into the depths of the earth to seek for the lost sheep, meaning the creature he had fashioned, and then ascend again to present to his Father this 'man' [humanity] thus regained?

IRENÆUS OF LYONS *Against Heresies*, III,19,3 (SC 211, p. 380)

A Jewish-Christian text of the second century, attributed to
Solomon in accordance with a practice common at that time in the
Jewish world, admirably expresses the *kenosis* of the incarnate and
crucified God. The word *kenosis* comes from the verb *ekenosen*, used
by Paul in the Epistle to the Philippians: 'Christ Jesus ... *heauton
ekenosen*' – that is, stripped, humbled, emptied himself – 'taking the
form of a servant, being born in the likeness of men' (Philippians
2.7). Jesus reveals to us the human face of God, a God who, in the
foolishness of love, 'empties himself' so that I may accept him in all
freedom and that I may find room for my freedom in him.

> His love for me brought low his greatness.
> He made himself like me so that I might receive him.
> He made himself like me so that I might be clothed in him.
> I had no fear when I saw him,
> for he is mercy for me.
> He took my nature so that I might understand him,
> my face so that I should not turn away from him.
>
> *Odes of Solomon 7 (The Odes and Psalms of Solomon* R.
> Harris and A. Mingana II, pp. 240-1)

The purpose of the incarnation is to establish full communion
between God and humanity so that in Christ humanity may find
adoption and immortality, often called 'deification' by the Fathers:
not by emptying human nature but by fulfilling it in the divine life,
since only in God is human nature truly itself.

> How could the human race go to God if God had not come to us?
> How should we free ourselves from our birth into death if we had
> not been born again according to faith by a new birth generously
> given by God, thanks to that which came about from the Virgin's
> womb?
>
> IRENÆUS OF LYONS *Against Heresies*, IV,33,4 (SC 100 bis, pp.
> 810-12)

> This is the reason why the Word of God was made flesh, and
> the Son of God became Son of Man: so that we might enter into
> communion with the Word of God, and by receiving adoption might
> become Sons of God. Indeed we should not be able to share in
> immortality without a close union with the Immortal. How could

we have united ourselves with immortality if immortality had not
become what we are, in such a way that we should be absorbed
by it, and thus we should be adopted as Sons of God?

IRENÆUS OF LYONS *Against Heresies*, III,19,1 (SC 211, p. 374)

In Jesus, however, the mystery is at the same time disclosed
and veiled. Because the inaccessible God reveals himself in the
Crucified, he is by that very fact a hidden and incomprehensible God, who upsets our definitions and expectations. The true
'apophatic' approach (*apophasis* means the 'leap' towards the mystery) does not rest solely, as is often thought, in negative theology.
That has only the purpose of opening us to an encounter, a
revelation, and it is this very revelation, in which glory is inseparable from *kenosis*, which is strictly unthinkable. The *apophasis*
therefore lies in the antinomy, the sharp distinction in character
between the Depth and the Cross, the inaccessible God and the
Man of Sorrows, the almost 'crazy' manifestations of God's love for
humanity, and a humble and unobtrusive plea for our own love.

He was sent not only to be recognized but also to remain hidden.

ORIGEN *Against Celsus*, 2,67 (PG 11,901)

By the love of Christ for us ... the Superessential gave up his
mystery, and manifested himself by assuming humanity. However,
in spite of this manifestation – or rather, to use a more divine
language, at the very heart of it – he loses nothing of his mysteri-
ousness. For the mystery of Jesus has remained hidden. No reason
and no intelligence have fathomed his essential nature. In whatever
way he is understood, he remains utterly mysterious.

DIONYSIUS THE AREOPAGITE *Letter 3, To Gaius* (PG 3,1069)

The incarnation is 'a mystery even more inconceivable than any
other. By taking flesh God makes himself understood only by
appearing still more incomprehensible. He remains hidden ... even
in this disclosure. Even when manifest he is always the stranger'.

MAXIMUS THE CONFESSOR *Ambigua* (PG 91,1048-9)

The Incarnation needs to be put back into the whole scheme
of creation. Human waywardness has certainly transformed it into

a tragic 'redemption', but the Incarnation remains above all the fulfilment of God's original plan, the great synthesis, in Christ, of the human, the divine and the cosmic. 'In him all things were created, in heaven and on earth, visible and invisible ... all things were created through him and for him. He is before all things, and in him all things hold together' (Colossians 1.16-17).

> Christ is the great hidden mystery, the blessed goal, the purpose for which everything was created ... With his gaze fixed on this goal God called things into existence. He [Christ] is the point to which Providence is tending, together with everything in its keeping, and at which creatures accomplish their return to God. He is the mystery which surrounds all ages ... In fact it is for the sake of Christ, and for his mystery, that all ages exist and all that they contain. In Christ they have received their principle and their purpose. This synthesis was predetermined at the beginning: a synthesis of the limit and the unlimited, of the measure and the immeasurable, of the bounded and the boundless, of the Creator and the creature, of rest and movement. In the fullness of time this synthesis became visible in Christ, and God's plans were fulfilled.
>
> MAXIMUS THE CONFESSOR *Questions to Thalassius*, 60 (PG 90, 612)

Everything in effect exists in an immense movement of incarnation which tends towards Christ and is fulfilled in him.

> That God should have clothed himself with our nature is a fact that should not seem strange or extravagant to minds that do not form too paltry an idea of reality. Who, looking at the universe, would be so feeble-minded as not to believe that God is all in all; that he clothes himself with the universe, and at the same time contains it and dwells in it? What exists depends on Him who exists, and nothing can exist except in the bosom of Him who is.
>
> If then all is in him and he is in all, why blush for the faith that teaches us that one day God was born in the human condition, God who still today exists in humanity?
>
> Indeed, if the presence of God in us does not take the same form now as it did then, we can at least agree in recognizing that he is in us today no less than he was then. Today, he is involved

with us in as much as he maintains creation in existence. Then, he mingled himself with our being to deify it by contact with him, after he had snatched it from death ... For his resurrection becomes for mortals the promise of their return to immortal life.

GREGORY OF NYSSA *Catechetical Orations*, 25 (PG 45,65-8)

Therefore the mystery of the Incarnation of the Word contains in itself the whole meaning of the riddles and symbols of Scripture, the whole significance of visible and invisible creatures. Whoever knows the mystery of the cross and the tomb knows the meaning of things. Whoever is intitiated into the hidden meaning of the resurrection knows the purpose for which God created everything in the beginning.

MAXIMUS THE CONFESSOR *Ambigua* (PG 91,1360)

The Incarnation was therefore the product of a long history, a fleshly fruit that had long been ripening on the earth. This was the point of view of Irenæus of Lyons who in the second century worked out a real theology of history expressed as a grand succession of covenants (with Adam, Noah, Abraham, Moses, and so on). Whilst humanity thus tested its freedom, an ever-diminishing 'remnant' meditated on and refined its expectations until a woman, Mary, by giving her indispensable assent, at last made possible the perfect union of the divine and the human. The history continues today; Life continues to be offered, not imposed. Today also, amidst the titanic undertakings of the modern age, people have desired 'to see even before becoming adult the disappearance of every difference between God and humanity'. The movement from the God-man to God-humanity is now possible only because of the patience of the saints, who have slowly established their communion.

People who will not wait for maturity are utterly unreasonable ... In their ignorance of God and of themselves these insatiable and ungrateful wretches would like ... to see, even before becoming adult, the disappearance of every difference between the uncreated God and humanity which has only just been created ... First of all creation had to appear. Only later did the mortal have to be vanquished and swallowed up in immortality, and humanity be fully conformed to the image and likeness of God, having freely discovered good and evil.

IRENÆUS OF LYONS *Against Heresies*, IV,38,4 (SC 100 bis, pp. 956-8)

So we can see the Nativity as a secret re-creation, by which human nature was assumed and restored to its original state. From then on all things were tending towards the predetermined end, which was already present in the heart of history like a seed of fire. Christ reveals to us, and we see in Christ, that perfect 'image of God' after which we are fashioned, and which attracts us like a magnet. It is now up to us to transform 'image' into 'likeness'. The next quotation from Gregory Nazianzen concludes with a picture of the crib, where on either side of the incarnate Logos stand the *alogoi* animals, that is, beasts which do not have the power of speech nor any understanding of its meaning. The entire universe, Origen said, is a *logos alogos*, a meaning not uttered, and therefore locked in absurdity. The Logos, the Meaning, is fully revealed by the incarnation.

I too will proclaim the greatness of this day: the immaterial becomes incarnate, the Word is made flesh, the invisible makes itself seen, the intangible can be touched, the timeless has a beginning, the Son of God becomes the Son of Man, Jesus Christ, always the same, yesterday, today and for ever ... This is the solemnity we are celebrating today: the arrival of God among us, so that we might go to God, or more precisely, return to him. So that stripping off the old humanity we might put on the new; and as in Adam we were dead, so in Christ we might be made alive, be born with him, rise again with him ... A miracle, not of creation, but rather of re-creation ... For this feast is my perfecting, my returning to my former state, to the original Adam ... Revere the nativity which releases you from the chains of evil. Honour this tiny Bethlehem which restores Paradise to you. Venerate this crib; because of it you who were deprived of meaning (*logos*) are fed by the divine Meaning, the divine Logos himself.

GREGORY NAZIANZEN *Oration 38, For Christmas* (PG 36,664-5)

We cannot celebrate the birth of the Word made flesh without glorifying Mary the 'Mother of God'. The Syriac hymn which follows heaps up paradoxes in accordance with the 'apophatic antinomy' which we have just described. Here it is the antinomy between God the Creator and a tiny baby.

> Blessed is she: she has received the Spirit who made her immaculate. She has become the temple in which dwells the Son of the heights of heaven . . .
> Blessed is she: through her the race of Adam has been restored, and those who had deserted the Father's house have been brought back . . .
> Blessed is she: within the bounds of her body was contained the Boundless One who fills the heavens, which cannot contain him.
> Blessed is she: in giving our life to the common Ancestor, the Father of Adam, she renewed fallen creatures.
> Blessed is she: she gave her womb to him who lets loose the waves of the sea.
> Blessed is she: she has born the mighty giant who sustains the world, she has embraced him and covered him with kisses.
> Blessed is she: she has raised up for the prisoners a deliverer who overcame their gaoler.
> Blessed is she: her lips have touched him whose blazing made angels of fire recoil.
> Blessed is she: she has fed with her milk him who gives life to the whole world.
> Blessed is she: for to her Son the saints all owe their happiness.
> Blessed be the Holy One of God who has sprung from thee.
> JAMES OF SARUG *Hymn to the Mother of God* (Bickell, I p. 246)

The virginity of the Mother of God does not deny *eros* but sets it free. It has always been recognized, from the ancient myths down to Freud himself, that love and death, *eros* and *thanatos*, are inseparable. In Mary's virginal motherhood, her fruitful virginity, we see transcendence intervening to snatch love out of the hands of death, and so fulfilling in embryo the expectation of humanity and of the cosmos, and setting in motion the universal transfiguration. We are born to die. Jesus is born to live a life without shadow and without limit, and to communicate this life to others. If he suffers and dies he does it willingly, in order to change death, in whatever shape it comes, into an approach to life. Gregory Nazianzen shows us the God-made-flesh assuming in a practical way all the weaknesses of our finite condition: temptation, hunger, thirst, fatigue, supplication, tears, mourning, the slavery that reduces us to a chattel, the cross, the tomb, hell; not because of some masochistic desire for pain (nothing could be more foreign to the Fathers' way of thinking) but in each case to correct and heal our nature, to set free our desires blocked by the multiplicity of needs, to overcome separation and death, and through the cross to transform the brokenness of creation into a spring of living water.

> He took our flesh and our flesh became God, since it is united with God and forms a single entity with him. For the higher perfection dominated, resulting in my becoming God as fully as he became man ... Here below he is without a father; on high he is without a mother: both these states belong to divinity ... He was wrapped in swaddling clothes, but when he rose from the tomb he laid aside the shroud ... 'He had no form or comeliness' (Isaiah 53.2), but on the mountain he shone with a splendour more dazzling than the sun – the foretaste of his future glory.
>
> As man he was baptized, but as God he washed away our sins. He had no need of purification, but he wished to sanctify the waters. As man he was tempted, but as God he triumphed, and he exhorts us to be confident because he has 'overcome the world' (John 16.33). He was hungry, but he fed thousands and he is 'the living bread which came down from heaven' (John 6.51). He was thirsty, but he cried, 'If any one thirst, let him come to me and drink,' and he promised that believers should become springs of living water (John 7.37f.). He knew weariness, but he is rest for 'all who labour and are heavy laden' (Matthew 11.28). He prays, but he answers prayers. He weeps, but wipes away tears. He asks where Lazarus has been laid, for he is man; but he raises him to life, for he is God. He is sold, dirt cheap, for thirty pieces of silver, but he redeems the world, at great cost, with his own blood ... He was weak and wounded, but he cures all infirmity and all weakness. He was nailed to the wood and lifted up, but he restores us by the tree of life ... He dies, but he brings to life, and by his own death destroys death. He is buried, but he rises again. He descends into hell, but rescues the souls imprisoned there.
>
> GREGORY NAZIANZEN *Third Theological Oration*, 19-20 (PG 36, 537-8)

This is possible because whilst Jesus is united both morally and ontologically with the whole human race (being 'consubstantial' with

us, a single being with us 'according to his humanity', in the words
of the Fourth Ecumenical Council), he nevertheless stays constantly
open to his Origin, the source of divinity, the Father who never ceases
to send down upon him the life-giving Spirit to act in him (for, as the
Council also said, Christ is 'consubstantial with the Father and the
Spirit according to his divinity').

> The Father was wholly in the Son when he fulfilled by his incar-
> nation the mystery of our salvation. Indeed, the Father was not
> himself incarnate, but he was united to the incarnation of the Son.
> And the Spirit was wholly in the Son, without indeed being incarnate
> with him, but acting in complete unity with him in his mysterious
> incarnation.
>
> MAXIMUS THE CONFESSOR *Questions to Thalassius*, 60 (PG 90,624)

So Christ's sacrifice was not in the least demanded by the Father,
as the only thing that could satisfy divine justice, appease the wrath
of God, and incline him favourably towards the human race. That
would be a regression to a non-biblical idea of sacrifice, as René
Girard has recently made clear. In the next quotation, Gregory
Nazianzen, opposing this way of thinking, meditates profoundly on
the readiness of Abraham to sacrifice his son.

Christ's sacrifice is a sacrifice of praise, of sanctification, of
restoration, by which he offers the whole of creation to the Father
so that the Father may bring it to life in the Holy Spirit. It is
truly a Pasch, the Passover, the 'passing over' of creation into the
Kingdom of Life. Because of the ontological unity of Christ with
the whole human race, just mentioned above, the sacrifice was a
bloody crucifixion. United with us in being and in love, Christ
took on himself all the hatred, rebellion, derision, despair – 'My
God, my God, why hast thou forsaken me?' – all the murders,
all the suicides, all the tortures, all the agonies of all humanity
throughout all time and all space. In all these Christ bled, suffered,
cried out in anguish and desolation. But, as he suffered in a human
way, so he was trustful in a human way: 'Father, into thy hands I
commit my spirit'. At that moment death is swallowed up in life,
the abyss of hatred is lost in the bottomless depths of love. 'A few
drops of blood' falling into the earth as into an immense chalice,
'have renewed the entire universe'.

> Why was the blood that was shed for us, God's most precious and
> glorious blood, this blood of the Sacrificer and of the Sacrifice,

why was it poured out, and to whom was it offered? . . . If it was a ransom offered to the Father, the question arises, for what reason? It was not the Father that held us captive. And then, why should the blood of his only Son be pleasing to the Father who refused to accept Isaac when Abraham offered him as a burnt offering, accepting instead the sacrifice of a ram?

Is it not evident that the Father accepts the sacrifice, not because he demands it or feels some need for it, but in order to carry out his own plan? Humanity had to be brought to life by the humanity of God . . . we had to be called back to him by his Son . . . Let the rest be adored in silence.

It was necessary for us that God should take flesh and die so that we might have new life . . .

Nothing can equal the miracle of my salvation; a few drops of blood redeem the whole universe.

GREGORY NAZIANZEN *Oration 45, For Easter*, 22,28,29, (PG 36, 653,661,664)

The sacrifice of Jesus accomplishes the Father's eternal plan to unite humanity with divinity, to bring alive and deify the depths of human nature, of the universe, of being. Never again should we be alone, shut out or lost. When we are in shame or despair, and there seems no way out, Christ is waiting for us in silent love. And he allows us to say *Abba*, Father, a word of childish tenderness. The Son's 'passion of love' precedes his incarnation and instigates it. It is inseparable from the Father's own mysterious 'passion of love'. For in giving his Son, the Father gives himself. And how could he have withheld him from the human race, seeing that the human race in the person of Abraham was ready to give his own son to God? This divine 'passion of love', which will cease only when the Kingdom has manifestly come, does not in the least impair the joy felt by the Father and the Son in the depths of their divine nature (and this joy is itself not impersonal, it is the Holy Spirit). A saint, whilst bearing within himself the immense joy of the divine presence, and precisely because he is bearing it, shares unreservedly in the distress of others. How much more is that true of our God and of his Christ, the 'Face of the Father', the pattern and focus of all sanctity!

If he came down to earth, it was out of compassion for the human race. Yes, he suffered our sufferings even before suffering the cross, even before taking our flesh. Indeed, if he had not suffered he would not have come to share our life with us. First he suffered, then he came down. But what is this passion that he felt for us? It was the passion of love. And does not the Father himself, the God of the universe 'slow to anger and abounding in steadfast love' (Psalm 103.8) also in some way suffer with us? Are you not aware that whilst governing human affairs he has compassion on our sufferings? Look how 'the Lord your God bore you, as a man bears his son' (Deuteronomy 1.31). In the same way as the Son of God 'bore our griefs', God bears with our behaviour. The Father is not impassible either . . . He has pity, he knows something of the passion of love, he has merciful impulses which it might seem his sovereign majesty would have forbidden him.

ORIGEN *Sixth Homily on Ezekiel*, 6, 6 (GCS 8,384-5)

None of all this would make sense if our faith did not teach us that Jesus, because he is the Person in communion, without in the least blurring the divine light (for the subject of his humanity is a Person who is divine and therefore perfect) is not separated from anything or anyone, but bears in himself the whole of humanity and the universe. The idea of 'human nature' in the Fathers is not philosophical but mystical, and denotes the unity of being common to all, the one and only Man broken by the fall and restored in Christ in the most literal sense.

The Word, in taking flesh, was mingled with humanity, and took our nature within himself, so that the human should be deified by this mingling with God: the stuff of our nature was entirely sanctified by Christ, the first fruits of creation.

GREGORY OF NYSSA *Against Apollinarius*, 2 (PG 45,1128)

The whole of humanity 'forms, so to speak, a single living being'. In Christ we form a single body, we are all 'members of one another'. Since humankind had imprisoned itself in death, it was necessary that God, by taking flesh, should allow himself to be imprisoned by death, in order to destroy his kingdom and to open to all flesh the way to resurrection. For the one flesh of humanity and of the earth 'brought into contact' in Christ 'with the fire' of his divinity, is henceforward secretly and sacramentally deified.

Our whole nature had to be recalled from death to life. God therefore stooped over our dead body to offer his hand, so to speak, to the creature lying there. He came near enough to death to make contact with our mortal remains, and by means of his own body provided nature with the capacity for resurrection, thus by his power raising to life the whole of humanity . . .

In our body the activity of any one of our senses communicates sensation to the whole of the organism joined to that member. It is the same for humanity as a whole, which forms, so to speak, a single living being: the resurrection of one member extends to all, and that of a part to the whole, by virtue of the cohesion and unity of human nature.

GREGORY OF NYSSA *Catechetical Orations*, 32 (PG 45,80)

How could humanity on earth, enslaved by death, recover its wholeness? It was necessary to give to dead flesh the ability to share in the life-giving power of God. Now the life-giving power of God is the Word, the only Son. He it was then whom God sent to us as Saviour and Liberator . . . He, though he is Life by nature, took a body subject to decay in order to destroy in it the power of death and transform it into life. As iron when it is brought in contact with fire immediately begins to share its colour, so the flesh when it has received the life-giving Word into itself is set free from corruption. Thus he put on our flesh to set it free from death.

CYRIL OF ALEXANDRIA *Homily on Luke*, V, 19 (PG 72,172)

The cross, inseparable from the descent into hell, the resurrection, and the ascension to the right hand of the Father, is seen as fundamentally life-giving. Its dimensions make of Christ the truly cosmic Man who transfigures the universe: 'Henceforward all is filled with light, the heavens, the earth and even hell', according to the Easter liturgy in the Byzantine rite. To be crucified in Christ is to die to one's own death in order to enter into the sacrifice that restores wholeness, and to understand, as St Paul says, 'the breadth and length and height and depth' of love (Ephesians 3.18-19).

'. . . that you may have power to comprehend with all the saints what is the breadth and length and height and depth' (Ephesians 3.18-19). The cross of Christ has all these dimensions. By the cross, in fact, 'when he ascended on high he led captivity captive' (Ephesians 4.8, Psalm 68.18). By it indeed 'he descended into the lower parts of the earth'. For the cross has a 'height' and a 'depth', and its 'breadth' and 'length' extend over all the immensity of the universe. Whoever is 'crucified with Christ', and knows the agony of this crucifixion, comprehends 'the breadth, the length, the height and the depth'.

ORIGEN Fragment of a *Commentary on the Epistle to the Ephesians* (Gregg p. 411-12)

These themes are taken up and developed in a very ancient Easter homily which is wholly permeated with the heat of the battle waged by the great champion of Life, and resounding with the joy of victory. The cross is truly the tree of life, the axis of the world brought back into line and giving a new stability to creation. Humanity is eagerly awaited and welcomed, no one is excluded from the marriage feast. The fruit of the tree of life is offered to all; the blood and the water flowing from Jesus's pierced side are the elements of a tremendous baptism, a baptism of fire and spirit. Indeed, the body of Christ crucified and risen is filled with the fire and wind of Pentecost. From now on the earth is secretly identified with this Body. There is no longer any separation. 'Life is poured out on all things'.

Jesus has shown in his own person all the fullness of life offered on the tree [the cross] . . .

For me this tree is a plant of eternal health. I feed on it; by its roots I am rooted; by its branches I spread myself; I rejoice in its dew; the rustling of its leaves invigorates me . . . I freely enjoy its fruits which were destined for me from the beginning. It is my food when I am hungry, a fountain for me when I am thirsty; it is my clothing because its leaves are the spirit of life . . . This tree of celestial dimensions rises up from the earth to heaven, an eternal plant deeply rooted in heaven and earth, the foundation of the universe, assembling together all the diversity of humankind, fastened by invisible nails of the Spirit, so that its links with the divine power may never again be broken . . .

Since the merciless battle that Jesus fought was victorious, he was first crowned with thorns in order to banish every curse from the earth, eradicating by his sacred head the thorns born of sin. Then having exhausted the Dragon's bitter gall, in exchange he completely opened for us the fountains of sweetness that spring from him . . . He opened his own side whence flowed the sacred blood and water, signs of the spiritual marriage, of adoption and the mystical new birth. Indeed, it is said, 'He will baptize you with the Holy Spirit and with fire' (Matthew 3.11): the water is the sign of the Spirit, the blood of the fire.

When the cosmic struggle was finished ... he remained steadfast at the edge of the universe, triumphantly displaying in his own person a trophy of victory. Then in the face of his long endurance the universe was overturned. There is little doubt that the whole world would have been annihilated ... if Jesus in his majesty had not breathed forth the divine Spirit, saying, 'Father, into thy hands I commit my spirit' (Luke 23.46). And when the divine Spirit ascended, the universe was given life, strength and stability.

O divine crucifixion, whose reach extends everywhere and to all things! O most singular of all things singular, thou art truly become all in all! May the heavens hold thy spirit and paradise thy soul! – for he says, 'Today I shall be with you in paradise' (cf. Luke 23.43) – but may the earth hold thy body. The indivisible was divided, so that everything might be saved, and even the underworld might know the divine coming ... That is why he gave himself up completely to death, so that the devouring beast might be secretly destroyed. It searched everywhere in his sinless body for food ... But when it found nothing in him that it could eat, it was imprisoned in itself, it was starved, it was its own death ...

O heavenly Easter! ... by thee the darkness of death has been destroyed and life poured out on every creature, the gates of heaven have been opened, God has shown himself as man and humanity has ascended and become God! Thanks to thee the gates of hell have been shattered ... Thanks to thee the great banqueting hall is full for the marriage feast, all the guests are wearing a wedding garment and no one, having no garment, will be cast out ... Thanks to thee the fire of love is burning in all, in spirit and body, fed by the very oil of Christ.

ANONYMOUS *Easter Homily* inspired by HIPPOLYTUS, *Treatise on Easter*,49,50,51,53,56,57,61,62 (SC 27, pp. 175-91)

In the crucified Christ forgiveness is offered and life is given. For humanity it is no longer a matter of fearing judgement or of meriting salvation, but of welcoming love in trust and humility. For God has allowed himself to be murdered to offer his life even to the murderers.

Christ's death on the cross is a judgement of judgement.

MAXIMUS THE CONFESSOR *Questions to Thalassius*, 43 (PG 90,408)

He who suspended the earth is suspended,
He who fastened the heavens is fastened,
He who fixed the universe is fixed on the wood,
God has been murdered . . .

God has clothed himself in humanity,
For me a sufferer he has suffered;
For one condemned he has been judged;
For one buried he has been buried;
But he is risen from the dead
And he cries:
Who will plead against me? I have delivered the one who was
    condemned,
I have given back life to him who was dead,
I have raised up one who was buried.
Who will dispute my cause? I have abolished death,
I have crushed hell,
I have raised humanity to the highest heavens,
Yes I, the Christ . . .

I am your forgiveness,
I am the Passover of salvation,
I am your light,
I am your resurrection.
MELITO OF SARDIS *Easter Homily* (SC 123, pp. 116,120,122)

Who can understand love
But he who loves?
I am united with my beloved,
My soul loves him.

In his peace,
That is where I am.
I am no longer a stranger,
For there is no hatred
With the Lord.

Because I love the Son
I shall become a son.
To cling to him who dies no more

Is to become immortal.
He who delights in life
Shall be alive.

Odes of Solomon, 3 (Harris-Mingana II, pp. 215-16)

Yesterday I was crucified with Christ; today I am glorified with him.

Yesterday I was dead with him; today I am sharing in his resurrection.

Yesterday I was buried with him; today I am waking with him from the sleep of death.

GREGORY NAZIANZEN *Oration I, For Easter*, 4 (PG 35,397)

The victory over death is a victory over biological death, which is henceforward transformed into a 'passing over', part of a great momentum of resurrection which must culminate in the manifestation of the Kingdom. The cosmos will be transfigured, in a manner no longer secret and sacramental, but open and glorious. In this universal metamorphosis persons, souls, will assume a bodily splendour, like Christ's at his transfiguration on the mountain, or after his resurrection.

Therefore, and most important of all, victory over death is also victory over spiritual death, which we experience daily and in which, left to ourselves, we should risk being imprisoned for ever. It is victory over hell. It is the certainty that henceforward no one will be separated from God, but that all will be – indeed, in a mysterious fashion, already are – immersed in his love. Victory over hell – this is the wonderful message that the ancient Church never ceased to proclaim.

[Christ speaks]
I have opened the gates that were bolted
I have shattered the bars of iron and the iron has become red-hot;
It has melted at my presence; and nothing more has been shut
Because I am the gate for all beings.
I went to free the prisoners; they belong to me
And I abandon no one . . .
I have sown my fruits in the hearts [of mortals]
And I have changed them into myself . . .

they are my members, and I am their head.
Glory to thee, Lord Christ, our Head! Alleluia!
Odes of Solomon, 17 (Harris-Mingana, pp. 289-90)

[Christ speaks]
I have stretched out my hands and offered myself to the Lord.
The stretching out of my hands is the sign of that [offering],
The stretching out on the wood
Where the Just One was hanged, by the roadside . . .
I am risen, I am with them,
I am speaking through their mouth . . .
I have laid on them the yoke of my love . . .
Hell saw me and was vanquished.
Death let me depart, and many with me.
I was gall and vinegar to it.
I descended with it to the depths of hell.
Death . . . could not bear my face.
I made of the dead an assembly of the living.
I spoke to them with living lips
so that my word should not be in vain.
They ran towards me, the dead.
They cried out, Take pity on us, O Son of God . . .
Deliver us out of the darkness that fetters us.
Open the gate for us that we may go out with thee.
We see that death has no hold on thee.
Deliver us also, for thou art our Saviour.
And I heard their voices and I traced my name on their heads.
So they are free and they belong to me.
Alleluia!
Odes of Solomon, 42 (pp. 403-5)

When he appears you shall say to yourself, 'My beloved speaks
and says, "Arise, my love, my fair one, and come away"' (Song
of Songs 2.10). I have opened the way for you, I have broken
your bonds, so come to me, my beloved. 'Arise, my beloved,
my fair one, my dove.' Why does he say 'Arise'? why 'Hasten'? For you I have endured the raging storms, I have borne
with the waves that would have assailed you; on your account
my soul became sorrowful even to death. I rose from the dead
after drawing the sting of death and loosing the bonds of hell.
Therefore I say to you, 'Arise, my fair one, and come away,

my dove; for lo, the winter is past, the rain is over and gone. The flowers appear on the earth'. I have risen from the dead, I have rebuked the storm, I have offered peace. And because, according to the flesh, I was born of a virgin and of the will of my Father, and because I have increased in wisdom and stature, 'the flowers appear on the earth'.

ORIGEN *Homilies on the Song of Songs*, 2,12 (SC 37, p. 101)

Today is the day of salvation for the world ... Christ is risen from the dead: arise with him. Christ returns to himself: you also must return to him. Christ has come forth from the tomb: free yourselves from the fetters of evil. The gates of hell are open and the power of death is destroyed. The old Adam is superseded, the new perfected. In Christ a new creation is coming to birth: renew yourselves.

GREGORY NAZIANZEN *Oration 45, For Easter*, 1,1 (PG 36,624)

Everything is summed up in the homily of John Chrysostom, still read today at the very heart of the Easter Vigil in Orthodox Churches.

Let every one who loves God rejoice in this festival of light!
Let the faithful servant gladly enter into the joy of his Lord!
Let those who have borne the burden of fasting come now to reap their reward!
Let those who have worked since the first hour receive now their just wage!
Let those who came after the third hour keep this festival with gratitude!
Let those who arrived only after the sixth hour approach with no fear: they will not be defrauded.
If someone has delayed until the ninth hour, let him come without hesitation.
And let not the workman of the eleventh hour be ashamed: the Lord is generous.
He welcomes the last to come no less than the first.
He welcomes into his peace the workman of the eleventh hour as kindly as the one who has worked since dawn.
The first he fills to overflowing: on the last he has compassion.
To the one he grants his favour, to the other pardon.

He does not look only at the work: he sees into the intention of
   the heart.

Enter then all of you into the joy of your Master.
First and last, receive your reward . . .
Abstinent and slothful celebrate this feast.
You who have fasted, rejoice today.
The table is laid: come all of you without misgivings.
The fatted calf is served, let all take their fill.
All of you, share in the banquet of faith: all of you draw on the
   wealth of his mercy . . .

Let no one weep for his sins: forgiveness is risen from the tomb.
Let no one fear death: the Saviour's death has set us free.
When it held him chained, he struck it down.
When he descended to hell, he plundered it.

He destroyed it for attacking his flesh, as Isaiah had foretold:
   hell was dismayed at his coming.
It was dismayed because it was trampled on; it was in bitterness
   because it was deceived.
It had taken hold of a body and was confronted by God.
It had taken hold of the visible, and the invisible had routed it.
Death, where is thy sting? Where, hell, thy victory?
Christ is risen and thou art brought to nothing.
Christ is risen and the devils are fallen.
Christ is risen and the angels rejoice.
Christ is risen and life has prevailed.
Christ is risen, and the dead are delivered from the grave.
For Christ, risen from the dead, is become the first fruits of those
   who sleep.
To him be glory and might for ever and ever. Amen.

JOHN CHRYSOSTOM *Paschal Homily* (Office of Matins for Easter in
the Byzantine Rite)

By the Ascension the Body of Christ, woven of our flesh and of
all earthly flesh, entered the realms of the Trinity. Henceforward the
creation is in God, it is the true 'burning bush' according to Maximus
the Confessor. At the same time it remains buried in the darkness
of death and separation because of humanity's hatred and cruelty
and irresponsibility. To become holy is to clear away this weight
of ashes and to uncover the glowing fire beneath, to allow life, in

Christ, to swallow up death. It is to anticipate the manifest coming of the Kingdom by disclosing its secret presence. To anticipate, and therefore to prepare and to hasten.

> Christ, having completed for us his saving work and ascended to heaven with the body which he had taken to himself, accomplishes in his own self the union of heaven and earth, of material and spiritual beings, and thus demonstrates the unity of creation in the polarity of its parts.
>
> MAXIMUS THE CONFESSOR *Commentary on the Lord's Prayer* (PG 90,877)

> Christ in his love unites created reality with uncreated reality – How wonderful is God's loving-kindness towards us! – and he shows that through grace the two are become one. The whole world enters wholly into the whole of God and by becoming all that God is, except in identity of nature, it receives in place of itself the whole God.
>
> MAXIMUS THE CONFESSOR *Ambigua* (PG 91,1308-9)

Henceforward the world is breached by an enclave of non-death. From now on we can enter into the resurrection, mark it with our own character according to our lives, and proceed by means of Christ's humanity to his divinity. For in Christ we have everything: he is 'the Way, the Truth and the Life'.

> 'The Word became flesh and dwelt among us' (John 1.14). By means of Christ who is man you proceed to Christ who is God. God is indeed beyond us. But he has become man. What was far from us has become, by the mediation of a man, very near. He is the God in whom you shall dwell. He is the man by way of whom you must reach him. Christ is at once the way you must follow and the goal you must reach. He is the Word who became flesh and dwelt among us. He put on what he was not, without losing what he was. In him humanity was revealed and God was hidden. Humanity was murdered, and God despised. But God disclosed himself and humanity rose again ... Christ is himself both man and God ... The whole of the Law depends on these commandments: 'You shall love the Lord your God with all your heart, and with all your soul, and with all your mind' and 'You shall love your neighbour as yourself. On these two commandments depend all the law and the

prophets' (Matthew 22.37-39). But in Christ you have everything. Do you wish to love your God? You have him in Christ ... Do you wish to love your neighbour? You have him in Christ.

AUGUSTINE OF HIPPO *Sermons*, 261,6 (PL 38,1206)

In Christ we have everything ...
If you want to heal your wound, he is the doctor.
If you are burning with fever, he is the fountain.
If you are in need of help, he is strength.
If you are in dread of death, he is life.
If you are fleeing the darkness, he is light.
If you are hungry, he is food: 'O taste and see that the Lord is good!
Happy are they who take refuge in him' (Psalm 34.8).

AMBROSE OF MILAN *On Virginity*, 16,99 (PL 16,305)

We are called to travel this way in the Holy Spirit. For Christ's humanity is the scene of an unending Pentecost. In Christ, we can receive the Spirit fully, drink the 'living water', the 'water welling up to eternal life'.

The Word made himself 'bearer of the flesh' in order that human beings might become 'bearers of the Spirit'.

ATHANASIUS OF ALEXANDRIA *On the Incarnation and Against the Arians*, 8 (PG 26,996)

A stream has welled up, it has become a torrent ...
It has flooded the universe, it has converged on the temple.
No bank or dam could halt it ...
It has spread over the whole face of the earth and replenished it completely.
All who were thirsty have drunk of it and their thirst has been quenched,
For the Most High has given them to drink.
By means of the living water they live for ever. Alleluia!

Odes of Solomon, 6 (Harris-Mingana, pp. 232-3)

The Holy Spirit is inseparable from our freedom. God remains in history the beggar who waits at each person's gate with infinite patience, begging for love. His silence, with which we sometimes reproach him, only shows his consideration for us. The cross and the resurrection coexist. 'Christ will be in agony to the very end of the world', he will suffer, according to Origen, until all humanity has entered the Kingdom.

> God has made himself a beggar by reason of his concern for us ... suffering mystically through his tenderness to the end of time according to the measure of each one's suffering.
>
> MAXIMUS THE CONFESSOR *Mystagogia*, 24 (PG 91,713)

> 'As for me, I am poor and in misery' (Psalm 70.6). It is Christ who utters these words, Christ who freely made himself poor for love of humanity, to make us rich.
>
> ORIGEN *Commentary on the Psalms*, Fragment 69,5-6 (Pitra, Analecta Sacra 3,88)

By that very fact Christ ensures our freedom. In the desert he rejected the temptations of riches, magic, and power that would have drawn people after him like tamed animals. He did not come down from the cross. He rose from the dead in secret, and is recognized only by those who love him. In the Holy Spirit, he walks at everyone's side, but he waits for the response of loving faith, that Yes like Mary's, by which our freedom is set free.

> The apostles gave a new testament of freedom to those who through the Holy Spirit had received a new faith in God.
>
> IRENÆUS OF LYONS *Against Heresies*, III,12,14 (SC 211, p. 244)

> In his great love God was unwilling to restrict our freedom, even though he had the power to do so. He has left us to come to him by the love of our heart alone.
>
> ISAAC OF NINEVEH *Ascetic Treatises*, 81 (Spanos, Athens 1895, p. 307)

4

God: Unity and Difference

The *kenosis* of the Son reveals the mystery of God who is Love. This gift of life is an extension of a mysterious exchange at the heart of the Deity. In God himself the One does not exclude the Other, it includes it. The Unity of God is so complete, so rich, that it is not solitude enclosed in itself, but rather the fullness of communion. And thereby, the source of all communion.

Christ reveals the Father, from whom he comes, whose Son and Word he is, and he breathes the mighty breathing of the Holy Spirit.

> I believe that if he is given the name 'Son', it is because he is of the same essence as the Father and also because he comes from the Father ... He is called Logos (Word) because he is, in relation to the Father, what the word is to the mind ... The Son makes known the nature of the Father quickly and easily, because everything begotten is an unspoken definition of the one who begot it. If, on the other hand, we wish to call him 'Word' because he is in everything, we shall not be mistaken: did not the Word create all that is? ... He is called 'Life' ... because he gives life to everything. Indeed, 'in him we live and move and have our being' (Acts 17.28) ... It is from him that we all receive the breath of life and the Holy Spirit, whom our soul contains to the limit of its openness.
>
> GREGORY NAZIANZEN *Fourth Theological Oration*, 20-1 (PG 36, 653-4)

The very name of Christ is a Trinitarian name: *Christos*, Messiah, means 'anointed' with the Messianic unction. Now the Father is the one who from all eternity 'anoints' the Son by causing the Spirit to rest on him, or rather in him, as an unction, the 'oil of gladness' of the psalm, because the Spirit is the joy of the divine communion.

> To name Christ is to confess the whole, for it is to point to God [the Father, the 'principle' of the godhead] who has anointed the Son; and to the Son who has been anointed, and to the unction itself, which is the Spirit. This accords with Peter's teaching in Acts: 'God anointed Jesus of Nazareth with the Holy Spirit' (Acts 10.38) and with the teaching of Isaiah: 'The spirit of the Lord is upon me, because the Lord has anointed me' (Isaiah 61.1). The Psalmist simply says, 'Therefore God, your God, has anointed you with the oil of gladness' (Psalm 45.7).
>
> BASIL OF CÆSAREA *On the Holy Spirit*, 12 (PG 12,116)

> By revealing the Father in the Spirit, Christ has disclosed for us the secret nature of the living God, showing us depths of love in the Trinity. To return to the great affirmations of the Gospel, only the Son knows the Father as the Father knows the Son, and as they are known by the Holy Spirit. In this wonderful unity of the godhead the One is never without the Other. For God is the infinite Unity of Persons, each of whom is a unique way of giving and receiving the divine essence.
>
> That God is, and that he is everywhere and fills the universe, is known by the angels and the saints who have purified themselves, because they are enlightened by the Holy Spirit. But where, how, and what he is, not one amongst all beings knows: only the Father knows the Son and the Son the Father, and the Holy Spirit knows the Father and the Son, since he is co-eternal and identical with them in essence. Indeed these Three who are only One know themselves, and are known by one another. As he himself said who is by nature God and Son of God, 'Who knows a person's thoughts except the spirit of a person which is in him? So also no one comprehends the thoughts of God except the Spirit of God' (1 Corinthians 2.11). And again: 'No one knows the Son except the Father, and no one knows the Father except the Son and any one to whom the Son chooses to reveal him' (Matthew 11.27).
>
> DIADOCHUS OF PHOTIKE *Catechesis*, 5 (SC 3 bis, p. 181)

The following hymn, rising at once to the mystery of the divine cosmic Logos, glorifies in a single sequence the Father as the principle of the godhead, and the Spirit as the 'bond of the Son and the Father'.

But this bond is himself a Person; nothing in God can be impersonal.
(Likewise the bond between a man and a woman is God himself, as
is seen in the face of their child.)

> O Christ, thine ineffable procreation
> preceded the beginning of the ages.
> Thou art the source of light,
> Thou art the shining ray of the Father.
> Thou scatterest the gloom
> to illuminate the souls of the saints.

> Thou art he who didst create the world
> and the orbits of the stars.
> Thou upholdest the centre of the earth.
> Thou art the Saviour of all.
> By thee the sun begins his course
> and lightens our days.
> By thee the crescent moon
> dispels the shadows of the night.
> By thine aid seeds sprout
> and flocks may graze.
> From thy never-failing fountain
> gushes the splendour of the life
> that gives fertility to the universe.
> And thou bringest forth
> the clear light of human intellect . . .
> As I sing thy glory thus,
> I praise thy Father too
> in his supreme majesty.
> I praise too the Spirit on the same throne,
> between the Begetter and the Begotten.
> As I sing the power of the Father
> my singing awakes in me
> the deepest of emotions.
> Hail, O source of the Son!
> Hail, O image of the Father!
> Hail, O dwelling of the Son!
> Hail, O imprint of the Father!
> Hail, O power of the Son!
> Hail, O beauty of the Father!
> Hail, O Spirit most pure,
> Bond of the Son and the Father!

O Christ, send down on me
This Spirit with the Father,
That he may sprinkle my soul with his dew
And fill it with his royal gifts.

SYNESIUS OF CYRENE *Hymns*, 5 (PG 66,1608-9)

The revelation of the Trinity has unfolded and continues to unfold in history. For Pentecost is a beginning, causing to spring up a river of life which flows, now underground, now on the surface, quickening its pace, which will one day – the Last Day – flow out into the sea, in the universal transfiguration.

The Old Testament has manifested the Father clearly, the Son only dimly. The New Testament has revealed the Son and implied the divinity of the Spirit.

Today the Spirit lives amongst us and makes himself more clearly known. It would actually have been dangerous openly to proclaim the Son while the divinity of the Father was not fully acknowledged, and then, before the divinity of the Son was accepted, to add as it were the extra burden of the Holy Spirit . . . It was more fitting that by adding a little at a time and, as David says, by ascending from glory to glory, the spendour of the Trinity should shine forth progressively.

GREGORY NAZIANZEN *Fifth Theological Oration*, 31,26 (PG 36, 161-4)

The Trinitarian revelation is included in the baptismal profession of faith. 'Go therefore and make disciples of all nations, baptizing them in the name of the Father and of the Son and of the Holy Spirit', was Christ's command to his apostles (Matthew 28.19). All our creeds are derived from baptismal confessions of faith and consequently exhibit a Trinitarian structure. The following is one of the oldest, dating from the second century, in which the Trinity is confessed in definite terms describing the relationships of the three Persons and their activity in the evolution of the universe and in history, creating, re-creating and sanctifying.

This is the rule of our faith, the foundation of the building, the stability of our manner of life.

Article I: God the Father, uncreated, who cannot be defined or seen, God, Creator of the Universe.

Article II: the Word of God, the Son of God, Christ Jesus our Saviour, who appeared to the prophets . . . according to the times and seasons ordained by the Father; by whom all things were made; who, above all, in the last days, to sum up all things in himself, became man amongst men, able to be seen and touched, to destroy death, to cause life to spring up, and to establish full communion between God and humanity.

Article III: the Holy Spirit, by whom the prophets prophesied, the Fathers received revelations, the righteous were led in the way of righteousness; and who in the last days was poured out in a new way on humanity, to renew it over all the earth and to bring it into union with God.

IRENÆUS OF LYONS *The Demonstration of the Apostolic Preaching,* 6 (PO 12,664)

The Trinitarian revelation is implicit also in the prayer which Christ himself taught us, the Lord's Prayer, of which the first three petitions invoke the three divine Persons. For the Son is the Father's eternal Name, which he hallowed to the point of death on a cross. And the Kingdom is identified with the Spirit, who is therefore both the unction of the Son and the Kingdom of the Father, as Paul Florensky observed.

Our Father, who art in heaven,
Hallowed be thy name.
Thy Kingdom come.

By these words the Lord is teaching those who pray to begin with the very mystery of God . . . The words of the prayer really point to the Father, the Father's name, and the Kingdom, to teach us . . . to honour, to call upon and to adore the One Trinity. For the name of God the Father, in its essential subsistence, is the only-begotten Son. And the Kingdom of God the Father, in its essential subsistence, is the Holy Spirit. For what Matthew calls 'Kingdom' another evangelist calls Holy Spirit: 'Thy Spirit come . . .' [Luke 11.2, variant reading].

MAXIMUS THE CONFESSOR *Commentary on the Lord's Prayer* (PG 90,884)

Thus the Trinity constitutes the inexhaustible fruitfulness of the Unity. From the Trinity comes all unification and all differentiation.

That is so, despite the fact that – as Dionysius insists elsewhere (*Divine Names*, II,11) – unity, in God, is always stronger than distinctions, so that 'distinctions remain indivisible and unified'.

> God, the divine Origin, is praised in holiness:
> whether as Unity, on account of the character of simplicity and unity proper to this Indivisible whose unifying power unifies us ourselves and assembles our different natures in order to lead us together ... to that unification which is modelled on God himself;
> or as Trinity, because of the thrice personal manifestation of this superessential fruitfulness whence all fatherhood in heaven and on earth receives its being and its name;
> or as Love for man, because ... the godhead has been fully imparted to our nature by one of its Persons calling humanity and raising it to himself, for Jesus mysteriously took flesh, and the eternal was thus introduced into time and by his birth penetrated the utmost depths of our nature.
>
> DIONYSIUS THE AREOPAGITE *Divine Names*, I,4 (PG 3,592)

One text from St Paul was tirelessly commented on by early Christian theologians. That is the passage in the Epistle to the Ephesians: 'One God and Father of us all, who is above all and through all and in all' (Ephesians 4.6). The Father is *God beyond all*, the origin of all that is. The incarnate Son is *God with us*, and he who becomes incarnate is none other than the Logos who gives form to the world by his creative words. The Spirit is *God in us*, the Breath, the *Pneuma*, who gives life to all and brings every object to its proper perfection. The Logos appears as order and intelligibility, the Pneuma as dynamism and life. Thus, as Maximus the Confessor said later, to contemplate the smallest object is to experience the Trinity: the very being of the object takes us back to the Father; the meaning it expresses, its *logos*, speaks to us of the Logos; its growth to fullness and beauty reveals the Breath, the Life-giver.

> Over all, the Father; and he is the head of Christ.
> Through all, the Word; and he is the head of the Church.
> In all the Spirit; and he is the living water given by the Lord to those who believe in him, love him, and know that there is only 'one God and Father of us all, who is above all and through all and in all'.
>
> IRENÆUS OF LYONS *Against Heresies*, V,18,2 (SC 153, p. 240)

The Father makes all things by the Word in the Spirit. So it is that the Unity of the Trinity is safeguarded. So it is that in the Church is proclaimed the one God who is 'above all and through all and in all' (Ephesians 4.6). He is 'above all' as Father, as author and source; 'through all' by the Word; 'in all' in the Holy Spirit.

ATHANASIUS OF ALEXANDRIA *Letters to Serapion*, I,28 (PG 26,596)

The Blessed Trinity is indivisible and enjoys Unity in regard to itself. You say 'the Father'. His Word is equally present; also the Spirit, who is in the Son.

You say 'the Son'. Now the Father is in the Son, and the Spirit is not external to the Word.

There is only one grace coming from the Father through the Son, and fulfilled in the Holy Spirit.

There is only one godhead . . . and there is only one God who is beyond all and through all and in all.

ATHANASIUS OF ALEXANDRIA *Letters to Serapion*, I,14 (PG 26,565)

St Basil in his *Treatise on the Holy Spirit* takes up this theme and links it with the passage in the psalm where the Son and the Spirit are described as the Word and the Breath of the Lord. The Breath carries the Word and enables it to find utterance; the Word makes the silence of the Breath heard, that silence of which Isaac the Syrian used to say that it is the 'mystery of the world to come'.

The Father is the origin of all, the Son realizes, and the Spirit fulfils. Everything subsists by the will of the Father, comes into being through the action of the Son, and reaches its perfection through the action of the Holy Spirit . . . 'By the word of the Lord the heavens were made, and all their host by the breath of his mouth' (Psalm 33.6). This refers . . . to the Word who was with God in the beginning, who is God. As for 'the breath of his mouth', this is 'the Spirit of truth, who proceeds from the Father' (John 15.26).

The number three therefore comes to your mind: the Lord who commands, the Word who creates, the Breath who confirms. And what can it mean to confirm, if not to make perfect in holiness?

BASIL OF CÆSAREA *Treatise on the Holy Spirit*, 16 (PG 32,136)

Gregory Nazianzen speaks of the Trinity as the unmoving movement of the One who neither remains imprisoned in his own solitude,

nor spreads himself indefinitely; for God is communion, not impersonal diffusion. The very fullness of the One demands the presence
in him of the Other; an Other who in absolute terms can only
be within the One and equal to him in infinity. But these two
are not opposed or combined in any mathematical way. For the
Third, who is Other but not Other, enables the fullness of Unity
to contain unending diversity without opposition; absolute differentiation coexists with absolute unity.

> The One enters into movement because of his fullness.
> The Two is transcended because the godhead is beyond all
> opposition.
> Perfection is achieved in the Three who is the first to overcome
> the compositeness of the Two.
> Thus the godhead does not remain confined, nor does it spread
> out indefinitely.
> GREGORY NAZIANZEN *Oration* 23,8 (PG 35,1160)

Gregory explains the Trinity by means of a double contrast. He
contrasts it on the one hand with the ancient pagan notion of diffused
divinity, and on the other with the God of Judaism who is totally
transcendent and distinct (although this statement would certainly
need qualification in the light of the mystical tradition of Judaism).
Today, from the same standpoint, we could contrast the mystery of
the Trinity with, on the one hand, the exoteric rigid monotheism
of popular Judaism and Islam, and, on the other, with Hinduism
and Buddhism and their transpersonal concept of divinity wherein
everything is engulfed, as in an immeasurable womb – which is why
India loves to speak of the 'divine Mother'.

Here too some qualification would be necessary in speaking
about both the 'way of love' in India and the various Buddhist
interpretations of grace. However, the mystery of personality and
inner life, a synthesis of which is sought with difficulty by the
various religions, seems to have been resolved in the doctrine of the
Three-in-One, where association is perceived within the absolute, or
rather the absolute within the association.

We are made in the image of God. From all eternity there is
present in God a unique mode of existence, which is at the same
time Unity and the Person in communion; and we are called to realize
this unity in Christ, when we meet him, under the divided flames
of the Spirit. Therefore we express the metaphysics of the person
in the language of Trinitarian theology. What could be called the

'Trinitarian person' is not the isolated individual of Western society (whose implicit philosophy regards human beings as 'similar' but not 'consubstantial'). Nor is it the absorbed and amalgamated human being of totalitarian society, or of systematized oriental mysticism, or of the sects. It is, and must be, a person in a relationship, in communion. The transition from divine communion to human communion is accomplished in Christ who is consubstantial with the Father and the Spirit in his divinity and consubstantial with us in his humanity.

> When I say God, it is of the Father, of the Son and of the Holy Spirit that I wish to speak without diluting the godhead beyond these limits, lest I should introduce a whole tribe of divinities, and without restricting it to something less than the three Persons, lest I be accused of impoverishing the godhead. Otherwise I should fall into the simplicity of the Judaizers or into the multiplicity of the Hellenizers . . .
> Thus the Holy of Holies, enveloped and veiled by the Seraphim, is glorified by a threefold consecration in the unity of the godhead.
> GREGORY NAZIANZEN *Oration 54, For Easter*, 4 (PG 36,628)

Gregory Nazianzen has been surnamed 'The Theologian' because he has spoken – or rather sung – of the very secret of God, 'theology' in the strict sense of the word, by celebrating the Trinity.

The mystery of the Three-in-One exceeds the bounds of fallen rationality, which knows only how to contrast or make the same. It does this with the aim of transfiguring it, transforming it into an understanding of the Person and of Love.

> I have hardly begun to think of the Unity before the Trinity bathes me in its splendour: I have hardly begun to think of the Trinity before the Unity seizes hold of me again.
> When one of the Three presents himself to me, I think it is the whole, so full to overflowing is my vision, so far beyond me does he reach. There is no room left in my mind, it is too limited to understand even one. When I combine the Three in one single thought, I see only one great flame without being able to subdivide or analyse the single light.
> GREGORY NAZIANZEN *Oration 49, On Baptism*, 41 (PG 36,417)

> When I speak of God, you should feel yourselves bathed in a single light and in three lights . . . There is undivided division,

differentiated unity. One only in the Three: such is the godhead. The Three as One only: they are the Three in whom is the godhead, or, to speak more precisely, the Three who are the godhead.

GREGORY NAZIANZEN *Oration 39*, 11 (PG 36,345)

In their expositions of the Trinity, St Basil and St Maximus the Confessor emphasize that the Three is not a number (St Basil spoke in this respect of 'meta-mathematics'). The divine Persons are not added to one another, they exist in one another: the Father is in the Son and the Son is in the Father, the Spirit is united to the Father together with the Son and 'completes the blessed Trinity' as if he were ensuring the circulation of love within it. This circulation of love was called by the Fathers *perichoresis*, another key word of their spirituality, along with the word we have already met, *kenosis*. *Perichoresis*, the exchange of being by which each Person exists only in virtue of his relationship with the others, might be defined as a 'joyful *kenosis*'. The *kenosis* of the Son in history is the extension of the *kenosis* of the Trinity and allows us to share in it.

Even if the godhead, which is beyond all, is worshipped by us as Trinity and as Unity, we know neither the three nor the one as numbers.

MAXIMUS THE CONFESSOR *On the Divine Names*, 13 (PG 4,412)

When we are speaking of unity we do not count by the method of addition to reach plurality, because we do not say 'one, two, three'; nor 'first, second, third'. 'I am the first and I am the last' (Isaiah 44.6). Of a second God we have not heard anything, seeing that when we worship a 'God from God' we confess the difference between the Persons who always remain in the Principle of Unity ... because in God the Father and in God the Only-Begotten we are contemplating only a single reality in the unchanging godhead reflected as it were in a mirror. The Son, indeed, is in the Father, and the Father in the Son, since the latter is like the former and the former is like the latter, so to that extent they are one. According to the distinction of Persons they are 'one' and 'one', but according to their unity of essence, the two are only one ... The Holy Spirit also is one and is unity; he also is spoken of separately; through the Son, who is one and is unity, he is united to the Father, who is one and is unity; and by himself he completes the Blessed Trinity

... The proof that he possesses the same nature as they derives not only from that, but also from the fact that he is said to be 'from God'. Not at all in the way in which all things are 'from God', but in such a way that he proceeds 'from God'; not by generation like the Son, but as Breath from the mouth of God.

'Mouth' here does not denote part of the body, nor does 'breath' denote a puff of air that is quickly spent. 'Mouth' here has to be understood in a manner worthy of God, and 'breath' describes a living essence, the effective cause of sanctification.

BASIL OF CÆSAREA *Treatise on the Holy Spirit*, 18 (PG 32,149-52)

The divine essence, the godhead, 'God', does not exist otherwise than in the Persons. The source of the godhead, the sole origin of the Son and of the Spirit is the Father. The early Church hardly ever spoke of 'God' in general, a God in whom the Persons could then be distinguished. It spoke of the Father, for 'the name Father is greater even than that of God'. The ocean of the divine essence springs from the fathomless depths of a Person, the Father. Yet through Christ we can, in the Holy Spirit, call him *Abba*, the word of trust and tenderness by which a small child calls his father. So the apophatic antinomy is also the paradox of the Father as Origin in unfathomed depths, and the Father as *Abba*, 'Daddy'.

In practice, the fact that the Father is the 'origin' of the Trinity does not imply any superiority or domination for his own advantage. As Christ will 'empty himself' on the cross, so the Father 'empties himself' for the benefit of the Son, to whom he gives all that he has and all that he is – the fullness of the divine unity – and on whom he causes his Spirit to rest, the Spirit by whom they love each other and find joy together. 'Spiritual fatherhood' after the likeness of the divine Fatherhood is sacrificial and liberating; it imparts the spirit of life and liberty. Dostoyevsky, in *The Brothers Karamazov*, has shown how spiritual fatherhood like this is the only answer to the dialectic of 'master' and 'slave', and to fatherhood in its degenerate form, which sons experience as tyranny and rivalry.

The following passages should be read in the light of this refusal of any 'subordinationism'. Irenæus of Lyons speaks of the Son and the Spirit as 'hands of God' (*the* God, par excellence, for the first Christians, is the Father). Dionysius depicts them as the shoots and flowers of the 'engendering' godhead. Gregory Nazianzen emphasizes that it is the Father who makes the Trinity a living unity: we cannot speak of the divine 'nature' or 'essence' except within the Three, within their communion which comes from the Father and returns to him.

As if God had no hands of his own! From all eternity he has with
him the Word and Wisdom, the Son and the Spirit. It is by them
and in them that he does all things.

IRENÆUS OF LYONS *Against Heresies*, IV,20,1 (SC 100 bis, p. 626)

The Father represents in the bosom of the deity the element of
generation, Jesus and the Spirit are after a fashion the divine shoots
of God's engendering deity, and as it were its superessential flowers
and radiance.

DIONYSIUS THE AREOPAGITE *Divine Names* II, 7-8 (PG 3,645)

The single nature of the Three is God. In regard to his oneness he
is the Father. The others come from him and return to him without
being confused with one another. They coexist with him, without
being separated in time, in purpose, or in power.

GREGORY NAZIANZEN *Oration* 42 (PG 36,476)

In a text already quoted Dionysius has reminded us that the
godhead is not spirit or sonship or fatherhood in the sense in which
we usually use these words. He goes on to explain that we must
learn to reason from the opposite direction. It is not a question of
thinking *about* the Trinity, but *in* it, starting from the Trinity as the
unshakeable foundation of all Christian thought.

Divine fatherhood and sonship are suggested to us by the gift of
that basic fatherhood and sonship, the gift by which spiritual beings
in conforming to God receive their being and the name of gods,
sons of gods, and fathers of gods.

DIONYSIUS THE AREOPAGITE *Divine Names*, II,8 (PG 3,645)

In particular the divine mystery transcends the distinction
between masculine and feminine. It integrates the symbolism of
both at the same time. The Bible repeatedly bears witness to
God's maternal tenderness; it speaks of his 'bowels of mercy', that
is *rachamim* in the visceral sense. St John mentions the 'Father's
bosom'. God is therefore at once father and mother, and the *Odes
of Solomon* call the Son and the Spirit the two breasts that feed us
with the milk of immortality.

By his mysterious divinity God is Father. But the tender love he has for us makes him become a mother. The Father in loving makes himself feminine.

CLEMENT OF ALEXANDRIA *Can a Rich Man be Saved?* 37 (PG 9,642)

Nevertheless, the ultimate predominance of fatherly symbolism indicates communion without confusion. The ultimate predominance of motherly symbolism (as is often the case in India) would indicate a confusion that obliterated the person.

At Pentecost the Father gives the Spirit 'in the name of the Son'. And the Spirit is the 'Spirit of the Son', the 'Spirit of Christ'. The Christian West has insisted on this basic truth. It has contemplated the 'movement' of the divine 'consubstantiality', the movement of love in the Trinity, going from Father to Son, then from Father and Son to the Holy Spirit who imparts it to us. However, St Augustine says that if the Spirit comes from the Son as well as the Father, (in Latin *Filioque*) he comes *principaliter* from the Father who remains the sole origin of the other divine Persons.

The Christian East, some of whose formulations – particularly those of the Alexandrian Fathers – are fairly similar to those we have considered, also stressed the giving of the Word by the Spirit. It was by the Spirit that the Word became flesh, it is by the Spirit that he makes himself present to the Church. Thus the relationship of the Son and the Spirit is seen to be one of mutual service. The Spirit comes from the Father in the Son and manifests him. The Son is born of the Father in the Spirit and is manifested by the Spirit. And both reveal the Father. In the Church the same reciprocity and the same mutual service must exist between the priesthood, which bears witness to the sacramental presence of Christ, and prophecy, which reveals the freedom of each conscience in the Holy Spirit.

Christ's existence is an existence in the Holy Spirit whose purpose is the 'pneumatization' of all flesh.

The coming of Christ? The Spirit precedes it. Christ's presence in the flesh? The Spirit is inseparable from it. Miracles and gifts of healing? It is the Spirit who bestows them. Demons driven out? In the Spirit of God . . . Sins forgiven? In the grace of the Spirit, for 'you were washed, you were sanctified, you were justified in the name of the Lord Jesus Christ and in the Spirit of our God' (1 Corinthians 6.11). Union with God? The Spirit effects it, since

'God has sent the Spirit of his Son into our hearts, crying "Abba! Father!"' (Galatians 4.6). The resurrection of the dead? It is brought about by the Spirit, for 'when thou sendest forth thy Spirit, they are created; and thou renewest the face of the earth' (Psalm 104.30).

BASIL OF CÆSAREA *Treatise on the Holy Spirit*, 19 (PG 32,157)

As for the conditions established for humanity by our great God and Saviour Jesus Christ in accordance with God's goodness ... all was effected by the Spirit.

He was present from the first in the flesh of the Lord when he made himself 'unction' and he is his inseparable companion, as it is written, 'He on whom you see the Spirit descend and remain ... is my beloved Son' (John 1.33; Matthew 3.17). Also: 'You know ... how God anointed Jesus of Nazareth with the Holy Spirit' (Acts 10.38). Then the whole of Christ's activity developed in the power of the Spirit. He was present also when Christ was tempted by the devil, for it is written: 'Jesus was led up by the Spirit into the wilderness to be tempted by the devil' (Matthew 4.1). He was still with him, inseparably, when Jesus performed his miracles, for, 'it is by the Spirit of God that I cast out demons' (Matthew 12.28). He did not depart from him after his resurrection from the dead. When the Lord, to renew man and to restore to him the grace received from the breath of God, breathed on the face of his disciples, what did he say? 'Receive the Holy Spirit' (John 20.22).

BASIL OF CÆSAREA *Treatise on the Holy Spirit*, 16 (PG 32,140)

Formulations are to be found in the Fathers or in ancient liturgical texts which, if we knew how to develop them, would enable us to harmonize the two approaches, Western and Eastern, to the 'procession' of the Holy Spirit. Thus, in the third century, at a time when Christian reflection was still fluid and diverse, Dionysius of Rome in a letter to his namesake at Alexandria notes that the Spirit proceeds from the Father *in* the Son (text quoted by St Athanasius in his *Letter on the Decrees of the Council of Nicæa*, 26).

In the following century Athanasius himself writes:

The Spirit is not external to the Word, but because he is in the Word it is through him that he is in God [God, here, denotes the Father as 'source of the godhead'].

Letter to Serapion, III (PG 26,633)

If the Father is mentioned, his Word is also present with him, and
equally the Spirit who is in the Son.
Letter to Serapion, I (PG 26,565)

We might ask whether the subsequent controversies did not
arise because people partly forgot the properly divine 'logic' which is
always simultaneously one and threefold, quite surpassing the fallen
rationality, the process of which remains binary. To say that the Spirit
'proceeds' from the Father is necessarily to name the Son, since from
all eternity the Father puts his Other in unity; so when he causes the
Spirit to 'proceed' he remains the Father *of the Son*. To say that the
Son is 'begotten' of the Father is necessarily to name the Spirit, the
Breath that carries the Word. For the Spirit, as Gregory of Nyssa for
example writes, is at the same time 'the Kingdom of the Father and
the Unction of the Son' (*Against Apollinaris*, 52 (PG 45,1249)).

The Byzantine liturgy for Pentecost admirably expounds this
'meta-logic' which is that of ineffable Love:

> Come, ye people, let us adore God in three persons:
> The Father in the Son, with the Holy Spirit.
> For the Father from everlasting begets the Word,
> who shares his Kingdom and his eternity,
> and the Holy Spirit is in the Father,
> glorified with the Son,
> a single power,
> a single essence,
> a single godhead.
> This it is whom we adore, saying:
> Holy God, who didst create all by thy Son with the aid of the Holy
> Spirit;
> Holy and Strong, by whom we have come to know the Father, by
> whom the Holy Spirit has come into the world;
> Holy and Immortal, Spirit of Consolation, who dost proceed from
> the Father and dwellest in the Son:
> Glory be to thee, O Holy Trinity!
> *Great Vespers of Pentecost in the Byzantine Rite*

The Church's existence also must be an existence in the Spirit:

And the Church? Is it not the work of the Spirit? For it is the
Spirit, Paul says, who has given to the Church 'first apostles, second

prophets, third teachers, then workers of miracles, then healers, helpers, administrators, speakers in various kinds of tongues' (1 Corinthians 12.28). The Spirit establishes this order in the distribution of his gifts.

BASIL OF CÆSAREA *Treatise on the Holy Spirit*, 16 (PG 32,141)

In God the Holy Spirit is almost anonymous (since God is entirely Spirit, entirely Holy). He is almost confused with the unmoving movement of love in the divine nature, with the divine 'common nature', as St Basil says. He is revealed as rich, 'variegated' with all the divine names, and so almost indistinguishable from the divine energies that he imparts to us, in our inmost depths. It is as if he were effacing himself.

When I think of the profusion of the names of the Spirit I am seized with dread: Spirit of God, Spirit of Christ, Spirit of Adoption. He renews us in baptism and resurrection. He blows where he wills. Source of light and life, he makes of me a temple, he makes me divine ... Everything that God does is done by the Spirit. He multiplies himself in tongues of fire and he multiplies his gifts, he raises up preachers, apostles, prophets, pastors, teachers ... He is another Comforter ... as if he were another God.

GREGORY NAZIANZEN *Fifth Theological Oration*, 29 (PG 36,165)

The Spirit is the hidden God, the inward God, deeper than our greatest depth. He gives life to all things and we breathe him without being aware of it. He is the breath of God in the breathing of the world, of humanity.

God has given to the earth the breath which feeds it. It is his breath that gives life to all things. And if he were to hold his breath, everything would be annihilated. His breath vibrates in yours, in your voice. It is the breath of God that you breathe – and you are unaware of it.

THEOPHILUS OF ANTIOCH *Three Books to Autolycus*, I,7 (SC 20, p. 72)

But this hidden God is not lost in immanence; he is entirely movement towards Christ, and, through Christ, towards the Father, in the same way as the energies that he imparts flow from the Father through the Son.

> The way to the knowledge of God leads from the Spirit in Unity through the Son in Unity to the Father of Unity, and, in the opposite direction, the fullness and the holiness of the divine essence, its royal dignity, comes from the Father by means of the Son to the Holy Spirit.
>
> BASIL OF CÆSAREA *Treatise on the Holy Spirit*, 18 (PG 32,153)

> The Father being the source and the Son being called a river, we can be said to drink the Spirit. For it is written: 'All were made to drink of one Spirit' (1 Corinthians 12.13). But, given the Spirit to drink, we drink Christ . . .
>
> And again: since Christ is the true Son, we, by receiving the Spirit, are transformed into sons, 'For you did not receive the spirit of slavery . . . but you have received the spirit of sonship' (Romans 8.15). Being transformed into sons by the Spirit, it is clear that it is into Christ that we are transformed . . .
>
> The Spirit has been given to us – as the Lord said: 'Receive the Holy Spirit' (John 20.22) – God is in us. This is actually what John wrote: 'If we love one another, God abides in us . . . by this we know that we abide in him and he in us, because he has given us of his own Spirit' (1 John 4.12-13). And God being in us, the Son is also in us, for the Son himself says, '[The Father and I] will come to him and make our home with him' (John 14.23).
>
> And again: the Son is the life – for he says: 'I am the life' (John 14.6) – and we are brought to life in the Spirit according to the saying: 'He who raised Christ Jesus from the dead will give life to your mortal bodies also through his Spirit which dwells in you' (Romans 8.11). And when we have been brought to new life in the Spirit, Christ himself lives in us: '. . . it is no longer I who live, but Christ who lives in me' (Galatians 2.20).
>
> ATHANASIUS OF ALEXANDRIA *Letter to Serapion*, I,19 (PG 26, 573-6)

A solitary God would not be 'Love without limits'. A God who made himself twofold, according to a pattern common in mythology, would make himself the root of an evil multiplicity to which he could only put a stop by re-absorbing it into himself. The Three-in-One denotes the perfection of Unity – of 'Super-unity', according to Dionysius the Areopagite – fulfilling itself in communion and becoming the source and foundation of all communion. It suggests the perpetual surmounting of contradiction, and of solitude as well, in the bosom of an infinite Unity. Each divine Person 'possesses unity through his relationship with himself' (St John of Damascus, *On the Orthodox Faith*, I,8). The best image of the Father, according to 'a monk of the Eastern Church', is the heart: 'Each heartbeat is an impulse by which the Father gives himself. These beats send towards us the Blood of the Son, given life by the breath of the Spirit' (*Jésus, simples regardes sur le Sauveur*, Chevetogne 1959, p. 144). It is in this rhythm of the heart that we are called to participate.

5

The Human Vocation

The human vocation is to fulfil one's humanity by becoming God through grace, that is to say by living to the full. It is to make of human nature a glorious temple. 'Do not forget that to live is glory', said Rilke on his deathbed. And it is a glory that overturns death, or rather, reverses it.

> 'The human being is an animal who has received the vocation to become God.'
> Words of BASIL OF CÆSAREA, quoted by GREGORY NAZIANZEN
> *Eulogy of Basil the Great, Oration 43, 48* (PG 36,560)

> Every spiritual being is, by nature, a temple of God, created to receive into itself the glory of God.
> ORIGEN *Commentary on St Matthew's Gospel, 16,23* (PG 13,1453)

The human being, God's image, has to attain to his likeness, which is at once meeting and sharing, keeping closely to the great Trinitarian sequence of the creation and re-creation of humanity.

> That is the order, the rhythm, the movement by which created humanity is fashioned after the image and likeness of the uncreated God. The Father makes the decisions and gives the commands, the Son carries them out and adapts them, the Spirit provides nourishment and growth, and humanity progresses little by little.
> IRENÆUS OF LYONS *Against Heresies, IV,38,3* (SC 100 bis, pp. 954-6)

This development both personal and collective – the collective being a dimension of the personal and not the other way round –

took on a tragic character with the 'fall' and 'redemption', but its basic movement and its goal did not change.

> It was necessary in the first place for human beings to be created; and having been created, to grow; and having grown, to become adult; and having become adult, to multiply; and having multiplied, to become strong; and having become strong, to be glorified; and having been glorified, to see their Lord. Indeed ... the vision of God obtains deliverance from death, the incorruptibility which is the expression of our union with God.
>
> IRENÆUS OF LYONS *Against Heresies*, IV,38,3 (SC 100 bis, p. 956)

In the incarnation humanity is the 'boundary' or 'frontier' between the visible and the invisible, the carnal and the spiritual, like a mediator between creation and the creator. This vocation is present also in the non-biblical religions and also in modern humanism, in the sciences and in the arts. But in these latter cases the vocation is limited either by the absorption of the human in the divine or by the assertion of the human being against God. It is the incarnation of the Word that fully reopens to humanity its creative destiny.

> The great Architect of the universe conceived and produced a being endowed with both natures, the visible and the invisible: God created the human being, bringing its body forth from the pre-existing matter which he animated with his own Spirit ... Thus in some way a new universe was born, small and great at one and the same time. God set this 'hybrid' worshipper on earth to contemplate the visible world, and to be initiated into the invisible; to reign over earth's creatures, and to obey orders from on high. He created a being at once earthly and heavenly, insecure and immortal, visible and invisible, halfway between greatness and nothingness, flesh and spirit at the same time ... an animal en route to another native land, and, most mysterious of all, made to resemble God by simple submission to the divine will.
>
> GREGORY NAZIANZEN *Oration 45, For Easter*, 7 (PG 36,850)

Humanity is called to take the world into itself, to 'comprehend' it with its intelligence and its love, in order to articulate the worship that the universe secretly offers, and to leave its own mark on the world, 'to name the creatures', according to Genesis. Humanity is at

the same time 'microcosm and *microtheos*' (Gregory of Nyssa), synthesis of the universe and offspring of God. Maximus the Confessor,
profoundly, prefers to call it 'macrocosm' (a great universe) since,
being the image of God, it exceeds even the cosmos in grandeur.
Being greater, it can take it into itself in order to give it life.

Indeed, humanity is quickened by a 'flash of the godhead', in
Gregory Nazianzen's vivid phrase, which seizes hold of it, draws
it along, will not leave it in peace, and denies it the possibility of
complete self-identification with the earth from which it was fashioned. 'Man is something infinitely greater than man', said Pascal.
No earth-bound conditionings could satisfy or define humanity.

The Fathers never ceased to glorify this irreducible greatness
of humanity, this 'fathomless depth' in the human being which is
where God is. Humanity is in the image of God because, like God
himself, it escapes all definition.

> An image is not truly an image if it does not possess all the
> characteristics of its pattern ... It is characteristic of divinity to
> be incomprehensible: this must also be true of the image. If the
> image could be essentially understood while the original remained
> incomprehensible, the image would not be an image at all. But our
> spiritual dimension, which is precisely that wherein we are the image
> of our Creator, is beyond our ability to explain ... by this mystery
> within us we bear the imprint of the incomprehensible godhead.
>
> GREGORY OF NYSSA *On the Creation of Man*, 11 (PG 44,155)

It could equally well be said that God is humanity's place, and
that this is more important than any facts of biology, sociology
or psychology precisely because it is the opening through which
God comes to dwell in humanity, and through which humanity
itself can ascend to God. This is the only answer to totalitarian
ideologies, that is, to 'social sciences', when they are tempted to
become all-embracing and reductionist.

> Understand that you are another universe, a universe in miniature;
> that in you there are sun, moon, and stars too. If it were not so,
> the Lord would not have said to his disciples, 'You are the light
> of the world' (Matthew 5.14). Do you still hesitate to believe
> that there are sun and moon in you when you are told that
> you are the light of the world?
>
> Do you wish to hear another text in order that you may not
> regard yourself as something small and worthless ... ?

This universe has its own Lord who rules it, who dwells in it and is God Almighty, as he himself declared by the prophets, 'Do I not fill heaven and earth?' (Jeremiah 23.24)

Hear then what God Almighty says of you – I mean of humanity: 'I will live in them and move among them' (2 Corinthians 6.16). And he adds the following, which applies to you: 'I will be a father to you, and you shall be my sons and daughters, says the Lord Almighty' (2 Corinthians 6.18).

ORIGEN *Fifth Homily on Leviticus*, 2 (GCS 6,336-7)

The Word of God took a lump of newly created earth, formed it with his immortal hands into our shape, and imparted life to it: for the spirit that he breathed into it is a flash of the invisible godhead. Thus from clay and breath was created humanity, the image of the Immortal . . . That is why in my earthy nature I am attached to life here below, while I also have in me a portion of the godhead; therefore my heart is tormented by the desire for the world to come.

GREGORY NAZIANZEN *Dogmatic Poems*, 8 (PG 37,452)

Know to what extent the Creator has honoured you above all the rest of creation. The sky is not an image of God, nor is the moon, nor the sun, nor the beauty of the stars, nor anything of what can be seen in creation. You alone have been made the image of the Reality that transcends all understanding, the likeness of imperishable beauty, the imprint of true divinity, the recipient of beatitude, the seal of the true light. When you turn to him you become that which he is himself . . . There is nothing so great among beings that it can be compared with your greatness. God is able to measure the whole heaven with his span. The earth and the sea are enclosed in the hollow of his hand. And although he is so great and holds all creation in the palm of his hand, you are able to hold him, he dwells in you and moves within you without constraint, for he has said, 'I will live and move among them' (2 Corinthians 6.16).

GREGORY OF NYSSA *Second Homily on the Song of Songs* (PG 44,765)

This capacity for transcendence that 'distances' us from the world, and makes us responsible for it, gives us the dignity of kings, or more precisely priest-kings, since our sovereignty is inseparable from offering. The image of God is revealed in us by our intelligence, by our vocation to express meaning, and by love, since God is wisdom, *logos*, and love. These patristic conceptions are not irrational but belong to a rationality which goes beyond the 'horizontal' connection of causes and effects, being enriched and broadened by a 'vertical' contemplation of the mystery and meaning of creatures and things, and their transparency to the divine *logoi*.

> The fact of being created in the image of God means that humanity right from the moment of creation was endowed with a royal character . . . The godhead is wisdom and *logos* [reason, meaning]; in yourself too you see intelligence and thought, images of the original intelligence and thought . . . God is love and source of love: the divine Creator has drawn this feature on our faces too.
>
> GREGORY OF NYSSA *On the Creation of Man* (PG 44,136-7)

Thus our higher faculties reflect divine qualities, and are called to bear fruit in 'virtues' which will be so many participations in the divine Names, in the modes of the divine presence. The image draws its essential power, however, from the 'principle of immortality', which arouses within us an attraction towards what transcends us, a 'desire for eternity'. Thereby we become greater than the universe into which we were born and which seeks to take possession of us. Thereby we assert our basic freedom. Ultimately, then, being in the image of God signifies personality, freedom.

> If humanity is called to life in order to share in the divine nature, it must have been suitably constituted for the purpose . . . It was essential that a certain kinship with the divine should have been mixed in human nature, so that this affinity should predispose it to seek what is related to it . . . That is why humanity was given life, intelligence, wisdom, and all the qualities worthy of the godhead, so that each one of them should cause it to desire what is akin to it. And since eternity is inherent in the godhead, it was absolutely imperative that our nature should not lack it but should have in itself the principle of immortality. By virtue of this inborn faculty it could always be drawn towards what is superior to it and retain the desire for eternity.
>
> That is summed up in a single phrase in the account of the creation of the world: 'God created man in his own image' (Genesis 1.27).
>
> GREGORY OF NYSSA *Catechetical Orations,* 5 (PG 45,21-4)

Humanity was free from the beginning. For God is freedom and humanity was made in the image of God.

IRENÆUS OF LYONS *Against Heresies*, IV,37,4 (SC 100 bis, p. 932)

He who created human beings in order to make them share in his own fullness so disposed their nature that it contains the principle of all that is good, and each of these dispositions draws them to desire the corresponding divine attribute. So God could not have deprived them of the best and most precious of his attributes, self-determination, freedom . . .

GREGORY OF NYSSA *Catechetical Orations*, 5 (PG 45,24)

In the West this mystery of freedom was distorted by the necessary but impetuous and exaggerated reaction of St Augustine to the voluntarism of Pelagius. Increasingly freedom and grace were contrasted by describing their respective roles in terms of causality. Can the free will of human beings be the cause of their salvation, as Pelagius claimed? Or is it the grace of God alone, as Augustine said? The latter's intuition – I am a wretch who has been saved gratuitously and so I sing *Alleluia* – is correct existentially, subjectively, but dangerous when stated objectively as part of a system. (In the 16th and 17th centuries, as is well known, this view hardened into the doctrine of twofold predestination, to salvation or to hell, without the individual being able to do much about it.) The Greek Fathers (and some of the Latin Fathers), according to whom the creation of humanity entailed a real risk on God's part, laid the emphasis on salvation through love: 'God can do everything except force man to love him'. The gift of grace saves, but only in an encounter of love. Grace envelops the individual, the whole person, like an atmosphere ready to seep in through the smallest breach. But only faith in its sovereign freedom can cause the breach to be made. Then it becomes an active opening-up, the beginning of abandonment to the divine life. And for the good of humanity as a whole some are 'set apart', for it is not the isolated individual but humanity in communion, or rather, all human beings together, who truly constitute the image of God. We can see that this 'complete Adam', this 'single man', is fragmented; we are continually breaking him in pieces. But Christ, the 'definitive Adam', puts him together again, the same but different, in the likeness of the Trinity. For St Gregory of Nyssa in particular the text 'Let us make man in our image' concerns humanity considered in its ontological unity.

It is the whole of [human] nature, extending from the beginning
to the end [of history], that constitutes the one image of Him who
is.

GREGORY OF NYSSA *On the Creation of Man*, 16 (PG 44,183)

To say that there are 'many human beings' is a common abuse of
language. Granted there is a plurality of those who share in the
same human nature . . . but in all of them, humanity is one.

GREGORY OF NYSSA *That there are not three Gods* (PG 45,117)

On the other hand, it is the whole human being, soul and
body, that is in the image of God. The body, by receiving the
life-giving breath of the Spirit, is enabled to be the visible expression
of the person: to be not a mask but a face. Like the Bible, the
Fathers assert that only the unity of soul and body constitutes the
human being. The visible aspect of humanity would not exist if
it were not *the invisible made visible*. Soul and body must mutu-
ally symbolize each other, according to Maximus the Confessor.
That is why the Saints, even when they are very ugly, are beautiful, with a beauty that springs from their intelligent and loving
hearts. The body is itself called to life and resurrection, therefore
similarly the cosmos, whose energies never cease to pass through
the body. In the 2nd century the Apostolic Fathers laid great emphasis on this dignity of the body. For them, Christianity proclaims, prepares and anticipates the resurrection of the flesh, as is
proved both by Christ's bodily resurrection and by his 'ascension',
which enabled earthly flesh (Merejkovsky's 'holy flesh of earth') to
penetrate into God himself. Such an idea is at the very opposite
pole from any ontological dualism, either the dualism of a degenerate Platonism where the body is the tomb of the soul and only
the soul is akin to the divine world, or that of Manicheism and
Gnosticism which regard bodily existence as the creation of an evil
Demiurge.

As a result early Christianity was fundamentally concerned not
with the immortality of the soul, which was regarded as incontro-
vertible but contrary to nature and only provisional, but with the
resurrection of the body, of the cosmos as a whole, the body of
humanity. The whole of the Church's life should be a 'laboratory
for the resurrection' (Dumitru Staniloae); it ought to vibrate with a
mighty resurrectional upsurge embracing all humanity and the whole
universe.

It is not in a part of [human] nature that the image is found, but nature in its totality is the image of God.

GREGORY OF NYSSA *On the Creation of Man*, (PG 44,185)

Spirits without bodies will never be spiritual men and women. It is our entire being, that is to say, the soul and flesh combined, which by receiving the Spirit of God constitutes the spiritual man.

IRENÆUS OF LYONS *Against Heresies*, V,8,2 (SC 153, p. 96)

Is it the soul, as such, that constitutes the human being? No. That is only the soul. Is it the body, then, that is called human? No. That is only the body. Consequently, since these two components, separately, do not constitute a human being, it must be the unity formed by the conjunction of both that alone deserves the name. It is the whole person, certainly, whom God has called to life and to resurrection, not merely a part. It is the human being, whole and entire, who is called, that is to say, the soul, but also the body. If that is so, how can it be conceded that one should be saved without the other when together they form an indissoluble union? Once the possibility of the flesh knowing a new birth has been admitted, what an unfair discrimination it would be for the soul to be saved without the body.

JUSTIN *Fragment 8* (in H. Lassiat, *L'Actualité de la catéchèse apostolique*, Sisteron 1979, p. 173)

If indeed the flesh possesses no useful function, why did Christ heal it? And why, in particular, did he go so far as to raise the dead to life? What was his purpose? Was it not to show us how the resurrection was to take place? How, moreover, did he raise the dead? Was it souls or bodies? Clearly, it was both together. If the resurrection was to be only spiritual, he would have to have shown, at his own resurrection, his body lying dead on one side, and his soul on the other in its risen state. But he did nothing of the sort. He rose with his body, convinced that the promise of life concerned it too. Why did he rise in his crucified flesh, if not to demonstrate the reality of the resurrection of the flesh? Wishing to convince his disciples who were refusing to admit that he had really risen with his body . . . he offered himself to be touched by them and showed them the marks of the nails in his hands. But because they still could not admit that it was he, in his own body, he asked to eat with them

... and he ate some honey and fish. Thus he proved to them that resurrection would come to our actual fleshly bodies. Furthermore, having declared that our dwelling-place will be in the heavens, he wanted to show that it is not impossible for the flesh to go to 'heaven'. Indeed, they saw him 'taken up into heaven' (Mark 16.19) just as he was, that is to say, in the flesh.

JUSTIN *Fragment 9* (in H. Lassiat, op. cit., p. 156-7)

At the inmost centre of the human being the great spiritual writers of the undivided Church see 'the heart'. This 'heart', which incorporates the organ so named without being wholly identified with it, is the site of a 'love-knowledge' in which the whole human being is at once gathered together and opened up. This 'Spirit-heart' is open to the Holy Spirit and receives the light of the godhead to communicate it to the body ... For the flesh can become spiritual, while on the other hand the highest intelligence, if it refuses to admit mystery, becomes fleshly.

Grace engraves on the heart of the children of light the laws of the Spirit. They must not therefore draw their confidence only from the Scriptures written in ink, for God's grace also inscribes the laws of the Spirit, the celestial mysteries, on the tables of the heart. The heart, in fact, directs and rules the whole body. Once grace possesses the pastures of the heart, it reigns over all its members and all its thoughts. For therein is the mind and all the thoughts of the soul and its hope. Through the heart, grace passes into all the members of the body.

PSEUDO-MACARIUS *Fifth Homily*, 20 (PG 34,589)

The account of the 'fall' in Genesis is given by several Fathers a very profound interpretation which rules out any 'jealousy' on God's part, and any idea of a terrifying godhead. The 'tree of life' was the tree of contemplation, the possibility of knowing the world in God. Adam and Eve would not have been able to approach it except after long preparation; if they had gone there in a state of childish innocence (a theme dear to St Irenæus), or in an attitude of egocentric greed, in order to plunder the world instead of reverencing it and offering it to God, they would have been burnt by the brilliance of the godhead. They needed to mature, to grow to awareness by willing detachment and by faith, a loving trust in a personal God.

Hence the prohibition, which the tempter insinuates to be a general and absolute ban, imposed by a jealous creator seeking to tyrannize over his creatures. Then they wish to 'take possession of the things of God without God'. And God keeps them away from the tree of life to avoid their being deified whilst in a state of falsehood and 'self-idolatry', which would mean an irremediable hell. Hence we have death, the result of the transgression, but also its remedy, since it makes humanity aware of its finiteness, and lays it open to grace. Hence also the 'tunics of skin' with which God, according to Genesis, clothed them after their fall. These are ambiguous, as death is, inasmuch as they signify a mortal life. For on the one hand they symbolize a certain opaqueness, that of a universe delivered up by humanity to death. On the other hand they represent an adaptation to this state of affairs, a protection that makes possible history, and that slow progress of revelation about which St Irenæus speaks. For the fall veiled but in no way destroyed the image of God in humanity. The symbolic account of the fall portrays an original condition which we cannot reach with our present understanding, because the conditions of time and space and material existence in it were utterly different (we can scarcely begin to imagine them except in Christ's transfigured humanity). What we call evolution is a merciful resumption by divine Wisdom of this fallen creation which was otherwise doomed to a 'flood' of disintegration. By evolution 'tunics of skin' were developed, so that humanity, stripped of the garment of paradisial light, might at last regain it.

The fall is permanent, as are all the principal acts of spiritual history. The Logos never ceases conquering death by death, bringing forth life in all its complexity, from a disintegrating universe. The cross and the resurrection are inherent in the very stuff of things. They are at work right up till the moment when the incarnation and the passion of the Word give rise, in this mortal life of victory and defeat, to an immortal life where humanity is invited to join . in the final complete victory.

> God placed man in paradise – whatever this paradise was – and gave him freedom, in order that the happiness of the beneficiary might be as great as that of the benefactor. He bade him watch over immortal plants, possibly divine thoughts . . . He gave him a law to exercise his freedom. This law was a commandment: he might pick the fruit of some trees, and one that he might not touch. This tree was the tree of knowledge. God had not planted it originally for the undoing of man and it was not out of jealousy that God forbade

him to go near it – let not the enemies of God intervene here; let them not imitate the serpent – no, it was of his goodness, if this prohibition be understood rightly. For that tree was, to my mind, the tree of contemplation, which only those could enter into without harm whose spiritual preparation had reached sufficient perfection. On the other hand, that tree could only be a source of misfortune for souls as yet too coarse, endowed with too bestial an appetite, just as solid food is harmful to babies who still need milk. When through the devil's hatred ... the first man had succumbed – alas! for my weakness, for that weakness of my distant ancestor is mine ... he was cut off from the tree of life, from paradise and from God himself. He clothed himself in tunics of skin. This can signify a flesh more dense, mortal and perverse. And for the first time he recognized his own loss of dignity and tried to hide from God. But he also gained us death ... so that evil should not be immortal. The penalty became in this way love for humanity. That, I think, is the divine way of punishing.

GREGORY NAZIANZEN *Oration 45, For Easter*, 8 (PG 36,850)

Having become God by deification, human beings would have been able to contemplate, with God himself, the works of God. They would have received knowledge of them in God.

MAXIMUS THE CONFESSOR *Questions to Thalassius*, Prologue
(PG 90,257)

Now human beings sought to take hold of the things of God without God, before God, and not after his will.

MAXIMUS THE CONFESSOR *Ambigua* (PG 91,1156)

Death is nothing else but separation from God ... and as a necessary consequence, death of the body.

MAXIMUS THE CONFESSOR *Centuries on Charity* II,93 (PG 90,425)

Thus God cannot be held responsible for evil, for he is the author of what is, and not of what is not. It is he who made sight, not blindness ... And that without subjecting us to his good pleasure by any violent constraint. He did not draw us towards what is good against our will, as if we were an inanimate object. If when the light shines very brightly ... someone chooses to hide his eyes by lowering his eyelids, the sun is not responsible for the fact that he cannot see it.

GREGORY OF NYSSA *Catechetical Oration* 7 (PG 45,32)

For his own part God could have given human beings the fullness right from the beginning, but they were incapable of receiving it because they were only little children.

IRENÆUS OF LYONS *Against Heresies*, IV,38,1 (SC 100 bis, p. 946)

It is precisely in this that God differs from humanity: God creates; humanity is created. He who creates is always the same, while they who are created must acknowledge a beginning, an intermediate state and a maturity ... They receive knowledge and progress towards God. For in so far as God is always the same, to that extent human beings found in God will always be making progress towards God.

IRENÆUS OF LYONS *Against Heresies*, IV,11,2 (SC 100 bis, p. 500)

How could you be God when you have not yet become human? How could you be complete when you have only just been created?

IRENÆUS OF LYONS *Against Heresies*, IV,39,2 (SC 100 bis, p. 964)

That is why God drove them out of paradise and carried them off far away from the tree of life. It was not because he refused them this tree of life out of jealousy, as some have had the audacity to maintain. No, it was because he acted out of compassion in order that human beings might not remain transgressors for ever, that the sin with which they found themselves burdened might not be immortal, that the evil should not be without end and therefore without remedy. God therefore halted them in their transgression by interposing death ... by setting them a term through the dissolution of the flesh which would take place in the earth, in order that human beings, by 'dying to sin' (Romans 6.2), should begin one day to 'live to God'.

IRENÆUS OF LYONS *Against Heresies*, III,23,6 (SC 211, pp. 460-2)

The resurrection therefore, through Christ, opens for humanity the way of love that is stronger than death. The image of God is restored, death becomes passover, adopted humanity receives the 'light of the Father'. The glory of the godhead comes to it through

the infinitely human presence of Christ. The fire by becoming incarnate acts as milk for humanity still a child. God's abasement
allows of humanity's elevation.

> Reproved first in many ways . . . corrected by the word, the Law,
> the prophets, by benefits, by threats, by chastisements, by water
> and fire, by victory, by defeats, signs coming from heaven, signs
> coming in the air, in men and nations, by unexpected upheavals,
> all of them aimed at breaking the power of evil, humanity needed a
> more effective remedy in the end to heal ills that were only growing
> worse . . . The last of these evils, which is also the first, is idolatry
> which transfers to creatures the worship due to the Creator alone.
> These misfortunes required more powerful aid if they were to be
> tackled effectively. That aid was not lacking. It was the Word of
> God himself, beyond time, beyond sight, beyond comprehension,
> incorporeal, principle born of principle, light sprung from light,
> fountain of life and immortality, faithful impression of the Pattern,
> invariable seal, representation of the Father in every way like him;
> humanity's purpose and *raison d'être*: the Word takes on the image
> of himself, he clothes himself in flesh to save our flesh, he is imbued
> with reasoning intellect on behalf of my intellect, purifying and
> correcting what is like himself . . . As God he committed himself
> to humanity, one single selfsame being sprung from two opposing
> principles, flesh and spirit, the one divine, the other accorded the
> grace of divinity. What a strange conjunction! What a paradoxical
> union! He who is, enters the contingent. The Uncreated One, the
> Unbounded, is introduced into the world . . . he occupies the middle
> ground between the subtlety of God and the density of the flesh. His
> richness wears the face of my poverty . . . that I may be enriched by
> his divinity . . . What is this mystery concerning my condition? I
> received the image of God and did not know how to keep it. God
> put on my flesh to save this image and to make the flesh immortal.
> He offers us a new covenant much more wonderful than the first.
>
> GREGORY NAZIANZEN *Oration 45, For Easter*, 9 (PG 36,851-2)

In the last times, when our Lord summed up all things in himself,
he came to us, not as he could have come, but as we were
capable of seeing him. He could, in fact, have come to us in his
inexpressible glory, but we were not yet able to bear it. Accordingly, as to children, the perfect Bread of the Father gave himself
to us under the form of milk – his coming as man – in order

that we should be fed so to speak at the breast by his incarnation and by this diet of milk be accustomed to eat and drink the Word of God. In this way we might be enabled to keep within us the Bread of Immortality which is the Spirit of the Father.

IRENÆUS OF LYONS *Against Heresies*, IV,38,1 (SC 100 bis, pp. 946-8)

It was in this way that the Father's light broke upon the flesh of our Lord. Then radiating from his flesh it came into us, and thus human beings had access to incorruptibility, enveloped as they were by the light of the Father.

IRENÆUS OF LYONS *Against Heresies*, IV,20,2 (SC 100 bis, p. 630)

The Son of God was made man so that man might become son of God.

IRENÆUS OF LYONS *Against Heresies*, III,10,2 (SC 211, p. 118); 16,3 (p. 298); 19,1 (p. 374); V,pref. (SC153, p. 14)

The Word was made flesh . . . to destroy death and give life.

IRENÆUS OF LYONS *Demonstration of the Apostolic Preaching*, 37 (PO 12,687)

In Christ, indeed, human nature is henceforward capable of receiving the Holy Spirit, the power of resurrection.

The Spirit also came down on the Son of God made Son of Man, and became accustomed to dwelling together with him in the human race and to taking his rest among humankind.

IRENÆUS OF LYONS *Against Heresies*, III,17,1 (SC 211, p. 330)

The Spirit abides in the Son from all eternity. He constitutes the Messianic unction of the Son come in the flesh. In the same way he alights on his Body the Church. The Spirit thus anoints all who seek consciously to live in Christ and thereby become other 'Christs', at once saved and saviours, to be set apart to work for the salvation of the world.

The countless lamps which are burning were all lit at the same fire, that is to say they were all lighted and are all shining through the action of one and the same substance. Thus Christians shine brilliantly through the action of the divine fire, the Son of God. Their lamps that have been lit are in the depth of their heart and they shine in his presence during the time they spend on earth, just as he himself shines brilliantly. Does not the Spirit say, 'God, your God, has anointed you with the oil of gladness'? (Psalm 45.7). He was called Anointed (*Christos*) in order that we might receive the unction of the same oil with which he was anointed, and might thereby become 'christs' also, being of the same nature as he and forming a single body with him. It is written likewise: 'He who sanctifies and those who are sanctified have all one origin' (Hebrews 2.11).

PSEUDO-MACARIUS *Great Letter* (PG 34,772)

By the Holy Spirit combining with our freedom we are able to move from the 'image' to the 'likeness'.

All of us who are human beings are in the image of God. But to be in his likeness belongs only to those who by great love have attached their freedom to God.

DIADOCHUS OF PHOTIKE *Gnostic Chapters*, 4 (SC 5 bis, p. 86)

By the baptism of regeneration grace confers two benefits on us, one of which infinitely surpasses the other. It gives the first immediately, for in the water itself it renews us and causes the image of God to shine in us ... As for the other, it awaits our collaboration to produce it: it is the likeness of God. When our spirit begins to experience the deep sensation of savouring the goodness of the Holy Spirit, then we should know that grace is beginning to overpaint the image with the likeness. Painters begin by sketching the outline of a portrait in a single colour, then they gradually add the lustre of one colour to the other until they copy their model, right down to the very hairs of its head. In just such a way, the grace of God in baptism begins by making the image once again what it was when man first came into existence. Then when grace sees us aspiring with our whole will to the beauty of the likeness, and standing naked and at peace in his studio, then he adds the lustre of one virtue after another, and, by raising the soul's beauty from splendour to splendour, makes it an unmistakable likeness. Our spiritual sensitivity shows us that we are in the process of being formed to the likeness. But we shall know its perfection only by illumination ... Indeed no one can attain to spiritual love unless he is brought to certainty by the light of the Holy Spirit ... And only the enlightenment of love, when it is added, shows that the image has completely attained the beauty of the likeness.

DIADOCHUS OF PHOTIKE *Gnostic Chapters*, 89 (SC 5 bis, p. 149)

And this 'likeness' has meaning only in the dynamism of the universal resurrection, in the immense river of life flowing from the communion of those who are at once saved and saviours, a communion that is openly offered and attractive to all. It is a longing of all Christians (and, no doubt, more or less consciously, of all human beings of good will) for the ultimate, for the moment when God will manifest himself – and be manifested by us – 'all in everyone' and 'all in all'. The 'likeness' is eschatological: it anticipates the fulfilment of history and of the cosmos and is to be understood in that light.

Human nature received the dignity of the image right from the beginning; but the likeness is reserved for the fulfilment ... St John the Apostle shows this truth still more clearly and in a more striking way when he says, 'Beloved, we are God's children now; it does not yet appear what we shall be, but we know that when he appears' (he is speaking without doubt of the Saviour) 'we shall be like him' (1 John 3.2).

And in the Gospel the Lord refers to this likeness as a blessing to come, and more precisely, as a blessing which his intercession will obtain for us when he asks his Father specifically on his disciples' behalf, 'Father, I desire that they also ... may be with me where I am' (John 17.24). 'As thou, Father, art in me, and I in thee, that they also may be in us' (John 17.21). In these words one can see how this likeness advances in some way until it reaches unity, opening before our eyes the prospect of the fulfilment or end of all things, when God will be all in all.

ORIGEN *On the Principles*, III,6,1 (GCS 5,280-1)

PART TWO

Initiation for Warfare

Ecclesia: A Place for Rebirth

1. *Bride and Mother*

The Ecclesia, the Church, is not primarily or fundamentally the concern of sociology. The institution is merely the visible aspect of the 'mystery'. Above all, the Church is the power of resurrection, the sacrament of the Risen One who imparts his resurrection to us; the new Eve, born from Christ's open side as Eve was born from Adam's rib. From Christ's pierced side indeed there flowed water and blood (John 19.34), the water of baptism and the blood of the Eucharist.

> Christ has flooded the universe with divine and sanctifying waves. For the thirsty he sends a spring of living water from the wound which the spear opened in his side.
>
> From the wound in Christ's side has come forth the Church, and he has made her his Bride.
>
> ORIGEN *Commentary on Psalm*, 77,31 (PG 17,141), *Commentary on Proverbs*, 31,16 (PG 17,252)

In its deepest understanding the Church is nothing other than the world in the course of transfiguration, the world that in Christ reflects the light of paradise. The paradise of his presence is in truth Christ himself, who could say to the thief full of faith who was crucified beside him, 'Today you will be with me in paradise' (Luke 23.43). The world-in-Christ, the new heaven and the new earth, means the heaven and the earth renewed, brought to us in the Church's sacraments and in the Scriptures which are also a sacrament. The different sacraments (or 'mysteries') are in any case only aspects of the sacramental character of the Church as a whole, whose heart and brightest light is the 'mystery of mysteries', the Eucharist.

> We need to take refuge with the Church, to drink milk at her breast, to be fed with the Scriptures of the Lord. For the Church has been planted in the world as a paradise.
>
> IRENÆUS OF LYONS *Against Heresies*, V,20,2 (SC 153 p 258)

In the Spirit the Church is the mystery of the Risen One, his sacramental presence. It might be called the Pneumatosphere, in which the preaching of the Apostles, the Good News, is always alive and present, continuing the 'witness of the prophets, the apostles and all the disciples'. Faithful and creative Tradition therefore is the life of the Holy Spirit in the Body of Christ; not passing things down, but 'newness of the Spirit', the newness that is constantly being renewed in persons. The Spirit abounds most plentifully in the sacramental body of Christ, but wherever the Spirit is at work in history and in the universe, the Church is secretly present. There is not a blade of grass that does not grow within the Church, not a constellation that does not gravitate towards her, every quest for truth, for justice, for beauty is made within her (even if the prophets and great creative spirits have sometimes been persecuted by the ecclesiastical institution), every scrap of meditation, of wisdom, of celebration is gathered in by her (even though Christianity has at certain times formed itself into a religious association that ignored or fought against other people).

> The Church's preaching is the same everywhere and remains true to itself, supported by the witness of the prophets, the apostles and all the disciples, from the beginning, through the middle, to the end, in a word, throughout the history of God's constant activity of saving humanity and making himself present to us in faith. This faith never ceases. We receive it from the Church and guard it under the action of the Spirit like a precious liquid that rejuvenates itself and the vessel containing it. The Church has been entrusted with this gift of God, just as God gave his breath to the flesh that he fashioned in order that all the members might receive its life. And this gift conveys the fullness of union with Christ, that is, the Holy Spirit, pledge of incorruptibility, confirmation of our faith, ladder of our ascent to God ... For where che Church is, there the Spirit of

God is also; and where the Spirit of God is, there the Church is, and all grace. And the Spirit is truth.

IRENÆUS OF LYONS *Against Heresies*, III,24,15 (SC 211, p. 470-1)

The Bride of Christ, the Church, in its human, all too human aspect, can be unfaithful to him. But he never ceases to give himself to her who is his body. He makes her mother of living truth for us, a place of rebirth.

2. *Scripture, the First Sacrament*

Already in Scripture there is an aspect of incarnation. Scripture embodies the Word, and the incarnation of the Word completes the transformation into Eucharist of the hearing or reading of the Word.

For true Christian thought is Eucharistic. The Eucharist of the mind – God must be loved with all one's mind – prepares us for the nuptial encounter of the sacrament. And the sacrament in its turn enlightens the mind.

We are said to drink the blood of Christ not only when we receive it according to the rite of the mysteries, but also when we receive his words, in which life dwells, as he said himself: 'The words that I have spoken to you are spirit and life' (John 6.63).

ORIGEN *Homilies on Numbers*, 16,9 (PG 12,701)

In truth, before Jesus, Scripture was like water, but since Jesus it has become for us the wine into which Jesus changed the water.

ORIGEN *Commentary on St John's Gospel*, 13,60 (GCS 4,294-5)

In this way Scripture forms the body of the Word. The ultimate meaning of the Old Testament is revealed in Christ by symbol and 'typology' that discern in the persons and events of the Bible 'types', in the sense of figures of the incarnate Word and his work of salvation. The context of Christian symbolism is the incarnation, the union of the divine and the human in the person of the Word. Now the whole of the Bible is one moment of the incarnation.

This is how you are to understand the Scriptures – as the one perfect body of the Word.

ORIGEN *Fragment of a Homily on Jeremiah* (PG 17,289)

In the two angels [who appeared in Christ's tomb] we can recognize the two Testaments . . . They have come together where the Lord's body is, because, by announcing in convergent fashion that the Lord took flesh, died, and rose again, the two Testaments are as it were seated, the Old at his head and the New at his feet. That is why the two cherubim who protect the mercy seat face each other . . . Cherub indeed means fullness of knowledge. And what do the two cherubim signify but the two Testaments? And what does the mercy seat represent but the incarnate Lord, of whom John says that he was made the propitiation for our sins? When the Old Testament foretells what the New Testament declares accomplished in the Lord, they face each other like the two cherubim, their gaze fixed on the mercy seat, because they are looking at the Lord between them and they . . . are recounting in harmony the mystery of his loving purpose.

GREGORY THE GREAT *Homilies on the Gospels*, 2,53,3 (PL 76,1191)

There are circles of initiation into the Word, and the narrower they become, the more intensely is its presence felt. The Bible is an 'evangelical preparation' and is concentrated in the Gospels. They in their turn find their completion in the Gospel of full initiation, that of St John. To enter into the Johannine message is to identify oneself with the Beloved Disciple. In it is made known the invocation of the Name, to the rhythm of the very beating of Christ's heart, John's head resting on his breast.

Jesus crucified, Mary and John on either side of the cross: that is actually the first Church (not yet Peter's but already John's) and Jesus commits to it his Spirit (Luke 23.46) and the sacraments (John 19.34).

No one has dared to give so pure a revelation of the divinity [of the Lord] as John. We must make bold to say the Gospels are the fulfilment of the whole Bible and John's Gospel is the fulfilment of the Gospels. No one can grasp their meaning unless he has rested on Christ's breast, unless he has received Mary from Jesus so that she has become his mother too.

ORIGEN *Commentary on the Gospel of John*, 1,6 (GCS 4,8-9)

The divine meaning of the Scriptures has to be gleaned from the letter of it and beyond the letter, through contemplation guided by the Spirit. In the Fathers we do not find any fundamentalism, but Scripture opened by the Spirit to its very heart, namely the mystery of the Trinity, the source of love, and Christ's victory over death and hell, the triumph of love.

If you try to reduce the divine meaning to the purely external signification of the words, the Word will have no reason to come down to you. It will return to its secret dwelling, which is contemplation that is worthy of it. For it has wings, this divine meaning, given to it by the Holy Spirit who is its guide . . . But to be unwilling ever to rise above the letter, never to give up feeding on the literal sense, is the mark of a life of falsehood.

ORIGEN *Commentary on Proverbs*, 23 (PG 17,221-4)

Origen, whose brilliant thought fertilized all Christian spirituality, especially, but not only, in the East, compares Scripture to an almond. He himself is an inspired interpreter of Scripture, and if his thought has had to be corrected on other points, it remains fully and directly nourishing in this field.

The bitter rind is the letter that kills and that has to be rejected.

The protecting shell is the ethical teaching, that, as a necessary part of the process of going into greater depth, requires a course of careful purification.

Then the spiritual kernel is reached, which is all that matters, which feeds the soul on the mysteries of divine wisdom.

The first aspect [of Scripture], that of the letter, is bitter enough. It prescribes circumcision of the flesh, regulates sacrifices and all that is meant by the 'letter that kills'. Reject all that as the bitter rind of the almond. In the second stage you will reach the defences of the shell, the moral teaching, the obligation of self-control. These things are needed to protect what is kept inside. But they have to be broken, and assuredly there will be found enclosed and hidden beneath these wrappings the mysteries of God's wisdom and knowledge that restore and nourish the souls of the saints. This threefold mystery is to be seen throughout all Scripture.

ORIGEN *Homilies on Numbers*, 9,7 (GCS 7,63-4)

Thus, from Origen to Cassian and Gregory the Great, the doctrine of the four meanings of Scripture was to be worked out more exactly. Four meanings, because the moral meaning is doubled, even as early as Origen, and made to apply not only to the ascetic teaching of the Bible but also to the life of the Word of God in the soul. Accordingly, as Henri de Lubac has admirably shown in his *Exégèse médiévale: les quatre sens de l'Ecriture* (3 vols, Paris 1959), it would be possible to distinguish the historical or literal meaning, the allegorical or typological meaning, the tropological or moral meaning and the anagogical or mystical meaning. This contemplative reading of the Bible would foster in the West over a long period a 'spiritual theology' which would counter scholasticism.

It happens that while listening to the Word the heart is touched by a particular saying and set on fire. Then one must stop and let the fire spread quietly.

> When a saying of the Lord's kindles the imagination of a hearer of the Word and makes him enamoured of the Wisdom that bursts into flames at the sight of any beauty, then 'the fire of the Lord is come down upon him'.
>
> ORIGEN *Commentary on Psalm* 104, 19 (Pitra, *Analecta sacra* 3,207)

Certainly one must 'knock and seek' to understand Scripture, to make out its historical context, and translate it from an archaic mentality into our own. That justifies the whole scientific apparatus of hermeneutics and exegesis. But science cannot give a meaning. If it tries to do that, it conveys a 'contraband type of philosophy'. The meaning is revealed only to prayer, and certainly to prayer with tears.

> For your part then apply all your zeal to the reading of Scripture, with faith and the good will that are pleasing to God. It is not enough for you to knock and seek. What is needed above all in order to obtain the understanding of divine matters is prayer.
>
> ORIGEN *Letter to Gregory Thaumaturgus*, 3 (PG 11,92)

> To penetrate to the very heart and marrow of the heavenly words, and to contemplate their hidden and deep mysteries with the heart's gaze purified, can be acquired neither through human

science nor through profane culture, but only by purity of soul, through the illumination of the Holy Spirit.

JOHN CASSIAN *Conferences*, XIV,9 (SC 54, p. 195)

If you wish to attain to true knowledge of the Scriptures, hasten to acquire first an unshakeable humility of heart. That alone will lead you, not to the knowledge that puffs up, but to that which enlightens, by the perfecting of love.

JOHN CASSIAN *Conferences*, XIV,10 (SC 54, p. 194)

Never approach the words of the mysteries that are in the Scriptures without praying and asking for God's help. Say, 'Lord, grant me to feel the power that is in them'. Reckon prayer to be the key that opens the true meaning of the Scriptures.

ISAAC OF NINEVEH *Ascetic Treatises*, 73 (Spanos, p. 288)

Scripture is an ocean that will never finish being explored. The encounter with the Word is always new. You know you are going the right way when your reading brings peace to your soul and fills it with sweetness. Sometimes you must leave a difficulty aside, and pray. The meaning will come through your being rooted in the Tradition, through being open to that river of life which is the communion of saints. Indeed, even if you are alone, all reading of Scripture is done with the Church; there is always a liturgical and eucharistic flavour to it. The Eucharist, where the encounter takes place, sheds light on it. The betrothal of Scripture achieves its full meaning and marriage in the Eucharist, where the Word is heard in the silence of love.

The soul marvels at the novelties it meets on the ocean of the mysteries of Scripture.

Even if the understanding that swims on the surface of the waters – the ocean of the Scriptures – is able to dive into the full depth of the meanings hidden in them, ... study, provided it so desires, suffices for it to become firmly attached to the unique thought of the mystery.

ISAAC OF NINEVEH *Ascetic Treatises*, 1 (p. 4)

When you approach Scripture, examine the intention of each word, in order to measure and understand with great discernment

the depth and holiness of meaning that it holds. Those who throughout their life have been led towards enlightenment by grace feel all
the time a kind of spiritual ray shining through the verses, and in the
spirit they identify the words and their deep meaning . . .

When a person reads the verses with a spirit of penetration, the
heart also is refined and satisfied. With a wonderful understanding
the divine power gives the soul a taste of abundant sweetness . . .

ISAAC OF NINEVEH *Ascetic Treatises*, I (p. 5)

Reading one and the same word of Scripture, one person is nourished by history only, another looks for the typical [from *typos*,
the 'figure' of Christ] meaning, another by means of this same
meaning reaches towards the contemplative meaning. Most often,
these three dimensions are found there at the same time . . . In
this way the words of God advance at the pace of the reader.

GREGORY THE GREAT *Homilies on Ezekiel*, I,7,8 (PL 76,843)

But for a Christian, Scripture is not a matter for esoteric study.
It is a Word of life for everyone; its concrete, direct language can
touch the simplest souls, sometimes the simplest especially. And the
mystery of it all will always be beyond the most erudite.

There is a diversity of approaches to suit all conditions. Equally
there are different stages on one and the same route. That is why
we need to know how to carry along with us, without trying too
hurriedly to explain them, the words that so far remain closed to us.
Life, the partial deaths that life brings, the better reception of grace,
all these may one day make us capable of understanding them.

Sacred Scripture . . . tests the strong with its more obscure sayings and gives satisfaction to the simple by its concrete language, . . . it is intelligible to readers who have little culture,
and educated people continually find new meanings in it. However, it also transcends all knowledge and all teaching by the
very way in which it expresses itself. For it unveils the mystery in one and the same language throughout all its writings.

GREGORY THE GREAT *Commentary on the Book of Job*, 20,1
(PL 76,135)

Those who are truly humble and really instructed are able,
when they approach the heavenly secrets, both to understand
certain of them that they have studied and to venerate others

that they have not understood in order to protect what they have not yet understood.

GREGORY THE GREAT *Commentary on the Book of Job*, 20,8,19 (PL 76,148)

3. *Baptism: Entry into New Life*

To be baptized is to die and rise again with Christ, in him. To die to the death that is so deeply entwined with our life. To cry out *de profundis* and to meet even in hell the crucified God who does not judge but welcomes us and who, in return for the least good will on our part (which is why faith is indispensable to baptism, or to its taking actual effect) raises us to life with himself.

Sanctify this water, that those who are baptized in it may be crucified with Christ, die with him, be buried with him, and rise again through adoption.

Apostolic Constitutions, 7,43 (F.X. Funk, I, p. 450)

Baptism is total immersion in the choking water of death, from which we emerge in the joy of breathing once again, of 'breathing the Spirit'. For the water, changed from lethal into life-giving, embodies the resurrectional power of the Spirit, of which it is a natural symbol.

Paul, the imitator of Christ, says, 'Be conformed to his death in order to attain to the resurrection of the dead' (cf. Romans 6.5). How then do we enter into the likeness of his death? By being buried with him in baptism. There is only one death and only one resurrection, of which baptism is the figure. That is why the Lord established the covenant of baptism, which contains the figure of death and life, the water being the likeness of death and the Spirit imparting life. The great mystery of baptism is performed with three immersions and as many invocations, so that the figure of death may be reproduced and that those who are baptized may be enlightened by the transmission of the knowledge of God.

BASIL OF CÆSAREA *On the Holy Spirit*, 15 (PG 32,128-9)

You were asked, 'Do you believe in God the Father almighty?'

You answered, 'I believe', and you were immersed in the water,
that is, buried. A second time you were asked, 'Do you believe in
our Lord Jesus Christ and in his cross?' You answered, 'I believe',
and you were immersed in the water and thereby you were buried
with Christ. A third time you were asked, 'Do you believe in the
Holy Spirit?' and you were immersed a third time, in order that the
threefold confession might destroy your repeated falls in the past.

AMBROSE OF MILAN *On the Sacraments*, III,7,20 (SC 25, p. 68)

The water closes over the neophyte like a tomb. For the tomb
to become a womb the Holy Spirit must supernaturally intervene.
The Spirit given 'from above' brings the human being to a new birth,
clothing with incipient but real light the whole being, the heart, the
mind, the desires, all the faculties, the very senses. Here the words
of Jesus to Nicodemus at the beginning of St John's Gospel should
be remembered: 'Truly, truly, I say to you, unless one is born anew,
he cannot enter the kingdom of God ... You must be born from
above [or 'anew']. The wind blows where it wills, and you hear the
sound of it, but you do not know whence it comes or whither it
goes; so it is with everyone who is born of the Spirit' (John 3.5
& 8). The Spirit, then, shapes the person who has been renewed
in water, which has become maternal, just as he brooded over the
original waters, but this time his work is *re*-creation. In the water
the hard growths of the soul, the callouses of the heart, are disolved.
The person becomes once again tractable and receives a form of light,
which is symbolized by the white garment put on after he or she
emerges, the symbol of the glorified body.

The threefold immersion signifies on the one hand the 'three
days' spent by Christ in the tomb, a tomb that was transformed,
according to the Easter liturgy, into a 'bridal chamber'. For baptism
recalls and re-enacts Good Friday and Holy Saturday and their
culmination in Easter Day (which is why in the ancient Church it
was conferred on the catechumens during the Easter Vigil, after the
long preparation of Lent). The lethal water becomes a womb by its
identification with the empty tomb.

On the other hand the threefold immersion signifies the three
Persons of the Trinity in whose name baptism is administered: 'Make
disciples of all nations, baptizing them in the name of the Father and
of the Son and of the Holy Spirit' (Matthew 28.19). The 'name'
signifies the presence. Baptism, which is conferred in Christ and
enables us to receive the Spirit, leads us into the Father's house. It
confers on us a Trinitarian mode of existence.

Baptism has a twofold purpose: to destroy the body of sin so that it can no longer produce fruit for death; and to live in the Spirit bearing fruits of holiness. The water appears as the image of death because it receives the body as if into a tomb; the Spirit infuses life-giving strength and renews our life, which is in a mortal state of sin, to the state of original life. This is being born again from above, of water and the Spirit. In the water we die, but the Spirit produces life in us. By three immersions and with three invocations the great mystery of baptism is accomplished, so that death is symbolically undergone, and the baptized are enlightened by the communication of the knowledge of God.

BASIL OF CÆSAREA *On the Holy Spirit*, 15 (PG 129-32)

The priest has to ask God to send the grace of the Holy Spirit on the water to make it the womb of a sacramental birth. For Christ said to Nicodemus, 'Unless one is born of water and the Spirit, he cannot enter the kingdom of God' (John 3.5). Just as in human birth the mother's womb receives a seed, but the hand of God fashions it, so in baptism the water becomes a womb for the one who is being born but the grace of the Spirit fashions the baptized in a second birth.

THEODORE OF MOPSUESTIA *Catechetical Homilies*, 14,9
(Tonneau-Devreesse p. 421)

Then you were led to the holy pool of baptism, just as Christ was taken down from the cross and laid in the tomb that had been prepared beforehand. Each one of you was questioned in the name of the Father, the Son and the Holy Spirit. You professed the saving faith and three times you were immersed in the water and three times emerged. This symbolized Christ's burial for three days. By this action you died and were born. The saving water was your tomb and at the same time a womb.

CYRIL OF JERUSALEM *Mystagogical Catecheses*, II,4 (SC 126,
pp. 110 & 112)

Chrismation, a later sacrament in the history of the Church, completes baptism (with which it forms a single rite in the Eastern Churches) by emphasizing its character of baptism in the Spirit. Incorporated into Christ by baptism, the candidate now receives the strength of the Spirit, the strength to 'realize' in a unique personal way the new being that has been received. But these two sacraments must not be separated unduly. For the humanity of Christ is suffused with the energies of the Holy Spirit.

> Christ was anointed with the oil of gladness, that is, with the Holy Spirit. The Spirit is so called because he is the source of joy. You also, you have received the sacramental anointing [the *myron*, sacrament of chrismation which in the West became the sacrament of confirmation]. You have in this way become companions and partakers of Christ.
>
> CYRIL OF JERUSALEM *Mystagogical Catecheses*, III,2 (SC 126, p. 124)

Thus life in the spirit means gradually becoming aware of 'baptismal grace', and this awareness transforms the whole person. The baptismal sequence of death and resurrection is repeated throughout our pilgrimage, enlightening its 'initiatory' moments. When everything seems lost, baptismal grace, if we pay heed to it, can convert a situation of death into one of resurrection, an apparent deadlock into a necessary breakthrough. We have to learn – and this is the whole meaning of ascesis – to get round obstacles, to tear away dead skin, to let the very life of Christ arise in us by the power of his resurrection. Each present moment has to become baptismal: a moment of anguish and death if I seek to cling to it and so experience its non-existence, but a moment of resurrection if I accept it humbly as 'present' in both senses of the word, almost like the gift of manna – but here we pass from the mystery of baptism to that of the Eucharist. We come finally to the moment of agony when we are overwhelmed by the waters of death. Through our baptism, according to the measure of our faith, they will be transformed into the womb of eternity.

The monk is one who of his own choice descends to death, who explores it during this life (in the desert, in the tombs – but where are the real deserts today?). The monk wears himself out sharing Adam's mourning and exile. His aim is to abandon himself without further delay to Christ who has conquered death: to see clearly in hell the dawn of baptism, and already here below to become aware of his own resurrection in the Risen One. The early Church named everyone who was truly spiritual (that is, filled with the Spirit) a 'risen one'.

'Baptism in the Spirit' is nothing other than this becoming aware of baptismal grace, when the water of tears is identified with the water of baptism and transforms the 'heart of stone' into a 'heart of flesh' on which the Spirit freely writes, whenever he chooses, the demands of love.

All the baptized are called, in one way or another, to take this monastic journey, in order to understand that their death is behind them; they have no more to fear from the death of the body. Were not Christians during the first centuries called 'those who have no fear of death'? Being now set free from anguish, we are able to love.

4. The Eucharist, Power to make Divine.

We pray in common, for ourselves and for everyone ... to attain to the knowledge of truth and grace ... to keep the commandments ... When the prayers are over we give one another the kiss of peace. Next, bread and a cup of wine mixed with water are brought to the president of the assembly of the brethren. He takes them, praises and glorifies the Father of the universe in the name of the Son and the Holy Spirit, then he utters a long eucharistic prayer as a thanksgiving for having been judged worthy of these blessings. When he has finished the intercessions and the eucharistic prayer all the people present exclaim Amen. Amen is the Hebrew word meaning 'So be it'. When the president has finished the thanksgiving and all the people have responded, the ministers whom we call deacons distribute the consecrated bread and wine to all who are present and they take some to those who are absent.

JUSTIN Apology, I,65 (PG 6,83)

'I am the living bread which came down from heaven; if anyone eats this bread, he will live for ever; and the bread which I shall give for the life of the world is my flesh ... Truly, truly, I say to you, unless you eat the flesh of the Son of Man and drink his blood, you have no life in you' (John 6.51-54).

The Fathers never ceased repeating these stupendous assertions of Jesus – Jesus is the 'bread of heaven', the 'bread of life' – the Risen One gives himself fully to us in the Eucharist which is thus resurrection food. Jesus is bread because his body is composed of the whole life of the cosmos kneaded together by human labour. He is also 'living bread', life-giving bread, because in him the divine life permeates the earth and the human race. The Eucharist is therefore a real power of resurrection, the 'leaven of immortality' as Ignatius of Antioch says. Certainly, it needs to be received in faith, and there needs to be an encounter within which the transmission of divine energy may take place, but its power is 'objective', and independent of our attitude to it. Our attitude can only encourage (or restrict) the spread of the eucharistic fire through our soul and body.

> The bread of heaven in Christ Jesus.
>
> HIPPOLYTUS OF ROME *Apostolic Tradition* (SC 11, p. 54)

> He is the bread of life. Whoever eats life cannot die . . . Go to him and take your fill, for he is the bread of life. Go to him and drink, for he is the spring. Go to him and be enlightened, for he is the light. Go to him and become free, for where the Spirit of the Lord is, there is freedom . . . 'I am the bread of life. Whoever comes to me shall not hunger, and whoever believes in me shall never thirst' (John 6.35).
>
> AMBROSE OF MILAN *Commentary on Psalm 118*, 18-28 (PL 15, 1203)

The sacramental realism of the Fathers is total. The bread is transformed absolutely into the body of Christ, the wine into his blood. The 'change' is complete and unquestioned.

> Christ himself declared, speaking of the bread, 'This is my body'. Who will dare then to hesitate in future? And when he himself asserts categorically that 'This is my blood', who will doubt it and say it is not his blood?
>
> CYRIL OF JERUSALEM *Mystagogical Catecheses*, IV,1 (SC 126, p. 134)

The eucharistic body is that of the historical Jesus as well as that of the risen Christ. It is the body of the Child in the crib, the body that endured the suffering on the cross – for the bread is 'broken', the blood 'poured out' – the body that is risen and glorified. The term 'body' covers the whole human nature. For God's human nature since the resurrection and the ascension encompasses the world and secretly transfigures it. However, Jesus's historical body, while allowing itself in the foolishness of love to be contained in a point of space and a brief moment of time, in reality already contained space and time in itself. For it was not the body of a fallen individual, crushing human nature in order to take possession of it. It was the body of a divine Person assuming that nature, with the whole universe, in order to offer them up. Incarnate, the Logos remained the subject of the *logoi*, the spiritual essences, of all created beings.

At the same time God-made-man had to accept into himself all our finiteness, our whole condition of separation and death, in order to fill it all with his light.

It is this deified humanity, this deified creation, this transfigured bread and wine, this body bathed in glory yet bearing for ever the wounds of the Passion, that the Eucharist communicates to us.

> The Magi adored this body lying in the manger . . . It is not now lying in a crib that I see thee but upon the altar.
>
> You should believe that today also it is the same meal over which Jesus presides. There is no difference between this [the Eucharist] and that.
>
> This is that same body that was covered in blood, pierced by the spear, pouring forth the saving streams of blood and water, for the whole world.
>
> Christ soared up from the depths of the abyss in dazzling light and leaving his rays there he went up to his throne in heaven. It is that body that he gives us to hold and to eat now.
>
> JOHN CHRYSOSTOM *Homily on First Corinthians*, 24,5 (PG 61,204), *Homily on Matthew*, 50,3 (PG 58,507), Homily on I Corinthians, 24,4 (PG 61,203-4)

Gregory of Nyssa, summarizing his teaching on this subject, recalls that the body of the Word was nourished with bread, so that bread can still today be integrated with and assimilated by the Body of the Word. And this deified bread is not so much consumed by us as we are consumed by it. 'The Eucharist transforms the faithful into itself', according to Maximus the Confessor.

> What then is this remedy? Nothing other than that glorious body which showed itself stronger than death and has become the source of life for us. Just as a little leaven, according to the Apostle's words, is mixed with all the dough, so the body that was raised by God to immortality, once it is introduced into our body, wholly changes it and transforms it into his own substance . . .
>
> The Word of God . . . once it became incarnate . . . provided his body with the means of subsistence in the usual suitable ways: he maintained its substance with the help of . . . bread. Even in normal conditions, when one sees bread, one sees in a sense the

human body, since bread absorbed by the body becomes the body itself. So here, the body in which God had become incarnate, since it was fed on bread, was in a sense identical with the bread – the food transforming itself, as we have said, to take on the nature of the body. It was recognized, in fact, that this glorious flesh possessed the property common to all human beings: like them it was maintained with the help of bread. But this body partook of the divine dignity because of the indwelling of the Word. We are therefore entitled to believe that the bread hallowed by the Word of God is transformed to become the body of the Word ...

As the bread transformed into that body was thereby raised to divine power, a similar change happens to the bread of the Eucharist. In the former case the grace of the Word hallowed the body that drew its substance from bread, and in a sense was itself bread. Likewise in the Eucharist the bread is hallowed by the Word of God and prayer ... It is transformed at once into his body ... as expressed in these words: 'This is my body' ...

That is why, in the economy of grace, he gives himself as seed to all the faithful. His flesh composed of bread and wine is blended with their bodies to enable human beings, thanks to their union with his immortal body, to share in the condition of incorruptibility.

GREGORY OF NYSSA *Catechetical Oration* 37 (PG 45,96)

The world was created as an act of celebration, so that it might share in grace and become Eucharist through the offerings of human beings. And that is precisely what Christ, the last Adam, has accomplished. By his death and resurrection he has brought glory to the universe. It is this transfigured creation that is offered to us in the Eucharist in order that we too may be able to join in this work of resurrection. 'The bread of the Communion,' St John Damascene said, 'is not mere bread but bread united with the godhead' (*On the Orthodox Faith*, IV,13). And it is united, not by a new process of incarnation but by integration with the body of Christ. The bread and the wine are transformed into Christ's body and blood and thereby 'plenified', made perfect, transfigured in accordance with their original purpose.

As far as we are concerned, our thinking accords with the Eucharist, and the Eucharist in its turn confirms our thinking. We offer to God what is his own, as we proclaim the communion and union of flesh and Spirit. For in the same way that earthly bread, after having received the invocation of God, is no longer ordinary bread but Eucharist, made up of two components, one earthly the other heavenly, so our bodies that share in the Eucharist are no longer corruptible, because they have the hope of the resurrection.

IRENÆUS OF LYONS *Against Heresies*, IV,18,5 (SC 100 bis, pp. 610-12)

Denials of the salvation and regeneration of the flesh are futile. For if there is no salvation for the flesh, then the Lord has not redeemed us by his blood, the cup of the Eucharist is not communion in his blood, and the bread which we break is not his body. For blood can issue only from veins, from flesh, from the whole human substance, and it is because he truly became all this that the Word of God redeemed us by his blood ... And because we are his members and are fed by means of created objects – things he himself provides for us by making the sun rise and the rain fall – he declared that the cup, part of creation, is his own blood by which our blood is strengthened. He likewise pronounced the bread, part of creation, to be his own body by means of which our bodies are strengthened.

IRENÆUS OF LYONS *Against Heresies*, V,2,2 (SC 153, pp. 30-2)

This union with Christ – one flesh in the coming together of two persons – is expressed in a nuptial symbolism that applies to the Church as a whole, as well as to every soul that makes itself 'ecclesial'. This symbolism extends as widely as the communion of saints: the marriage at Cana, the marriage supper of the Lamb, and the symbolism of the Song of Songs describing the wine of the Eucharist as intoxication with the divine *eros*.

For those acquainted with the hidden meaning of the Scriptures, the invitation to the mystery that was given to the apostles is identified with that of the Song of Songs: 'Eat, O friends, and drink deeply'. In both cases, in fact, it is said, 'Eat and drink deeply' ... and the intoxication is Christ himself.

GREGORY OF NYSSA *Homilies on the Song of Songs*, 10 (PG 44,985)

The Eucharist requires the memorial (or *anamnesis*) of the whole history of salvation. This is epitomized in its central point, the life-giving cross, the cross of Easter. These events which are written in the 'memory' of God are made present, actual and active by the 'memory' of the Church. In this living 'memorial' the priest is the image of Christ, an 'other Christ', as St John Chrysostom says. He bears witness to Christ's unshakeable fidelity to his Church. Through the one who sums up the people's prayer and constitutes for them the sign of Christ, Christ our one high priest accomplishes the Eucharist. And everything is done in the Holy Spirit. It is in the Holy Spirit that the Church is the 'mystery' of the Risen Christ, the world in process of transfiguration. The Spirit 'broods' on the waters at the beginning and 'hovers' over them like a great bird. In order to make the human being live, God breathes his Spirit into the clay. The Spirit comes down on the Blessed Virgin in order that the Word may take flesh in her. He rests on Jesus as his Messianic anointing and it is in him that Jesus thrills with joy and multiplies the 'signs' of the Kingdom. It is by the life-giving power of the Spirit that God raises Jesus (Romans 1.4). Likewise when the people are assembled to offer themselves in the offertory of the bread and wine, the Spirit comes upon them to 'manifest' the body and blood of Christ through the bread and wine (the word 'manifest' is found in the eucharistic liturgy of St Basil). The Spirit thereby integrates the people in the glorified humanity of the Lord. So the memorial is effected by the coming of the Spirit in response to the Church's *epiclesis* (a word that means 'invocation'). All the faithful ratify this invocation by their *amens*. In this respect they are concelebrants of the liturgy. But only the apostolic witness of the bishop (or of the priest representing him) can testify to the *epiclesis* being heard, to the fullness of God's faithfulness.

Christ, through the priest, fulfils the Eucharist by the memorial. That is the dimension that the Latin Church was to emphasize.

Everything is fulfilled in the Holy Spirit for whom the priest asks the Father in close communion with the people. That is the dimension that the Christian East was to emphasize.

Two inseparable dimensions are today on the way to reunion after a long history of separation.

The priest says, 'This is my body', and these words change the nature of the offerings. Thus the word of the Saviour, pronounced once, has sufficed and will suffice to fulfil the most perfect sacrifice on the altar of every church, from the Last Supper of Jesus Christ right up till our time and till his coming again.

The bread becomes the bread of heaven, because the Spirit comes to rest upon it. What is there in front of us is not the work of any human power. He who did this at the Last Supper still does it now. For our part, we hold the rank of servants: it is he who sanctifies and transforms.

There is only one Christ, whole and entire now as then, a single body ... We do not offer another victim as the high priest of those days did [in the Old Testament]. It is always the same victim, or rather we make a memorial of the sacrifice.

JOHN CHRYSOSTOM *Homily on the Treachery of Judas*, 1,6 (PG 49, 380), *Homily on John*, 45,2 (PG 59,253), *Homily on Matthew*, 82,5 (PG 58,743), *Homily on Hebrews*, 17,3 (PG 63,131)

We pray God to send the Holy Spirit on the gifts laid here, to make the bread the body of Christ and the wine the blood of Christ. For the Holy Spirit sanctifies and transforms all that he touches.

CYRIL OF JERUSALEM *Mystagogical Catecheses*, V,7 (SC 126, p. 154)

The bread and wine of the Eucharist before the holy invocation are ordinary bread and wine, but after the invocation the bread becomes the body of Christ and the wine the blood of Christ.

CYRIL OF JERUSALEM *Mystagogical Catecheses*, I,7 (SC 126 p. 94)

To communicate in the risen Christ is to enter the realm of an unending Pentecost. In fact the body of Christ is a 'spiritual' body, *pneumatikon*, according to St Paul. It is not dematerialized, but brought fully to life by the energies of the Spirit. *The Body of God where the Spirit blazes* [*Le Corps de Dieu où flambe l'Esprit*], to quote the title of a fine book by Daniel Ange.

We are fed with the bread from heaven, our thirst is quenched by the cup of joy, the chalice afire with the Spirit, the blood wholly warmed from on high by the Spirit.

An anonymous *Homily* inspired by HIPPOLYTUS *Treatise on Easter*, Exordium 8 (SC 27, pp. 133 & 135)

Fire and the Spirit are in our baptism. In the bread and the cup also are fire and the Spirit.

EPHRAIM OF SYRIA *On Faith* (Lamy I, p. 413)

From now on you will be eating a pure and spotless Passover meal, leavened bread, bread of perfection kneaded and cooked by the Spirit – the body and blood of God himself that is offered for all humanity.

EPHRAIM OF SYRIA *Second Sermon on Holy Week*, (Lamy, I, p. 390)

To communicate in Christ is therefore to communicate in the Spirit.

Every·time you drink, you receive the forgiveness of your sins and you are intoxicated with the Spirit. That is why the Apostle said, 'Be not drunk with wine, but be filled with the Spirit'. For one who is drunk with wine totters and reels. But one who is intoxicated with the Spirit is rooted in Christ.

AMBROSE OF MILAN *The Sacraments* V,13,17 (SC 25, p. 92)

The Eucharist anticipates the Parousia, Christ's return, or rather that of the world to Christ. So it is all pointing towards the final fulfilment. That is why the Aramaic word *Maranatha* – 'Come, Lord!' – was a specifically eucharistic prayer in the early Church. What Scriabin at the beginning of our century was content to dream of, the expression of a mystery in a musical composition so beautiful that at its last chord the world would actually be transfigured, the Church of the earliest centuries was praying and hoping for at every celebration of the Eucharist. 'May the Lord come and the world pass away,' the *Didache* teaches us to pray: the world, that is, of illusion and death. The creation, by contrast, being wholly good, will arrive at fulfilment when God is 'all in all'. So the Eucharist constitutes the Church as a people of the Exodus on its way to the Kingdom, already fed by it with eschatological 'manna', a 'manna' of eternity.

O our most holy Passover, Christ, Wisdom, Word and Power of God, enable us to participate in thee still more clearly in the unquenchable light of thy Kingdom to come.

Prayer after Communion, in the Liturgy of St Basil

5. *The Eucharist, Foundation of the Church*

The very being of the Church is eucharistic.

> Thy hand holds up the world
> and the universe rests in thy love.
> Thy life-giving body is at the heart of thy Church;
> thy sacred blood protects the Bride.
>
> CYRILLONAS *Supplication to God* (Bickell I, p. 26)

By the Eucharist the community is integrated into the body of Christ. And the body is inseparable from the head. 'The least separation would bring about our death,' says John Chrysostom in another passage.

> Just as the head and the body constitute a single human being, so Christ and the Church constitute a single whole.
>   This union is effected through the food that he has given us in his desire to show the love he has for us. For this reason he united himself intimately with us, he blended his body with ours like leaven, so that we should become one single entity, as the body is joined to the head.
>
> JOHN CHRYSOSTOM *Homily on I Corinthians*, 30,1 (PG 61,279), *Homily on John*, 46,3 (PG 59,260)

> Let us learn the wonder of this sacrament, the purpose of its institution, the effects it produces. We become a single body, according to Scripture, members of his flesh and bone of his bones. This is what is brought about by the food that he gives us. He blends himself with us so that we may all become one single entity in the way the body is joined to the head.
>
> JOHN CHRYSOSTOM *Homily on John*, 46 (PG 59,260)

'Of the same blood' with Christ, 'incorporated into him', 'grafted' on to his body, a 'single plant', a 'single entity' with him, the faithful are also 'members one of another'. These powerful Pauline expressions, with their unmistakable eucharistic associations, have been tirelessly commented on and developed by the Fathers. The Eucharist renews, strengthens and deepens the 'consubstantiality', the ontological unity of all human beings. They all form one and the same being in Christ, one and the same life through time and space. In this way the Eucharist is the basis of the 'catholicity' of the Church, its existence *kath-holon*, in accordance with the whole, in accordance with the fullness of a truth that is life and love, the communion of saints rooted in communion by the 'holy things', namely, the body and blood of Christ.

> As this broken bread once scattered over the mountains has been gathered together to make a single entity, so gather thy Church together from the ends of the earth into thy Kingdom.
>
> *Didache*, IX,4 (SC 248, p. 176)

> When the Lord calls his body bread, made from the collection of a large number of grains, he is pointing to the unity of our people. And when he calls his blood wine, which is pressed from a large number of clusters of grapes to form a single liquid, he signifies that our flock is made up of a multitude gathered into unity.
>
> CYPRIAN OF CARTHAGE *Letter* 69, V,2 (Correspondance, Belles Lettres 1961 II, p. 242)

> Although we are distinguishable by our very different personalities, as were for instance Peter, or John, or Thomas, or Matthew, yet we are merged as it were in a single body in Christ by feeding on his unifying body.
>
> CYRIL OF ALEXANDRIA *Commentary on John*, 11,11 (PG 74,560)

> Of the one and of the other, Christ makes a single body. Thus he who lives in Rome looks on the Indians as his own members. Is there any union to be compared with that? Christ is the head of all.
>
> JOHN CHRYSOSTOM *Homily 61*, 1 (PG 59,362)

> Men, women, children, deeply divided as to race, nationality, language, class, work, knowledge, rank and fortune ... are all created afresh by the Church in the Spirit. On all alike she impresses a divine form. All receive from her a unique unbreakable nature, a nature that does not allow any account to be taken henceforward of the manifold and deep differences which distinguish them. Thereby all are united in a truly catholic way. In the Church no one is in any way separated from the community. Everyone is, so to speak, merged into everyone else, by the simple and indivisible power of faith ... Christ is thus everything in everyone, Christ who incorporates everything in himself in accordance with the infinite and all-wise power of his goodness. He is the centre upon which all

lines converge so that the creatures of the one God may not remain strangers or enemies to one another for lack of common ground on which to display their friendliness and their peace.

MAXIMUS THE CONFESSOR *Mystagogia*, I (PG 91,665-8)

The early Church saw this unity as analogous to the unity of bread or wine that is made up of many grains of wheat or many grapes, each of which must be crushed, like the ascetical overcoming of the egocentric self in baptism. Cyprian of Carthage prefers the analogy of the water that the priest pours into the wine when he prepares the 'holy gifts' before the the eucharistic celebration. But it is always a question of the integration of the Christian people in Christ.

Because Christ embodies us all, we see that the water represents the people, and wine the blood of Christ. When therefore the water is mixed with the wine in the chalice, it is the people being mixed with Christ. The multitude of the faithful are being united with him in whom they believe. This mixture, this union of the wine and the water in the cup of the Lord, is indissoluble. Likewise the Church, that is to say the people in the Church who persevere faithfully and constantly in their faith, can never be separated from Christ, but will remain attached to him by a love which will make of the two one being. But when the cup of the Lord is consecrated, water alone can never be offered, any more than wine alone can be offered. For if wine alone is offered, the blood of Christ is present without us. But if water alone, the people are there without Christ. On the other hand, when the two are mixed and by blending together form a single entity, then the mystery is completed. The cup of the Lord then is not water alone or wine alone without any mingling of the two, any more than the body of the Lord could be flour alone or water alone without the mingling of the two and their union to form bread. In a similar way also the unity of the Christian people is represented: just as many grains brought together, ground and mixed with one another, make a single loaf of bread, so in Christ, who is the bread of heaven, we are well aware there is only one body in which our multiplicity is united and blended together.

CYPRIAN OF CARTHAGE *Letter* 63, 13 (Belles Lettres II, pp. 207-8)

The earthly liturgy is united with the heavenly liturgy that the angelic powers celebrate. During the eucharistic liturgy the congregation is 'lifted up to heaven', or rather finds itself in a dimension of resurrection where there is no longer any separation between heaven and earth, or between angels and human beings, or between the living and the dead (who are not dead but preparing themselves also for the resurrection, or, in the case of the saints, preparing us for it).

> On high the armies of the angels are giving praise. Here below, in the Church, the human choir takes up after them the same doxology. Above us, angels of fire make the thrice-holy hymn resound magnificently. Here below is raised the echo of their hymn. The festival of heaven's citizens is united with that of the inhabitants of earth in a single thanksgiving, a single upsurge of happiness, a single chorus of joy.
>
> JOHN CHRYSOSTOM *On Ozias, Homily 4,* 1 (PG 56,120)

The 'one, holy, catholic and apostolic' Church is fully manifest in the eucharistic congregation presided over by the bishop, who delegates to his priests the responsibility of representing him in their various parishes. As the image of Christ the bishop gathers the local people together to form a eucharistic body. The bishop therefore incorporates the Church. But the Church equally incorporates the bishop, who is a servant of her communion. The body of priests grouped round their bishop makes up the *presbyterium*.

> Each one individually and all of you together are united in one and the same faith in Jesus Christ, Son of Man and Son of God, in obedience to the bishop and the *presbyterium*, in harmony, breaking one loaf of bread which is the medicine of immortality, an antidote to death that gives eternal life in Jesus Christ.
>
> IGNATIUS OF ANTIOCH *To the Ephesians,* 20,2 (SC 10, p. 90)

> The Church is the people in union with their bishop . . . Thus you must know that the bishop is in the Church and the Church in the bishop.
>
> CYPRIAN OF CARTHAGE *Letter 66,* 8,3 (Belles Lettres II, p. 226)

These eucharistic congregations combine with one another to form the universal Church, since there exists through time and space a single Eucharist celebrated by Christ, our High Priest. This unity of the many is expressed in a whole catena of Trinitarian analogies. It takes effect around centres of communion that have the 'care', that is, the responsibility of circulating information, witness, life and love amongst local congregations. For a local congregation shows the unity of the Church only in so far as it is in communion with all the others, just as the divine Persons exist in one another.

These Trinitarian analogies are to be found in the *Thirty Fourth Canon of the Apostles*, as it is called (in fact, in its present form certainly a third century document). The ministry of the leading bishop, analogous to the role of Father in the Trinity, is one of 'kenosis' designed to ensure a loving 'perichoresis' between the local churches.

These 'centres of harmony' are arranged hierarchically from the region (the ecclesiastical province with its metropolis) to the patriarchate which can be either an area of civilization or, in the modern age, a nation. Already at the beginning of the second century, St Ignatius of Antioch in the prologue to his Letter to the Romans praises the vocation of the church of Rome to exercise a universal oversight to ensure the communion of all the local Churches. He calls the Bishop of Rome 'the person in charge of charity'. St Irenæus specifies the role of this Church as the privileged witness of the apostolic Tradition.

The reunion in depth of all Christians today largely depends, as is well known, on the ability of the Church of Rome, the Church of Peter and Paul, to recover her vocation to exercise the *kenosis* of charity in the service of all the sister Churches.

> The bishops of each people need to know which among them is the first, and look upon him as their head. And they should do nothing of importance without consulting him, since each of them has the duty of undertaking only what concerns his own diocese and its rural dependencies. But let the leader on his part do nothing without consulting all. In this way there will be harmony, and God will be glorified through Christ in the Holy Spirit.
>
> *Thirty Fourth Canon of the Apostles, Apostolic Constitutions,* 8,47 (Funk I, pp. 572-574)

> With this Church [of Rome], because of its pre-eminent origin, every Church must necessarily be in agreement, that is to say, the faithful everywhere. For therein has been preserved for all time, to the benefit of all, the Tradition that comes from the apostles.
>
> IRENÆUS OF LYONS *Against Heresies*, III,3,2 (SC 211, p. 32)

The 'sacrament of the altar' is reflected and extended in the 'sacrament of our brother', as St John Chrysostom repeats continually. No one can receive God's pardon and peace in the Eucharist without also becoming a person of pardon and peace. No one can take part in the eucharistic feast without becoming a person prepared to share. In the Church of the first three centuries many of the faithful brought with them to the eucharistic gathering not only the bread and wine necessary for the celebration, but also the wealth that they wished to share.

> Then comes the distribution and sharing out of the eucharistic gifts among all, and the absent are sent their share by the ministry of the deacons. Those who have plenty and wish to give, give freely according as they wish. The whole of what has been collected is handed over to the president and he gives help to orphans, widows, those who are in need because of illness or for some other reason, prisoners, strangers passing through; in short, he gives succour to all who are in need.
>
> JUSTIN *Apology*, I,67 (PG 6,84)

The Eucharist not only establishes the existence of the Church and the communion of Christians among themselves, but determines the manner in which these are present in the world. For everyone is called 'to give thanks in all circumstances' (1 Thessalonians 5.18), to become a 'eucharistic person'. Making the Eucharist part of oneself, especially by the invocation of the name of Jesus, is one of the fundamental themes of Christian spirituality. The eucharistic celebration is an apprenticeship in new relations among people, and between people and things; it cannot but have a prophetic dimension.

> Venerate the nature of the offering itself. Christ is there, sacrificed. And for what purpose was he sacrificed? To bring peace to the things of heaven and earth, to reconcile you with the God of the universe and make you his friend . . . What the Son of God has done in this way, you must do too as far as your human strength allows, by being a builder of peace both for yourself and for others . . . That is why at the moment of the sacrifice, the only commandment of which he reminds you is to be reconciled with your brother. Thus he shows you that this is more important than the others.
>
> JOHN CHRYSOSTOM *On the Treachery of Judas, Homily 1, 6*
> (PG 49,381)

> Do you wish to honour the body of the Saviour? Do not despise it when it is naked. Do not honour it in church with silk vestments

while outside you are leaving it numb with cold and naked. He who said, 'This is my body', and made it so by his word, is the same that said, 'You saw me hungry and you gave me no food. As you did it not to one of the least of these, you did it not to me.' Honour him then by sharing your property with the poor. For what God needs is not golden chalices but golden souls.

JOHN CHRYSOSTOM *On Matthew, Homily 50, 3* (PG 58,508)

6. *Eucharistic Practices*

The Eucharist, which is the basis of the Church, necessarily had, for the Christians of the first centuries, a character of unanimity and community. Not in the sense of an anonymous 'mass meeting', because at the same time it was completely personal, often with the priest using the formula 'the servant of God N. communicates'. It was precisely this that established the person in communion; that made of the individual a distinct being but in communion, after the image of the Trinity. In the symbolism of the week, which is more primitive than that of the year, every Sunday is Easter and is therefore the eucharistic day par excellence, on which all the faithful exchange the kiss of peace and form themselves into the Church by sharing together in the eucharistic feast. Christ rose on the day after the sabbath, on the 'first day of the week', as the New Testament calls it. The first day is also the eighth – and the last – day. 'Day One', when time began, as Basil of Cæsarea says, (*Treatise on the Holy Spirit*, 27) is the original day of creation, the Easter dawning of the 'day with no sunset' on which we welcome Life sprung from the tomb.

We all assemble on the day of the sun [Sunday] because that is the first day, the day on which God drew matter out of darkness and created the world. It is also the day on which Christ our Saviour rose from the dead.

JUSTIN *Apology*, I,67 (PG 6,84)

According to some of the Fathers, Clement of Alexandria in particular, this first and last Day, which makes Christians 'sons of the Day' (1 Thessalonians 5.5), also symbolizes the eternal birth of the Word 'through whom every creature has come to the light of existence' (*Miscellanies* 6,16). For the Word is that 'beginning'

(Genesis 1.1) and the Word incarnate is that 'new beginning' in which God creates and re-creates 'the heavens and the earth'. The resurrection resumes the work of creation, in order to associate us with the coming of the eighth day, and make us sons of the Son.

All the same, more frequent communion, often daily, is also well attested in the apostolic and patristic ages, with the idea that every day ought to be a festival and share in the grace of the 'Day of the Lord', a biblical expression denoting the coming of the Kingdom. The bread asked for in the Lord's Prayer in daily anticipation of the last Today (this bread called in the gospel *epiousios*, that is, 'bread of the world to come', a 'supersubstantial' bread), is very clearly the Eucharist. There is no question of 'deserving' the Eucharist, as we shall see clearly in the texts that will be quoted on faithfulness and humility. 'Anyone who is considered unworthy to receive the Eucharist every day will be no less unworthy to receive it once a year,' St Ambrose of Milan said. It is a question of becoming aware of one's unworthiness, of taking one's place amongst those 'sick persons' for whom Jesus said he came, and who need for their survival the 'bread of life', the 'daily bread', the 'medicine of immortality'. There were some, ascetics in the desert, who could receive the Eucharist once only, at the end of their life. But they received it then with the radiance of a divine flash of lightning. The Christian people, however, were not ascetics, but lived under the influence of the Eucharist, sustained by the life of the Other. They had no fear of 'trivializing' holy communion because they knew that the mystery of Christianity, the paradox of it, is precisely the coming of God in the seeming triviality of our daily life.

On this fundamental point there is no difference between the Latin and the Greek Fathers. St Ambrose speaks of daily communion with a view to giving every day the spiritual flavour of the Today of the Kingdom.

> You hear it said that every time the sacrifice is offered, the Lord's death, resurrection and ascension are represented, the forgiveness of sins is offered, and yet do you not receive this bread of life every day? Anyone who is wounded looks for healing. For us it is a wound to be liable to sin. Our healing lies in the adorable heavenly sacrament . . .
>
> If you receive it every day, every day becomes for you Today.
>
> If Christ is yours today, he rises for you today. Today has come.
>
> AMBROSE OF MILAN *The Sacraments*, V,2-26 (SC 25, pp. 95-96)

St Basil speaks no differently. And his letter shows that in the fourth century, in a period that was already 'Constantinian', when mass coversions were taking place, the ancient custom still existed (attested by the Fathers and in the first place by the *Didache*) whereby on Sunday people were allowed to take away consecrated bread and wine to keep at home, so that each could communicate every day or the father could give communion to his family.

> To communicate also every day, to receive one's share of the sacred body and precious blood of Christ is an excellent and beneficial practice, because the Lord himself says clearly, 'He who eats my flesh and drinks my blood has eternal life'. Who, in fact, could doubt that to partake continually of life is to live fully? We on our part communicate four times a week, on Sunday, Wednesday, Friday and Saturday; but also on other days if the memorial of a saint is being kept. As for the need to take communion with our own hands, to which we may be reduced in time of persecution, if there is no priest or deacon, it is superfluous to show that this is in no way against the rule, since the practice is confirmed by immemorial usage attested by history ... At Alexandria and all over Egypt each believer may keep the Eucharist at his home and give it to himself when he wishes. As soon in fact as the priest has offered the sacrifice and distributed the sacrament, anyone who has once received the whole is right to believe that when he takes part of it each day he is continuing to partake of the sacrifice and is receiving it from the hands of the priest who gave it to him. In church indeed the priest gives the amount for which he is asked. The person who receives it is free to keep it and put it to his mouth with his own hand.

BASIL OF CÆSAREA *Letter 93* (PG 32,186-7)

It seems that in the sixth and seventh centuries, with the barbarian invasions and the disappearance or attenuation of the cultured laity, people partly lost their sense of the life of the Church, and communion, in both East and West, became an exceptional event, from once to three times a year. The eucharistic celebration was transformed into a sacred spectacle performed in the presence of an 'ignorant' people by clergy who effectively reserved the communion for themselves. The Eucharist was thoroughly 'sacralized', in a setting of reverence and fear, and approach to it became an individual matter, no longer communal.

At the same time the traditional way of communicating, attested for example by the text that follows from Cyril of Jerusalem, was reserved from then on to the clergy, while the faithful were treated rather like children and received the communion from the hand of the priest. This was done directly in the West where only the consecrated bread was distributed to the layfolk, or by means of a spoon in the East, where communion in both kinds continued to exist.

It must be admitted that the attitude described by St Cyril seems more in keeping with the spirit of the Gospel. It bears witness on the one hand to an extreme veneration for the sanctifying power of the Eucharist, and on the other hand to the trust placed in adults consciously sharing in the offering of the liturgy.

> When you approach, do not present your hands spread out nor your fingers separated, but make a throne with your left hand for your right hand since it has to receive the King, and receive the body of Christ in the hollow of your hand, saying 'Amen'. Take care then to hallow your eyes by the touch of the sacred body, then consume it and make sure that you do not lose any portion of it . . .
>
> So after having received the body of Christ in communion, approach also the chalice of his blood. Do not stretch your hands out, but bowing in an attitude of respect and adoration and saying 'Amen', hallow yourself by taking also the blood of Christ. And while your lips are still wet, brush them with your hands and hallow also your eyes, your forehead and your other senses.
>
> CYRIL OF JERUSALEM *Mystagogical Cathecheses*, V,21 & 22 (SC 126, pp. 170 & 172)

Fasting and a regular discipline of penance are indispensable as preparation for communion. In the early Church the fast began at dusk the evening before (the beginning of the liturgical day) and ended with communion in the early morning. Its aim was, and still is, to deepen a person's hunger for God who gives us himself for food. One cannot communicate without being hungry.

> The mystic feast is prepared for by fasting . . . It is bought at the price of hunger and the cup of sober intoxication is gained by thirst for heavenly sacraments.
>
> AMBROSE OF MILAN *On Elijah and Fasting*, 10,33 (PL 14,708)

The attitudes of the first centuries make up the Tradition of the undivided Church, a Tradition that corresponds much better to the spiritual condition of our own times than that of the times of Christendom, however moving and worthy of respect the customs then adopted may have been. Those attitudes could provide useful guidance in the reforms that are needed or are already developing in the Christian world today. They would help to avoid either a strangely individualistic, sacralizing objectivization, or a perfunctory Eucharist without preparation or mystery, which risks being the expression of the dominant euphoria of a particular group.

7. *Stones and People*

'God built humanity so that humanity might build for him': churches, yes, but also societies, culture, the visible or invisible networks which sustain a 'eucharistic' relationship between human beings and the earth. God comes near to us unendingly in the bread of life, the food of resurrection. Everything has to be built up round this seed of fire.

> When three are gathered together in thy name they already form a church. Watch over the thousands here assembled. Their hearts had prepared a sanctuary before our hands built it to the glory of thy name. May the temple of stone be as beautiful as the temple of our hearts. Deign to bless both alike with thy Spirit. Our hearts, like these stones, are marked with thy name . . .
>
> God built humanity so that humanity might build for him. Blessed be his loving-kindness who has so loved us! He is infinite; we are limited. He builds the world for us. We build a house for him. It is good that human beings can build a dwelling for him who is present everywhere . . .
>
> He dwells tenderly in our midst. He draws us to him in the bonds of love. He stays with us and calls us to take the path to heaven to dwell with him . . .
>
> God came among human beings so that they might meet him . . .
>
> Thine is the kingdom of heaven: ours is thy house! . . . There the priest offers the bread in thy name and thou givest thine own body to all for food . . .
>
> Thy heavens are too high for us to be able to reach them. But behold, thou comest to us in the church, so close.
>
> Thy throne rests on fire; who would dare approach? But the

Almighty lives and dwells in the bread. Anyone who wishes may approach and eat.

BALAI *For the consecration of a new church* (Bickell I, pp. 77-82)

A church brings out the meaning of the world by restoring to the world its spiritual dimension, opening it up to the mystery. And then the world looks like a church.

The church is the perfect image of the sensible world. For sky it has the divine sanctuary, and for earth the nave in all its beauty. And vice versa the world is a church. For sanctuary it has sky and for nave the grandeur of the earth.

MAXIMUS THE CONFESSOR *Mystagogia*, 3 (PG 91,669)

Equally, the church expresses the significance of human beings, their bodies, their souls, their hearts and their minds. They themselves become a church, making a nave of their bodies – learning by ascesis to transform their vital energy into love – and a sanctuary of their souls, where they offer to God the *logoi*, the spiritual essences of things – which is the contemplation of the cosmos in God. Finally they make an altar of their minds, where everything including themselves is united to the godhead – and that is the vision of God, perfect communion, 'deification'.

The church is like a human being. For soul it has the sanctuary, for mind the divine altar, for body the nave. The church is the image and likeness of the human being who himself has been created in the image and likeness of God. By its nave, as by the body, it enables the gaining of practical wisdom; by its sanctuary, as by the soul, it gives a spiritual interpretation of the contemplation of nature; by the divine altar, as by the mind, it reaches the vision of God. Conversely, the human being is a mystical church. By the nave of his body he enlightens his active powers . . . by the sanctuary of his soul he offers to God the spiritual essences of things . . . by the altar of his mind he invokes the silence in the heart of the divine word, with a loud voice that surpasses all knowledge. There, as far as is allowed to humanity, he is united to the godhead . . . and receives the imprint of its dazzling splendour.

MAXIMUS THE CONFESSOR *Mystagogia*, 6 (PG 91,684)

Nevertheless, *metanoia*, repentance, the turning of the intellect and heart, is necessary for the Church as it is for each of its members.

The power of resurrection is given definitively to the Church in the Eucharist and offered to human beings; it is then up to them to live in that power, and often the fruits are pitiful. Not only is their witness feeble, it is discredited. For there are two sides to the Church: on the one hand, its sacramental depth, the centre of which is the Eucharist, by which it is the mystery of the Risen Christ, and the vehicle of resurrection; and on the other hand, its human side, where people exercise their freedom in laziness or misbehaviour or rebellion, forcing the Spirit into a kind of 'kenosis', while Christians monopolize or disfigure or reject the mystery instead of letting it shine through. This is the history of human fidelity and infidelity where, nevertheless, there never ceases to be a witness to the the absolute fidelity of God in the 'golden chain' of holiness, often hidden but never broken . . . The Church, Origen says, is the harlot whom Christ unendingly washes with his blood to make her his spotless bride.

> There are not only 'wars' outside the Church. There are also 'seditions' inside the Church.
> As there are many sinners amongst the pagans, so there are also many such amongst us members of the Church. That is why the Lord complains and laments over our sins, saying: 'Alas for me, I am like a man harvesting straw' (Micah 7.1). If Jesus had good reason to weep over Jerusalem, he will have much better reason to weep over the Church. It was built to be a house of prayer, but its shameful greed and the hateful stupidity of some people – if only prelates were not among them! – have made it a 'den of thieves', so that Jesus can repeat, in regard to the sinners dwelling in the living sanctuary that he had built, the words of the Psalmist: 'What profit is there in my death, if I go down to the pit?' (Psalm 30.9).
> He comes looking for fruit to gather and discovers only a few pitiful bunches of shrivelled grapes. No fruit that might be good, very little fruit at all. Who among us would be able to offer the grapes of virtue? Who might bear fruit by the grace of God?
> ORIGEN *Commentary on Matthew*, 35 (GCS 11,68), *Homily on Jeremiah*, XV,3 (PG 13,432), *Commentary on Matthew's Gospel*, 16,21 (PG 13,1445)

Ambrose of Milan, a layman whom the clergy and laity of the city had elected bishop much against his will – he actually fled and they had to compel him – has left us this wonderful prayer, in which the loftiest vocation of the bishop is expressed. In it he asks first of all for the grace of compassion, for the ability to weep with the

sinner whose confession he is hearing, whom he is correcting and
consoling.

> Where do I find the grace of hearing thee say: 'Her sins, which
> are many, are forgiven, for she loved much'? (Luke 7.47). I have
> to confess, my debts were greater, the sins that have been forgiven
> me more numerous, because I have come to the priesthood from
> the uproar of the law courts and the responsibilities of public life.
> Therefore I am afraid of being ungrateful. My sins have been more
> numerous – and I have loved less.
>
> Guard thy work, Lord, preserve in me the grace which thou
> hast granted me, in spite of my flight. I believed I was not worthy
> of the episcopate . . . but by thy grace I am what I am, the least,
> and indeed the last, of bishops.
>
> Since thou hast granted me to work for thy Church, guard the
> fruits of my labour. Thou calledst me to the priesthood when I was
> a lost child. Let me not lose myself now that I am a priest.
>
> Above all give me the grace of compassion. Grant me to be able
> to have compassion on sinners from the depth of my heart: for that
> is the supreme virtue . . . Grant me to have compassion every time
> that I witness the fall of a sinner. Let me not arrogantly reprove
> him, but let me suffer and weep with him. Do thou cause me when
> I weep for my neighbour to weep for myself as well, and to apply
> to myself the words: the harlot is more righteous than you are.
>
> AMBROSE OF MILAN *On Penance*, II,8,67 & 73 (PL 16,431)

The eucharistic community only makes sense if it tries to live
truly as brothers and sisters, following the pattern of the first Church
at Jerusalem which practised the sharing of possessions. When the
faith of the Christian people grows weak, the monks take over, as is
shown by the following text of St Basil, one of those who established
monasticism as a visible element in the Christian community. But the
monks have to be an example and a leaven to lead back the eucharistic
communities to become once again centres of welcome and of mutual
help, where people may recover their energy in an atmosphere of
beauty and loving-kindness. They must be restorative cells capable
of neutralizing the cancers that are gnawing at our societies.

> A fraternal community then is a stadium where athletes are in
> training, a good path for progress, a continual stimulus, a constant
> concern for God's commandments. Its purpose is the glory of God
> according to our Lord's commandments. But it also follows the

example of the saints, of whom the Acts of the Apostles tell us that 'all who believed were together and had all things in common', and again, 'The company of those who believed were of one heart and soul, and no one said that any of the things which he possessed was his own, but they had everything in common'.

BASIL OF CÆSAREA *Longer Rules*, 7,4 (PG 30,347)

Why has the Church been spoken of at such length if not because, as Maximus the Confessor so forcefully says, the spiritual life has no other aim but to transform the human being into Church, the temple of the Holy Spirit?

2

The Interior Combat

Ascesis means exercise, combat. 'Spiritual combat, harder than men's battles', Rimbaud says. As free human beings with a capacity to 'create positively', we are challenged to keep faith with the great transformation in Christ, such that we transform likewise, in the Holy Spirit, the relationship that in this world we necessarily have with material things – our genetic inheritance, psychological and social background – so that finally we transform the materials themselves.

> God did not create death; he did not create evil; but he left to human beings, as to angels, freedom in everything. Thus through their freedom some rise to the highest good, others rush headlong into the depths of evil. But you, man, why do you reject your freedom?
>
> Why this reluctance to have to make an effort, to toil, to fight, to become the artificer of your own salvation? 'My Father is working still,' it is written, 'and I am working' (John 5.17).
>
> Are you then reluctant to work, you who were created in order to create positively?
>
> ORIGEN First Homily on Ezekiel, 3 (GCS 8,326).

Ascesis then is an awakening from the sleep-walking of daily life. It enables the Word to clear the silt away in the depth of the soul, freeing the spring of living waters. The Word can restore to its original brightness the tarnished image of God in us, the silver coin that has rolled in the dust but remains stamped with the king's likeness (Luke 15.8-10). It is the Word who acts, but we have to co-operate with him, not so much by exertion of will-power as by loving attentiveness.

Each one of our souls contains a well of living water. It has in it ... a buried image of God. It is this well ... that the hostile powers have blocked up with earth ... But now that our Isaac [Christ] has come, let us welcome his coming and dig out our wells, clearing the earth from them, cleansing them from all defilement ... We shall find living water in them, the water of which the Lord says: 'He who believes in me, out of his heart shall flow rivers of living water' (John 7.38) ...

For he is present there, the Word of God, and his work is to remove the earth from the soul of each one of you, to let your spring flow freely. This spring is in you and does not come from outside because 'the kingdom of God is in the midst of you' (Luke 17.21). It was not outside but in her house that the woman who had lost her silver coin found it again (Luke 15,8). She had lighted the lamp and swept out the house, and it was there that she found her silver coin. For your part, if you light your 'lamp', if you make use of the illumination of the Holy Spirit, if you 'see light in his light', you will find the silver coin in you. For the image of the heavenly king is in you. When God made human beings at the beginning he made them 'in his own image and likeness' (Genesis 1,26). And he does not imprint this image on the outside but within them. It could not be seen in you as long as your house was dirty, full of refuse and rubbish ... but, rid by the Word of God of that great pile of earth that was weighing you down, let the 'image of the heavenly' shine out in you now ... The maker of this image is the Son of God. He is a craftsman of such surpassing skill that his image may indeed be obscured by neglect, but never destroyed by evil. The image of God remains in you always.

Origen *Homily on Genesis*, 1,4 (GCS 6,113-21)

The purpose of ascesis is thus to divest oneself of surplus weight, of spiritual fat. It is to dissolve in the waters of baptism, in the water of tears, all the hardness of the heart, so that it may become an antenna of infinite sensitivity, infinitely vulnerable to the beauty of the world and to the sufferings of human beings, and to God who is Love, who has conquered by the wood of the cross.

Spiritual fat is the obtuseness with which evil cloaks the intelligence.

Evagrius of Pontus *Centuries*, IV,36 (Frankenberg, 287)

Ascesis is not obedience to some abstract categorical imperative. It frees human nature to follow its deep instinct to ascend towards God. It enables a person to pass from a state 'contrary to nature' to a state 'in harmony with nature', in harmony, that is, with that human (and cosmic) material united in Christ with the godhead, without separation or confusion. This is the testimony of St Benedict, the father of Western monasticism, and of an *Amma*, a 'mother' of the desert, St Syncletica, whose teaching is marked by a very feminine directness, and always close to real life.

If justice leads us to propose some mild constraint in order to correct vices and to preserve love, do not at once fly in dismay from the path of salvation, which one cannot enter except through a narrow gate. For as you advance gradually in a holy life and in faith, your heart is enlarged and you run the way of God's commandments in an ineffable sweetness of love.
BENEDICT OF NURSIA *Rule*, Prologue, 47-49 (Centenario, p. 8)

Amma Syncletica said, 'Great endeavours and hard struggles await those who are converted, but afterwards inexpressible joy. If you want to light a fire, you are troubled at first by smoke, and your eyes water. But in the end you achieve your aim. Now it is written: "Our God is a consuming fire". So we must light the divine fire in us with tears and struggle.'
Sayings of the Desert Fathers Amma Syncletica, 2 (SO 1, p. 299)

And everything is done in Christ. He excites and sustains our effort. Ascesis is a response of love. It is a positive abandonment enabling Christ to purify us 'as gold in the fire'. For he is the goldsmith and the fire is that of the Holy Spirit.

I share everything with Christ, spirit and body, nails and resurrection.
Christ . . . thou art for me my native land, my strength, my glory, everything.
Christ is my strength and my breath and the wonderful prize for my running.
It is he who enables me to run well.
I love him as my purest love because for those whom he loves he is faithful beyond all that we can conceive.

> In him is my joy even if he chooses to send me some suffering,
> because I aspire to be purified as gold in the fire.
>
> GREGORY NAZIANZEN *Theological Poems*, (PG 37,623-4)

The Fathers discern three main stages in the spiritual way:

1. *Praxis*, the practice of ascesis, the purpose of which is to transform the vital energy that has gone astray and been 'blocked' in idolatrous 'passions'. *Praxis* gives birth to the virtues, which love will then synthesize. These virtues, let us remember, are both human and divine. They represent so many participations in the Divine Names, and in the brilliance of the godhead in whose image we are made. This is not a matter, then, of mere morality. Not only do the virtues enable us to avoid idolatry – above all self-idolatry – and to gain the inner freedom that makes love possible, but they have a mystical flavour. In this chapter and the two following, it is this praxis with which we shall be mainly concerned.

2. 'Contemplation of nature', that is, some intimation of God in creatures and things.

3. Direct personal union with God.

Now, these three stages follow in succession in Christ. Evagrius and Maximus the Confessor relate virtue and freedom to the flesh of Christ, according to an idea that is not only Christological but also eucharistic. For Evagrius the contemplation of nature is connected with the blood of Christ (from whose pierced side the earth was sprinkled and received its transparency). For Maximus it is connected with the soul of Christ; and we know that the Bible establishes a close relation between the soul and blood.

As for union with God, Maximus describes it under two aspects. First, our union with the Spirit of Christ (the spirit being the heart and summit of his deified humanity), secondly, our transition from the humanity of Christ to his divinity. In a wholly Johannine interpretation of this latter stage, Evagrius refers to the breast of Christ; any one who rests on it and feels the beating of God's human heart (note the reappearance of Maximus's symbolism of spirit and heart) is initiated into the divine life, as John was when he rested on Christ's breast.

> The virtues acquired are the flesh of Christ and whoever eats it will
> find inner freedom.
> The contemplation of creatures is the blood of Christ and whoever
> drinks it will be enlightened by him.

The knowledge of God is the breast of Christ and whoever rests
on it will be a theologian.

EVAGRIUS OF PONTUS *Mirror for Monks*, 118-20 (Gressman p. 163)

Whoever passes from ascesis to inner freedom is able to contemplate
in the Holy Spirit the truth of creatures and things. It is as if he
passed from the flesh of Christ to his soul.

Another, through this symbolic contemplation of the world,
passes to the more naked mystical initiation that is 'theology'. It
is as if he passed from the soul of Christ to his spirit.

Another, through this state, is mystically led to the ineffable
state where all definition is overridden by a radical negation. It is
as if he passed from the spirit of Christ to his divinity.

MAXIMUS THE CONFESSOR *Ambigua* (PG 91,1360)

The Fathers adopted the Platonic and Aristotelian conception of
the soul's faculties, giving it added depth. They distinguish the *nous*
(the mind or intellect), the *thumos* (courage and gallantry that can
turn to aggression and anger), and finally *epithumia* (desire that is
in danger of being converted into lust). In the deep sense the *nous*
is identified with what Mark the Ascetic calls the 'altar of the heart',
that relationship with God that nothing in human nature can destroy,
even if it is unperceived or rejected. But the light of the *nous* can
refuse to make itself known, and it is at this subtle high point of the
soul that Satanic pride is born.

If we seek some approximate equivalents in modern psychology,
the domain of the *nous* might be that explored by Frankl and the
'existential psychologists', for whom the unconscious reveals a spiritual dimension that points to God. The domain of the *thumos*
would be more like Adler's idea of the desire, that is at the centre
of the unconscious, to assert oneself, to prove one's worth. Finally
epithumia calls to mind the Freudian *libido*.

For most ascetical authors, although these classifications vary
considerably and need to be understood in context, there exist two
overriding 'mother-passions'. One concerns the irrational faculties
(*thumos* and *epithumia*), namely gluttony in the sense of fundamental
greed; the other concerns *nous*, namely pride. Pride and greed form an
alliance in a sort of metaphysical usurpation that annexes the whole
being to the ego. Spiritual writers, especially Maximus the Confessor,
speak here of *philautia*, self-love, self-centredness, that snatches the
world away from God to annex it, making neighbours into things.

There is no longer the Other, nor other people, only the absolute I. 'Whoever has *philautia* has all the passions', according to Maximus.

Greed unleashes debauchery as an expression of sexuality. The two together, to satisfy themselves, breed avarice. Avarice produces depression – grief at not possessing everything – and envy – of those who possess. Thus arises anger, against anyone who threatens my goods, or who forestalls me in securing something that I covet.

Pride, in its turn, begets 'vain glory', the display of riches and temptations, followed by anger and depression when the sought-for admiration and approval is lacking. So we come back, through the deep desire to monopolize, to greed. The two circles meet and form an ellipse with two poles.

In the unleashing of passions others accord a privileged position to the 'three giants': forgetfulness, spiritual insensitivity, and a kind of ignorance or stupidity. We forget that God exists, that we can receive him at every moment; we ignore our neighbours; we lose the capacity for wonder; and we end by living like sleep-walkers.

It will do no harm to quote two passages from St John Damascene, who, although he falls just outside my chronological limits, has in this case the merit of summing up the earlier tradition very clearly.

We should know that according to the Fathers there are eight kinds of thought that attack us. The first is gluttony; the second, lust; the third, avarice; the fourth, depression; the fifth, anger; the sixth, despair; the seventh, vain glory; the eighth, pride.

JOHN OF DAMASCUS *The Eight Spirits of Evil* (PG 95,80)

We should commit no sin if these powerful giants had not appeared at the beginning, as Mark the wisest of sages says, namely forgetfulness, spiritual insensitivity, and ignorance . . . The primary cause, the baleful mother of them all, so to say, is *philautia* – love of self.

JOHN OF DAMASCUS *On Virtues and Vices* (PG 95,88)

Perhaps however Maximus the Confessor goes deepest when he notes:

The cause of this deviation [of the natural energies into destructive passions] is the hidden fear of death.

MAXIMUS THE CONFESSOR *Questions to Thalassius*, 61 (PG 90,633)

Then:

We who constitute a single nature devour one another like serpents.
MAXIMUS THE CONFESSOR *Questions to Thalassius*, Introduction
(PG 90,260)

And the reason:

Only love overcomes the fragmentation of human nature.
MAXIMUS THE CONFESSOR *Centuries on Charity*, (PG 91,396)

It is now possible to understand the function of *praxis*. It aims
to transform, in love, with the object of making love possible, the
intelligence and the passions of human nature.

Praxis is a spiritual method for purifying the part of the soul
that is concerned with the passions.
EVAGRIUS OF PONTUS *Practical Treatise, or The Monk*, 78 (SC 171,
P. 666)

A prayer that is specially loved and used a great deal in the
Orthodox Church, St Ephraim's prayer, gives an idea of the working
of this transformation:

Lord and Master of my life,
take far from me the spirit of laziness, discouragement, domination,
    and idle talk;
grant to me, thy servant, a spirit of chastity, humility, patience,
    love;
yea, my Lord and King, grant me to see my sins, and not to judge
    my neighbour,
for thou art blessed for ever and ever. Amen.
EPHRAIM OF SYRIA *Prayer for the season of Lent in the Byzantine
Rite*

'Laziness' here is to be identified with forgetfulness, with the
'hardness' of heart that makes a person see no further than appearances, 'sense-data', what we can 'get our teeth into', as we vividly put
it. It is the condition of the anti-poet, of the anti-mystic, of the 'spiritual bourgeois', to use Nicholas Berdyaev's words. It gives rise to the
spirit of domination that was the object of Christ's third temptation,
and comes close to pride. As for the 'idle talk', this is the 'care-
less words' of the Gospel (Matthew 12.36): words of lying, magic,

possession, profit-making, death. More deeply, however, they are words of discouragement, of despair, of fascination with nothingness. This is the 'accidie' well known to the greatest ascetics, but which in our time has become the everyday expression of a general nihilism.

The second part of the prayer develops in counterpoint the operation of the virtues. Faith that overcomes *philautia*; chastity that is not necessarily continence, since marriage can be chaste, but rather means the integration of desire in a personal relationship; humility and patience that apply the faith to everyday matters and strengthen it with an invincible hope. And clear self-knowledge, the basis not of a guilt-inducing obsession but of a greater confidence; the refusal to judge others; and finally the seal of the blessing, exchanged between humanity and God for the sanctification of the whole of life.

The basis of *praxis* is the 'keeping of the commandments'. These 'commandments' refer less to the Decalogue – except to the extent that Jesus disclosed and made incarnate their spiritual meaning – than to the injunctions and the actions of Christ, and above all the Sermon on the Mount, the Beatitudes. For the Beatitudes describe Christ himself, his beauty – and through him the very mystery of the God of *kenosis* and love. To obey Christ's commandments is to love him, and to beseech him, aided by our very weakness, to take possession of us and transform our life with his.

> Whoever knows the power of God's commandments and under-stands the faculties of the soul is aware of the way in which the former heal the latter and are the way to true contemplation.
>
> EVAGRIUS OF PONTUS *Centuries*, II,19 (Frankenberg, p. 143)

We can see the essentials of the commandments in the sober and practical arrangement of the Benedictine Rule. In every line we find the example and the words of Jesus, whether he is taking up an Old Testament commandment and illuminating it or delivering the Sermon on the Mount or the parable of the Last Judgment in the twenty-fifth chapter of St Matthew's Gospel: 'I was hungry and you gave me food, I was thirsty and you gave me drink, I was a stranger and you welcomed me, I was naked and you clothed me, I was sick and you visited me, I was in prison and you came to me . . . as you did it to one of the least of these my brethren, you did to me' (Matthew 25.39-40).

The monk becomes little by little a centre of blessing. His trust in God's infinite mercy enables him to hope. Knowing himself to be fundamentally loved, he feels himself not only able but obliged to serve his neighbour and love his enemy. The fear of God is the discovery someone makes who is terrified by the realization that to be completely identified with this world is to be lost in a false existence. Meditation on hell enables us to understand *from what* Christ came to save us, provided we cling with all our strength to his salvation.

(Certain themes such as the systematic repression of negative thoughts will be studied in the fourth chapter of this part.)

What are the rules for living a good life?
— In the first place to love the Lord with all one's heart, with all one's soul and with all one's strength.
— Then to love one's neighbour as oneself.
Then not to kill.
Not to commit adultery.
Not to steal.
Not to covet.
Not to bear false witness.
— To respect all people.
— And not to do to others what one would not wish to have done to oneself.
— To deny oneself in order to follow Christ.
— To be master of one's own body . . .
— To help the poor.
To clothe the naked.
To visit the sick.
To bury the dead.
To assist those in distress.
To console the afflicted . . .
— Not to let anything come before the love of Christ.
— Not to give rein to one's wrath.
— Not to meditate revenge.
— Not to harbour deceit in one's heart.
Not to offer a pretended peace.
Not to forsake charity.
Not to swear, for fear of perjury.
To speak the truth from heart and mouth.
— Not to render evil for evil.
— Not to commit injustice but to bear patiently what is done to oneself.
— To love one's enemies.
Not to render cursing for cursing, but rather blessing.

To endure persecution for righteousness' sake . . .

To place one's hope in God.

If one sees any good in oneself, to ascribe it to God, not to oneself.

To fear the day of judgment.

To dread hell.

To desire eternal life with all one's heart and soul.

Every day to keep death present before one's eyes . . .

— Not to hate anyone.

— Not to entertain jealousy.

— Not to give oneself up to envy . . .

To respect the aged.

To love the young.

— In the love of Christ to pray for one's enemies.

— After a disagreement, to make peace before the sun goes down.

And never to despair of God's mercy.

— Such are the tools of the spiritual art.

BENEDICT OF NURSIA *Rule*, IV (Centenario, pp. 20-6)

Diadochus of Photike, a great bishop, both a humanist and a contemplative, offers a more condensed form of the 'keeping of the commandments'. The path goes from faith to love by way of hope, detachment, humility, respect for others, and chastity, meaning the integrity of spirit that makes it possible to integrate the whole being in love.

First definition: faith. A thought about God free of idolatry.

Second definition: hope. A loving pilgrimage of the spirit towards what is hoped for.

Third definition: patience. Ceaseless perseverance in seeing with the inner eye the Invisible as if it were visible.

Fourth definition: absence of avarice. To be as eager not to possess as people usually are to possess.

Fifth definition: knowledge. To disregard oneself in the effort to ascend to God.

Sixth definition: humility. Never thinking about what one deserves.

Seventh definition: absence of irascibility. The ability to avoid anger.

Eighth definition: integrity (or interior chastity). The inward sense constantly united to God.

Ninth definition: love. An increased friendliness towards those who insult us.

Tenth definition: total transformation. In the enjoyment of God
the anguish of death becomes joy.

DIADOCHUS OF PHOTIKE *Gnostic Chapters*, Preamble (SC 5 bis,
84-5)

Maximus the Confessor emphasizes that the 'keeping of the
commandments' makes it possible to overcome the spirit of aggression and greed, and consequently to enlighten the vital force
(the *thumos*) and desire (the *epithumia*).

The believer is seized with a holy trembling.
Whoever believes thus finds humility.
Whoever finds humility receives gentleness,
and thus overcomes the influence of unnatural aggression and
    covetousness.
Whoever is gentle keeps the commandments.
Whoever keeps the commandments is purified.
Whoever is purified is enlightened.
That person is judged worthy to enter with the Word into the
    nuptial chamber of the mysteries.

MAXIMUS THE CONFESSOR *Theological Chapters*, 16 (PG 90,1089)

Ascesis requires discernment. To move from the blessings of this
life, which are fundamentally good, to a radical demand to go beyond
them, we must first have become aware of a higher perfection, and
have received a pledge of God's 'sweetness' (even if later he has to
withdraw it and ask us to go through the desert places). Lacking
this discernment, ascesis is apt to be self-interested or Pharisaical,
in danger of withering purposelessly between earth and heaven.

To eat and drink with thanksgiving to God all that is served up or
prepared for one is not in any way opposed to the rule of knowledge.
For 'everything is very good' (Genesis 1.31).
    But voluntarily to abstain from what is agreeable and abundant
is a sign of great discernment and higher knowledge. We do not
readily despise the delights of this life if we do not taste with
complete satisfaction the sweetness of God.

DIADOCHUS OF PHOTIKE *Gnostic Chapters*, 44 (SC 5 bis,
pp. 110-11)

The whole of *praxis* is symbolized by the fast, provided that this
includes spiritual as well as bodily fasting, as the Fathers teach. In

the test made by God of Adam's freedom and trust, the early Church perceived the commandment of fasting. Human beings, instead of hurling themselves on the world as on to their prey, ought to have learned to see it as a gift from God and a ladder by which to reach him. From this point of view sin now appears as exploitation and selfishness, the desire to make use of and consume the world instead of transfiguring it. Christ, by contrast, fasted for forty days in the desert to show the tempter that 'man shall not live by bread alone, but by every word that proceeds from the mouth of God' (Matthew 4.4), and the world also is a word which comes from the mouth of God.

Fasting therefore signifies a radical change in our relation with God and with the world. God – not the self – becomes the centre, and the world is his creation, a dialogue amongst ourselves and with the Creator. Fasting prevents us from identifying ourselves with the world in order merely to possess it, and enables us to see the world in a light coming from elsewhere. Then every creature, every thing, becomes an object of contemplation. Fasting puts between ourselves and the world a wondering and respectful distance. It enables us to hunger for God as well, and to welcome our bodily hunger as an echo, the 'sighing' of creation.

And so for the Fathers fasting from food is inseparable from prayer and almsgiving, from the loving relationship re-established with God, and from spontaneous, inventive sharing with one's neighbour. That was the real meaning of almsgiving in the first centuries.

> Let us cherish fasting, for fasting is the great safeguard along with prayer and almsgiving. They deliver human beings from death. Just as Adam was driven out of paradise for having eaten, refusing to trust, so it is by fasting and faith that they who wish to enter paradise do so.
>
> ATHANASIUS OF ALEXANDRIA *On Virginity*, 6 (PG 28,260)

> Fasting lightens the body, prepares it for resurrection, and opens it to healing grace. It makes the soul more readily transparent and predisposes it to the study of Wisdom, to listening to the Word. It makes sharing and mutual help possible.

> God did not give the body to be an obstacle by means of its weight ... A lighter flesh he will raise more quickly to new life.
>
> TERTULLIAN *On Fasting*, 17 (PL 2,978)

Fasting is food for the soul, nourishment of the spirit.
AMBROSE OF MILAN *On Elijah and Fasting*, 2,2 (PL 14,698)

[One who fasts] feeds like Moses on familiarity with God and his word. He experiences the truth of the text, 'Man shall not live by bread alone, but by every word that proceeds from the mouth of God'.
JEROME *Letter 130*, 10 (PL 22,1115)

We have the days of Lent devoted to fasting. We have Wednesday and Friday every week . . . And the Christian is free to fast at any time, not out of superstition but in voluntary detachment . . . How could anyone in fact study the Holy Scriptures, or devote himself to knowledge and wisdom, if he were not master of his own mouth and his own belly? But there is another reason, also spiritual, that some apostles have praised in their letters . . . Blessed are they that fast for the sake of feeding the poor.
ORIGEN *Homilies on Leviticus*, 10,2 (PG 12,528)

Fasting makes prayer easier.

The prayer of one who fasts is an eagle in full flight. That of the wine-bibber is made heavy with satiety and dragged down to earth.
PSEUDO-NILUS (Evagrius of Pontus) *On the Eight Spirits of Evil*, 1 (PG 79,1145)

Yet the emphasis is always on the whole nature of fasting and its purpose, and on moderation.

If the enemy suggests to you an extreme ascesis that risks making your body feeble and useless, you must moderate your fasting.
ATHANASIUS OF ALEXANDRIA On Virginity, 8 (PG 28,261)

Just as the body if it is burdened with a multitude of foods makes the spirit slack and lazy, so if it is enfeebled by excessive abstinence it breeds despondency and aversion in the contemplative part of the soul. It is necessary therefore to regulate the soul's nourishment in accordance with the state of the body, so that when the body is in good health it may be suitably controlled, and when it is weak it can be reasonably strengthened. The athlete must not be in poor physical shape.

DIADOCHUS OF PHOTIKE *Gnostic Chapters*, 45 (SC 5 bis, p. 111)

Fasting is capable of making us bad-tempered, or of giving us the good conscience of a Pharisee. Hence the constant call for respect for one's neighbour, for the struggle against backbiting, and also for sharing with the poor, and for the works of righteousness.

Abba Pambo asked Abba Anthony, 'What ought I to do?'
     The old man told him, 'Do not put any trust in your righteousness, do not worry about the past, keep a tight rein on your tongue and your belly.'
Sayings of the Desert Fathers, Anthony 6 (SO 1, p. 21)

If you fast, but fail to keep watch over your mouth so as to refrain from evil speaking and angry words, from lying and perjury; if you slander your neighbour, even if the words come from the mouth of one who is fasting, your fast will be of no avail and will be labour lost.

ATHANASIUS OF ALEXANDRIA *On Virginity*, 7 (PG 28,260)

What is the use of keeping a fast for forty days without considering the meaning of it? What is the use denying oneself banquets, then spending one's time in litigation? What is the use of not eating the bread one possesses if one has to steal that of the poor? ... The Christian's fasting ought to foster peace, not quarrels. What advantage is there in making one's stomach holy with fasting and defiling one's lips with lies? Brother, you will be able to come to church only if your feet are not entangled in the snares of usury. You will have the right to pray only if envy does not make an obstacle in your heart ... The money you give to the poor man will be given in all righteousness only if you have not extorted it from another poor man ...
     So, let us imitate as far as possible Christ's fasting by our practice of the virtues, in order that grace may come upon us through the twofold fasting of body and spirit.

MAXIMUS OF TURIN *Sermon for Lent*, Homily 44,8 (PL 57,135-6)

All ascesis, in fact, is magnetic attraction by love, by which we are conformed to the crucified Christ. But the cross cannot be separated from Easter and, suffering or triumphant, its meaning is always love. 'He who says he abides in him ought to walk in the same way in which he walked . . . He who loves his brother abides in the light' (I John 2.6 & 10).

> The first and greatest commandment is love. Thanks to love the spirit sees the original Love, namely God. For by our love we see God's love for us, as the psalm says, 'He teaches his ways to those who are gentle.'
>
> EVAGRIUS OF PONTUS *Letter 56* (Frankenberg, p. 605)

The key to spiritual progress according to the greatest exemplars of ascesis is, therefore, evangelical love for one's enemies. That is, first of all – something very simple but very difficult – the refusal to judge, the refusal to assert oneself by despising or condemning others. Only such an attitude of mind brings detachment and peace. The rest is secondary.

> A brother asked Abba Poimen, 'What ought I to do? I lack courage when I am praying alone in my cell.'
>
>   The elder told him, 'Do not despise, condemn or blame anyone. God will grant you peace and you will meditate in tranquillity.'
>
> *Sayings of the Desert Fathers*, in Thomas Merton, *The Wisdom of the Desert*, p. 46

Make no mistake, however. Christian ascesis is not only or even especially moderation, self-control, wisdom. It is the folly of those who in Christ fling themselves into the furnace of the spirit, of those who themselves have something in common with fire.

> Abba Lot came one day to see Abba Joseph and said to him, 'Father, I keep my little rule to the best of my ability. I observe my modest fast and my contemplative silence. I say my prayers and do my meditation. I endeavour as far as I can to drive useless thoughts out of my heart. What more can I do?'
>
>   The elder rose to answer and lifted his hands to heaven. His fingers looked like lighted candles and he said, 'Why not become wholly fire?'
>
> *Sayings of the Desert Fathers*, Joseph of Panepho, 7 (PG 65,229)

To climb a mountain it is not enough to have a map. A guide is necessary. Hence the importance of the 'spiritual father' in the tradition with which we are concerned.

The spiritual father is above all a 'spiritual' person, one in whom the Spirit dwells. And the Spirit makes him an icon of the divine fatherhood, a fatherhood that as we have seen is sacrificial and liberating.

Only self-mortification, long, hard and crucifying, makes possible this acquisition of the Spirit, in accordance with the monastic saying 'Give your blood and receive the Spirit'. The 'spiritual father' thus obtains the spiritual gift of 'compassion' (in its full sense of 'suffering with') and along with it the gift of a humble and respectful understanding of hearts. People come to him asking for a 'word of life'. And his word cuts open the hidden abscess, frees and awakens them, sometimes with a touch of humour, like that of the experienced monk who commanded a young brother who was eager to have his own way to recite the Lord's Prayer, saying not 'Thy will be done' but 'My will be done'. The 'spiritual father' is above all a man of gentleness, kindness and unlimited charity. And thus he brings home to a person who hates himself how much he is in fact loved.

The spiritual father is able give guidance because he knows the paths. His role is to keep a little way in front. He does not have to lay down rules, but be an example. He is not a master, a 'guru', since for Christians the only master is Christ. The destiny of the spiritual father is that of St John the Baptist: 'He [Christ] must increase, but I must decrease.'

A brother asked Abba Poimen, 'I am living with some brothers. Do you want me to be in charge of them?' The elder said to him, 'No. Do your own work first, and if they want to survive they will provide what is needed themselves.' The brother said to him, 'But it is they themselves who want me to be in charge of them.' The elder said to him, 'No. You must become their example, not their legislator.'

Sayings of the Desert Fathers, Poimen, 188 (SO 1, p. 253)

An example like that does not draw attention to himself. Only those who wish will follow.

A young man came to see an old ascetic to be instructed in the way of perfection. But the old man said not a word to him.

The other asked him the reason for his silence. 'Am I your superior to give you orders? Do what you see me doing if you like.' From then on the young man imitated the ascetic in everything and learned the meaning of silence.

Sayings of the Desert Fathers, in P. Evdokimov, *La paternité spirituelle*, 'Contacts', 58, 2nd quarter, 1967

Sometimes it is enough to enter into the silent radiance of a presence which, without trying, allows God to shine through.

Three brothers were in the habit of going to see the blessed Anthony every year. The first two would ask him questions about their thoughts and the salvation of the soul. But the third would keep silence without asking anything. Eventually Abba Anthony said to him, 'You have been coming here to see me for a long time now and you never ask me any questions.' The other replied, 'One thing is enough for me, Father, to see you.'

Sayings of the Desert Fathers, Anthony, 27 (PG 65,84)

To have complete confidence in one's spiritual father is to know that he will keep you in his prayers, that he will concentrate on you the prayer that he extends over the whole world. For he is one of those whose prayer defends and protects the world, saves it from falling apart, and becomes the life-blood of truly creative undertakings, in the Church as in society. Being 'poor in spirit', meaning emptied of themselves, of their personalities, of their functions in society, they allow the suffering of the world to enter into them, they enable the power of the resurrection to pervade history, to penetrate the blind passions of human beings.

All the days that our father Pachomius was with us in the body, he prayed day and night for the salvation of our souls and those of the whole world.

Coptic Life of St Pachomius

There is no doubt that the whole world owes its continuing existence to the prayers of monks.

Rufinus of Aquileia *History of the Monks*, Prologue (PL 21,389)

There are tears of another sort, those we are made to shed by the hardness of heart and the sins of others. Samuel wept thus over

Saul. So too in the Gospel we see our Lord weeping over Jerusalem; and in earlier times Jeremiah: 'O that my head were waters, and my eyes a fountain of tears, that I might weep day and night for the slain of the daughter of my people' (9.1) . . .

These are the tears of the righteous man crushed under the weight of the troubles, the anguish and the sorrows of this world.

This is shown clearly by the title of the psalm, 'A prayer of the afflicted, when he is faint and pours out his complaint before the Lord'. The person thus introduced is that poor man of whom the Gospel says: 'Blessed are the poor in spirit, for theirs is the kingdom of heaven'.

JOHN CASSIAN *Conferences*, IX,29 (SC 54, pp. 64-5)

Sometimes one who is advanced in the spiritual life is set free, in Christ, from the fallen and divisive limitations of space and time, and shares in the apparently incomprehensible ways of God.

Two brothers were going to see Anthony. On their journey they ran out of water and one of the two died. The other was at death's door. At the end of his strength he lay down on the ground awaiting death. Anthony, sitting on the mountain side, called two monks who were there and urged them, 'Take a jug of water and hurry to the road from Egypt. Two brothers were coming. One of them is already dead, and the other is going to die unless you are quick. This has just been revealed to me in prayer.' The monks went and found the dead monk and buried him. Then they refreshed the exhausted one with a drink of water and took him to the elder. The distance was a day's journey. Someone perhaps will ask, 'Why did not Anthony speak before the first monk died?' That would be wrong. It was no business of Anthony's to determine the time of his death. That is reserved to God, and God decreed death for the one and revealed to Anthony the danger in which the other was.

ATHANASIUS OF ALEXANDRIA *Life of Anthony*, 59 (PG 26,927)

The tender compassion of the great spiritual guide has something maternal about it. It is as if he had become a complete human being reconciling in himself the animus and the anima, the masculine and the feminine dimensions of humanity.

Some elders came to see Abba Poimen to ask him, 'If we see some brothers dozing in the congregation, do you want us to reprove them so that they stay awake?' He said to them, 'For my part, when I see a brother dozing, I lay his head on my lap and let him rest.'

Sayings of the Desert Fathers, Poimen, 92 (PG 65,344)

The spiritual father is wise. First of all he welcomes his 'son' into his prayer. The latter must not bother him with trivial details of his daily life but must consult him especially when a particular thought becomes persistent and obsessive. The exception occurs only at certain times when a rigorous and detailed opening of the heart proves indispensable.

Brother, nothing is to be gained by consulting your spiritual father about all the thoughts that come into your mind. Most of them quickly disappear. You need to ask about those that persist and make war on you.

BARSANUPHIUS *Letter 165* (Correspondance, Solesmes 1971, p. 141)

Brother, do not try yourself to discern the thoughts that come into your mind. You are not capable ... If they worry you ... cast your powerlessness before God, saying, 'Lord, I am in thy hands, come to my help.' ... As for the thought that persists in you and makes war on you, tell it to your Abba and by God's grace he will cure you.

BARSANUPHIUS *Letter 142*, (Correspondance, Solesmes 1971, p. 174)

The refectorian had a habit that intrigued me greatly. He always carried a notebook hanging from his belt, and I discovered that he noted in it all the thoughts that came to him so as to report them to his spiritual father every day.

JOHN CLIMACUS *The Ladder of Divine Ascent*, 4th step, 32(43) p. 39

The 'father' leads his 'spiritual son' to freedom, for

In the One
there is no longer master or disciple
but all are gods.

EVAGRIUS OF PONTUS *Centuries*, IV,58 (Frankenberg, p. 297)

3

Confidence and Humility

Christian ascesis is distinct from 'techniques' of self-control, serenity, inner life, that enable one to enjoy a methodically acquired euphoria; it is at the service of a personal relationship. Personal loyalty to a hidden and revealed personal presence requires faith and humility, which are therefore the most important things. Humility is not the will to be nothing in order to become all: rather it is the acceptance of self in openness to the Other.

For a Christian the divine cannot be reduced to the exploration of one's own inner life or the acquisition of cosmic 'powers'. The divine has nothing to do with scientism, however spiritualistically inclined. It is Someone who comes to us in the sovereign freedom of his love. Grace does not come to order. We can only prepare ourselves to receive it, making ourselves attentive to the possibility of a meeting.

> Can a person or a thing, regarded in its solidity, avoid being seen when it comes before our eyes? The higher divine realities on the other hand, even when they are in front of us, can be perceived only with their own consent. It depends entirely on them whether they are seen or hidden.
>
> It was by grace that God revealed himself to Abraham and the other prophets. The eye of the heart itself did not allow Abraham to see God, but the grace of God was offered spontaneously to the gaze of that righteous man. This is true not only of God the Father but also of our Lord and Saviour, and of the Holy Spirit ...
>
> So let us too make an effort so that from today God may appear to us, as we have been promised by a text of Scripture that says: 'He manifests himself to those who do not distrust him' (Wisdom 1.2).
>
> ORIGEN *Homily 3 on Luke*, 1,11 (CGS 9,20-3)

Faith is the way – with the risk that it entails. The cards are not turned up before they are played. Only faith and interior purification can open the eyes of the heart to contemplation, which is never more than a partial anticipation of what we shall see in the Kingdom.

'I am the way, and the truth, and the life' (John 14.6). Faith is our way, contemplation is the truth and the life. 'For now we see in a mirror dimly' (I Corinthians 13.12). This is faith. 'But then face to face.' This is contemplation. Paul says again: 'Christ dwells in our hearts according to the inner man by faith.' That is the road along which we can catch glimpses only. But he adds: 'You will know the love of Christ which surpasses all knowledge and you will be filled with all the fullness of God' (cf. Ephesians 3.16-19). Contemplation is this fullness ... 'You have died,' he says again, 'and your life is hid with Christ in God.' That is faith. But 'when Christ who is our life appears, then you also will appear with him in glory' (Colossians 3.3-4). That is the vision of God.

'Beloved,' John says, 'we are God's children; it does not yet appear what we shall be.' That is faith. But he goes on: 'We know that when he appears we shall be like him, for we shall see him as he is.' (I John 3.2). That is contemplation ...

'Jesus then said to the Jews who had believed in him, "If you continue in my word, you are truly my disciples, and you will know the truth and the truth will make you free"' (John 8.31-32). They had faith. They were beginning to walk in Christ as along a road. That is why he invites them to walk along it right to the end. What end? He tells them, 'The truth will make you free.' Free from what ... if not from corruption and death?

This journey, this road, faith, obliges me to repeat those words of the apostle: 'Since we have these promises, beloved, let us cleanse ourselves from every defilement of body and spirit, and make holiness perfect in the fear of God' (2 Corinthians 7.1).

There are some who would like to discover pure and unchanging truth by themselves before believing. But only a heart that has been purified can enable them to contemplate it. 'Blessed are the pure in heart, for they shall see God' (Matthew 5.8). Otherwise they would be like blind men thinking they can be cured by turning their unseeing eyes towards the sun. Who can possibly contemplate its light before recovering his sight?

AUGUSTINE OF HIPPO *Sermons*, 346,2 (PL 38,1523-4)

We have no other way but Christ. To him we cling in all our anguish, in all our inability to repent, to purify ourselves, to pray. For he is our repentance, our cleansing, our prayer. It is in him that 'anguish for death' becomes 'anguish for God'. For God incarnate, descending to hell, chose the way of horror in order to set us free. The two greatest spiritual masters of the golden age, St Isaac of Nineveh and St John Climacus, bear converging witness on this point. We need to listen to Isaac's cry, his supplication *de profundis* – and we are reminded of that other Isaac, the original one when he saw his father's knife flashing over him, and God intervened . . .

Lord Jesus, our God,
who wept for Lazarus,
and shed for him tears of grief and compassion,
accept the tears of my bitterness.
By thy sufferings assuage my suffering.
By thy wounds heal my wounds.
By thy blood cleanse my blood.
Pour out on my body the perfume of thy life-giving body.
For the gall that thou wast given to drink changes the bitterness
     of my soul into sweetness . . .
May thy body stretched on the wood of the cross draw to thee my
     spirit crushed by the demons . . .
May thy sacred hands pierced with the nails snatch me from the pit
     of damnation and bring me back to thee, as thou hast promised.
May thy face which suffered blows and spittle enlighten my face
     that is defiled by my wrongdoing.
May thy soul which on the cross thou didst give back to thy
     Father lead me by thy grace to thee.
I have no broken heart to start me on the quest for thee,
no penitence, no tenderness . . .
I have no tears with which to pray to thee.
My spirit is in darkness . . . my heart is cold . . .
I know not how to make it warm again by tears of love for thee.
But thou, Lord Jesus Christ, my God,
do thou give me complete repentance, the breaking of my heart,
that with my whole soul I may set out in quest of thee.
Without thee I should be without all reality . . .
May the Father who in his womb begot thee in eternity
renew in me thine image.
I have forsaken thee. Do not thou forsake me.
I have wandered far from thee. Do thou set out in quest of me.

Lead me back to thy pastures with the sheep of thy flock.
Feed me together with them on the fresh grazing of thy mysteries
  where the pure heart dwells,
the heart that bears in it the splendour of thy revelations . . .
May we be worthy of such splendour through thy grace
and by thy love for humankind, O Jesus Christ our Saviour,
for ever and ever. Amen.

ISAAC OF NINEVEH *Ascetic Treatises*, 2 (Spanos, pp. 10-11)

We need to exercise ourselves greatly, to lay upon ourselves many
hidden labours after a life of negligence, in order that our spirit
which resembles a greedy and irritable dog may attain purity and
vigilance through simplicity, gentleness and fervour. However, be
of good heart. If the passions lord it over us and we are weak,
let us with great confidence offer to Christ our spiritual weakness
and our impotence; let us confess them before him. He will help
us irrespective of what we deserve, on the sole condition that we
descend continually to the bottom, into the abyss of humility.

JOHN CLIMACUS *The Ladder of Divine Ascent*, 1st Step, 17 (21)
p. 16

Faith is to know that we are loved. It is to answer love with love.
'Love me with love, you who are loved.' To love God is not a duty
but a cry of recognition, when we understand that he has first loved
us, even to the horror of the cross, of hell. Then our timid liberty is
stirred, our heart is moved and all that matters henceforward is that
wound by which life comes to us. 'I walk with a song in my heart
for thy love has wounded me,' as St John Climacus says.

The Bride says, 'I am wounded by love' (Song of Songs 2.5). By
these words she designates the arrow that sinks deep into her
heart. Love is the archer. Now love is God . . . God shoots his
chosen arrow, his only begotten Son, first moistening the three
tips of its point with the life-giving Spirit. Now the point is faith,
and faith makes not only the arrow but the archer also to penetrate its target, in accordance with the word of the Lord: 'My
Father and I are one and we shall come to him and make our
dwelling in him' (John 14.23).

Thus the soul is uplifted by this divine elevation and sees in
itself the sweet arrow of love with which it has been wounded, and
glories in its wounding in the words; 'I am wounded by love'.

GREGORY OF NYSSA *Homilies on the Song of Songs*, 4 (PG 44,852)

Keep my secret, you who are kept by it.
Keep my faith, you who are kept by it.
Learn what I know, you whom my truth has known.
Love me with love, you whom I have loved.
Pray without ceasing, dwell in the love of the Lord,
you who are loved in the Well-beloved,
you who are living in the Living one,
saved by him who has redeemed you.
So will you escape from death, throughout all ages,
in the name of your Father. Alleluia!

Odes of Solomon, 8 (Harris-Mingana, pp. 254-5)

And this exchange of love if we do not want it to be illusory
must be confirmed by an infallible test, brotherly love.

Two men who wanted to see the sunrise would be very foolish
to argue about the place where it will appear and their means of
looking at it, then to let their argument degenerate into a quarrel,
from that to come to blows and in the heat of the conflict to gouge
out each other's eyes. There would no longer be any question then
of contemplating the dawn . . .
    Let us who wish to contemplate God purify our hearts by faith
and heal them by means of peace; for the effort we make to love one
another is already a gift from him to whom we raise our eyes.

Augustine of Hippo *Sermons*, 23,18 (PL 38,162)

Ascetic tenacity, even if it is not masochism or lust for self-
destruction, runs the risk of being an extreme example of the will
to power and possession – Lucifer's own special temptation. Ascesis
then becomes the most dangerous of idols. That is why God expects
from us, basically, love and humility.

An elder replied, 'I tell you, many have ruined their bodies with
no discernment and gone away without finding anything. We may
have evil-smelling breath because of our fasting, we may know the
Scriptures by heart, we may recite all the psalms . . . and still lack
what God is looking for – love and humility.

Anonymous Sayings of the Desert Fathers, 90 (SO 1, P. 357)

The mixture of sin and humility is worth more than the mixture
of virtue and pride. The God of the Pharisee in the Gospel, and of all
like him, is no doubt only his good conscience. The humility of the

publican, the man doubly excluded, for political and for religious
reasons, truly makes room for the divine. 'I came not to call the
righteous, but sinners,' Christ said.

Imagine two chariots. Harness virtue and pride to one, sin and
humility to the other. You will see the chariot drawn by sin
outstrip that of virtue . . . To understand why one of these vehicles
is faster than the other, remember the Pharisee and the publican
. . . One relied on his own righteousness, on his own fasting and
the tithes that he paid. The other needed to say only a few words
to be free of all his sins. That was because God was not only
listening to his words, he also saw the soul of him who spoke
them, and finding it humble and contrite he judged him worthy
of his compassion and love . . .

That is precisely what Christ wanted to demonstrate when he
said: 'Come to me, all who labour and are heavy laden, and I will
give you rest' (Matthew 11.28). So it is that he calls to us; let us
not keep our distance. If our sins are countless that is all the more
reason for going to him, for we are the sort of person he is calling. In
fact he says: 'I came not to call the righteous, but sinners' (Matthew
9.13) . . . He is called the God of consolation, of mercy, because
unceasingly he consoles and encourages the unfortunate ones and
the afflicted, even if they have committed thousands of sins.

Let us then be content to surrender and go to him and never
to leave him.

JOHN CHRYSOSTOM *On the Incomprehensibility of God*, 5 (PG 48,
745)

God himself is humble because he is love. God humbled himself
out of love. Therefore not only does humility open us to God: it
clothes us with Christ, the humbled God.

Humility is the ornament of the godhead. The Word clothed
himself in it when he became man. By it he lived among us in
the flesh . . . And anyone who wraps himself in it truly makes
himself like him who came down from on high and clothed his
grandeur and glory in humility, lest the created world should
dissolve at the sight of him. Indeed, the created world would not
have been able to contemplate him if he had not taken it to himself
and in this way lived within it.

ISAAC OF NINEVEH *Ascetic Treatises*, 20 (p. 76)

The Lord who went down to hell, now, the moment I call to
him, comes to seek me in the midst of the darkness in which I am
struggling.

It was not said: I have fasted, I have kept awake, I have slept
on the hard ground. Rather it was said: I have humbled myself and
at once the Lord has saved me.

JOHN CLIMACUS *The Ladder of Divine Ascent*, 25th Step, 14 (p. 118)

Ascesis ought to make a person ready to welcome this coming
to him of Another, a wholly undeserved coming, one which no ascesis
will ever earn.

I have seen some of them, sick in soul and body, haunted by
their sins, engaging in contests beyond their strength ... To them
I say, God judges our *metanoia* not by our efforts but by our
humility.

JOHN CLIMACUS *The Ladder of Divine Ascent*, 26th Step, 2nd part,
9 (108) p. 138

The ultimate sin is to despair of God's mercy. That is to limit
it, to make our ego its limit, whereas it is boundless.

The mercy of God has no limits, nothing is too great for it.
That is the reason why anyone who despairs of it is the author of
his own death.

JOHN CLIMACUS *The Ladder of Divine Ascent*, 5th Step, 23 (46)
p. 58

Trust, childlike trust, enables the power of the resurrection to
dwell in us. For the God who was made man never ceases to be with
us.

O smallest of human creatures, do you want to find life?
    Preserve in yourself faith and humility and ... in them you will
find the one who protects you and dwells secretly with you ...
    When you come before God in prayer, be in your thought like
an ant, like something crawling on the ground, like a child lisping.
And in his presence make no pretence of knowledge. Approach God
rather with the heart of a child. Go into his presence to receive the

loving care with which fathers look after their little children. It has
been said, 'The Lord protects little children.'. . .

When God sees that in all purity of heart you are trusting in
him more than in yourself . . . then a strength unknown to you will
come to make its dwelling in you. And you will feel in all your
senses the power of him who is with you.

ISAAC OF NINEVEH *Ascetic Treatises*, 19 (p. 67)

It is by the 'depths of the humbled heart' and not by some
conceited 'ascent' that a person really rises, ascending from the
crucified Christ to the glorified Christ. One should read again here the
account of humility to be found in the Rule of St Benedict. The degrees
of humility lead us from the fear of God – which draws us up out of
the mire – eventually to the love that banishes the fear. Obedience,
patience, silence: these are attitudes appropriate to monks but also
to all those who are trying to practise an 'interior monasticism'.

If we wish to attain the summit of humility, we must by our actions
set up the ladder that appeared in a dream to Jacob and on which
he saw angels descending and ascending. This descent and ascent
show us that by trying to climb we descend and by humility we
ascend. Now, this ladder thus set up is our life in this world, and
when the heart is humbled the Lord raises it to heaven. The sides
of the ladder are our body and soul, and on these sides God's call
has fixed the steps of humility for us to climb . . .

The first degree of humility consists in always keeping present
in the mind the fear of God and absolutely avoiding forgetfulness
of it . . .

The second degree of humility is not to love one's own will,
not to take pleasure in fulfilling one's own desires, but in one's
actions to imitate the Lord when he says: 'I have come down from
heaven, not to do my own will, but the will of him who sent me'
(John 6.38) . . .

The third degree of humility is to subject oneself in all obedience
to a superior for the love of God, imitating the Lord of whom the
apostle says: 'He became obedient unto death' (Philippians 2.8).

The fourth degree of humility consists in keeping patience and
tranquillity of spirit, even when hard and repugnant commands are
given or one is unjustly treated . . .

The fifth degree of humility consists in disclosing to the abbot
in humble confession the evil thoughts that come into the heart,
or the wrong done in secret . . .

The sixth degree of humility is when the monk is happy in the worst of conditions, and whatever requests are made of him he still sees himself as a bad and unworthy worker . . .

The seventh degree of humility is to know oneself the meanest and most despicable of men, not merely by saying so but by believing it with heartfelt conviction . . .

The eighth degree of humility is when the monk does nothing save what is commanded him by the common rule of the monastery and the example of his seniors.

The ninth degree of humility is when the monk has control of his tongue and remaining silent only speaks when he is questioned . . .

The tenth degree of humility is when we are no longer disposed to laugh easily; for it is written: 'A fool raises his voice when he laughs' (Ecclesiasticus 21.20).

The eleventh degree of humility is when the monk utters but few words when he speaks, words, however, of wisdom spoken quietly without scoffing, humbly and with gravity; for it is written: 'The wise man is recognized by the fewness of his words.'

The twelfth degree of humility is when the monk not only in his heart but also in his outward bearing suggests humility to those who see him . . .

Once these steps have been climbed the monk will soon come to that perfect love of God which drives out fear. Thanks to this love he will begin to observe, as though naturally and from habit, everything which at first he was afraid to look at; no longer for fear of hell, but for love of Christ, and through good habits and delight in virtue.

BENEDICT OF NURSIA *Rule*, VII (Centenario, pp. 32-42)

It is especially profitable not to boast, not to put oneself forward, carefully to refrain from speaking about one's own ascetic practices, to give the glory to God, and not to oneself, for every good thing that seems to happen in or because of oneself. In this way any narcissistic tendencies will be converted into self-forgetfulness and trustful self-abandonment.

Those who fear the Lord do not boast of their good observance. They consider that everything good in them comes not from themselves but from the Lord. They glorify him who is acting in them, saying with the prophet: 'Not to us, O Lord, not to us, but to thy name give the glory.'

BENEDICT OF NURSIA *Rule*, Prologue, 29-30 (ibid. p. 6)

One day in the Vale of the Hermitages, when a feast was being celebrated, the brethren were eating together in their place of assembly. A certain brother said to those who were serving at table, 'I won't eat anything cooked, just a little salt on my bread.'

The one who was serving at table called to another brother and said in the presence of the whole gathering, 'This brother is not eating anything cooked. Bring him just a little salt.'

Then one of the elders rose and said to the brother who had asked for salt, 'It would have been better for you today to eat meat alone in your cell, rather than to publish what you are doing to so many of the brethren.'

Sayings of the Desert Fathers, Anonymous series, 124 (SO 1, p. 366-7)

Whatever miracle may be worked in us is worked by God. In the healing of a soul or a body it is better to tell a lie in order to remain unknown than to be accorded the fame of a wonder-worker. Healing is by God alone, and the faith of the person who is healed. 'Your faith has healed you,' says Jesus.

A woman who had cancer of the breast heard of Abba Longinus and sought to meet him. Now, he dwelt at the ninth milestone beyond Alexandria. When the woman came looking for him he was gathering firewood by the sea. Approaching him the woman said, 'Abba, where does Abba Longinus the servant of God live?' She had no idea it was he. His reply was, 'Why are you looking for that impostor? Don't go to him. He is an impostor. What is the matter with you?' The woman showed him her trouble. He made the sign of the cross over the place and sent her away, saying, 'Go, and God will heal you, for Longinus cannot be any use to you.' The woman trusted these words and was healed on the spot. Later, when she was recounting the episode to others and describing the old man, she discovered that he was the Abba Longinus.

Sayings of the Desert Fathers, Longinus, 3 (PG 65,256-7)

A great monk, when he is dying, confesses that he has not even begun to serve God. The stories from the Egyptian desert tell us that the brothers gathered round Abba Sisoes when he was dying.

They asked him for a 'word'. 'How can I give you a word,' replied Sisoes, 'when I have not yet myself begun to repent?' Truly, that was the word.

Abba Pambo delivers the same message to us in the following brief narrative.

> It is related that at the hour of his death Abba Pambo said to the monks around him, 'Ever since I arrived here and built myself a cell in which I have lived, I do not remember ever having eaten bread that I have not earned with my own hands, or having uttered a word that I have had to regret. Yet I go to the Lord as someone who has not even begun to serve God.'
>
> *Sayings of the Desert Fathers*, Pambo, 8 (PG 65,369)

Humility makes forgiveness possible and is identified with it, or at least with silence when an injury has been received.

> A brother asked one of the elders for a definition of humility and he replied, 'It is to pardon our brother who has wronged us before he himself asks our pardon.'
>
> One of the elders was asked by a brother, 'What is humility?' and he answered, 'It is to do good to those who do evil to us.' The brother put a further question, 'If one cannot go as far as that, what should one do?' The elder replied, 'Flee those who offend us and keep silent.'
>
> *Sayings of the Desert Fathers*, Anonymous series, 171 & 173 (SO 1, p. 382)

But we must not be content with words, or with too much talk about love. Humility should be practical and realistic.

> A brother went to see Abba Matoes and said to him, 'How were the solitaries of Scete able to do more than Scripture requires, by loving their enemies more than themselves?'
>
> Abba Matoes answered him, 'For my part I do not yet love the one who loves me, as much as I love myself.'
>
> *Sayings of the Desert Fathers*, Matoes, 5 (PG 65,292)

Humility is closely connected with interior silence. Any obsession with guilt must be rejected but we must be able to keep silence and say nothing in the face of insults, as Jesus did. We remember his silence before Pilate. The loving power of that silence has been portrayed by Dostoyevsky in *The Legend of the Grand Inquisitor*.

A brother asked Abba Bessarion, 'What am I to do?' The answer: 'Keep silence and do not judge yourself.'

Sayings of the Desert Fathers, Bessarion, 10 (PG 65,141)

I do not pray any longer not to sin, but for thirty years I have been repeating, 'Lord Jesus, shield me from my tongue.' Yet despite this my tongue trips me up every day, and I commit sin because of it.

Sayings of the Desert Fathers, Sisoes, 5 (PG 65,393)

Abba Agathon carried pebbles in his mouth for three years, not to become an orator but to learn to keep silence.

Sayings of the Desert Fathers, Agathon, 15 (PG 65,113)

If someone accuses you of something you have done, or not done, and you keep silent, this is in conformity with the nature of Jesus.

If you answer: 'But what have I done?' that is not according to his nature.

If you answer back word for word, that is contrary to his nature.

Sayings of the Desert Fathers, Abba Isaiah, Logos 25,51 (CSCO 294, p. 438)

Silence is receptivity. It makes us attentive and allows a conversation with God that goes beyond words.

The friend of silence comes close to God.
In secret he converses with him and receives his light.

JOHN CLIMACUS *The Ladder of Divine Ascent*, 11th Step 4 (5) (p. 78)

Humility and silence are so many aspects of interior poverty and renunciation. A person uprooted from a settled life, heads for the desert, to become God's nomad. The real desert is within us. A vast city can be a strange kind of desert.

Spiritual deepening necessarily passes through 'mindfulness of death'. This 'mindfulness' is a 'reminder', an *anamnesis* in the strictest sense of the word, something not intellectual but existential. Our whole being is shaken and we experience the anguish and bitterness of our narrow finiteness, the condition of alienation, error, horror, hatred of others and of self. Everything seems precarious and about to overwhelm us, physical death seems imminent, and we feel the threat, already partially experienced, of spiritual death – this is real agony.

Then we discover, nearer still, the Christ who is conqueror of death and hell. And the 'mindfulness of death' becomes a blessed 'mindfulness of God', of God who is incarnate, crucified, bound with the chains of hell, risen. And all of a sudden there is no longer anything but resurrection. The anguish is changed into trust and the bitterness into sweetness.

The 'mindfulness of death' in spite of appearances does not come automatically. It has to be asked for and received as a grace.

> An elder said: 'The man who keeps the image of death continually before his eyes will always overcome his faint-heartedness.'
> *Sayings of the Desert Fathers* (in T. Merton, p. 113)

> Perfect awareness of death is free of all anguish.
> JOHN CLIMACUS *The Ladder of Divine Ascent*, 6th Step, 16 (p. 60)

> Mindfulness of death gives to the soul's activity something incorruptible.
> JOHN CLIMACUS *The Ladder of Divine Ascent*, 6th Step, 21 (p. 61)

> Mindfulness of death is a grace added to the other gifts that God gives us. If it were not so, why should we often stand by tombs without feeling the least emotion, whereas our heart can be deeply moved when we are far from the sight of them?
> JOHN CLIMACUS *The Ladder of Divine Ascent*, 6th Step, 22 (p. 61)

> It is impossible to spend the coming day in faith if we do not think of it as the last day of our life.
> JOHN CLIMACUS *The Ladder of Divine Ascent*, 6th Step, 26 (p. 62)

The 'mindfulness of death' should be linked with the Name of Jesus, the name of death's conqueror. Then I know at once *what* I am saved from and *by whom*. And if go to sleep each night like this, I introduce into my sleep, which is at once an image of death and also a kind of self-abandonment, a tang of the resurrection. The name of Jesus shuts up the infernal depths from which illusions come into the soul; and it opens the soul to the 'superconscious', which is penetrated by baptismal grace and visited by bright dreams.

Let the mindfulness of death be present when you fall asleep and when you wake up. In this way you will be protected during your sleep.

JOHN CLIMACUS *The Ladder of Divine Ascent*, 15th Step, 51 (p. 91)

The 'mindfulness of death' is thus the way to the most profound contemplation.

The mindfulness of death is the first thought by which the love of God leads the soul to life and fills the heart . . . When the power of God wants to manifest life in a person's heart, it plants this thought there as a foundation. If it is not quenched by the complexities and vanity of this life, if it is allowed to grow in peace . . . it leads him to the most profound contemplation, too profound for words.

ISAAC OF NINEVEH *Ascetic Treatises*, 39 (p. 167)

The experience of humility and the 'mindfulness of death' is bound up with the 'gift of tears'. The heart is broken and exults in the Spirit with immense joy. The joy is 'sorrowful' because it is inseparable from the cross, but it is the sign that all the strength of human suffering, crucified and risen, is being healed, pacified, and transfigured in a kind of ontological tenderness. The whole being is wonderfully torn apart, and the heart of stone becomes a heart of flesh; discreet and gentle tears begin to flow, not distorting the face. This 'emotion' of the heart, that everyone feels at certain moments when experiencing compassion or love or beauty, from now on becomes a settled state.

The tears are at first those of bitterness and despair, when the Spirit makes us aware of our 'unlikeness', of our complicity in hatred and destruction. Then they become tears of gratitude and fervour because 'the cross is the judgment of judgment' and 'Christ is risen'.

Pray first of all to receive the gift of tears in order to soften the hardness of your heart by 'breaking' it.

EVAGRIUS OF PONTUS *On Prayer*, 5 (Philokalia I,177)

Conversion and humility direct the soul aright.
Compassion and gentleness make it strong.

EVAGRIUS OF PONTUS *The Mirror of Monks*, 53 (Gressman, p. 157)

Sadness weighs us down,
self-disgust is unbearable.
But tears before God are stronger than either.

EVAGRIUS OF PONTUS *The Mirror of Nuns*, 39 (Gressman, p. 149)

The water of tears is a return to the source, to the water of baptism, and so to the waters of creation that are amenable to the Spirit. The 'baptism of tears', this conscious realization of baptismal grace, is the same thing as 'baptism in the Spirit'.

So anguish, by becoming prayer, is turned with all its ardour into peace and light.

Nothing is so well calculated to dispel sloth and negligence as anguish that gathers the spirit together from all sides and makes it return into itself. Anyone who prays in anguish will be able, after his prayer, to know a great joy in his soul. Just as clouds when they gather begin by making the day dark, then, once they have poured out all the water they contained, the atmosphere is serene and light; so anguish, as it builds up in our heart, plunges our thoughts into darkness, but then, when it has vented all its bitterness through prayer and accompanying tears, it brings to the soul a great light. God's influence irradiates the soul of the one who is praying, like a ray of sunlight.

JOHN CHRYSOSTOM *On the Incomprehensibility of God*, Sermon 5 (PG 48,744)

The mystery of tears fashions us after the mystery of Golgotha, of the sacred agony in which all the sorrow of the world is gathered up and all its joy is inaugurated. We have to stand, like St John, with Mary, at the foot of the cross.

Abba Joseph used to relate what Abba Isaac said: 'One day I was sitting near Abba Poimen and I saw him in ecstasy, and as I enjoyed great freedom of speech with him, I prostrated myself and besought him saying, "Tell me, where were you?" And he replied in embarrassment, "My thoughts were there where Mary was, the holy Mother of God, weeping over the cross of the Saviour. And for my part I wish I could always be thus weeping."'

Sayings of the Desert Fathers, Poimen 151 (SO 1, p. 246-7)

Little by little, through the tears there comes a smile, something familiar to the child but forgotten by the adult.

One who goes on his way to God with interior tears never ceases keeping festival.

JOHN CLIMACUS *The Ladder of Divine Ascent*, 7th Step, 38 (41)
(p. 65)

One who is clothed with blessed tears for a wedding dress knows the soul's spiritual smile.

JOHN CLIMACUS Ibid. 44(41) p. 66

At the beginning of the spiritual life God is accustomed to reveal himself clearly. But the person who is still inexperienced mixes these experiences with his imagination and takes them too seriously. Then there comes the exodus through the wilderness, the 'sadness for God' and the tears of sorrow, then the tears 'without sorrow'. And he receives the true joy as a grace that is indeed a 'free gift', a joy that he can now welcome in complete humility, one which radically re-creates him. As the world was created from the primordial waters, so is man re-created from the water of his tears.

The initial joy is one thing, the joy that consummates is another. The former is vulnerable to imagination, the latter has the strength of humility. Between the two comes a blessed sadness, and tears without sorrow.

DIADOCHUS OF PHOTIKE *Gnostic Chapters*, 60 (SC 5 bis, p. 120)

A 'stranger on earth', the spiritual person's dwelling is found in God. *Eros* is transfigured and illumined by the contemplation of the human face of God. Then comes the experience of the true joy, pure and fundamental, joy in the Father and the Son, joy that is almost the Spirit himself, in the Kingdom of the Father to which the Son admits us.

The Father of all things is a well-beloved kingdom.
Anyone who is in him,
anyone who establishes his dwelling in him,
finds his joy in living as a stranger
because he has for delicious food
the beauty of God's face.

EVAGRIUS OF PONTUS *Centuries*, Suppl. 57 (in Hausherr p. 186)

The name of the Son of God is great, majestic, upholding the whole world. Now consider those whom he upholds. They are those who bear his name in the depths of their heart. He then becomes their support, he maintains them in joy because they are not ashamed to bear his name.

HERMAS *The Shepherd*, 91, 5-6 (SC 53, p. 326)

A text of the second century which shows the Christian awareness of fundamentals emphasizes that joy is the true condition of humanity.

Clothe yourself then in joy where God delights to be. Make it your delight. For every joyful person acts well, thinks rightly, and tramples sadness underfoot. The gloomy person on the other hand always acts badly. In the first place such a one does wrong by grieving the Holy Spirit who is given to us as joy. Then ... the gloomy person is guilty of impiety in not praying to the Lord ... for prayer offered in sadness lacks the strength to ascend to the altar of God ... Sadness mingled with prayer prevents it from rising, just as vinegar mingled with wine robs it of its flavour ... Purify your heart then of the sadness that is evil, and you will be living for God. And all those who have stripped themselves of sadness in order to put on joy will likewise be living for God.

HERMAS *The Shepherd*, 42, 1-4 (SC 53, p. 190)

With trust and humility, in a joy that is peaceful and strong, we find our true stature as sons in the Son, crowned with flames of the Spirit. We attain the true royalty which is our freedom.

Be like a king in your heart, on the throne of humility. You bid laughter: 'Go', and it goes. You bid sweet tears: 'Come', and they come. You bid your body that is both servant and tyrant: 'Do this', and it does it.

JOHN CLIMACUS *The Ladder of Divine Ascent*, 7th Step, 40(43) (p. 66)

4

Passions Transfigured,
Thought Transcended

To 'see' God one must purify one's 'heart', one's 'spirit'. Some speak more of the 'heart', others more of the 'spirit': Jerusalem and Athens? Perhaps ... Indeed it was soon perceived that this separation is a sign of the fallenness of humanity, but that in the crucible of grace it becomes possible to unite 'heart' and 'spirit'. This 'heart-spirit' is purified and reconciled with itself, and little by little becomes aware of the fire it contains. The decisive element here is the blessed state of 'the pure in heart, for they shall see God.' Even before there is any question of an ascetical method, what matters is to change one's life: 'poverty' and 'justice' are not to be kept apart, as the text of the Beatitudes in St Luke's Gospel underlines. And as St Augustine reminds us in the following reflections, sand is thrown in the eyes of the heart not only by a multiplicity of images, not only by association of ideas, but also by the refusal to serve one's neighbour in practical ways. To be too busy filling the coffers prevents one from emptying one's heart so as to make it attentive to the 'interior Master'. For 'where your treasure is,' says Jesus, 'there will your heart be also.'

> To purify yourself, have faith. You would like to see God. That desire is good, it is noble, and I challenge you to make trial of it. You would like to see him? 'Blessed are the pure in heart, for they shall see God' (Matthew 5.8). Think first of all about purifying your heart ... You believe that God is evident to the eyes like the light ... But if your eyes were clogged with sand, would you not have to wash them out before you could see the light?
>
> Your heart is defiled also. And avarice spreads its murkiness there ... Do you not realize that by hoarding in this way you are

covering your heart with mud? How then will you see him whom
you desire?

You say to me, 'Show me your God.' . . .

I answer you, 'Take a look at your heart. Everything you see
in it that might sadden God, remove. God wants to come to you.
Listen to Christ your Lord: "My Father and I will come to him and
make our home with him" (John 14.23). That is God's promise. If
I were to tell you I was coming to stay with you, you would clean
your house. Now it is God who wants to come into your heart. Do
you not hasten to purify it? How could he dwell with avarice? . . .
God has commanded you to clothe the naked. But avarice induces
you to strip the one who is clothed . . . I am looking at your heart.
What do you have in it? Have you filled your coffers but thrown
away your conscience? . . . Purify your heart.'

AUGUSTINE OF HIPPO *Sermons*, 261,4 (PL 38,1203-4)

Beyond that, however, everything resolves itself, including the
basic motives of our actions, into those *logismoi* or *dialogismoi* of
which Jesus speaks in the Gospels. The usual translation is 'thoughts'.
More precisely they are the seeds of the 'passions', those suggestions
or impulses that emerge from the subconscious and soon become
obsessive. In the ascetic sense, remember, the 'passions' are blockages,
usurpations, deviations that destroy the human being's basic desire.
They are forms of idolatry, of that 'self-idolatry' that deflects towards
nothingness our capacity for transcendence.

What is it then to be a fool for Christ? It is to control one's
thoughts when they stray out of line. It is to make the mind empty
and free so as to be able to offer it in a state of readiness when
Christ's teachings are to be assimilated, swept clean for the words
of God that it needs to welcome.

JOHN CHRYSOSTOM *On the Incomprehensibility of God*, Sermon 5
(PG 48,710)

It is therefore essential to let the 'heart-spirit' settle like calm
water. Then it becomes a tranquil lake in which the sky is reflected, in which the face of Christ can be seen and thereby the
true face of one's neighbour also.

One of the Fathers said, 'In the same way as you cannot see

your face in troubled water, the soul, if it is not emptied of foreign thoughts, cannot reflect God in contemplation.'

Sayings of the Desert Fathers (in T. Merton, p. 77)

It is important to learn how to lead back 'into the house of the body' the mind that is scattered, pulled this way and that, put to all kinds of wrong uses. The whole art is to confine the incorporeal within the corporeal, as St John Climacus was to put it, with the intention of making it faithful and vigilant, like the virgins in the parable whose lamps were full of oil in expectation of the Bridegroom's arrival (Matthew 25.1-13). One must learn to keep awake in the silence of the heart.

Let the soul collect its scattered thoughts as if it were recalling stray children back home to the body. Let it await unceasingly in sobriety and love the day on which its Lord will come truly to visit it ... In this way sin will do no harm to people living in hope and faith awaiting the Redeemer. When he comes he transforms the thoughts of the heart ... he teaches true prayer that remains firm and unshakeable. Fear not. 'I will go before you and level the mountains, I will break in pieces the doors of bronze and cut asunder the bars of iron' (Isaiah 45.2). And: 'Keep watch on yourself that no word in the silence of your heart may make you an object of reprobation.'

PSEUDO-MACARIUS *Thirty First Homily*, 1 (PG 34,728)

The heart that is not purified is a dark abyss, an immensity of the subconscious, that is not merely individual but pan-human, even cosmic, containing all the dark side of the world. In the 'upward' direction it is shut off by death, and in the 'downward' direction given over as prey to the 'powers of darkness'. Faith and humility, on the contrary, open the 'upward' way for the heart through the risen Christ to the 'image of God' that might be termed the 'superconscious'. Thus the divine light penetrates the abyss, and Christ triumphs there anew over the murderous powers of evil. The abyss of the heart opens on to the abyss of God.

To refrain from evil is not perfection. Perfection is to enter into a spirit of humility and to put to death the serpent that is making its nest and practising murder below even the spirit, deeper than the abode of thought, in the treasury and storehouse of the soul. For the heart is an abyss.

PSEUDO-MACARIUS *Eighteenth Homily* (PG 34,633)

This penetration of the light into the subconscious manifests itself, as we have already suggested, in the form of dreams full of joy and peace, that are sometimes prophetic. Diadochus of Photike here describes the criteria that make it possible to distinguish dreams like this from those which display diabolical forces.

Dreams appearing to the soul in the love of God are sure signs of a healthy soul. They do not skip lightly from one image to another. They do not alarm the senses . . . They fill the soul with spiritual happiness. Even after awakening, the soul seeks with an ardent desire the joy of the dream. Diabolical apparitions behave in contrary fashion. They change rapidly . . . they speak loudly, utter great threats, overwhelm the soul with their cries. Then the spirit, if it has been purified, recognizes them and awakens the body . . . It may happen that good dreams do not bring joy to the soul but cause it sadness and tears without pain. That is the case with those who are making great progress in humility.

DIADOCHUS OF PHOTIKE *Gnostic Chapters*, 37 (SC 5 bis, p. 106)

It is therefore necessary to possess 'discernment of spirits': not only to know how to progress through the flood, or jungle of thoughts without being dragged helplessly along by them, but also to know how to sift the 'good' from the 'bad'. In the good our true nature is at work, attracted by grace, but in the bad the foreign powers envelop the soul in a strait-jacket and interpose themselves between the spirit and the heart.

This attention to one's thoughts, this particularly fruitful 'fishing' in the silence of the night, when the subconscious becomes accessible, must all be placed in the context of prayer. For it is only by his relation with God that a person can break free from external conditioning.

And this prayer must be discreet, indeed secret. 'Go into your room and shut the door,' says Jesus – for fear of being ostentatious and causing embarrassment to others.

This is the true foundation of prayer: keeping watch over your own thoughts and giving yourself to prayer in great tranquillity,

in great peace, in such a way as not to disturb others ... You
will then have to wage war on your own thoughts and cut back
their rampant growth ... push ahead towards God, refrain from
doing as your thoughts would have you do, but on the contrary
lead them back from their dispersion, sifting the natural thoughts
from those that are bad. The soul subjected to sin advances as if
across a river choked with reeds and sedge ... Anyone wishing to
cross over must reach out with his hands and laboriously root out
by force the obstacles in his way. Thus do thoughts from the enemy
power imprison the soul as in a strait-jacket. It requires great zeal
and great alertness to discern them.

PSEUDO-MACARIUS *Sixth Homily*, (PG 34,520)

In most of the texts the 'heart' is understood as the centre of the
personality where all our faculties meet. It is the 'heart-spirit' already
purified, especially by baptismal grace. So it is necessary to practise
'custody of the heart' by the discerning of the thoughts.

Be the door-keeper of your heart and do not let any thought come
in without questioning it. Question each thought individually: 'Are
you on our side or the side of our foes?' And if it is one of ours,
it will fill you with tranquillity.

EVAGRIUS OF PONTUS *Letter 11* (Frankenberg, p. 575)

An ambiguous 'thought' is put in parenthesis, some way off,
and is bombarded with rays of prayer until it is harmonized or it
disintegrates.

Wake up, keep watch! If the thought that comes to you is a
good thought you should know that God wants to open up a way
of life for you ... But if the thought is dark, if you are in two minds
because you cannot see clearly whether it is to help you or deceive
you – since an evil thought can be hidden under an appearance of
good – keep watch night and day in the ardour and intensity of
prayer so as to prepare yourself to fight it. Do not chase after it
and do not accept it either, but pray about it earnestly. Do not
cease to call on the Lord and he will show you whence it comes.

ISAAC OF NINEVEH *Ascetic Treatises*, 34 (Spanos, p. 148)

Invocation of the name of Jesus is habitual in these exercises
of discernment. It is important that the 'natural' thought giving

expression to the deep but still blind yearning of the soul should be enlightened and strengthened by being clothed with the name of Christ. Any idolatrous or obsessive idea is dashed against this name. For example the name of Jesus may be invoked faster and faster until the soul is quieted. This is how the monks used to interpret the psalm of the exiles that recommends the dashing of the 'children of Babylon' against the rocks. The children symbolize negative thoughts. The rock is Christ.

On this point too it will be seen that Benedictine monasticism is hardly distinguished from Eastern monasticism.

> He who acts righteously . . . is he who drives the devil from his heart. He seizes this brood of devilish thoughts and dashes it to pieces against Christ.
>
> BENEDICT OF NURSIA *Rule*, Prologue 28 (Centenario, p. 6)

Sometimes it is preferable, instead of tackling 'thoughts' head on, to break off all contact with them and to take refuge in Christ. Witness a moving passage about such a 'little way' from that giant of ascesis, Isaac of Nineveh.

> There is no need to set oneself against the thoughts. Better take refuge in God. If we refrain from opposing the thoughts sown in us by the devil, and in prayer to God break off all contact with them, that is the sign that the intelligence has discovered the wisdom that comes from grace, and that true knowledge has freed us from too much action. Thus we have mastered the shortest route.
>
> ISAAC OF NINEVEH *Ascetic Treatises*, 33 (p. 144)

After all, it is not the human being acting alone, but the coming of the Spirit that cleanses the soul of all the dust of 'reasonings and thoughts'. The 'true recollection' is not so much mastered as received. But we must prepare to receive it.

> The Holy Spirit taking pity on our weakness visits us even when we are still not purified. Provided only that he finds our intelligence simply praying with a desire for true recollection, he comes down upon it and scatters the whole troop of reasonings

and thoughts that are besieging it and leads it to love and to the achievement of spiritual power.

EVAGRIUS OF PONTUS *On Prayer*, 63 (Philokalia I,182)

Clearly it is not only a question of discerning between good and bad thoughts, but also of escaping from the flux of our psychic processes in which so often 'something thinks', 'something speaks' in spite of us. The spirit soars up to God beyond the visible and the intelligible, up even beyond its own flight – pure *ek-stasis* of the person up to the personal God. Then we can say with the bride of the Song of Songs: 'I slept, but my heart was awake' (Song of Songs 5.2).

A woman who is asleep can remain impervious to the uproar of a storm, but will be woken by a sigh from her baby in the next room. A sleeper who is indifferent to the noises in the street immediately hears the light footsteps of the one he loves. Lighter still are the footsteps of the 'One who comes'. But the heart wakes for him.

When the spirit wants to think, it goes down beneath itself and plunges into thoughts one at a time. For the thoughts are below the thinker, precisely because they are being thought and are thus limited. They constitute a scattering, a dismemberment of the spirit. For the spirit is simple, without division. Thoughts on the other hand are innumerable and scattered, the units, so to speak, of which the spirit is made . . . But the spirit is united by the movement by which it raises itself up to that which is above it, namely when it devotes itself to the contemplation of God, when in ecstasy it is transported beyond the visible and the natural and even beyond its own movement.

JOHN OF SCYTHOPOLIS *On the Divine Names of Dionysius the Areopagite*, 7 (PG 4,344)

In ordinary sleep the sleeper is not awake, and the one who is awake is not asleep, but both sleeping and wakefulness succeed each other alternately, taking each other's place . . . But here we find an unheard of and paradoxical union and mixture of contraries. For the Bride says: 'I slept, but my heart was awake' (Song of Songs 5.2). What can these words mean? Sleep resembles death. For in sleep all visible activity of the body comes to a halt . . . The body is entirely relaxed. It also induces forgetfulness of those preoccupations that a person carries about with him, it puts fear to sleep, it pacifies anger, it soothes bitterness and makes us insensible to all pain.

We see from this how high the soul rises above itself when it
says: 'I sleep but my heart is awake' . . . Enjoying the contemplation
solely of that which is . . . but allowing all bodily activity to sleep,
it receives in the unclothed nakedness of the spirit the revelation of God in divine wakefulness. May we make ourselves also
worthy of it, by attaining through sleep to wakefulness of soul.

GREGORY OF NYSSA *Sermons on the Song of Songs*, 10 (PG 44,
992-3)

Having reached interior freedom, where the 'passions' cease, or
are transformed into love, and participate in God's pure 'passion of
love', we let the light of God transfix us. In this light, whose source
is utterly elsewhere, we then see, beyond the stirring of 'thoughts',
our heart-spirit as an interior heaven, sapphire in colour. It is an
abyss of light or, better, of transparent glory, inwardly azure, as a
sign that the world is becoming interior to the spiritual person. To
descend into the heart, say the ascetics, is thereafter to climb Sinai,
where God revealed himself to Moses.

If you wish to see the transparency of you own spirit you must rid
yourself of all thoughts, and then you will see yourself looking like
sapphire or the colour of heaven. But to do that without interior
freedom [*apatheia*] is not possible. Human beings need God's help
in filling their emptiness with light and strength.

EVAGRIUS OF PONTUS *Centuries*, Suppl. 2 (Frankenberg p. 425)

Anger (where the strength of the soul, the *thumos*, is inflamed
and distorted) and greed (where desire, the *epithumia*, is inflamed and
distorted) are major passions to be overcome, major energies to be
transformed.

If you are armed against anger you will never allow greed to master
you. For it is greed that fuels anger, and anger that blurs the eye of
the spirit, so wrecking the state of prayerfulness.

EVAGRIUS OF PONTUS *On Prayer*, 27 (Philokalia I,179)

To come before God in prayer is to see oneself in his clear
and sober light with the eyes of a child. So one feels oneself being
weighed and judged, and this leads to self-judgement, and any resentment fades away like something laughable.

And how can one pray, or escape from the demon of sadness,
if one has wounded a brother or sister in anger?

If you receive some provocation or contradiction that irritates you, and you feel your anger leading you to reply in kind and retaliate, then remember prayer and the judgment that is awaiting you, and at once your unruly emotion will subside.

EVAGRIUS OF PONTUS *On Prayer*, 12 (Philokalia I,178)

It is a question not only of preserving one's calm outwardly – since resentment is worse than an outburst of anger – but also of allowing the Holy Spirit to pacify the soul.

The Holy Spirit calms the soul. Anger rouses the heart. Nothing is so opposed as anger to the coming of the Holy Spirit to us.

JOHN CLIMACUS *The Ladder of Divine Ascent*, 8th Step, 16(18)
(p. 71)

I have seen people preserving a calm exterior ... while beneath an appearance of quiet they are nourishing internal resentment. I regard them as more pitiable than those who give vent to their feelings. Their dreary character puts the Dove, the Holy Spirit, to flight.

JOHN CLIMACUS *The Ladder of Divine Ascent*, 8th Step, 17(20)
(p. 71)

Then we come to the gentleness of those who are strong, whether they are in the desert or amongst other people.

Better a man living in the world if he is gentle than a monk who flies into fits of anger.

EVAGRIUS OF PONTUS *Mirror of Monks*, 34 (Gressmann, p. 156)

However, it is not a question of abolishing aggressiveness, of unmanning anyone, of assuming an attitude of nihilistic indifference. There can be a good use for aggressiveness when we use it calmly against hatred and stupidity.

Anger, more than the other passions, is wont to trouble and upset the soul. But even anger sometimes renders the soul great benefits. When, in fact, we use it calmly against error or stupidity, to denounce and save, we obtain for the soul additional gentleness, since we are furthering the purposes of justice and divine goodness. And also when we rouse ourselves strongly against evil we often make more masculine what is feminine in the soul ... Therefore one who makes temperate use of anger out of zeal for truth will no doubt be found better, in the time of judgement, than one who out of inertia was never stirred to anger.

DIADOCHUS OF PHOTIKE *Gnostic Chapters*, 62 (SC 5 bis, p. 121)

It is the same with desire as it is with strength. *Eros* has to be transformed into eagerness for a meeting, for the content of a personal relationship. The texts we are considering, being monastic in character, speak only of the metamorphosis of *eros* in relation to the personal God. But one might think here also of its metamorphosis in the relationship of a man and a woman, each of them in the light of God recognizing the other as a person.

I have seen impure souls who threw themselves headlong into physical *eros* to a frenzied degree. It was their very experience of that *eros* that led them to interior conversion. They concentrated their *eros* on the Lord. Rising above fear they tried to love God with an insatiable desire. That is why, when Christ spoke of the woman who had been a sinner, he did not say that she had been afraid, but that she had loved much and had easily been able to surmount love by love.

JOHN CLIMACUS *The Ladder of Divine Ascent*, 5th Step, 6(28) (p. 57)

Thus God must be loved *also* with all the strength of *eros*. Then *eros* is transformed and subsumed in *agape*, the spiritual love that comes from above. The Fathers do not oppose these terms. *Agape* without *eros* would remain weak, powerless, mere moonshine, just as *eros* without *agape* would be a dark destructive force. This opposition is brilliantly described by Dostoyevsky in *The Idiot* where he compares the unarmed agape of Mushkin with the blind *eros* of Rogozhin – both qualities bring death to the woman who aroused pity only or desire only ... Together *eros* and *agape* constitute a creative virility, like the sun, joining heaven to earth.

Human nature cannot express the overflowing abundance of divine love. Accordingly it is symbolized by what is most violent in the passions that excite us, I mean the passion of love, in order that we may learn thereby that the soul, which has its eyes on the beauty of the divine nature, must be as much enamoured of it as the body is with that which is akin to it, changing passion into detached joy, so that our soul is 'erotically' on fire in us with the flame of the Holy Spirit only.

GREGORY OF NYSSA *Sermons on the Song of Songs*, I (PG 44, 777)

It is not a question of crushing the life in us but of restoring to the soul its spiritual youthfulness.

We are not asked to tear out or annihilate the natural activities of the soul but to purify them. That means we have to rid it of the defilements and impurities with which our negligence has covered it, so that it may be restored to its natural youthful brightness with the native vigour that belongs to it.

ORIGEN *Sermons on Joshua*, 22,4 (GCS 7,436)

Nothing exists – anger or lust – that does not have some share in what is good. That fact is the basis of metamorphosis. Good in the Greek sense is, of course, the fullness of being. Even a blind desire for a better life should be respected. What is necessary is not to eliminate desire but to free it by showing that its impetus is opposed to death and that only the resurrection of Christ can satisfy it.

Without some share in what is Good nothing has ever existed, nothing does exist and nothing could exist. Take lust, for example. It is devoid of Good because of its senseless covetousness ... but that does not prevent it taking its share in what is Good by means of the feeble echo that remains in it of fellowship and tenderness. Likewise anger has a share in what is Good because of its innate impulse, the desire to improve what seems evil and bring it back to what appears a better state. Even the person who desires the worst of lives, in so far as the desire is to live, and to live what seems a better life, by the very desiring, by the desire to live and by the aiming at a higher life, that person has a share in what is Good. If what is Good were entirely suppressed, there would no longer be any life, nor desire, nor purpose, nor anything else.

DIONYSIUS THE AREOPAGITE *Divine Names*, IV, 20 (PG 3,720)

Detachment gives a person royal power, thus it is said that 'The city belongs to you'. Indeed, 'It is the gateway to God', but only the gateway.

Once upon a time there was a Greek philosopher who told one of his disciples to give money to anyone who insulted him,

for three years. At the end of this period of testing the master said
to him, 'Now you may go to Athens to learn wisdom.'

Entering Athens the disciple met a wise man who was sitting
by the city gate insulting all the passers-by. He did the same to
the disciple who immediately burst out laughing. 'Why do you
laugh when I insult you?' demanded the wise man. 'Because for
three years I have been giving money to those who insulted me,
and now you are doing it for nothing.' 'Come into the city; it
belongs to you', replied the wise man.

Abba John who was in the habit of recounting this story would
add: 'That is the gateway to God.'

Sayings of the Desert Fathers (in T. Merton, p. 60)

Truth is metamorphosis. All our powers of life and of passion
are unified in the crucible of 'insatiable love'.

In one whose whole spirit is inwardly turned towards God, even
covetousness gives strength to the burning love for God, even the
power of anger is directed with a single impulse towards divine
love. That person has become, through sharing in the divine light
over a long period, full of light himself. The power of the elemental
forces, thus unified, is transformed into a burning insatiable love.

MAXIMUS THE CONFESSOR *Centuries on Charity*, II,48 (PG 90,1000)

The soul is made perfect when its powers of passion have been
completely directed towards God.

MAXIMUS THE CONFESSOR *Centuries on Charity*, III,98 (PG 90,1048)

It is exactly in this way that the destructive passions are set aside
– less by exhausting oneself struggling against them, than by opening
oneself to a fullness of life and joy and awareness that removes their
limitations and harnesses their power.

It is not by fighting against the passions that one prevents them
entering the heart. That is achieved rather by the gratification of
conscience, by the knowledge with which the soul is filled, and by
the desire for its own acts of contemplation.

ISAAC OF NINEVEH *Ascetic Treatises*, 38 (p. 165)

PART THREE

Approaches to Contemplation

1

On Prayer

1. *What is Prayer?*

Any increase in the depth of existence, any perception of mystery in the presence of love or of beauty or of death, leads to prayer. Yet for there to be prayer in the Christian sense of the word a specifically personal relationship has to be established with the living God, a 'conversation' as Evagrius puts it. The word should be taken in a broad sense. It may be silent listening, a cry of distress, a celebration; it may also be Job's plaintive challenge. The disposition we need to cultivate, even when care weighs heaviest, is that of remembering that God exists and loves us; that we are not alone, lost, ridiculous in the presence of nothingness or horror; that there is Another whom we may approach in union with Christ, in him, in the depths of our being.

> Prayer is a conversation of the spirit with God. Seek therefore the disposition that the spirit needs, in order to be able to reach out towards its Lord and to hold converse with him without any intermediary.
> EVAGRIUS OF PONTUS *On Prayer*, 3 (Philokalia I, 177)

Prayer does not seek to draw God towards us since, as St Augustine says, he is closer to us than we are to ourselves. Its purpose is to bring us close enough to him for dialogue, and to make us aware of his nearness. 'Lord, all is in Thee and I myself am in Thee; do thou receive me,' says the pilgrim Macarius in Dostoyevsky's *The Adolescent*.

> It may be true that the divine principle is present in every being, but not every being is present in him. We ourselves will

come to dwell with him if we call on him with very holy prayers and a tranquil mind. For his indwelling is not local, as if he could change position ... If we were on a ship, and to rescue us ropes attached to a rock were thrown to us, obviously we should not draw the rock any nearer to ourselves, but we would pull ourselves and our ship nearer to the rock ... And that is why ... in prayer we need to begin, not by drawing to ourselves that Power that is everywhere and nowhere, but by putting ourselves in his hands and uniting ourselves to him.

DIONYSIUS THE AREOPAGITE *Divine Names*, III,1 (PG 3,680)

True prayer is not only of the mouth, it is of the heart, that is, of the whole being. It is a cry *de profundis*, out of the deep. There is a correspondence between the depths of the heart and the heights of heaven, understood not in a physical sense but in the sense of a 'beyond' in relation to the centre. So it was that Pascal had recourse to the hidden God, when the discoveries of Copernicus and Galileo had demonstrated the emptiness of the 'infinite spaces'.

By prayer I mean not that which is only in the mouth, but that which springs up from the bottom of the heart. In fact, just as trees with deep roots are not shattered or uprooted by storms ... in the same way prayers that come from the bottom of the heart, having their roots there, rise to heaven with complete assurance and are not knocked off course by the assault of any thought. That is why the psalm says: 'Out of the deep have I called unto thee, O Lord' (Psalm 130.1).

JOHN CHRYSOSTOM *On the Incomprehensibility of God*, Sermon 5 (PG 48,746)

Prayer upholds the virtues and is itself upheld by them. It expresses the gratitude that arises in us in the presence of the crucified God who restores us to life. And the heart is moved with an ontological tenderness.

Prayer is the daughter of gentleness ...
Prayer is the fruit of joy and gratitude.

EVAGRIUS OF PONTUS *On Prayer*, 14,15 (Philokalia I,178)

In the admirable formula that follows, Evagrius gives us the key to the collaboration in prayer of grace and freedom. God gives prayer to whoever, overcoming natural tendencies to rebelliousness or torpor, makes it a rule to pray, and thus works together with the deepest current of his or her being that is created in the image of God. For the image feels the magnetic pull of its model.

> If you want to pray, you need God, who gives prayer to one who prays.
>
> EVAGRIUS OF PONTUS *On Prayer*, 59 (Philokalia I,181)

Macarius develops the same theme in a sermon. We cannot do anything by ourselves but calls out like a child that does not yet know how to walk and cries to attract its mother's attention. It is not exactly salvation by faith (especially as we are taught that faith itself is a gift: what can the human contribution be then?). It is salvation by love and humility.

> It is not true, as some maintain who are led astray by error, that the human being is irremediably dead and can no longer do anything good. A small child is incapable of anything; it cannot run to its mother on its own legs; it tumbles on the ground, cries out, sobs, calls out to her. And she is gentle with it, she is touched to see her baby seeking her so impatiently with so many sobs. It cannot reach her but cries out to her tirelessly, and she goes to it overcome with love, she kisses it, presses it to her heart and feeds it, with unspeakable tenderness. God loves us and he behaves like her towards the soul that seeks him and cries out to him. In the eagerness of that infinite love that is his . . . he takes hold of our spirit, unites himself to it, and we become 'one spirit with him', as the apostle says (I Corinthians 6.17). The soul is linked with the Lord, and the Lord, full of compassion and love, unites himself to it and it dwells in his grace. Then the soul and the Lord are one spiritually, they form one life, one heart.
>
> PSEUDO-MACARIUS *Forty-sixth Homily*, (PG 34,794)

Prayer and theology are inseparable. True theology is the adoration offered by the intellect. The intellect clarifies the movement of prayer, but only prayer can give it the fervour of the Spirit. Theology is light, prayer is fire. Their union expresses the union of the intellect and the heart. But it is the intellect that must 'repose' in the heart, and theology must transcend it in love.

If you are a theologian you will pray truly; and if you pray truly you are a theologian.

EVAGRIUS OF PONTUS *On Prayer*, 61 (Philokalia I,182)

When the intellect is filled with love towards God, it tears this world of death apart, it breaks away from images, passions, reasoning, in order to be no longer anything but gratitude and joy. For it experiences, in this way, victory over death.

When your intellect, in an ardent love for God, sets itself gradually to transcend, so to speak, created things and rejects all thinking ... at the same time filling itself with gratitude and joy, then you may consider yourself approaching the borders of prayer.

EVAGRIUS OF PONTUS *On Prayer*, 62 (Philokalia I,182)

Little by little, beyond its secondary forms, prayer has to make a void that waits on God, an attentive, recollected, loving void. 'A void where the internal straining has nothing external corresponding to it,' says Simone Weil. Poverty. *Nada* of the Spanish mystics.

The 'living creatures' of Ezekiel are the four 'animals' that symbolize cosmic, angelic powers. They are covered with eyes. Likewise, the human being at prayer must become sheer listening, sheer gazing. Then Christ comes to dwell in him and the Spirit is united with him, to pray another sort of prayer that is no longer merely human.

To pray there is no need of gestures, nor cries, nor silence, nor kneeling. Our prayer that is at once tranquil and fervent ought to be a waiting upon God, for God to come and permeate all its approaches, all its ways, all its senses. Enough of groanings and sobs. Let us seek in our prayer only the coming of God.

When we are at work, do we not apply the whole of our body to the task? Do not all our limbs take part in it? Likewise, let our soul devote itself wholly to its praying and to the love of the Lord. Do not let it be distracted or torn this way or that by thoughts. Let it become, I say, completely a waiting upon Christ.

Then Christ will enlighten it, he will teach it true prayer, he will endow it with ... adoration 'in spirit and in truth' (John 4.24) ...

The Lord instals himself in a fervent soul, he makes it his throne of glory, he seats himself there and dwells there. The prophet Ezekiel speaks of the four Living Creatures harnessed to the Lord's chariot. He says that they had countless eyes. In the same way the soul that seeks God – rather I mean the soul that is sought by God – is no longer anything but gazing.

PSEUDO-MACARIUS *Thirty-Third Homily*, (PG 34,741)

That is why to reach this stage of prayer we have to banish all thoughts and tricks (as if we could deceive God or prevail over him!). The intellect is concentrated, words are suspended.

In your prayer time, rid yourself of everything that harasses you ... be an ignorant and simple and at the same time a pensive child ... Banish tricks and devices and behave like a child just weaned from its mother.

EVAGRIUS OF PONTUS *Pareneticus* (Frankenberg, p. 560)

Let your tongue pronounce no word when you betake yourself to prayer.

EVAGRIUS OF PONTUS Fragment preserved in Syriac
(*Orientalia Christiana*, XXX, p. 50)

John Cassian recommends a dialogue with God that is silent, relaxed and trustful, when a person 'shuts the door of his room', as Jesus requires, that is the door of his inner sanctuary, of his 'heart-spirit'. He suggests frequent prayers but short ones because of their very intensity, to avoid distraction.

We have to take particular care to follow the Gospel precept that bids us go into our inner room and shut the door to pray to our Father.

This is how to do it.

We are praying in our inner room when we withdraw our heart completely from the clamour of our thoughts and preoccupations, and in a kind of secret dialogue, as between intimate friends, we lay bare our desires before the Lord.

We are praying with our door shut when, without opening our mouth, we call on the One who takes no account of words but considers the heart.

We are praying in secret when we speak to God with the heart alone and with concentration of the soul, and make known our state of mind to him alone, in such a way that even the enemy powers themselves cannot guess their nature. Such is the reason for the deep silence that it behoves us to keep in prayer . . .

Thus our prayers should be frequent but short, for fear that if they are prolonged the enemy might have an opportunity to insinuate distraction into them. This is true sacrifice: 'A broken and a contrite heart, O God, thou wilt not despise' (Psalm 51.17).

JOHN CASSIAN *Conferences*, IX,35-6 (SC 54, p. 71)

So comes the Spirit who prays in us, as St Paul says, 'with sighs too deep for words'. Interior tears, a need for silence.

When the Holy Spirit acts in the soul he sings psalms and prays with complete relaxation and sweetness in the secret places of the heart. This disposition is accompanied by interior tears, then by a sort of fullness, eager for silence.

DIADOCHUS OF PHOTIKE *Gnostic Chapters*, 73 (SC 5 bis, p. 132)

All prayer shares, consciously or not, in the prayer of the incarnate Word, in his relationship with the Father, in his 'state of sacrifice' as Cyril of Alexandria puts it. Consequently all one's praying is done 'in Church', in the communion of the angels and the saints.

Anyone who prays shares in the prayer of the Word of God, who is present even among those who do not know him and is not absent from anyone's prayer. The Son prays to the Father in union with the believer whose mediator he is. The Son of God is, in fact, the high priest of our offerings and our advocate with the Father. He prays for those who pray and pleads for those who plead . . .

The high priest is not alone in uniting himself to those who are genuinely praying. There are the angels as well, of whom Scripture asserts that 'there will be more joy in heaven over one sinner who repents than over ninety-nine righteous persons who need no repentance' (Luke 15.7). Likewise, the souls of the saints who have fallen asleep . . . The chief of all the virtues, according to the divine Word, is love of neighbour. It must be admitted that the saints who are already dead practise it more than ever towards those who are struggling in this life, much more than those can do who come to the aid of the weaker while they themselves remain subject to human weakness. For 'if one member suffers, all suffer together; if one member is honoured, all rejoice together' (1 Corinthians 12.26). That is what is accomplished by those who love their brothers and sisters.

But one can equally apply to the love that is practised beyond the present life the apostle's words: 'my anxiety is for all the churches. Who is weak, and I am not weak? Who is made to fall, and I am not indignant? (2 Corinthians 11.28b-29). Does not Christ himself say that he is ill with those who are ill, that he is with those who have neither clothes nor house, that he is hungry and thirsty alongside hungry and thirsty human beings? Who among those who have read the Gospel does not know that Christ makes all human suffering his own?

ORIGEN *On Prayer*, 10-11 (PG 11,448)

2. Trials

The masters of ascesis put us on our guard against images, apparitions and visions. For Satan 'disguises himself as an angel of light' – which is what he is, except for pride. Especially at the beginning of the spiritual life, when the soul attains to true prayer, it receives exquisite visions (here it is necessary to use the terms of taste), and these visions make the soul believe it has arrived at union. It runs the risk, then, of succumbing to delusion and vainglory.

Once the intellect has arrived at true and pure prayer it is likely that the demons ... will offer it an illusory vision of God beneath a form pleasing to the senses, so as to make it believe that it has fully attained the goal of its prayer. Now all of that, as an admirable gnostic said, is the work of the passion of vainglory and of a demon whose assaults make the brain reel.

EVAGRIUS OF PONTUS *On Prayer*, 73 (Philokalia I,183)

When you are faced with the exquisite image, react in the same way as you do to the interior uproar unleashed by the demons when they see themselves unmasked, and take refuge in God in all poverty and trust. If the temptation persists, recite over and over again at an increasing rate the *Kyrie eleison* ('Lord, have mercy') or any other short prayer, preferably one containing the name of Jesus.

One who strives after pure prayer will hear noises and uproar, voices and insults. But he will not be dismayed nor lose his composure if he says to God, 'Thou art with me, I fear no evil.'

EVAGRIUS OF PONTUS *On Prayer*, 97 (Philokalia I,185)

At the moment of such a temptation use a short intense prayer.

EVAGRIUS OF PONTUS *On Prayer*, 98 (Philokalia I,185)

On the journey there are 'dark nights' that are not merely loss of contact with the visible and intelligible but trials of anguish and despair. Then it is important to fall, not into nothingness, but at the feet of the Crucified who went down to hell. One must identify oneself with Christ in his agony when he said not only, 'My God, my God, why hast thou forsaken me?' but also, 'Father, into thy hands I commit my spirit'.

Trials such as these are the crucible of humility, the exodus into the desert that is faith alone. Each of them is the introduction to a 'consolation' – that is, to a perceptible presence of the Consoler, of the Holy Spirit – and the greater the nakedness in which one welcomes him, the greater the consolation received.

There are three stages in the life of those who are converted: the beginning, the middle, and perfection. At the beginning, those converted encounter the enticements of sweetness; in the middle, battles against temptation; at the end, the perfection of fullness. Sweetness at first to strengthen them; then bitterness to test them; finally the delight of the ultimate joy to establish them.

GREGORY THE GREAT *Commentary on Job*, 20,11,28 (PL 76,302)

Let us not be troubled when it befalls us to be plunged into darkness, especially if we are not responsible for it. You must realize that this darkness enshrouding you has been given you by God's providence for reasons known to him alone. Sometimes indeed our soul is engulfed by the waves and drowned. Whether we give ourselves to the reading of Scripture or to prayer, whatever we do we are increasingly imprisoned in darkness ... it is an hour filled with despair and fear. The soul is utterly deprived of hope in God and the consolation of faith. It is entirely filled with perplexity and anguish.

But those who have been tested by the distress of such an hour know that in the end it is followed by a change. God never leaves the soul for a whole day in such a state, for then hope would be destroyed ... rather he allows it to emerge very soon from the darkness.

Blessed is he who endures such temptations ... For, as the Fathers say, great will be the stability and the strength to which he will come after that. However, it is not in one hour or at one stroke that such a combat is concluded. Nor is it at one moment, but gradually, that grace comes to take up its dwelling completely in the soul. After grace, the trial returns. There is a time for trial. And there is a time for consolation.

ISAAC OF NINEVEH *Ascetic Treatises*, 57 (Spanos, p. 232-3)

All the drama of the Song of Songs is there, as the mystics of the early centuries have shown in their profound commentaries, in particular Origen and Gregory of Nyssa. The Bridegroom approaches and then disappears, and to find him again the Bride needs great patience. Similarly, in the old fables the betrothed is unexpectedly left alone and has to put on iron shoes and wear them, or weave a garment without uttering a word, in order to find her beloved again.

Then she [the Bride in the Song of Songs] looks longingly for the Bridegroom who has shown himself and then disappeared. This happens often throughout the Song of Songs and can be understood by anyone who has experienced it himself. Often, as God is my witness, I have felt that the Bridegroom was drawing near to me and was as close to me as possible. Then all of a sudden he has gone away and I have not been able to find the object of my search. Once again I have begun to desire his coming and sometimes he returns. And when he appears to me and I am holding him with my hands, once more he escapes me, and when he has vanished I begin to seek him again. This happens often until I hold him truly and arise, leaning on my beloved.

ORIGEN *Sermons on the Song of Songs*, 1,7 (SC 37, P. 75)

These trials form part of what Diadochus of Photike calls 'educative desolation'. The divine light veils itself in order that the human being may break free from illusion and pride, and from all masks including that of the ascetic, and may become a pure receptacle for the grace which is able to fashion a new creature.

Educative desolation does not in any way deprive the spirit of the divine light. Only, grace hides its presence from the spirit in order to make it go forward ... to have recourse in great fear and in great humility to God's help ... It is like a mother who sees her child rebel against the regular routine of feeding and so keeps it away from her arms for a while, so that when it is

frightened by the intimidating aspect of men or animals it may
return to nestle in its mother's bosom . . .

Educative desolation brings to the soul humiliation, grief and
a proper despair in order that the part of the soul that seeks glory
and is easily exalted may return to humility. But it leads the
heart immediately to the fear of God, to tears, and to a keen
desire for the beauty of silence.

DIADOCHUS OF PHOTIKE *Gnostic Chapters*, 87 (SC 5 bis, p. 146-7)

God calls the heart and makes it exult; then he disappears; and
then he reveals himself again. By the test of renunciation and a more
lively 'feeling' of God, a person escapes gradually from the attacks of
evil: light penetrates and protects his or her nature more and more.
But God refuses to provide an overwhelming proof of his presence.
If he did he would actually be destroying the very possibility of a
meeting and the free offer of his love. God introduces the soul that
has been made holy to a rhythm of alternate enstasy and ecstasy,
of contentment and of a yearning for an irreducible otherness, so
that the soul does not cease to renew its love and spread itself in the
inexhaustible store of God's riches.

When people are baptized, grace hides her presence until the soul
makes a decision. When the whole person has turned to the Lord,
then with an unspeakable tenderness she reveals her presence to the
heart. Then once again she awaits a movement of the soul while
allowing the darts of the devil to reach even its inmost senses, in
order that the soul may seek God again with more fervour and
humility. Then if that person begins to make progress by keeping
the commandments and calling continually on the Lord Jesus, the
fire of divine grace spreads also to the outward motions of the
heart. As a result the arrows of the devil fall short and hardly
scratch the vulnerable part of the soul any more. Finally when the
fighter contains all the virtues, and especially the most complete
renunciation, grace enlightens the whole person with the deepest
feeling, engendering an ardent love for God. From then on the
arrows of the devil are quenched without touching the bodily senses.
For the wind of the Spirit that is blowing within the heart destroys
the darts of the devil while they are still in flight. However, even
one who has reached this stage is sometimes abandoned by God to
the malice of the devil, and is left without any light for the spirit, so
that this freedom of ours may not be entirely shackled by bonds

of grace ... for the human being ought to be able still to make progress in the spiritual life. For what we regard as perfection is still imperfect in the presence of the richness of God, this God who with all the eagerness of his love longs to be our teacher.

DIADOCHUS OF PHOTIKE *Gnostic Chapters*, 85 (SC 5 bis, p. 144-5)

The more the Inaccessible shares with us, the more inaccessible he shows himself to be. By reminding us of the distance between him and us he keeps us from idolizing the mystical state. It is a spirituality not of fusion or commixture but of communion, in which the Other remains the more unknown the more he makes himself known. This is the way into a living eternity where progress in love never comes to an end.

When the soul at the call of its beloved goes out to look for him whom no name can reach, it learns ... that it is enamoured of one who is inaccessible, and is desirous of one who cannot be grasped. These words strike the soul and wound it with despair, because it believes its search for fullness will never come to an end ... But the veil of its sadness is taken away from it when it is taught that to go forward continually in its search, and never to cease raising its sights, constitutes the true enjoyment of what it desires. Each time its desire is fulfilled the desire for higher realities is engendered.

So when the veil of its despair has been taken away, and it has seen that the invisible and infinite beauty of him whom it loves is shown to increase in beauty to all eternity, it is animated by a still stronger longing for its beloved and opens to him ... the state of its heart, saying that, after having been smitten with God's shaft, it has been wounded to the heart by the point of faith and has been mortally wounded by love. Now according to John, love is God. To him be glory and power for ever and ever.

GREGORY OF NYSSA *Sermons on the Song of Songs*, 12 (PG 44, 1036-7)

3. *Times and postures for prayer*

In the following very ancient text, the sanctification of time is related to the principal moments of the Passion and Easter. It thereby gives a new meaning to cosmic praise. The cross and the resurrection have inaugurated the 'last times', marked by the reversal of the symbolism usually ascribed to day and night. The day, despite its proud self-sufficient brightness, is connected henceforward with Christ's suffering and death – midday becomes darkness. The evening sees the dawn of the spirit appear with the sacramental water and blood that flow from the side of the Crucified. The night is filled with paschal light, 'the poles are reversed', and the dawn, coming with cock-crow, looks forward to the breaking of the day with no sunset, the day of the Kingdom.

We should notice also, in this apostolic period when it was not yet necessary to be a monk to be fully Christian, as people in later Christian centuries came to believe, the assurance that married life even in its sexual expression is not in any way opposed to the spiritual life, but can be organized to promote it.

Let us notice finally the profound conception, well attested in the ancient Church, according to which at certain times, and especially in the dead of night which is the moment of resurrection, the whole cosmos becomes Church – stars, plants and animals gather together in a sort of prayer.

> If you are at home pray at the third hour [nine o'clock] and praise God. If you are elsewhere at that moment praise God in your heart, for at that hour Christ was nailed to the Cross . . . You will pray likewise at the sixth hour [midday] remembering Christ hanging on the cross while . . . the darkness reigned. At that hour you will offer a very fervent prayer to imitate him who prayed for his executioners when the universe was plunged in darkness. At the ninth hour [three o'clock in the afternoon] resume your prayer and praise . . . At that hour Christ, his side pierced, poured out water and blood. He illumined the declining daylight until evening and offered a symbol of the resurrection with the return of the light.
>
> Pray also before your body goes to sleep.
>
> Towards the middle of the night get up, wash your hands in water, and pray. If your wife is there, pray together. If she is not yet a Christian, withdraw into another room to pray, then go back to bed.
>
> Do not be negligent over your prayer. One who is married is in no way defiled. 'He who has bathed does not need to wash . . . but he is clean all over' (John 13.10). If you make the sign of the cross with your moist breath your body will be clean all over, right down to your feet. For the gift of the Spirit and the water of baptism, flowing as from a spring, have cleansed the believer, if he has received them with a heart full of faith.

We have to pray at this hour because the men of old from whom we have received this tradition have taught us that all creation rests then for a moment in order to praise the Lord. The stars, the trees, the rivers stop for an instant and, together with the choir of angels and the souls of the righteous, sing the praises of God. And so praying at this hour ought to be precious to the faithful.

The Lord himself bears witness to that when he says: 'Behold, the bridegroom! Come out to meet him' (Matthew 25.6). And at the end: 'Watch therefore, for you know neither the day nor the hour' (Matthew 25.13). Towards cock-crow get up again and pray in the same way . . . We are looking for the day of the resurrection of the dead in hope of eternal light.

Apostolic Tradition, 35 (Botte, p. 69)

A Christian, if he cannot pray in the dead of night, should try, by means of the attitude we have described, to let Christ's presence permeate his sleep while creation keeps watch in the clear angelic light.

Evening Hymn

We bless thee now, O my Christ, thou Word of God,
Light of Light without beginning, Bestower of the Spirit.
We bless thee, threefold light of undivided glory.
Thou hast vanquished the darkness and brought forth the light,
to create everything in it.

Thou hast given solidity to matter,
moulding the face of the world
and the shape of its beauty therein.
Thou hast enlightened the human spirit,
endowing it with reasoning and wisdom.
Everywhere is to be found the reflection of eternal light,
so that in the light the human spirit
may find its splendour and become entirely light.

Thou hast illumined the sky with spangled lights.
The night and the day thou hast commanded to alternate in peace
by giving them, for rule, brotherly love.
Night puts an end to the body's toil,
Day awakens us again to our work,

to our business that engrosses us.
But we are fleeing the darkness,
we are hastening to the day that never wanes,
to the day that will never know the sorrow of the dusk.

Grant to mine eyelids a light sleep,
that my voice remain not long dumb.
Thy creation shall keep watch to sing psalms with the angels.
May my sleep be ever peopled by thy presence . . .
Even parted from the body my spirit sings thy praise
O Father, Son and Holy Spirit.
To thee be glory and power
for ever and ever.
Amen.

GREGORY NAZIANZEN *Dogmatic Poems* (PG 37,311-14)

The following Syriac hymn emphasizes the same symbolism of reversal of day and night. Christ's descent into hell has filled everything with light. Each night recalls Easter. Each dawn announces Christ's return.

Death had laid its snares
for our humanity.
But he in his mercy came
to rescue us therefrom.

Praise be to thee, Lord of the angels;
the sight of thee has brought joy
to the unfortunates of hell.

From that time night has been far removed.
Night has vanished.
For his light is risen upon his creatures.

He has come down from the heights and set us free.
He has gone up again and, behold,
he is seated at the right hand of God once more.

They burn to go to meet him
at the time of his return,

all they who waited for him,
faithful to his name.

He entered into hell
and the brightness of his light
scattered the darkness from the souls departed.

The fruit that Adam ate
had slain him.
The Fruit that comes from above
descended for his salvation.

He has broken open the tombs
and restored the dead to life,
mystical figure of the day of his power.

It approaches, it is coming,
the day of resurrection.
Happy is he who waits for it to come.

Great is the day of his coming
when all things that are hidden
shall be revealed.

Those who lie in darkness
shall hear his voice.
On the day of resurrection
they shall go forth to meet him.

Adam is restored to life
and, seized with admiration,
he returns to the domain
of utter felicity.

Syrian hymn attributed to James of Sarug (Evening Office in the
Maronite liturgy)

Let us be precise about the symbolism of standing or kneeling:
for praise, worship and thanksgiving, pray standing up with out-
stretched hands; for penitence or intercession, pray kneeling.

However, there is nothing mechanical or magical about this.
Christianity knows nothing of the oriental technique of postures.

They are only one of many possible languages for communication, so they have only a relative value. The same applies to place. When possible it is good to have a peaceful place at one's disposal for prayer, one furnished no doubt with sacred pictures. But it is possible to pray anywhere at all.

> Certainly there are countless attitudes of the body, but that in which we stretch out our hands and lift our eyes to heaven is to be preferred for expressing with the body the dispositions of the soul during prayer. That at least is the way we should act when there are no obstacles. But circumstances may lead us to pray sitting down, for example when we have a pain in the legs; or even in bed because of fever. For the same reason, if for example we are on board ship or if our business does not allow us to withdraw to perform our duty in regard to prayer, it is possible to pray without taking up any particular outward attitude. In regard to kneeling for prayer, this is essential when we are accusing ourselves of our sins before God and entreating him to heal and absolve us. It symbolizes the prostration and humility of which Paul speaks when he writes: 'For this reason I bow my knees before the Father, from whom every family in heaven and on earth is named' (Ephesians 3.14). That is spiritual kneeling, so called because every creature adores God in the name of Jesus and prostrates itself humbly before him. The Apostle seems to be alluding to this when he says: 'At the name of Jesus every knee should bow, in heaven and on earth and under the earth' (Philippians 2.10). As for the place, you should realize that every place is suitable for prayer ... However, in order to pray undisturbed it is possible to choose a particular place in one's house, if practicable, as a kind of hallowed spot, and to pray there.
>
> ORIGEN *On Prayer*, 31 (PG 11,549-52)

In the following text another symbolism appears, just as primitive, since according to the Gospels Christ rose on the day after the Sabbath, on 'the first day of the week'. In the symbolism of the week, Sunday is Easter, the first and the eighth day, restoring the origin and anticipating the fulfilment in Christ, the 'Alpha and Omega'. On that day the faithful should remain standing like sons or daughters, like people set free, on the road to the Kingdom. A person standing upright, head held high, bears witness to his true royalty, the upward movement of his soul toward the heavenly realm. Kneeling and prostration, by contrast, bear witness to our humiliation which we turn into humility. For to prostrate oneself and then to get up again is a symbol of resurrection.

That is why the First Ecumenical Council forbade kneeling on Sundays.

Daily prayer is made turned towards the East as a symbol of paradise lost – lost and regained: the sun rises in the East. And it is made standing up, though punctuated with prostrations.

We all look toward the East to pray but very few among us realize that we are seeking again our ancient native land, the paradise that God planted in the East towards Eden. We make our prayer standing up on the first day of the week [Sunday] but not all of us know the reason: it is not only because, being risen with Christ and being bound to seek the things that are above, we are reminding ourselves, by standing upright on the day consecrated to the resurrection, of the grace that has been given to us, but it is also because this day is in some way an image of the age to come ... This day is, in fact, also the eighth day and it symbolizes the fullness that will follow the present time, the day that never closes ... the age that will never come to an end ... It is therefore necessary that the Church should bring up her children to pray standing upright on this day, so that with a continual reminder of life without end we should not forget to make ready our food for the journey ... The upright posture ... makes our soul, so to speak, emigrate from the land of the present to that of the future.

By contrast, every time we kneel and get up again we show by our actions that sin has cast us to the ground and the love of our Creator has called us back to heaven.

BASIL OF CÆSAREA *Treatise on the Holy Spirit*, 27 (PG 32,192)

The following text from the second century adds detail to the symbolism of the upright posture with the hands stretched out, by likening it to the appearance of the life-giving cross, the whole person having become a sign of the cross.

I have stretched out my hands in offering to the Lord.
The hands stretched out are a sign thereof,
upright with hands stretched out,
the wood of the cross set up.
Alleluia!

Odes of Solomon, 27 (Harris-Mingana, p. 356)

To pray everywhere is not only possible, it is a duty, because the universe is primarily a place of worship. Prayer, by going deep into transcendence and so demonstrating the human being's transcendence, enables grace to penetrate the creation and reveal its secret holiness.

> Every Christian, even if he lacks any education, knows that every place is a part of the universe and that the universe itself is the temple of God. He prays in every place with the eyes of his senses closed and those of his soul awake, and in this way he transcends the whole world. He does not stop at the vault of heaven but reaches the heights above it, and, as though out of this world altogether, he offers his prayer to God, led by God's Spirit.
>
> ORIGEN *Against Celsus*, 7,44 (PG 11,1485)

The 'circular motion' mentioned by Dionysius the Areopagite symbolizes and facilitates the soul's concentration and its unification in ecstasy. This description tallies with the suppliant posture of Elijah referred to in the Bible, and resulted in one of the positions for the 'prayer of Jesus': sitting on a low stool, the person praying bows low with his face between his knees.

When he rises again his soul expands in a 'spiral motion' through the outflow of the divine glory. Then by a 'longitudinal motion' he is accessible to all creation, which appears to him as a body of symbols, a theophany.

> The soul moves with a circular motion when it enters into itself and turns away from the outside world; when it gathers together its capacities of understanding, and unifies them in a concentration that saves it from all bewilderment; when it distances itself from the multiplicity of external objects, so as to concentrate on itself. When it has reached interior unity ... it is led towards the Beautiful-and-Good ...
>
> The soul moves with a spiral motion, in so far as it is enlightened, in a way appropriate to it, by divine knowledge.
>
> Its motion finally is longitudinal when, rather than return into itself and aim at spiritual union (for then as we have just seen its motion is circular), it turns towards the things around it, and relies upon the outer world as on a complex body of symbols, in order to rise to contemplation.
>
> DIONYSIUS THE AREOPAGITE *Divine Names*, IV,9 (PG 3,705)

Sometimes physical solitude is needed where nature itself becomes prayer – on the 'high places'.

For one who is acquainted with the mystery of grace the
mountain is better than the city. On the peaks the chamois does
not fall into the hands of the shearer! Flee the settled dwellings,
man of the mountains!

EPHRAIM OF SYRIA *Sermon on Monks*, 3 (Lamy 4,150)

In this way it will be possible by degrees to walk in the hubbub
of the city carrying the silence of the mountains in one's heart.

In the world there are many things obscuring the view and disturbing taste and hearing. That is why it is necessary . . . to run away
from all excitement and take refuge in the desert where tranquillity
is total, serenity complete, noise does not exist, where eyes are fixed
on God alone and ears attentive to hearing only the divine words.
The ears delight to hear the symphony of the Spirit whose power
over the soul is so strong that, once anyone has been touched by
this music, he can no longer prefer either food or drink or sleep to
it. Henceforward neither the crowd nor the bustle of this world's
affairs can distract one whose attention is so engaged . . . So those
who have climbed to the mountain top no longer hear more of
what is going on in the cities than an insignificant and irritating
noise resembling the buzzing of bees.

JOHN CHRYSOSTOM *Second Sermon to Stelechius on Compunction*
(PG 47,411)

4. *How to pray?*

The fundamental part of meditation that can pierce the heart suddenly, no matter where, no matter when – in the way a lover
remembers the beloved and is filled with immense joy – consists in
recollecting that God exists and that he lòves us. He, the unfathomed
deep beyond all, takes us to himself as a father his child. He admits us
to an area of non-death, of positive inspiration free of anguish and
hatred, the place of the Holy Spirit. In the Eucharist he gives us an
earnest of the Kingdom. Then his sweetness invades our heart, we
thirst for him, we long for all humankind to share this joy of ours,
and we pray that all may be saved.

I will not deny thy love
for it is thou who didst form me from the earth,
it is thou who dost stretch out thy hand and support me.
That must be the point of my meditation in my time of prayer.

EVAGRIUS OF PONTUS *Protrepticus*, (Frankenberg, p. 556)

The holy Abba Evagrius commented thus on the prayer that is in the Gospel according to Matthew: Our Father who art in heaven . . .

Our Father who art in heaven: these are the words of those who enjoy intimacy with God, like a son in the bosom of his father.

Hallowed be thy name: that is to say, may it, being glorified through our witness, be hallowed among us, by people who will say: these are true servants of God.

Thy Kingdom come: the Kingdom of God is the Holy Spirit. We pray that he may be sent down upon us.

Thy will be done on earth as it is in heaven: the will of God is the salvation of every soul. What is accomplished among the powers of heaven we pray may come about for us on earth.

Our bread for tomorrow is what we shall inherit from God. We pray that we may have an earnest of it today, that is, that his sweetness may make itself felt in us in this world, causing a burning thirst.

EVAGRIUS OF PONTUS *Catenae on the Gospels*, Coptic Documents
(Lagarde, p. 13)

After the Lord's Prayer, the immemorial prayer of the Church, come the psalms following the sequence of Hebrew prayer. Psalmody gives its rhythm to the life of a monk and each of the faithful ought to practise it to some extent. All Tradition applies the psalms to Jesus. At the same time, as Cassian explains, the psalms ought to be our own; they ought to enter into and illuminate our most tragic experiences; they ought to be our cry to God over all the contradictions of our destiny, our violence, our despair, our fervour.

When we listen to the psalms . . . we must pay attention to seeing Christ, to discerning him. Apply yourself to this psalm with us, let us seek Christ in it. Yes, he will show himself to those who seek him, he who appeared to people who were not seeking him. He who saved those who scorned him will not shun those who desire him.

AUGUSTINE OF HIPPO *Commentary on Psalm 98* (PL 37,1258)

Penetrated by the same feelings in which the psalm was composed, it is as if we became the authors of it and we run ahead of its thought rather than follow it. We grasp the meaning before reading the words. The sacred words reawaken our experience reminding us of the assaults we have undergone and still undergo every day, of the marks of our negligence or, on the contrary, of our fervour, blessings of divine visitation or wiles of the enemy, the havoc wrought by the forgetfulness that is so ready to creep into our soul, our frailty ... and our blindness. All these feelings we find expressed in the psalms. They are the bright mirror in which we become more deeply conscious of what is happening to us. We are made sensitive by our own experience. It is no longer a question of what we have merely heard. We are in touch with the reality. We understand it completely. It is no longer simply entrusted to our memory; we give birth to it in the depth of our heart as an intuition that forms part of our being. Reading throws light on experience. By this method our soul arrives at the purity of prayer ... The soul pours out its prayer to God with unspeakable groaning.

CASSIAN *Conferences*, X,11 (SC 54, P. 92).

When a phrase or a word in a psalm, or in personal prayer, takes hold of our soul or makes the heart exult, we should stop and go deep into this 'intuition of God'. We should cease to multiply words, and find rather the silence in the heart of the word, the Spirit at rest in the Word. Liturgical prayer is of limited assistance here, as happens in every language when symbol becomes reality. Multiplicity of words from elsewhere or from afar has not the same value as that interior cry, that sigh perhaps, that betokens the dizzying nearness of the Other.

The excellence of prayer does not consist in its quantity but in its quality, as is shown ... by this word: 'In praying, do not heap up empty phrases', and so forth (Matthew 6.7).

EVAGRIUS OF PONTUS *On Prayer*, 151 (Philokalia I, 189)

If a profitable reflection comes to you, let it take the place of psalmody. Do not reject God's gift for the sake of maintaining the tradition [your rule]. A prayer with no inkling of the intuition of God and no intellectual vision is only a weariness of the flesh. Do not take pleasure in a multiplicity of psalms. It

casts a veil over your heart. A single word in intimacy is worth
more than a thousand at a distance.

EVAGRIUS OF PONTUS *Pareneticus* (Frankenberg, p. 561)

We must learn first of all to bring wayward thoughts back
to the body. The body is the cell for anyone seeking Christ in
the silent depths of the heart. Serious thankful attention to the
humblest feeling, as we shall see, also constitutes a way of contemplating God through things.

A hesychast [from *hesychia*: silence, peace, sweetness of union
with God] is one who seeks to confine the incorporeal within
the corporeal . . . the actual limits of his body are the hesychast's
cell. There is an abode of wisdom there.

JOHN CLIMACUS *The Ladder of Divine Ascent*, 27th step, 5(7) &
10(12) (p. 150)

To concentrate the mind and give it peace, to parry the incon-
sequent yet obsessive flux of 'thoughts' or indeed to dry up the flow
of them, the repetition of a short formula can be a help. It is not a
mantra that is efficacious of itself as in India, but a word addressed
to someone, the expression of a relationship, a cry for help, a link
with him whom Augustine calls the 'interior Master'. Here Cassian
gives a formula that was to be retained by Western monasticism.

This is what happens in fact. Our thoughts wander from spiritual
contemplation and run hither and thither. When we return to
ourselves like people waking up, we look for something to revive
our memory of God. But while we are seeking, time passes. Before
we have found anything we are wandering again . . .
    The cause of this confusion is quite clear: we do not possess
anything precise, as a formula for instance would be . . . to which
we can recall our wandering mind . . . one thought succeeds another
without stopping, in a perpetual flux in which the soul neither
perceives the origin of its thoughts nor is aware of their flight and
disappearance . . .
    Here is that formula for praying that you are looking for.
Every monk who is aiming at a continual recollection of God
should accustom himself to using it in meditation, and that will
enable him to banish other thoughts . . . It is a secret that the few
survivors of the Fathers of the early days taught us and which we

in turn confide to the small number of souls who are really thirsting to know it. To keep yourself continually mindful of God's presence you should set this formula before yourselves: 'Haste thee, O God, to deliver me: make haste to help me, O Lord.' (Psalm 70.1). This short verse expresses all the feelings that human beings can have. It adapts itself to every situation ... in adversity, for deliverance; in prosperity, for it to continue without inducing pride; ... at work, in your various occupations; on a journey you can also repeat it; ... let sleep close your eyes on these words and you will end by saying them even in your sleep; meditate on them according to Moses's precept 'when you sit in your house, and when you walk by the way, and when you lie down, and when you rise' (Deuteronomy 6.7).

JOHN CASSIAN *Conferences*, X, 8 & 10 (SC 54, pp. 83, 85-6)

The ascetics of the Christian East made use of a similar formula in which the appeal for help is made in trustful abandonment: 'Lord as thou wilt and as thou knowest best, have mercy'. Or simply, 'Lord have mercy', *Kyrie eleison*. Still today the use of this formula in Eastern monasticism is much preferred to the invocation of the name of Jesus, out of humility.

They asked Abba Macarius, 'How should one pray?' The old man replied, 'There is no need to lose oneself in words. It is enough to spread out the hands and to say, "Lord, as thou wilt and as thou knowest best, have mercy." If the battle is fierce, say, "Help!" He knows what is suitable for you and he will take pity on you.'
Sayings of the Desert Fathers, Macarius, 19 (PG 65,269)

Brief formulae of this kind make it possible to pray coming and going and while working. We then discover that there is much more time for prayer than we might imagine.

I will show you how I do not cease praying, simply by going on with my work. I am there sitting in God's presence. And when I put my little leaves to soak and when I start to weave a rope I say, 'Have mercy on me, O God, according to thy steadfast love' (Psalm 51.3). Is not that a prayer?
Sayings of the Desert Fathers, Lucius (PG 65,253)

Invocation of the name of Jesus comes next, in a variety of formulae, as will be seen from a reading of the texts that follow. The prayer 'Lord Jesus, Son of God, have mercy upon me, a sinner' does not seem to have taken definite shape before the thirteenth century. It was to be combined with a method that satisfies, though in a quite different dimension, the modern concern for efficiency.

In a quite natural way the invocation of the name of Jesus is combined with the rhythm of breathing. Pray as you breathe.

[Anthony] called his two companions ... and said to them, 'Always breathe Christ'.

ATHANASIUS OF ALEXANDRIA *Life of Anthony*, XCI (PG 26,969)

Let your calling to mind of Jesus be continually combined with your breathing and you will know the meaning of silence.

JOHN CLIMACUS *The Ladder of Divine Ascent*, 27th step, 2nd part, 26 (62), (p. 156)

The name does not contain the presence (as is the case in magical formulae or in the religions of antiquity) but it summons it. The presence of Christ is thus the presence of the Trinity ('Christ', let us remember, means 'the Anointed', and it is the Father who anoints and the Spirit who is the unction). Since human beings are in the image of God and this image is restored in them and activated by baptismal grace, the presence is already in them, in their 'heart', in that most central of centres, that deepest of depths, which is also openness to transcendence (the physical heart symbolizes and incorporates the spiritual heart without being entirely identified with it). But this presence in the heart is unconscious; to call upon it is to make it gradually more perceptible by uniting heart and intellect.

Let us keep our eyes always fixed on the depths of our heart with an unceasing mindfulness of God.

DIADOCHUS OF PHOTIKE *Gnostic Chapters*, 56 (SC 5 bis, p. 117)

The Holy Spirit, the Breath of God, is linked to the Word from all eternity. Therefore when a person's intellect and breathing utter the name of the Incarnate Word – Jesus – they are united with the Holy Spirit, and the person breathes and thinks in the Spirit.

The intellect, strengthened by the invocation, finds its connection with the heart again, and this, or rather the presence in it, becomes conscious. Intellect and heart together form that heart–spirit in which a person collects, opens, unifies, harmonizes and enlarges himself infinitely. It properly constitutes the 'place of God'.

Abba Evagrius said, 'I was tormented by the thoughts and passions of the body, so I went to find Abba Macarius. I said to him, "Father, give me a word to live by." Abba Macarius said to me, "Secure the anchor rope to the rock and by the grace of God the ship will ride the devilish waves of this beguiling sea . . ." I said to him, "What is the boat? What is the rope? What is the rock?" Abba Macarius said to me, "The ship is your heart; keep guard over it. The rope is your mind; secure it to our Lord Jesus Christ, who is the rock who has power over all the waves . . . because it is not difficult, is it, to say with each breath, "Our Lord Jesus, have mercy on me: I bless thee, my Lord Jesus, help me."'

PSEUDO-MACARIUS *Coptic Cycle of Sayings*, (*Annales du Musée Guimet* XXV, p. 160)

Then we see, marvellous consciousness of consciousness, beyond that, the light of our own depths encompassing the world. 'The heart that is purified becomes in itself a heaven with a sun, moon and stars . . .' according to Philotheus of Sinai (*On Sobriety*, 27). But this light is such only because it is open to the Uncreated Light, the light of the Transfiguration, of Easter, of the Parousia. The 'descent' of the heart corresponds to Moses's 'climbing' of Sinai. The heart-spirit is an interior Sinai on which God reveals himself in translucent darkness. We, in order to endure a fire like this without dying, hide in the cleft of a rock that is, in fact, the humanity of Jesus. The Light, in this tradition, is never either 'enstasy' of the intellect alone or a fullness in itself. It radiates from the face of Christ crucified and glorified. It is a manifestation of the Father. It is almost the same as the Holy Spirit. 'The mirror of the soul by its very nature is destined to receive the features and the luminous image of Christ' (*On Sobriety*, 23).

When the spirit, having put off the old man, has put on the man of grace, he will see his own condition at the moment of prayer, like the colour of sapphire or the sky – what the Scripture calls the place of God, seen by the Ancients on Mount Sinai.

EVAGRIUS OF PONTUS *Practical Chapters*, 70 (PG 40,1243)

The spirit, when we close all its outlets by our concentration on God, demands of us expressly some task that may satisfy its need for activity. It should therefore be given the Jesus Prayer as the only occupation that answers fully to its purpose. It is, in fact, written that 'No one can say "Jesus is Lord" except by the Holy

Spirit' (I Corinthians 12.3) . . . Those who meditate on this holy and
glorious Name continually in the depths of their heart can see also
the light of their own spirit. For if it is entertained with great care by
the mind, the Name with intense emotion destroys all the impurities
that cover the surface of the soul. In fact, it is said: 'The Lord your
God is a devouring fire' (Deuteronomy 4.24). Consequently the
Lord now transports the soul to a great love . . . This Name . . . is the
pearl of great price; on discovering it, one rejoices with unspeakable
joy, and sells all one's possessions in order to purchase it.

DIADOCHUS OF PHOTIKE *Gnostic Chapters*, 59 (SC 5 bis, p. 119)

When the soul calls on the 'Lord Jesus' it does so in the Holy
Spirit. For it is only in the Holy Spirit, St Paul says, that we can
confess that Jesus is the Lord . . . It is a loving dialogue that never
ceases, not even in the silence of perfect light, for this light is, in
fact, the substance and, as it were, the halo crowning a meeting of
which we shall never tire.

Grace joins the soul in crying, 'Lord Jesus', like a mother
teaching her child the word 'father' by their repeating it together.
The apostle says: 'The Spirit helps us in our weakness; for we do
not know how to pray as we ought, but the Spirit intercedes for
us with sighs too deep for words' (Romans 8.26).

DIADOCHUS OF PHOTIKE *Gnostic Chapters*, 61 (SC 5 bis, p. 121)

The signs of entry into *hesychia*, that is, into the silence, the
peace, the sweetness of union with God, are indicated by St Isaac of
Nineveh in some remarkable words about to be quoted – the sudden
coming, through a verse or a word, of a silence that then remains
– an emotion pervading the whole being, sober, detached, with
charismatic tears dropping quietly from the eyes, without distorting
the face – the momentary union of the intellect and the heart. This last
element is important, showing that it is not a question of mechanical
technique, making the syllables of the prayer coincide with the
beating of the heart, but of praying 'with all one's heart'. Then,
but only by pure grace and 'for a moment', can come the 'plunge'
of the intellect into the heart.

When you give yourself to prayer, if you are, as far as possible, free
from all distraction, and if the verse comes suddenly to a halt on
your tongue and immobilizes your soul in the silence, and if,

independently of your will, this silence remains in you, be sure you have entered the peace you seek . . .

And again: if in every thought that arises in your soul, and in every remembrance and point of contemplation that come to you in this peace, you find tears filling your eyes and flowing with no effort down your cheeks, be sure that the wall before you is down . . .

And if you find from time to time your intellect has become immersed in your heart without your having foreseen it and apart from any regulation, and if it remains there for a moment . . . if, after that, you feel your limbs seized, as it were, by a great weakness and peace reigns over your thoughts, if this state continues, be sure that the cloud has begun to cover your dwelling with its shadow.

ISAAC OF NINEVEH *Ascetic Treatises*, 12 (Spanos, p. 47)

Intense meditation on the Lord's Prayer, namely, on our adoption in Christ, can enable us for an instant to escape from time to share in the eternal relationship of love between the Father and the Son. Beyond all language and beyond the motion of prayer itself, the soul experiences what Cassian calls the 'prayer of fire', fulfilment in the abyss of light and love of the Trinitarian life.

The various kinds of prayer [petition, promise, intercession, pure praise] are followed by a higher state still . . . it is the contemplation of God alone, an immeasurable fire of love. The soul settles in it and sinks into its depths. It converses with God as with its own Father, very familiarly, with special tenderness. That we have a duty to aim for this state, we are taught by the very text of the Lord's Prayer, since it says, 'Our Father'. We thereby profess that the God and Lord of the universe is our Father, and therefore express the certainty that we have been called from the condition of slaves to that of adopted children.

JOHN CASSIAN *Conferences*, IX, 18 (SC 54, p. 55)

The prayer 'Our Father' raises those who make themselves familiar with it to that prayer of fire which very few know from experience. It is an ineffable state that is far above all human feeling, without the sound of any voice, without any movement of the tongue, without any articulate word. The soul is wholly filled with light and no longer makes use of human language, which is always limited. But it engrosses the whole person and becomes an abundant spring from which prayer flows and soars

in an ineffable fashion up to God. It says so many things in this
brief space of time that it cannot easily express them or even
remember them when it returns to itself.

JOHN CASSIAN *Conferences*, IX,25 (SC 54, p. 61-2)

St Isaac of Nineveh for his part distinguishes simple prayer, with
its many different forms, from the prayer of contemplation, in which
a person remains 'like a body without breath', in a sort of ecstasy
which none the less is still perceived as prayer. In the end when
all activity of the tongue, the intellect and the heart ceases there
comes the ineffable state, complete silence, for the Trinity himself
takes up his abode in the soul.

It is at the moment when a person is praying and beseeching
God, talking to him and struggling to gather his thoughts together
from all directions . . . that he is open to God alone and his heart
is filled with God. He comprehends then the incomprehensible.
For the Holy Spirit . . . breathes on him until, in the height of
concentration, the very motion of his prayer stops. His spirit in
its wonderment is struck with amazement and filled with love, and
forgets its own desires and petitions. Its movements are plunged into
deep inebriation. It is no longer of this world. It no longer makes
any distinction between soul and body and objects of memory.
The great and godly Gregory has said so: 'Prayer is the purity
of the spirit. It stops of its own accord when the light of the
Holy Trinity ravishes it in wonder.'

ISAAC OF NINEVEH *Ascetic Treatises*, 32 (p. 134-40)

The joy of prayer is one thing; the prayer of contemplation is
another. The latter is more precious than the former, as an adult
is more advanced than a child. The verses of a psalm may be very
delightful on the tongue, and the singing of a single verse during
prayer may prevent us from continuing and passing on to another
verse, so inexhaustible is it. But it may also happen that prayer
gives rise to contemplation, which interrupts what the lips are
saying. Then the person is in ecstasy. Contemplation makes him
as it were a body without breath. This is what we call the prayer of
contemplation . . . but there is still a measure in this contemplation
. . . it is always a prayer. The meditation has not yet reached the
point where there is no longer any prayer. It has not yet arrived at
the higher state. In fact, the movements of the tongue and of the heart

are keys. And what comes next is entry into the treasure house. Here every tongue and every mouth falls silent and the heart too, that gathers together the thoughts, and the spirit that governs the senses, and the work of meditation. They are like a flutter of impudent birds. Let their activity cease ... for the Master of the house has come.

ISAAAC OF NINEVEH *Ascetic Treatises*, 31 (p. 134)

This fullness, however, does not do away with the intellect, rather it fertilizes it. The spirituality of the Fathers is not anti-intellectual. For them the human being is *logikos*. He is the image of the Logos, able to make out the meaning and consequently capable of sound reasoning. The more the intellect is imbued with the light and the love of God, the more it is purified, refined, broadened, and cognisant of conscientious and beautiful thoughts, which Hesychius of Batos compares to dolphins. Just as the dolphin in its leaping interweaves the sky and sea, so the thoughts of the sanctified intellect combine the human and the divine. (The dolphin, of course, for the first Christians symbolized Christ, in whom the two natures are united.)

Prayer without distraction is the highest intellection of the intellect.

EVAGRIUS OF PONTUS *On Prayer*, 35 (Philokalia I, 180)

The heart that is freed from imaginings ends up by producing in itself holy and mysterious thoughts, as on a calm sea you see fish leaping and dolphins gambolling.

HESYCHIUS OF BATOS *On Sobriety and Virtue*, 156 (Philokalia I, 165)

5. *To Become Prayer*

Ultimately prayer becomes spontaneous, continuous; it encounters and liberates the deepest impulses of our nature and the hidden glorification of objects. It puts an end to glory's exile. The very pulsing of the blood, the intuitions of the heart, the thoughts of the mind never cease to 'sing in secret to the hidden God'.

When the Spirit dwells in a person, from the moment in which that person has become prayer, he never leaves him. For the Spirit himself never ceases to pray in him. Whether the person is asleep or

awake, prayer never from then on departs from his soul. Whether
he is eating or drinking or sleeping or whatever else he is doing,
even in deepest sleep, the fragrance of prayer rises without effort
in his heart. Prayer never again deserts him. At every moment
of his life, even when it appears to stop, it is secretly at work
in him continuously. One of the Fathers, the bearers of Christ,
says that prayer is the silence of the pure. For their thoughts are
divine motions. The movements of the heart and the intellect that
have been purified are the voices full of sweetness with which such
people never cease to sing in secret to the hidden God.

ISAAC OF NINEVEH *Ascetic Treatises*, 85 (p. 347)

Through ascetic *praxis*, namely the 'virtues' that are already
divine-human and clothe us with Christ, and then through perception
of the mystery of creatures and things, prayer becomes a state. A
person does not pray any more in the sense of a voluntary action
that is often difficult, he *is* prayer. He gives meaning and voice to the
dumb and painful prayer of created things. And prayer perfecting
the 'virtues' shines out from him in welcoming tenderness.

We go to the virtues to discover the 'principles' [*logoi*] of created
beings, in sight of the Lord who gives rise to them. For his part
he is accustomed to reveal himself, once prayer has become a
state.

EVAGRIUS OF PONTUS *On Prayer*, 52 (Philokalia I, 181)

The human being, this traveller on the earth, this exile, then
realizes that there is no other place than God. He makes his abode
in the unity of the Father and the Son, a unity that is the actual site
of the Holy Spirit. Already here below he is borne up by this breath of
unity, this Trinitarian fullness. He is henceforward the great celebrant
of life.

This is the moment in which we shall realize in ourselves the prayer
that our Saviour addressed to the Father for his disciples: 'That
the love with which thou hast loved me may be in them, and I
in them' (John 17.26) . . . The utter love with which 'God first
loved us' (I John 4.10) enters our heart through the fulfilment of
this prayer of the Lord . . . And this will be the sign of it: God will
be our love and our longing, our study and our thinking. He will
be our life. The unity of the Father with the Son and of the

Son with the Father takes possession of our feelings and of our mind. And in the same way that God loves us completely, we shall be united with him by a love that will never grow less, to the point that we shall be breathing, thinking and speaking in him.

So we shall arrive at the goal of which we spoke and which the Lord desires for us in this prayer of his: 'That they may be one even as we are one, I in them and thou in me, that they may become perfectly one' (John 17.22-23). 'Father I desire that they also whom thou hast given me, may be with me where I am' (John 17.24).

Such should be our aim: to achieve, already in this life, this breathing in unity as a foretaste of the life and the glory of heaven. Such is the goal of perfection ... that the whole of our life and all the motions of our heart may become one single uninterrupted prayer.

JOHN CASSIAN *Conferences*, X,7 (SC 54, p. 81)

Some men of the desert become pillars of prayer, settled or wandering. They reject all domestication, even that of monastic communities, in order to opt for the untrammelled liberty of the wild animals. 'Men of the hills' on the heights and in freedom.

The desert is much better than inhabited places for one who is seeking the glory of God, and the mountains are indeed preferable to cities for anyone aware of the grace that is given him.

Consider the little things. The animals of the desert are not subject to the whip and the mountain goats are not victims of shearers. Look at the wild ass in the desert; no one rides on his back. Watch the roebuck in the wild; he does not lose his freedom. Look at the stags on the rocks; they do not have to bear the yoke. Think of the wild beasts; they do not have to have their food doled out to them ...

If an eagle makes its nest in a house its eyes suffer from the smoke. If the wild ass and the roebuck come down into the plain they are haunted by fear. If a ravening beast comes near city walls it forfeits its skin. A stag that goes down to the valley loses its antlers. If a mountain goat is attacked by dogs it escapes only with its fleece in tatters ... The splendour and the beauty of wild beasts vanish on the plains. The strongest lions are overpowered, tamed and put in cages. So look to the animals, O man of the hills, and keep away from the dwellings of humanity. Do not relax.

EPHRAIM OF SYRIA *Sermon on Monks*, 3 (Lamy 4,150)

But the true desert is within, as Amma Syncletica remarked with very feminine sagacity.

> Amma Syncletica said, 'Many live on the mountains and behave as if they were living amidst the uproar of a city, and they are lost. It is possible while living amongst a crowd to be inwardly solitary, and while living alone to be inwardly beset by the crowd.'
>
> *Sayings of the Desert Fathers*, Syncletica, I (SO 1, p. 299)

Nor is the quest for the 'state of prayer' confined to anchorites. The whole existence of a Christian can, even in its most everyday concerns, become prayer, if hope and faith support it through all its vicissitudes, if in its entirety it is interpreted in the light of the cross and the resurrection. Then the human being becomes capable of extending the liturgy into culture and society. He is able to 'offer the Eucharist in all things', as St Paul required.

> He prays unceasingly who combines prayer with necessary duties and duties with prayer. Only in this way can we find it practicable to fulfil the commandment to pray always. It consists in regarding the whole of Christian existence as a single great prayer. What we are accustomed to call prayer is only a part of it.
>
> ORIGEN *On Prayer*, 12 (PG 11,452)

> Prayer is continuous when the spirit clings to God with deep emotion and great longing, and remains for ever attached to him by faith and hope in all the actions and events of its destiny.
>
> MAXIMUS THE CONFESSOR *Asceticism*, 25 (PG 90,932)

> How is the fullness of God's glory achieved in each one of us? If what I do and say is for the glory of God, my words and deeds are full of God's glory. If my plans and undertakings are for the glory of God, if my food and drink and all my actions are for the glory of God, then it is to me also that the words are addressed: 'The earth is full of his glory'.
>
> ORIGEN *Homilies on the Visions of Isaiah*, 4,1 (PG 13,252)

2

The Glory of God Hidden
in His Creatures

Contemplation begins only after the completion of ascetical exercises (*praxis*), the aim of which is the achievement of interior freedom (*apatheia*), that is to say, the possibility of loving. Contemplation consists of two stages: direct communion with God is the aim, of course, but first we must come to 'knowledge of creatures' or 'contemplation of nature' (*physike theoria*), that is, the contemplation 'of the secrets of the glory of God hidden in his creatures'.

> Faith is the doorway to the mysteries. What the eyes of the body are for physical objects, faith is for the hidden eyes of the soul. Just as we have two bodily eyes, so we have two spiritual eyes, and each has its own way of seeing. With one we see the glory of God hidden in creatures: with the other we contemplate the glory of God's holy nature when he deigns to give us access to the mysteries.
>
> ISAAC OF NINEVEH *Ascetic Treatises*, 72 (p. 281)

People who know nothing of God – and there are plenty of them in our time – none the less have an inkling of him through the things he has created, when they look at them, apart from their practical uses, in their sheer beauty and their strange gratuitousness. Then they are filled with wonder. For the real miracle, as Wittgenstein said, is that things exist! The cosmos – a word that for the ancient Greeks meant at the same time order and ornament – by the continual process of death changing into life and decay into growth, bears witness specifically to an intelligence at work, which, in a time of apparently continuous scientific advance, our intelligence is able to decipher. 'Ever since the world began, his invisible attributes, that is to say his everlasting power and deity, have been visible to the eye of reason in the things he has made' (Romans 1.20). As Dumitru

Staniloae emphasizes in his *Dogmatic Theology* (Bucharest 1978)
the very rationality of the world would be inexplicable without an
eternal Subject. It 'presupposes the rational, the more than rational,
the apophatic depth of an eternal Person, and has meaning only if
it is addressed by that eternal Person to persons with rational and
more than rational powers, so as to bring about an agreement and
a communion of love with them'.

All things would tend to nothing in virtue of their nature if they
were not governed by God.

GREGORY THE GREAT *Commentary on the Book of Job*, 16,37,45
(PL 75,1144)

For the Fathers there is a question here not so much of natural
theology as of an original revelation, a covenant with the Logos 'through
whom all things were created' (Colossians 1.16), a covenant that has
been renewed and wonderfully deepened by the incarnation of the
Logos. Evagrius makes it clear that the Wisdom and the Power of God,
of which St Paul goes on to speak, are the Son and the Spirit. Making
sense of the universe is only possible with the Trinity. For the purpose
of the universe is revealed by the Logos, and it is the Spirit, the life-giving
breath, who is causing each thing and the universe as a whole to tend in
the direction of that purpose. The world, for a Christian, is a Trinitarian
text, or better it is a woven cloth: the fixed threads of the warp symbolize
the Logos, the moving threads of the woof the dynamism of the *Pneuma*.

Besides this, the cosmos, as we have seen, has been mysteriously preserved and strengthened by the cross. In Christ it has been
drawn into a 'union without absorption' with God (Dionysius the
Areopagite). The first Christians who did not dare to make direct
representations of the cross, because it was an object of disgust and
opprobrium, used to see it in all manner of things – in the flight of
a bird, in the spread of a tree's branches, in the shape of a mast with
its sail, in the complete human figure. Today we are discovering that
the cross is written into the very stuff of matter, as is shown by
contemporary physics which can only tackle its subject by multiplying antinomies. The rhythm of death-and-resurrection recurs in
the whole evolution of the cosmos. It transmutes horror into a kind of
sacrifice and finds its completion in the ultimate mutation of Easter.
All the life and all the suffering of the world are taken up into it. This
vision of the 'Sacrifice of Love' ought to permeate the way we look at
creatures and objects every day. 'You are looking at the sun? Then
think of Him who is the Light of the World, albeit shrouded in

darkness. You are looking at the trees and their branches growing green again each spring? Then think of Him who, hanging on the wood of the cross, draws everything to himself. You are looking at rocks and stones? Then think of the stone in the garden that was blocking the entrance to a tomb. That stone was rolled away and since then the door of the sepulchre has never been shut' (A Monk of the Eastern Church, *Love without Limits*, Chevetogne 1971 pp.27-28).

> As for those who are far from God . . . God has made it possible for them to come near to the knowledge of him and his love for them through the medium of creatures. These he has produced, as the letters of the alphabet, so to speak, by his power and his wisdom, that is to say, by his Son and by his Spirit . . .
>
> The whole of this ministry is performed by creatures for the benefit of those who are far from God.
>
> EVAGRIUS OF PONTUS *Letter to Melania* (in Hausherr, p. 84)

The contemplative, like the illiterate person, does without books. Creatures and things in their delicacy and infinite subtlety continually speak to him of God. 'All are yours; and you are Christ's; and Christ is God's' (I Corinthians 3.22). This could be put the other way round: 'God is Christ's; and Christ is yours; and you belong to all things.'

> One of the wise men of that time went to find the holy man Anthony and asked him, 'Father, how can you be happy when you are deprived of the consolation that books can give?'
>
> Anthony replied, 'My philosopher friend, my book is the nature of creatures; and this book is always in front of me when I want to read the words of God.'
>
> EVAGRIUS OF PONTUS *Practicus or The Monk* (SC 171, p. 694)

The world is the gift of God. We must know how to perceive the giver through the gift. More precisely, since the time of the incarnation, the Passion and Easter, we can see the earth as an immense memorial, the tomb/womb in which Christ was buried and to which he gave resurrected power through the power of his own resurrection. And the tree of the cross, which has become the tree of life, secretly identifies the earth with paradise and gives proof once again of the sacramental nature of things.

> I cannot show you my God, but I can show you his works. 'Everything was made by him' (John 1.3). He created the world

in its newness, he who has no beginning. He who is eternal created
time. He who is unmoved made movement. Look at his works and
praise their maker.

AUGUSTINE OF HIPPO *Sermon 261*, 2 (PL 38, 1203)

The Most High has wounded me with his Spirit,
filled me with his love,
and his wounding has become my salvation . . .
All the earth is like a memorial to thee,
a presence of thy works . . .
Glory to thee, O God,
thou who art for ever the delight of Paradise.
Alleluia!

Odes of Solomon, 11 (Harris-Mingana, II, p. 266)

The book of the cosmos (the world, St Augustine says, is a
'first Bible') and that of the Scriptures match each other, since
they have the same author. Both of them find their full revelation
✓ in Christ who, after writing them, made them his body and his
face. The incarnate Logos frees the speechless tongue of creation
and unites it with the world as *logos alogos*. Christ has become
the direct divine-human subject of the cosmic *logoi*. He confers
on them their deepest meaning, their paschal nature, the power
of the resurrection to work in them. He reveals their roots in the
abyss of the three-Personed God.

Origen, within the limits of the knowledge of his time, looks at
creation with amazement and admiration. He sees its infinite complexity, brought into harmony by syntheses which are increasingly
complex and rich. Dionysius the Areopagite celebrated the 'sympathy' that holds all creation together and transforms its contradictions
into living tensions. Here is the Trinitarian fabric once again. Every
✓ creature, however lowly in itself, yet expresses an infinite intelligence.
Humanity must be united with every creature in order to make the
praise of its tongue-tied nature to be heard. For 'prayer like a sigh
has always resided in the mystery and essential nature of creation'
(Basil Rozanov, *The Apocalypse of our Time*). The person of prayer
understands that 'everything is praying, every creature is singing the
glory of God.' 'I learned thus,' the 'Russian Pilgrim' adds, 'what the
Philokalia calls "the knowledge of the language of creation" and I
saw how it is possible to converse with God's creatures.'

In what a wonderful way the tremendous discoveries of Western
science – undoubtedly made possible and mysteriously made fruitful

by this contemplative gaze – permit us today to widen the scope of this celebration!

> The divine art that is manifested in the structure of the world is not only to be seen in the sun, the moon and the stars; it operates also on earth on a reduced scale. The hand of the Lord has not neglected the bodies of the smallest animals – and still less their souls – because each one of them is seen to possess some feature that is personal to it, for instance, the way it protects itself. Nor has the hand of the Lord neglected the plants of the earth, each of which has some detail bearing the mark of the divine art, whether it be the roots, the leaves, the fruits or the variety of species. In the same way, in books written under the influence of divine inspiration, Providence imparts to the human race a wisdom that is more than human, sowing in each letter some saving truth in so far as that letter can convey it, marking out thus the path of wisdom. For once it has been granted that the Scriptures have God himself for their author, we must necessarily believe that the person who is asking questions of nature and the person who is asking questions of the Scriptures are bound to arrive at the same conclusions.

ORIGEN *Commentary on Psalm* 1,3 (PG 12,1081)

> The Word both hides and reveals himself in visible forms as much as in the words of Scripture. The visible is the invisible written down. The divine idea, the *logos*, which produces, develops and attracts to itself every creature, is both silent and self-revelatory in it. It is silent in the negligence and greed of humanity. It is self-revelatory when humanity 'names' living things, like a poet on fire with love. Matter is infra-visible, the interplay of energies, a mathematical abstraction; form bears witness to the invisible.

> In the Scriptures we say the words are the clothes of Christ and their meaning is his body. The words veil, the meaning reveals. It is the same in the world where the forms of visible things are like the clothing, and the ideas according to which they were created are like the flesh. The former conceal, the latter reveal. For the universal creator and law-maker, the Word, both hides himself in his self-revelation and reveals himself in his hiding of himself.

MAXIMUS THE CONFESSOR *Ambigua*, (PG 91,1129)

'Lift up your eyes, and see how the fields are already white for harvest' (John 4.35). The Word is in the midst of his disciples. He is asking his hearers to lift up their eyes toward the fields of the Scriptures and toward that other field where the Word is present in every creature, however small, so that they may perceive the whiteness and the brilliant radiance of the light of Truth which is everywhere.

ORIGEN *Commentary on St John's Gospel*, 13,42 (GCS 4,269)

The nature of matter is good. In reality, since matter is an abstraction, it is the fruitful flesh in which the Spirit is incarnate. The material nature of 'materials', in the sense the artist-craftsman gives to the word, is an incarnation. By means of form it participates in the order, the beauty, the realm of the Good-and-Beautiful where God can be discerned.

It is just as false to repeat the commonplace that it is in matter as such that evil resides. For to speak truly, matter itself also participates in the order, the beauty, the form ... How, if it were not so, could Good be produced from something evil? How could that thing be evil when it is impregnated with good? ... If matter is evil how can one explain its ability to engender and nourish nature? Evil as such engenders and nourishes nothing. It does not produce or preserve anything. If it be objected that matter ... leads souls towards evil, how could that be true when many material creatures turn their gaze towards the Good?

DIONYSIUS THE AREOPAGITE *Divine Names*, IV,28 (PG 3,792)

And so every creature is a gift of the invisible, a palpable mystery.

When someone whose mind is but partially developed sees something clothed in some semblance of beauty, he believes that this thing is beautiful in its own nature ... but someone who has purified the eyes of his soul and is trained to see beautiful things ... makes use of the visible as a springboard to rise to the contemplation of the spiritual.

GREGORY OF NYSSA *On Virginity*, (PG 46,364)

The ancient Greeks, to symbolize a true meeting, used to use a split ring whose two separate halves were joined together again. In

Christ the world is joined together again in symbol, in a profusion of symbols. The invisible part appears in the visible: the visible draws its meaning from the invisible. Each symbolizes the other in the 'house of the world', of which God is the 'eccentric centre', being radically transcendent. God transcends the intelligible as well as the visible, but through the incarnation of the Logos he penetrates them both, transfigures and unites them. The world is a vast incarnation which the fall of the human race tries to contradict. The *diabolos*, the opposite of the *symbolon*, is continually trying to keep apart the separated halves of the ring; but they come together in Christ. Christian symbolism expresses nothing less than the union in Christ of the divine and the human – of which the cosmos becomes the dialogue – displaying the circulation in Christ of glory between 'earth' and 'heaven', between the visible and the invisible.

> God's love for humanity wraps the spiritual in the perceptible, the superessential in the essence. It gives form ... to what is formless and, through a variety of symbols, it multiplies and shapes Simplicity that has no shape.
>
> DIONYSIUS THE AREOPAGITE *Divine Names*, I, 4 (PG 3,592)

> The world is one ... for the spiritual world in its totality is manifested in the totality of the perceptible world, mystically expressed in symbolic pictures for those who have eyes to see. And the perceptible world in its entirety is secretly fathomable by the spiritual world in its entirety, when it has been simplified and amalgamated by means of the spiritual realities. The former is embodied in the latter through the realities; the latter in the former through the symbols. The operation of the two is one.
>
> MAXIMUS THE CONFESSOR *Mystagogia*, 2 (PG 91,669)

> The divine apostle says: 'Ever since the creation of the world his invisible nature ... has been clearly perceived in the things that have been made' (Romans 1.20). If the invisible things are seen by means of the visible, the visible things are perceived in a far greater measure through the invisible by those who devote themselves to contemplation. For the symbolic contemplation of spiritual things by means of the visible is nothing other than the understanding in the Spirit of visible things by means of the invisible.
>
> MAXIMUS THE CONFESSOR *Mystagogia*, 2 (PG 91,669)

God himself is simple and unlimited, beyond all created things . . .
because he is free of any interdependence.

MAXIMUS THE CONFESSOR *Ambigua* (PG 91,1296)

So everything is symbolic: all creatures, however lowly, and
their relationships, their balance, in which life springs unceasingly
from death. The purity of matter, that point of transparency at the
heart of things, reaches its perfection in Mary's fruitful virginity.
Alongside the utilitarian use of objects, or rather by means of it,
one must learn to contemplate the flowering of heavenly realities in
them. There is not only the horizontal concatenation of cause and
effect. Each created object when contemplated 'vertically' expands
to infinite horizons. Only this 'vertical' knowledge can clarify the
scientific quest and limit and guide its technical power. *Homo faber*
(Man the Maker) suffocates himself and suffocates the world if he
is not in the first place *homo celebrans* (Man the Worshipper).

The apostle Paul teaches us that God's 'invisible nature' has been
'clearly perceived in the things that have been made' (Romans 1.20):
what is not seen perceived in what is seen. He shows us that this
visible world contains teaching about the invisible world, and that
this earth includes certain 'images of celestial realities' . . . It could
even be that God who made the human race 'in his own image and
likeness' (Genesis 1.27) also gave to other creatures a likeness to
certain celestial realities. Perhaps this resemblance is so detailed that
even the grain of mustard seed, 'the smallest of all seeds' (Matthew
13.31), has its counterpart in the kingdom of heaven. If so, by
that law of its nature that makes it the smallest of seeds and yet
capable of becoming larger than all the others and of sheltering
in its branches the birds of the air, it would represent for us not a
particular celestial reality but the kingdom of heaven as a whole.

In this sense it is possible that other seeds of the earth likewise
contain an analogy with celestial objects and are a sign of them.
And if that is true for seeds it must be the same for plants. And if
it is true of plants it cannot be otherwise for animals, birds, reptiles
and four-footed beasts . . . It may be granted that these creatures,
seeds, plants, roots and animals, are undoubtedly at the service
of humanity's physical needs. However, they include the shape
and image of the invisible world, and they also have the task of
elevating the soul and guiding it to the contemplation of celestial
objects. Perhaps that is what the spokesman of the Divine Wisdom
means when he expresses himself in the words: 'It is he who gave

me unerring knowledge of what exists, to know the structure of the world and the activity of the elements: the beginning and end and middle of times, the alternations of the solstices and the changes of the seasons, the cycles of the year and the constellations of the stars, the natures of animals and the tempers of wild beasts, the powers of spirits and the reasonings of men, the varieties of plants and the virtues of roots; I learned both what is secret and what is manifest' (Wisdom 7.17-21). He shows thus, without any possible doubt, that everything that is seen is related to something hidden. That is to say that each visible reality is a symbol, and refers to an invisible reality to which it is related.

ORIGEN *Commentary on the Song of Songs*, 3 (GCS 8,208-9)

For anyone who reflects, the appearances of beauty become the themes of an invisible harmony. Perfumes as they strike our senses represent spiritual illumination. Material lights point to that immaterial light of which they are the images.

DIONYSIUS THE AREOPAGITE *Celestial Hierarchy*, I,3 (PG 3,121)

The interpretation of the world as a theophany, that grand contribution of the ancient religions to understanding, thus finds its full place in Christianity. But it has been freed from the danger of idolatry and has become the poetical expression of a communion. The marvellous hymn composed by Dionysius the Areopagite should be read: the brilliance of the sun symbolizes and incarnates the life-giving radiation of the divine glory. The sun by its prolific splendour testifies to a different Sun. The Good-and-Beautiful, spreading its presence like the sun, initiates a Trinitarian game of separation and conjunction; it gives each object its limits and at the same time its urge towards communion, its leap in the light towards the fount of the sunshine, towards the centre where the lines converge. This quotation from the Areopagite reminds one of Van Gogh writing from Arles, at the height of August, to his brother Theo: 'Anyone here who does not believe in the sun is a complete infidel'.

What praise is not demanded by the blaze of the sun? For it is from the Good that its light comes, and it is itself the image of the Good. Thus we give glory to the Good by calling it Light . . . Indeed, just as the goodness proper to the deity permeates everything that exists, . . . so that it illumines every creature and gives it life, . . . and is its height and breadth, its cause and its purpose; so likewise with the image in which divine Goodness is revealed, that great sun which is wholly light, and whose brightness is unceasing . . . It is the sun that enlightens everything and pours out upon the whole visible world the brightness of its rays . . . It is the sun that allows bodies to develop, bestows life on them, purifies and renews them . . . And just as Goodness moves all things, and just as God the Creator gathers together all things that are scattered, turning them towards himself as their source and centre and perfect fulfilment; and as according to the Scriptures everything receives from the Good its structure and existence . . . and as every object finds its own proper borders in the Good and all objects aim at the Good – the intelligent by way of knowledge, the sensible by way of the feelings, the merely animate by natural instinct, the inanimate by their simple share in existence – so, likewise, the light uses its property of revelation through images to gather together and draw to itself . . . everything that receives its rays. That is why it is called 'sun' [*helios*] because everything is gathered together [*aolles*] in the light and the light reunites what has been scattered. It is towards this light that all perceptible realities are tending . . . I am certainly not asserting in the manner of the ancients that the sun actually governs the visible world as god and maker of the universe. But since the creation of the world, the invisible mysteries of God, thanks to his eternal power and godhead, are grasped by the intellect through creatures. (cf. Romans 1.20)

DIONYSIUS THE AREOPAGITE *Divine Names*, IV,4 (PG 3,697-700)

The angels are the mediators of glory, ministers of this symbolic structure of created being. Perceiving their presence we learn to fathom the depth of nature and its belonging to another world, its being rooted in God:

> Angels, bearers of the Divine Silence,
> Lights of revelation set by the Inaccessible
> to reveal him on the very threshold of his sanctuary.

DIONYSIUS THE AREOPAGITE *Divine Names*, IV,2 (PG 3,696)

Interior freedom – *apatheia* – makes possible that attentive gaze, stripped of covetousness, which perceives the outward appearance of each object and its secret, and honours it. Claudel must be quoted here: 'A pure eye and a fixed gaze see every object becoming transparent in front of them' (*La Ville*) 'Only a soul that has been made pure will understand the fragrance of the rose' (*L'oiseau noir dans le soleil levant*). And his allusion to Japanese art is pertinent because, let us repeat, the 'contemplation of nature' makes it possible to accommodate in the 'barque' of the Church, in its memory, the experiences of the cultures that are fed by a cosmic symbolism: 'All the art of the old Japanese painters (who in almost all periods were monks) is explained if it is understood that, for them, the visible world was a perpetual allusion to Wisdom, like that great tree which, with unutterable majesty, says No to evil for us' (*ibid.*).

> Wisdom consists in seeing every object in accordance with its true nature, with perfect interior freedom.
>
> MAXIMUS THE CONFESSOR *Centuries on Charity*, II,64 (PG 90,420)

Here is a little spiritual exercise: by means of the humblest of sensations – of breathing, of rejoicing under the blue sky, of touching a stone, or the bark of a tree, of gazing, as Claudel or Heidegger would say, at the majesty of a tree – I try to reach the transcendence of a thing. The object is visible and at the same time invisible; I must seek its inner self, let myself be led by it.

> We may gain some inkling of what God is if we attempt by means of every sensation to reach the reality of each creature, not giving up until we are alive to what transcends it . . .
>
> CLEMENT OF ALEXANDRIA *Miscellanies*, V,XI (PG 9,112)

The aim of the exercise becomes more specific: the mystery of the object, progressively laid bare, leads us to Christ. The Word, by becoming incarnate, has reopened for us the paradisial dimension of the world. Opaque but transparent, the earth is the paradise which we can re-enter by dying and rising with Christ.

> By meditation . . . we are no longer considering the physical properties of an object, its dimensions, its thickness, length or breadth. What is left from now on is only a sign, a unity provided, if I may so put it, with a position . . . Beyond, we discover the immensity of Christ, and there, by means of his holiness, we advance toward the depth of his infinity until we glimpse the Almighty . . . The grace of understanding comes to us from God through his Son. Solomon bears eloquent witness to that when he says: 'I have not the understanding of a man . . . Every word of God proves true . . . Do not add to his words' (Proverbs 30.2 & 5-6). Moses also calls Wisdom by the symbolic name 'tree of life' (Genesis 2.9) and it was planted in paradise.

But is not this paradise also the world in which are all the elements of creation? There the Word was made flesh; there he flowered and bore fruit; there he has given life to those who taste of his goodness.

CLEMENT OF ALEXANDRIA *Miscellanies*, V,XI (PG 9,109)

So it is that a person in whom all the strength of the passions has been crucified and transfigured radiates the peace of paradise. Around him wild beasts are calm, and human beings also, who can sometimes be wild beasts. In truth he is another Orpheus, like the young Christ of the Mausoleum of Galla Placida at Ravenna.

The humble man confronts murderous wild beasts. From the moment they see him their savagery is tamed, they approach him as if he were their owner, nodding their heads and licking his hands and feet. They actually scent coming from him the fragrance that Adam breathed forth before the Fall when they came to him in paradise and he gave them their names.

ISAAC OF NINEVEH *Ascetic Treatises*, 20 (Spanos, p. 78)

For such a person the beauty of the body no longer arouses lust, but rather praise.

Someone, I was told, at the sight of a very beautiful body [a woman's] felt impelled to glorify the Creator. The sight of it increased his love for God to the point of tears. Anyone who entertains such feelings in such circumstances is already risen . . . before the general resurrection.

JOHN CLIMACUS *The Ladder of Divine Ascent*, 15th step, 58 (p. 168)

If objects give us an inkling of God, then drawing near to God we can receive the full revelation of their *logoi*, their spiritual natures, their infinite meanings. The Logos is the divine subject of all logoi, of all the subsistent 'words' that support the world. The *logikos* man, personal image of the Logos, is called to become their human subject. The meeting is fully brought about in the God-Man who enables us to fathom the spiritual essences of objects, not in order to possess but in order to offer them to the Logos after having 'given them their names', marked them with our own creative spirit. The world then becomes a momentous dialogue between the Logos and the *logikos* man. (It is also necessarily a dialogue of human beings among themselves, since they exist as persons only according to their relationship with one another.) All history, all cultures, animated by the presence of the cosmic Logos, form the setting; but the only place where there can be neither confusion nor separation is Christ.

> Just as at the centre of a circle there is a single point at which all the radii meet, so one who has been judged worthy to reach God recognizes in him, by a direct awareness and without formulating thoughts, all the essences of created objects.

MAXIMUS THE CONFESSOR *Gnostic Centuries*, II,4 (PG 90,1125-8)

> In knowledge, the spirit offers the spiritual essences of the universe as so many gifts which it makes to God. In existence, the spirit receives the gifts, making explicit by its life all the splendour of the divine wisdom that is invisibly immanent in creatures.

MAXIMUS THE CONFESSOR *Questions to Thalassius*, 51 (PG 90, 480-1)

As for the Saints, it is in union with God that they receive spiritual awareness of created objects. They see the world in God, permeated by his light and forming a whole in the hollow of his hand. This is what St Benedict was doing when he contemplated the whole universe gathered up in a ray of the divine glory.

> While the disciples were still sleeping, Benedict the man of God was already keeping vigil, anticipating the hour of the night office. Standing in front of his window in the dead of night he was praying to the Lord Almighty when suddenly he saw a light shining, and it dispelled the darkness and sparkled with such brilliance that it would have outshone the light of day. While he was watching it something extraordinary happened. As he described it later, the whole world was gathered up before his eyes as if in a ray of sunlight . . .
> How is it possible for the whole world to be seen in this way by a human being? . . .
> To one who sees the Creator, the whole of creation is limited. But one glimpse of God's light makes everything that has been created seem too narrow. The light of interior contemplation in fact enlarges the dimensions of the soul, which by dint of expanding in God transcends the world. Should I say this? The soul of the contemplative transcends itself when, in God's light, it is transported beyond itself. Then, looking below itself, it understands how limited is that which on earth seemed to it to have no

limits. Such a seeker ... could not have had that vision except
in God's light. It is not surprising that he should have seen the
whole world gathered up in his presence, since he himself in the
light of the Spirit was lifted up out of this world. When it is said
that the world was gathered up before his eyes that does not
mean that heaven and earth were contracted. No. The soul of
the seer was expanded. Enraptured with God he was able to see
without difficulty everything that is under God.

GREGORY THE GREAT *Dialogues*, II,35 (PL 66,198-200)

The sun that rises and illumines the world makes itself visible as
well as the objects it illumines. It is the same with the Sun of righteousness. When he rises in a mind that has been purified, he makes
himself seen in addition to the *logoi* of the objects he has created.

MAXIMUS THE CONFESSOR *Centuries on Charity*, I, 95 (PG 90)

Deep within Shinto temples in Japan you find only a mirror. It is
a symbol and a riddle. The risk there is of turning in upon the Self. But
the Christian knows that the Self is the image of Christ. And Christ
is the faithful mirror who reflects the truth not only of creatures and
objects, but also of the Self that is no longer an undifferentiated abyss
but the interior expression of a face.

See! The Lord is our mirror:
open your eyes,
look into it,
learn what your faces are like!
Odes of Solomon, 13 (Harris-Mingana, II,276)

From that moment on nothing is profane. Nor is anything sacred
of itself any more. The real division is between the profane and
the sanctified. And everything can be sanctified: not only cosmic
realities, but objects produced by human beings apparently for the
most ordinary uses. This surprising importance of the commonplace,
which some artists of our time try to bring out – for example by
putting some utilitarian object on a pedestal – is perceived by the
spiritual person, who quite naturally respects it.

Look upon all the tools and all the property of the monastery as
if they were sacred altar vessels.
BENEDICT OF NURSIA *Rule*, XXI, 10 (Centenario, p. 76)

The person who is sanctified in this way includes all created things in his love and in his prayer. His charity extends to the cosmos. Reading the lines that follow from St Isaac of Nineveh we are reminded of certain Buddhist texts. Yet from the biblical point of view created things are not 'temporary aggregations', they are perfectly real. And their suffering is real too, the horror that is multiplied by the powers of darkness, to which the world is continually given over as prey by our sin. About this agony it might be said that Christ, and the saints with him, are perpetually being crucified in order to impart to all things, 'even to serpents', a life freed from all forms of death, an aspect stressed by St Isaac.

> What is purity, briefly? It is a heart full of compassion for the whole of created nature ... And what is a compassionate heart? He tells us: 'It is a heart that burns for all creation, for the birds, for the beasts, for the devils, for every creature. When he thinks about them, when he looks at them, his eyes fill with tears. So strong, so violent is his compassion ... that his heart breaks when he sees the pain and the suffering of the humblest creature. That is why he prays with tears every moment ... for all the enemies of truth and for all who cause harm, that they may be protected and forgiven. He prays even for serpents in the boundless compassion that wells up in his heart after God's likeness.'
>
> ISAAC OF NINEVEH *Ascetic Treatises*, 81 (p. 306)

The 'contemplation of nature' can give spiritual flavour to our lives even if we lay no claim to be in any way 'mystics' in the rather particular sense that this word has acquired in the West. A little loving attention in the light of the Risen Christ is enough. The humblest objects then breathe out their secret. The person becomes the priest of the world at the altar of his heart, celebrating that 'cosmic liturgy' of which Maximus the Confessor speaks. Language, work, art, culture, the humanities, find their meaning there because the Logos,

> while hiding himself for our benefit in a mysterious way, in the *logoi*, shows himself to our minds to the extent of our ability to understand, through visible objects which act like letters of the alphabet, whole and complete both individually and when related together. He, the undifferentiated, is seen in differentiated things, the simple in the compound. He who has no beginning is seen in things that must have a beginning; the invisible in the visible; the intangible in the tangible. Thus he gathers us together in himself,

through every object ... enabling us to rise into union with him,
as he was dispersed in coming down to us.

MAXIMUS THE CONFESSOR *Ambigua* (PG 91,1288)

However, we are continually tempted to appropriate the world,
to take possession of it as a kind of prey. We thus increasingly
enslave it to death, and today we are in danger simultaneously
of collectively committing suicide, and destroying nature. But by
the intervention of the mystery of Christ and of the witness of his
followers a state of death is transformed into a state of resurrection.
In Christ the world becomes Eucharist. In him we can transfigure the
world by integrating it into the human consciousness of the Risen
Christ, who offers resurrection to everyone and everything. It is up
to Christians to show people that the cross, all the crosses of history,
call upon us to advance from possession to sharing and offering,
to discover the Giver through the gift. They invite us to respect
nature and spiritualize it, and to share the blessings of the earth like
brothers and sisters, because, as Dumitru Staniloae, whose thought
is summarized here, writes, 'They are destined to serve interpersonal
communion' (*Dogmatic Theology*, I,344). Sanctity imparts the divine
light not only to our bodies but to the whole cosmic environment.
Today, when history itself is raising the ultimate questions, we are
called to what Simone Weil termed a 'holiness of genius' that is
able to communicate the light to the very foundations of culture.

Two passages from contemporary writers underline the reality of
a similar form of contemplation. Pierre Emmanuel in *L'Arbre et
le vent* shows the need to experience the depth of the universe
in order to awaken the depth in oneself. He continues: 'In the
countryside this dimension is everywhere to be seen: in the plain
extending all the way to Ventoux; in the distance to the evening
star at dusk; in the trunk of the majestic umbrella pine; in the
flight of the kestrel; in the hooting of the owl at night. These
objects that are at once visible and invisible exist as much as I
do, and more so, each in its own order ... They are all symbolic
– even the scorpion that I am careful not to squash and which I
like to see basking on the wall. Man's true measure is in these
objects. It consists in making their true nature his own, taking
part in their praise, hearing it in them, merging it into himself.'

And Vladimir Maximov in *Les Sept Jours de la création*: 'Mi-
raculously ... it was if I were seeing the forest for the first time. A
fir tree was not only a fir but also something else much greater. The

dew on the grass was not just dew in general. Each drop existed on its own. I could have given a name to every puddle on the road.'

Thus the person of prayer, the person for whom knowledge stands for life and life for immortality, becomes capable of 'feeling everything in God'. He can feel on every object, in every object, the blessing of God. Thereby he is able to bless everything and to see in everything a miracle of God. By so seeing he is able, without seeking to do so, to work the miracle of materiality restored to health, weightless, splendid, belonging to the new Jerusalem.

What is knowledge? – The feeling of eternal life.

And what is eternal life? – Feeling everything in God.

For love comes from meeting him. Knowledge united to God fulfils every desire. And for the heart that receives it, it is altogether sweetness overflowing on to the earth. For there is nothing like the sweetness of God.

Isaac of Nineveh *Ascetic Treatises*, 38 (p. 164)

3

Enstasy – Ecstasy

1. *Into the Unknown*

In the battle of ascesis and the offering of creatures to God in the cosmic liturgy, our will must cooperate with divine grace. But the ultimate knowledge, the love-knowledge of the Trinity, takes hold of us by grace alone. We prepare for it by a stripping away of our being until we become nothing but expectation. In Simone Weil's admittedly approximate expression, we must 'de-create' ourselves, and descend even below the level of plants and stones, to those luminous deep waters on which the Spirit breathes: to the waters of baptism, the waters of creation. Then the Spirit comes as he came upon Mary and the person is created afresh in 'an ineffable peace and silence'.

> It is in the power of our spirit to gain the spiritual understanding of objects. But to understand the Holy Trinity is not only not in the power of our spirit but it requires a superabundant grace from God.
>
> EVAGRIUS OF PONTUS *Centuries*, I,79 (Frankenberg, p. 355)

> To progress in thinking about creatures is painful and wearisome. The contemplation of the Holy Trinity is ineffable peace and silence.
>
> EVAGRIUS OF PONTUS *Centuries*, I,65 (Frankenberg, p. 105)

Certainly, as we have seen, God, can be known by way of every reality. And to know him is to be taken into the *perichoresis*, the

Trinity's continuous movement of love, which sends us back to creatures. Yet the soul aspires to direct unity with him so that 'nothing may interpose itself between the soul and God' as St Augustine said. And he is witness to such an uninterrupted meeting – so intense that in his thought the cosmos loses all importance. The true knowledge of God appears then as an unknowing, because it takes place beyond the frontiers of any human capacity to understand or rationalize, and because it is communion with Another whose otherness remains irreducible. The person, going beyond the borders of the intellect, meets the living God who also, in his love, 'goes out' of himself, leaves his inaccessible transcendence. By this interweaving, in Christ, of the two 'ecstasies', the uncreated light sets the soul ablaze and draws it into the depths of the Trinity. The unknowing is not simply negative theology: it is a soaring of the personality towards that personal God who was led by love to assume the condition of a slave and to die on a cross. To get a proper sense of this mystery of Christ we need the remarkable apophatic algebra of the Areopagite.

> God is known both in all objects and outside all objects. God is known both through knowing and through unknowing ... He is nothing of what is, and therefore cannot be known through anything that is; and yet he is all in all. He is nothing in anything; and yet he is known by all in all, at the same time as he is not known by anything in anything.
>
> It is no mistake then to speak of God and to honour him as known through all being ... But the way of knowing God that is most worthy of him is to know him through unknowing, in a union that rises above all intellect. The intellect is first detached from all beings, then it goes out of itself and is united to rays more luminous than light itself. Thanks to these rays it shines in the unfathomable depths of Wisdom. It is no less true, however, as I have said, that this Wisdom can be known from every reality.
>
> DIONYSIUS THE AREOPAGITE *Divine Names*, VII, 3 (PG 3,872)

Augustine understood the experience of the Eastern *en-stasis* in the form Plotinus gave it, and he converted it into an encounter with the absolute Thou, as is emphasized by the well-known sentence of the *Confessions*: 'But Thou, Lord, wast more within me than my inmost being, and higher than what is highest in me' (*Tu autem, Domine, eras interior intimo meo et superior summo meo*). God is more transcendent than the 'One' of Plotinus, with whom humanity identifies itself, and he is more within than the Self, whom Eastern mysticism identifies as the Absolute. Augustine's ecstasy at Ostia, a year after his conversion to Christ, bears witness, in a language that is still that of Plotinus, to an aspiration towards the God who is inaccessible and yet quite suddenly perceptible to the heart with an overwhelming immediacy. This God, who is touched for an instant 'for a whole heartbeat', is then simultaneously glimpsed as an 'abyss of inward joy' and as the Other, as my Creator, in whose presence I am and who is speaking to me. Whereas a fleeting, purely Plotinian experience a year earlier at Milan ended like withdrawal from drugs, in 'an immense confusion', the ecstasy at Ostia takes place in the great longsuffering of faith and fertilizes it with hope. On the other hand, it must be emphasized, it is not solitary. The presence of his mother suggests ecclesial communion.

> Shortly before the day on which thy servant [Monica, Augustine's mother] was to leave this world . . . it so happened that she and I were alone, standing by a window from which could be seen the garden of the house in which we were living at Ostia . . . Our conversation was a very happy one. We dismissed the past and took ourselves with all that we were into the future ahead of us. We sought in the light of that eternal present that is thyself, Lord, what the immortal life of the saints might be, that life that eye has not seen nor ear heard nor heart grasped. We opened our hearts wide to drink the waters of thy heavenly spring, that spring of life that is in thee, so that by filling ourselves as best we could we might have some inkling of that higher life . . .
>
> We were exalted by an ever more burning desire and we ascended through the whole range of physical creation right up to the sky, whence the sun the moon and the stars send their light upon the earth. Then we rose higher still, thinking inwardly of thee, speaking of thee and marvelling at thy works. Thus we arrived at our souls, and went on beyond them to reach that region of inexhaustible plenty . . . where life is that very Wisdom by which was made everything that is and everything that has been and everything that will be. But that Wisdom itself was not made, for it is today such as it has been and such as it will be – more precisely such as it is, for it is eternal . . . And while we were speaking and desiring intensely to attain to this sovereign Wisdom we touched it slightly for a whole heartbeat.

Then, with a sigh, we left in heaven those first fruits of our spirit and came back to the word that is uttered and that has a beginning and an end ...

We said therefore: Suppose someone imposed silence within himself upon the tumults of the flesh and shut his eyes to the spectacle of earth, sea and sky; suppose he imposed silence on his own soul without allowing it to stop at itself or think about itself; suppose he rid himself of the dreams and the imaginings of memory and forgot all language, all words, all that is mutable (for if he listened to those things they would tell him, 'We did not make ourselves: he who abides for ever made us.'); suppose he paid no more heed to these creatures after they had invited him to listen to their Creator, and God alone had spoken to him and he had heard divine words not uttered by a tongue of flesh nor by the voice of an angel, nor by a peal of thunder, nor by the language of figures and symbols, but by the Creator himself, whom we love in his creation, speaking in a wholly spiritual fashion, as in the wholly spiritual contact that was effected just now between our thought when it was ravished to heaven and the eternal Wisdom ... if then that ecstasy continued ... and if the one who was enjoying it were absorbed by that contemplation alone in the abyss of interior joy, in such a way that eternal life resembled that brief moment of transport after which we have sighed so longingly – surely this would be the fulfilment of that word of the Gospel: 'Enter into the joy of your Lord'.

AUGUSTINE OF HIPPO *Confessions*, IX,X 23-5 (Belles Lettres p. 227-9)

The specifically Christian treatment of the theme is developed by Augustine in his commentary on Psalm 41. There again is the worship of the personal God beyond self, beyond the Self, beyond the fine point of the soul. But the path to him is more explicitly described: it is the Church, whose liturgy, interiorized, enables the soul to hear (rather than to see, though the distinction is purely relative for mystics and artists) some fragments of the celestial liturgy. How bewitching is the attraction of that divine music, that sharing in the eternal festival! Then suddenly through the music – the transition from hearing to seeing – there blazes forth the face of God, the face of Christ.

Note the realism of Augustine, his candour, free of the conventional style preferred by the Christian Orient. The soul, after having glimpsed the full reality, though only in a flash, falls back into the

shadows of everyday routine. The vision becomes again something
to be waited for. But hope has taken the place of despair.

This realism with its tragic overtones was to leave its mark on
the West. It would prevent it from falling asleep on its way back
to the original. It would make it a pilgrim to the ultimate.

I sought the substance [of God] in myself, as if it were similar
to what I am; and I did not find it.

I sense then that God is well beyond my soul. To touch him
then, 'I pondered on these things and I stretched out my soul above
itself'. How in fact could my soul reach what it needs to look for
beyond itself if it did not stretch out above itself? If my soul were
to remain within itself it would not see anything but itself and,
within itself, it would not see its God ... 'I stretched out my soul
beyond myself' and only my God remains for me to grasp. It is
there, in fact, above my soul, that the dwelling of my God is. That
is where he dwells, from there he sees me, from there he created
me ... from there he raises me up and calls me, from there he
guides me and steers me into harbour.

He who dwells in the highest heavens in an invisible abode
possesses also a tabernacle on earth. His tabernacle is his Church
still on its journey. It is there he must be sought because in the
tabernacle is found the way that leads to his abode. Actually when
I stretched out my soul above myself to reach my God, why did I
do it? 'Because I will enter into the place of the tabernacle', the
marvellous tabernacle, even to the house of God ... The tabernacle
of God on earth is made up of faithful people ... The prophet
[David] entered the tabernacle and from there arrived at the house
of God. While he was marvelling at the saints, who are as it were
different parts of this tabernacle, he was led to the house of God,
carried away by a certain delight, a kind of secret charm, as though
from the house of God were coming the bewitching sounds of a
musical instrument. He walked in the tabernacle and hearing this
music within, whose sweetness drew him on, he set himself to
follow what he heard ... and he arrived at the house of God
... How did you come to the secret of that abode? The reply:
amidst songs of gladness and praise, amidst the joyful harmonies
of the holiday-makers ... in the house of God it is always a
holiday ... it is celebrated by the choirs of angels, and the face
of God, seen unveiled, gives rise to a joy beyond description.
There is no beginning to that day of festival, nor any end. Of
this eternal festivity some ineffable sound is heard in the ears

of the heart, provided that no human noise is mixed with it. The harmony of that festival enchants the ear of anyone who is walking in this tabernacle and contemplating the marvels that God has worked for the redemption of the faithful. It leads the hart to the waterbrooks.

But we see God from a distance. Our body that is doomed to corruption weighs our soul down and our spirit is troubled by many thoughts. Sometimes, spurred on by the longing that scatters the vain images that surround us, we succeed in hearing those divine sounds . . . However, since we are weighed down by our heaviness we soon fall back into our habitual ways. We let ourselves be dragged back to our usual way of living. And just as when we drew near to God we found joy, so when we fall back to earth we have reason to groan. 'Why art thou so heavy, O my soul: and why art thou so disquieted within me?' We have just tasted a secret sweetness, we have just been able with the fine point of the spirit to glimpse, very briefly, it is true, and in a flash only, the life that does not change. Why then are you still distressed? Why this sadness? You do not doubt your God. You are not at a loss for an answer to those who ask you, 'Where is your God?' Already I have had a foretaste of the immutable. Why are you still distressed? Hope in God. And the soul replies in secret: 'Why am I in distress, unless it is because I am not yet in that abode where this sweetness into whose bosom I was fleetingly transported is for ever enjoyed? Can I perhaps from now on drink from this fountain without fear? . . . Am I even now secure against all my inordinate desires? Are they tamed and vanquished? Is not the devil, my enemy, on the watch for me? And you would have me untroubled while I am still exiled from God's house!' Then . . . the reply comes: 'Hope in God. While awaiting heaven find your God here below in hope . . . Why hope? Because I shall witness to him. What witness will you give? That he is my God, the health of my countenance. My health cannot come to me from myself. I will proclaim it, I will bear witness to it: My God is the health of my countenance . . .'

AUGUSTINE OF HIPPO *Commentary on Psalm 41* (PL 36,464-7)

In the contemplative life there is a great straining of the soul when it is lifting itself towards the heavenly heights, endeavouring to transcend all that it can see with the body, and pulling itself together in order to expand. Sometimes it is victorious and overcomes the resistance of the darkness of its own blindness. Then it attains, briefly and in a covert manner, something of the light that knows no bounds. Yet it quickly falls back into itself, and quits that light, repulsed, and returns with sighs to the darkness of its own blindness.

GREGORY THE GREAT *Homilies on Ezekiel,* 2,2,12 (PL 76,955)

St Gregory of Nyssa also, the poet and dramatist of darkness, mentions those brief thoughts that come to us from a fullness beyond our reach. Beyond our reach, yes, but 'a few drops of night' are enough to inebriate us.

The advantage you will gain from having welcomed me and enabled me to dwell in you will be the dew with which my head is covered and the drops of night that trickle from my locks . . .
    Let whoever has gained access to the invisible sanctuary rejoice if its fullness sprinkles his spirit with dark insubstantial thoughts.

GREGORY OF NYSSA *Homilies on the Song of Songs,* 11 (PG 44, 1002)

To catch a glimpse of the divine light as if through a narrow loophole is none the less to broaden the soul prodigiously. A gleam is enough for everything to be transformed.

In the splayed windows [of the temple in Ezekiel's vision] the part by which the light enters is only a narrow opening, but the interior part that receives the light is wide. In the same way the souls of those who contemplate see only a feeble gleam of true light and yet everything in them seems to expand widely . . . What they see of eternity in their contemplation is almost nothing, yet it is enough to broaden their inward vision and to increase their fervour and their love. Although they are receiving the light of truth as if through a loophole only, everything in them seems to be broadened.

GREGORY THE GREAT *Homilies on Ezekiel,* 2,5,17 (PL 76,995)

Noverim me, noverim te (if I knew myself, I should know thee), says Augustine. In Christ the awareness of the subject leads on to that of the divine Thou. And he sees in the soul's faculties, in the memory, the intelligence and the will, the image of the Trinity. To the Fathers, the image of God in humanity restored in Christ leads on to the Trinitarian light, towards the Kingdom. When a person by faith, humility, and the appropriate ascesis perfects the purifying of the image, it attains to a resemblance of participation. It becomes wholly translucent to the Archetype.

'The kingdom of God is within you' (Luke 17.21). From this we learn that by a heart made pure . . . we see in our own beauty the image of the godhead . . . You have in you the ability to see God. He who formed you put in your being an immense power. When God created you he enclosed in you the image of his perfection, as the mark of a seal is impressed on wax. But your straying has obscured God's image . . . You are like a metal coin: on the whetstone the rust disappears. The coin was dirty, but now it reflects the brightness of the sun and shines in its turn. Like the coin, the inward part of the personality, called the heart by our Master, once rid of the rust that hid its beauty, will rediscover the first likeness and be real . . . So when people look at themselves they will see in themselves the One they are seeking. And this is the joy that will fill their purified hearts. They are looking at their own translucency and finding the model in the image. When the sun is looked at in a mirror, even without any raising of the eyes to heaven, the sun's brightness is seen in the mirror exactly as if the sun's disc itself were being looked at. You cannot contemplate the reality of the light; but if you rediscover the beauty of the image that was put in you at the beginning, you will obtain within yourself the goal of your desires . . . The divine image will shine brightly in us in Christ Jesus our Lord, to whom be glory throughout all ages.

GREGORY OF NYSSA *Homilies on the Beatitudes*, 6 (PG 44, 1270)

The Fathers distinguish here, without in any way separating them, the inaccessible essence of God and the energy (or energies) by means of which his essence is made inexhaustibly capable of being shared in. It is a distinction that is inherent in the reality of the divine Persons and it points, on the one hand, to their secret nature and, on the other hand, to the communication of their love and their life. The essence does not imply a depth greater than the Trinity; it means the depth in the Trinity, the depth, that cannot be objectivized, of personal existence in communion. The inaccessibility of the essence means that God reveals himself of his own free will by grace, by a 'folly of love' (St Maximus's expression). God in his nearness remains transcendent. He is hidden, not as if in forbidden darkness, but by the very intensity of his light. It is only God's inaccessibility that allows the positive space for the development of love through which communion is renewed. God overcomes otherness in himself without dissolving it and that is the mystery of the Trinity in Unity. He overcomes it in his relations with us, again without dissolving it, and that is the distinction-identity of the reality and the energies. '*God is altogether shared and altogether unshareable*', as Dionysius the Areopagite and Maximus the Confessor say. The energy is the expansion of the Trinitarian love. It associates us with the *perichoresis* of the divine Persons.

God as inaccessible essence – transcendent, always beyond our reach.

God as energy capable of being shared in – God incarnate, crucified, descended into hell, risen from the dead and raising us up, that is, enabling us to share in his life, even from the starting point of our own enclosed hell – God always within our reach.

The energy – or energies – can therefore be considered from two complementary standpoints. On the one hand is life, glory, the numberless divine Names that radiate eternally from the essence. From all eternity God lives and reigns in glory. And the waves of his power permeate the universe from the moment of its creation, bestowing on it its translucent beauty, masked partially by the fall. At the same time, however, the energy or energies denote the actions of God who is living and active, operations that create and maintain the universe, and then enable it to enter potentially into the realm of the Spirit, and to be offered the risen life. All these operations therefore are summed up in Jesus, the name that means 'God saves', 'God frees', 'God sets at liberty'. In his person humanity and all creation are 'authenticated', 'spiritualized', 'vivified', since, as St Paul says, 'in him [Christ] the whole fullness of deity dwells bodily' (Colossians 2.9). The energy as divine activity ensures our share in the energy as divine life, since what God gives us is himself. The energy is not an impersonal emanation nor is it a part of God. It is that life that comes from the Father through the Son in the Holy Spirit. It is that life that flows from the whole being of Jesus, from his pierced side, from his empty tomb. It is that power that is God giving himself entirely while remaining entirely above and beyond creatures.

It may be said in all truth that the pure in heart see God and, at the same time, that no one has ever seen God. In fact that part

of his nature that is invisible becomes visible through the energies
that are thus revealed about his nature.

GREGORY OF NYSSA *Homilies on the Beatitudes*, 6 (PG 44,1269)

We declare that we know God in his energies but we hardly
claim to approach him in his very essence. For his essence remains
inaccessible, whereas his energies reach down to us.

BASIL OF CÆSAREA *Letter* 234 (PG 32,869)

God's unique nature, while remaining entirely one, multiplies itself
in powers that communicate being and life ... and all these mu-
nificent gifts of Goodness ... make it possible for the unsharable
character of the Shared to be glorified in the sharers as well
as in the shares that are given.

DIONYSIUS THE AREOPAGITE *Divine Names*, II, 5 (PG 3,644)

We can share in what God communicates to us of his nature, but
his nature in itself remains incommunicable.

MAXIMUS THE CONFESSOR quoted by Euthymius Zygabenus
Dogmatic Panoply, 3 (PG 130,148)

'We shall see God as he is': that means ... that we shall
understand the beauty of the divine nature of the Father by contemplating the glory of him [Christ] who has shone forth from
him.

CYRIL OF ALEXANDRIA *Commentary on the Gospel of John*, 16,25
(PG 73,464)

The energy of the divine nature is common to the Persons [of the
Trinity] while belonging properly to each one of them in a mode
that is fitting to each ... The energy belongs to the Father, but
through the Son and in the Spirit. It belongs to the Son, but as
power of the Father ... it belongs to the Spirit, inasmuch as he is
the Spirit of the Father and the Son.

CYRIL OF ALEXANDRIA *On the Holy and Consubstantial Trinity*, VI
(PG 75,1056)

The distinction-identity of nature and energy must be understood dynamically. The more the soul is filled, satiated with God,

the more God calls it further beyond. Transfiguration and transcendence, *enstasis* and *ecstasis*, never cease alternating. The more
God is known, the more he is found to be unknown. (And it is
the same with our neighbour.) The more God makes it possible
for us to share in him (this is 'energy'), the more we aspire to reach
him who eludes us (this is his 'nature'). Thus the soul advances
'from beginning to beginning'. Eternity is inaugurated already here
below in that rhythm of fullness and aspiration. The theology of
the nature and the energy of God reveals itself in this way as an
astonishing metaphysic of communion, of 'relational being'. This has
been propounded in this century by Russian and Greek philosophers
– in particular by Christos Yannaras in his magisterial work *Person
and Love*, but also in France by Gabriel Marcel and Maurice Zundel,
and by that unassuming and profound French-speaking philosopher
from the Lebanon, René Habachi.

> The unlimited reality of the godhead that cannot be circumscribed
> remains beyond all comprehension . . . Thus great David when he
> was seeking exaltation in his heart and was going 'from strength to
> strength' (Psalm 84.7) nevertheless cried to God: 'Thou, O Lord,
> art on high for ever' (Psalm 92.8). By that, I think, he meant to
> convey that for all eternity, world without end, anyone who is
> hastening towards thee grows ever greater and rises continually
> higher, each moment making progress by the addition of graces,
> whilst 'Thou, O Lord, art enthroned for ever; thy name endures
> to all generations' (Psalm 102.12) . . . At each instant, what is
> grasped is much greater than what had been grasped before, but,
> since what we are seeking is unlimited, the end of each discov-
> ery becomes the starting point for the discovery of something
> higher, and the ascent continues.
>
> Thus our ascent is unending. We go from beginning to begin-
> ning by way of beginnings without end.
>
> Nor, whilst ascending, do we cease to desire more, knowing
> what we know. Rather, as we rise by a greater desire to one
> still higher, we continue on our way into the infinite by increasingly
> higher ascents.
>
> GREGORY OF NYSSA *Homilies on the Song of Songs*, 8 (PG 44,
> 940-1)

> When the soul has become simple, unified, really like God, it
> finds fulfilment . . . it clings to the One who alone is really lovable
> and desirable. It is unified with him by the living activity of love.

It is transformed into that which it apprehends, continually making fresh discoveries.

GREGORY OF NYSSA *Dialogue on the Soul and Resurrection* (PG 46, 93)

Thus the sanctified soul becomes, as Jean Daniélou wrote, an 'expanding universe'.

Sharing in the divine fullness is such that it makes whoever achieves it ever greater, more illimitable, so as never to cease growing. Because the spring of all reality flows ceaselessly, the being of anyone who shares in it is increased in grandeur by all that springs up within, so that the capacity for receiving grows along with the abundance of good gifts received.

GREGORY OF NYSSA *Dialogue on the Soul and Resurrection* (PG 46, 112)

2. *Love and Inebriation*

The spiritual person is drunk with the wine of love and that wine is the Spirit, the wine of power and life. It is to comprehend at last, without any sentimentality, the great Johannine declaration: 'God is love'. It is the internalizing of the Eucharist; it is to become Eucharist. It is the breathing, beyond space and time, of the air of the resurrection.

One who has found love feeds on Christ every day and at every hour and he becomes immortal thereby. For Jesus said: 'Whoever eats this bread that I shall give him shall never see death' (cf. John 6.58). Blessed is he who eats the bread of love that is Jesus. For whoever feeds on love feeds on Christ ... as John bears witness saying: 'God is love' (I John 4.8). Therefore one who lives in love receives from God the fruit of life. He breathes, even in this world, the air of the resurrection ... Love is the Kingdom ... Such is the 'wine to gladden the heart of man' (Psalm 104.15) Blessed is he who drinks of this wine ... the sick have drunk of it and become strong; the ignorant have drunk of it and become wise.

ISAAC OF NINEVEH *Ascetic Treatises*, 72 (Spanos, p. 282)

It is a matter of unity between the Lord and the 'heart that is aware' – the heart like a chariot of fire goes up to the Lord and the Lord comes down into it and absorbs it, as the Eucharist

absorbs the communicant. Meister Eckhart's words come to mind:
'The eye with which I see God and the eye with which God sees
me are one and the same eye.'

> In union with God,
> the heart absorbs the Lord and the Lord the heart,
> and the two become one.
>
> *Quotation attributed to St John Chrysostom by Callistus and*
> *Ignatius Xanthopoulos, 52 (Philokalia IV,252)*

If we are capable of loving, it is because we are responding to
God's love: God first loves us. Love becomes incarnate and comes
to us in Jesus. The Holy Spirit is this love that is poured out in our
hearts. Thus we are loving God by means of God; the Spirit enables
us to share in the love with which the Father loves the Son and
the Son the Father. Love casts us into the Trinitarian realms; the
Trinitarian realms are those of love.

Augustine, almost brutally, cites the example of erotic passion.
If no personal love enters into it the passion subsides. Yet the body
of the other is just as desirable. For that which is loved, and that
by which it is loved, is love, invisible love. Invisible, but the only
thing that enables one to see.

To love God, Augustine says finally, is to sing his glory; or better,
it is to become, ourselves, a song of glory.

He teaches us in this way to understand God as the life of our
life, the soul of our soul, the love of our love.

> We only love if we have first been loved. Hear what the apostle
> John has to say. He it was who leant on the Master's heart and
> resting there drank in heavenly secrets ... Among the other secrets
> which the great seer drew from that source he showed us this:
> 'We love him because he first loved us' (1 John 4.10). Ask how
> anyone can love God and you will find no other answer than this:
> God first loved us. He whom we love has given himself first. He
> has given himself so that we may love him. What was his gift?
> The apostle Paul states it more clearly: 'God's love has been
> poured into our hearts'. By what means? Through us perhaps?
> No. Through whom then? 'Through the Holy Spirit which has
> been given to us' (Romans 5.5).
> Full of this testimony let us love God through God ... The
> conclusion imposes itself on us and John states it for us still more
> succinctly: 'God is love and he who abides in love abides in God, and

God abides in him' (1 John 4.16). It is not much to say, 'Love comes from God'. But who among us would dare to repeat these words: 'God is love'? They were spoken by someone from experience. Why does the human imagination with its superficial attitude represent God to itself? Why do human beings fashion an idol according to their desire? . . . God is love . . . We see nothing of him and yet we love him . . . Let us seek below what we shall discover on high. Love that is attached only to physical beauty does none the less move us to more profound feelings. A sensual and lecherous man loves a woman of rare beauty. He is carried away by the loveliness of her body, yet he seeks in her, beyond her body, a response to his tender feelings for her. Suppose he learns that this woman hates him. All the fever, all the raptures that those lovely features aroused in him subside. In the presence of that being who fascinated him he experiences a revulsion of feeling. He goes away and the object of his affections now inspires him with hatred. Yet has her body changed in any way? Has her charm disappeared? No. But while burning with desire for the object that he could see, his heart was waiting for a feeling that he could not see. Suppose, on the contrary, he perceives that he is loved. How his ardour redoubles! She looks at him; he looks at her; no one sees their love. And yet it is that which is loved, although it remains invisible . . .

You do not see God. Love and you possess him . . . for God offers himself to us at once. Love me, he cries to us, and you shall possess me. You cannot love me without possessing me.

O brethren, O children, O catholic seedlings, holy and heavenly plants, you who have been regenerated in Christ and born in heaven, listen to me or rather listen through me: 'Sing to the Lord a new song!' (Psalm 149.1) . . . and let not your life bear witness against your tongue. Sing with your voice, sing with your heart, sing with your mouth, sing with your life, 'sing to the Lord a new song'. But how ought you to love him whom you are praising? Without any doubt the one whom you love is the one whom you are seeking to praise. You want to be aware of his glory in order to praise him . . . You all want to be aware of his glory. 'His praise in the assembly of the faithful' (Psalm 149.1). The glory of him who is praised is no other than the singer of the praise. Do you want to sing glory to God? Be yourselves what you sing.

AUGUSTINE OF HIPPO *Sermon 34 on Psalm 149,2-6* (PL 38,210)

John Climacus also uses the intensity of human love to convey the intensity of the *eros* that ought to unite us to God, which is God himself. The image of love and the image of inebriation overlap. The divine *eros* quenches and renews our thirst at the same time – a humble repetition of the enstasy-ecstasy rhythm celebrated by Gregory of Nyssa in his commentary on the Song of Songs.

> Love: its nature is like God . . . its action: inebriation of the soul . . . its proper strength: spring of faith, abyss of patience, ocean of humility.
>
> Love and interior freedom and adoption as sons are distinct from one another only in their names, like light and fire and flame.
>
> If the face of someone we love . . . makes us happy, how great will be the power of the Lord when he comes secretly to dwell in the soul that is pure?
>
> Love is an abyss of light, a fountain of fire. The more it flows the more burning the thirst for it becomes . . . that is why love is an everlasting progression.
>
> JOHN CLIMACUS *The Ladder of Divine Ascent*, 30th step, 3(7) & 4(9) (p. 167), 10(16) (p. 168), 18(37) (p. 169)

The goal of the ascetic life is not to see the translucence of one's own soul. For the love that permeates the spirit comes from Another, whose very transcendence calls for love. Anyone who loves God with the whole of his being receives a 'total sensation of certainty of heart', a heart in which intellect, strength and desire are transfigured in the crucible of grace.

> There is no question that the spirit, when it begins to be frequently under the influence of the divine light becomes wholly translucent, to the point of itself seeing the fullness of its own light . . . But St Paul clearly teaches that everything which appears to it in bodily shape . . . comes from the malice of the enemy, when he says that the enemy disguises himself as an angel of light (2 Corinthians 11.14). The ascetic life must not therefore be undertaken with such a hope in mind . . . its sole purpose is to come to love God with a sensation in the heart of total certainty, which means 'with all your heart, and with all your soul, and with all your strength, and with all your mind' (Luke 10.27).
>
> DIADOCHUS OF PHOTIKE *Gnostic Chapters*, 40 (SC 5 bis, p. 108)

And now, a purple passage from Gregory of Nyssa. The banqueting house, the wine cellar, the must fermenting with a gurgling sound and a heavy scent rising from it, the eager mouth rejecting a cup in order to suck straight from the bung-hole of the barrel, staggering everywhere, a dark red whirlpool, a breaking away from everyday restraints, inebriation with the divine *eros*. One needs to be a vine-grower to understand this text, its sparkling symbolism, the September plenty, the crushed grape, the bodies drenched in must, the new wine . . . it is the poem of a strict ascetic and a mad drunkard. It is a poem of *ekstasis*, of going out of self, when a person is wrenched away from everyday order and convention, and enters into the whole power and spontaneity of the true life.

> The soul then says: 'Bring me into the banqueting house. Spread over me the banner of love' (Song of Songs 2.4) . . . Her thirst has become so strong that she is no longer satisfied with the 'cup of wisdom' (Proverbs 9.2). The whole content of the cup poured into her mouth no longer seems able to quench her thirst. She asks to be taken to the cellar itself and apply her mouth to the rim of the vats themselves that are overflowing with intoxicating wine. She wants to see the grapes squeezed into the vats and the vine that produces these grapes, and the vinedresser of the true vine who has cultivated these grapes . . .
>
> That is why she wants to enter the cellar where the mystery of the wine is performed. Once she has entered she aspires still more highly. She asks to be put under the banner of love. Now love, John says, is God.
>
> GREGORY OF NYSSA *Homilies on the Song of Songs*, 4 (PG 44,845)

And this wine is the living water of which the Gospel speaks. It is the joy of the resurrection becoming consciously ours, and breaching the absurd and the nothingness, making an enclave of non-death in which to leap and dance, as Christ on the fresco of a Byzantine church in Constantinople is dancing and trampling down the gates of hell.

> Deep water has approached my lips,
> springing from the superabundant fountain of the Lord.
> I drank, I am drunk
> with the living water that never dies.
>
> *Odes of Solomon*, 9 (p. 207)

3. *Darkness and Light, God's House, Inward Birth*

We have said that the 'descent' into the heart corresponds to Moses's 'ascent' of Sinai. Moses penetrated then into the darkness where God was. Likewise we, in so far as we are personal existence in relationship, by going beyond any vision of the mind or the body, penetrate into the divine Darkness. It is the symbol and the experience of a presence that cannot be grasped, a night in which the Inaccessible presents himself and eludes us at the same time. It is the nocturnal communion of the hidden God with the person who is hidden in God.

This darkness does not deny the glory that flows from it. It is not the absence of light: rather it is 'more than luminous'. Or again, *coincidentia oppositorum*, the coincidence of opposites (which in their very unity remain opposites): the darkness is simultaneously both the brightest light, dark through excess of brightness, and the blackest obscurity because it is 'transluminous'.

Likewise the darkness does not deny the Word but reaches the Silence in the very heart of the Word.

The divine darkness is entered by 'closing the eyes', that is by renouncing a gaze that is diffusive, objectifying, possessive, and by learning to look inward – or simply with the eyes shut, as in the state of loving abandon.

> At first the revelation of God to Moses is made in light. Then God speaks to him in the cloud. Finally, by climbing up higher, Moses contemplates God in the darkness.
>
> See what we learn from this. The passage from darkness to light is the initial separation from lying and erroneous views about God.
>
> The more attentive awareness of hidden objects, guiding the soul by means of visible things to invisible reality, is like a cloud obscuring the whole perceptible world, leading the soul and accustoming it to the contemplation of what is hidden.
>
> Finally the soul, which has travelled by these ways towards the things that are above and has abandoned everything that is accessible to human nature, penetrates into the sanctuary of the knowledge of God that is wrapped on all sides in darkness. There, as everything perceptible and intelligible has been left outside, there remains for the soul's contemplation only what cannot be grasped by the intellect. It is there that God dwells according to the words of Scripture: 'Moses drew near to the thick darkness' (Exodus 20.21).

GREGORY OF NYSSA *Life of Moses* (PG 44,376-7)

Superessential Trinity, more than divine and more than good, thou that presidest over divine Christian wisdom, lead us not only beyond all light, but even beyond unknowing, up to the highest peak of the mystical Scriptures, to the place where the simple and absolute and incorruptible mysteries of the godhead are revealed, in the more-than-luminous darkness of the Silence. For it is in that Silence that we learn the secrets of the Darkness that shines with the brightest light in the bosom of the blackest obscurity and, while remaining itself utterly intangible and utterly invisible, fills with a brightness more beautiful than beauty the minds that know how to shut their eyes.

DIONYSIUS THE AREOPAGITE *Mystical Theology*, I, 1 (PG 3,997)

Darkness indicates the ultimate meeting, when the human being, in a state of ontological poverty, becomes pure movement towards God, who comes down infinitely lower than his own transcendent state, retaining nothing of himself but the poverty of love. All 'essence' is surpassed, by God in a 'trans-descent', by the human being in a 'trans-ascent'. There is now only an inexpressible communion of persons.

Exercise yourself unceasingly in mystical contemplation; abandon feelings; renounce intellectual activities; reject all that belongs to the perceptible and the intelligible; strip yourself totally of non-being and being and lift yourself as far as you are able to the point of being united in unknowing with him who is beyond all being and all knowledge. For it is by passing beyond everything, yourself included, irresistibly and completely, that you will be exalted in pure ecstasy right up to the dark splendour of the divine Superessence, after having abandoned all, and stripped yourself of everything.

DIONYSIUS THE AREOPAGITE *Mystical Theology*, I, 1 (PG 3, 997-1000)

Instead of speaking of darkness it is equally possible to speak of light, provided that we specify that it is uncreated light issuing inexhaustibly from the Inaccessible. It is more-than-dark light from the hidden God that makes it possible to share in him: energy of the essence that comes from the Father through the Son in the Holy Spirit.

Light like this is inseparable from fire. The chariot by which a person speeds into glory is a heart on fire. (In Jewish mysticism also

one finds this identification of the burning heart with the chariot of
fire by which the prophet Elijah was taken up.) As the icons suggest,
the whole person becomes vision, filled with the light that issues
from the face of the transfigured Christ. The 'food of the Spirit'
and the 'water of life' refer to the inner content of the 'mysteries' –
mysteries of the Name of Jesus, of Scripture, of the Eucharist, of the
baptismal garment of light. To enter into the inner content of these
mysteries is to find immortal life already here below.

> If you have become the throne of God, and the heavenly driver
> has used you for his chariot, and your whole soul has become
> spiritual vision and total light, if you have been fed on the food
> of the Spirit, if you have drunk the water of life and put on the
> garments of indescribable light, if your inner personality has been
> established in the experience and the perfection of all these things,
> then indeed you are truly living eternal life.
>
> PSEUDO-MACARIUS *First Homily*, 12 (PG 34,461)

Like the strange 'living creatures' (cosmic and angelic) in
Ezekiel's vision the soul becomes all eye, meaning pure translucence.
(According to the ancients the eye could only see because it was itself
light.) The soul is filled with the light of Christ, such light as can
almost be identified with the Holy Spirit. All eye, and so all face – a
sign at once of the meeting with God who for us has given expression
to himself, and of an unbounded welcome for one's neighbour.

> The soul that has been judged worthy to share in the Spirit in
> his light, and has been illumined by the splendour of his ineffable
> glory becomes all light, all face, all eye, and no part of it remains
> any longer that is not filled with spiritual eyes and light. That means
> that it has no longer anything dark about it but is wholly Spirit and
> light. It is full of eyes, no longer having a reverse side but showing
> a face all round, for the indescribable beauty of Christ's glory and
> light have come to dwell in it. In the same way as the sun is the
> same all round and does not have any reverse side or lower part
> but is wholly and completely resplendent with its light . . . so the
> soul that has been illumined with the ineffable beauty and the
> glorious brightness of Christ's face and has been filled with the Holy
> Spirit, the soul that has been found worthy to become the dwelling
> and the temple of God, is all eye, all light, all face, all glory and all
> Spirit, since Christ is adorning it in this way, moving it, directing it,

upholding it and guiding it, thus enlightening it and embellishing it
with spiritual beauty.

PSEUDO-MACARIUS *First Homily*, 2 (PG 34,451)

Another profoundly evangelical theme is the 'abiding' or 'indwelling' of God in us. His 'indwelling' makes us temples of God. We
not only listen to the words of Jesus but we welcome his silence into
our hearts, the mysterious presence of the Father and of the Spirit.

It is better to keep silent and to be, rather than to speak but not
to be. One who truly possesses Christ's words can also hear his
silence in order to be perfect ... Nothing is hidden from the
Lord but our very secrets are close to him. Let us do everything
in him who dwells in us so that we may become his temples.

IGNATIUS OF ANTIOCH *Epistle to the Ephesians*, 15,1-3 (SC 10,
p. 84)

The person becomes the unlimited place where God is.

Fear not the coming of your God; fear not his friendship. He will
not straiten you when he comes; rather he will enlarge you. So that
you might know that he will enlarge you he not only promised to
come, saying, 'I will dwell with them,' but he also promised to
enlarge you, adding, 'and I will walk with them.' You see then,
if you love, how much room he gives you. Fear is a suffering that
oppresses us. But look at the immensity of love. 'God's love has
been poured into our hearts' (Romans 5.5).

AUGUSTINE OF HIPPO *Sermons*, 23, 7 (PL 38,157)

God's coming brings joy, happiness, infinite tenderness. And
grace penetrates the body as well as the soul, for man is a living
unity. 'Do you not know that your bodies are members of Christ?
... Do you not know that your body is a temple of the Holy
Spirit?' (1 Corinthians 6.15 & 19)

If you renounce the life you are leading today and if you persevere
in your prayer, you will feel that your effort is securing you great
restfulness. You will discover in these slight pains and fatigues a joy
and a happiness that are immense. God's tender love is ineffable. He
offers himself to those who with all their faith believe that God can
dwell in the human body and make it his glorious abode.

God built heaven and earth to be the dwelling place of the human race. But he also built the human body and soul to make them his own abode, so that he might dwell therein and rest there as in a well kept house . . . 'We are his house' (Hebrews 3.6).

In their houses human beings carefully accumulate their wealth. The Lord in his house, our soul and body, amasses and stores up the heavenly riches of the Spirit.

PSEUDO-MACARIUS *Forty Ninth Homily* (PG 34,813-4)

The astronomical discoveries of the 17th century showed that the physical heavens are empty (but not limitless – curved, Einstein was to say, and contained, but in what?). The technical revolution of our century has finally emancipated the human race from the bosom of the earth, seen now as only a derisory planet circling a mediocre star . . . God and the human race have lost any place in the visible universe. But those places were only symbols. God is the hidden God who transcends the perceptible no less than the intelligible. And amongst us his place is the saint. Or rather, his place is the human being, the image of God, incapable of being limited to this world, who cannot be defined except as indefinable. Holiness proves that. Thus God is the abode of the human race.

And the human being can deliberately become the abode of God.

The Spirit is the place of the saints
and the saint is the place of the Spirit.

BASIL OF CAESAREA *Treatise on the Holy Spirit*, 26 (PG 32,184)

God is the beggar knocking at the door of our soul asking for love. In the following text which forms a counterpoint to that of Gregory of Nyssa, quoted in the preceding section, it is not God who is the banqueting house for us, it is the human being who ought to be the banqueting house for God. In order to welcome the Word the soul must be inebriated with the Holy Spirit.

'Bring me into the banqueting house' (Song of Songs 2.4). Why have I been standing outside for so long? 'Behold, I stand at the door and knock; if anyone . . . opens the door I will come in to him and eat with him, and he with me' (Revelation 3.20). 'Bring me in.' The Word of God is still saying the selfsame thing today ... It is to you he is saying, 'Bring me in' – not just into the house but into the 'banqueting house' – that your soul may be filled with the wine of joy, the wine of the Holy Spirit; and thus you may lead the Bridegroom, the Word, Wisdom, Truth, into your house. So these words may be said even to those who are not yet perfect: 'Bring me into the banqueting house.'

ORIGEN *Homilies on the Song of Songs*, 2,7 (SC 37, p. 92)

Union with God may also be expressed in terms of inward birth. The soul corresponds to the Blessed Virgin. It recalls the mystery of the incarnation. And the incarnation is spiritually extended to holy souls who are thereby preparing for Christ's return. All the mysteries of the Gospel are not only performed in the liturgy but take possession of us in the spiritual life. The Word is continually being born in the stable of our heart. 'Even if Christ were to be born a thousand times at Bethlehem', Angelus Silesius wrote, 'if he is not born in you, you are lost for eternity.' To ensure this birth of Christ in us is the true function of liturgical times and seasons, interpreted inwardly by ascesis, prayer and contemplation.

What came about in bodily form in Mary, the fullness of the godhead shining through Christ in the Blessed Virgin, takes place in a similar way in every soul that has been made pure. The Lord does not come in bodily form, for 'we no longer know Christ according to the flesh', but he dwells in us spiritually and the Father takes up his abode with him, the Gospel tells us.

In this way the child Jesus is born in each one of us.

GREGORY OF NYSSA *On Virginity* (PG 46,324 & 838)

In order that the dispositions of the Gospel and the things of the Holy Spirit may develop in us, their author has to be born in us.

GREGORY OF NYSSA *Against Eunomius* (PG 45,585)

God always wishes to become incarnate in those who are worthy of it.

MAXIMUS THE CONFESSOR *Questions to Thalassius*, 22 (PG 90,321)

To be deified is to enable God to be born in oneself.

DIONYSIUS THE AREOPAGITE *Ecclesiastical Hierarchy*, II, Intro.
(PG 3,392)

4. *The Embrace of the Infinite; the Birth of the Glorious Body*

Through its own transparent 'bareness', the spirit can experience
the infinite, and thus be launched on to the boundless ocean of the
godhead. Essential mysticism, if you wish. What comes to mind here
is the 'bottomless sea of the godhead' of which Ruysbroek speaks
in the *Spiritual Marriage*, and also Angelus Silesius, noting in his
Cherubic Pilgrim that 'in God nothing is known; he is a unique Unity.
Whatever is known in him cannot but be ourselves.' However, in
Maximus (more clearly than in Evagrius, whom he seems here to
be quoting) the divine essence – or the outpouring of its radiance–
is situated within a personal presence, and is contemplated at the
heart of a meeting, of a communion. Moreover, if we manage to look
behind differences in terminology and our own assumptions about
what is meant, we shall see that the Western 'essential mystics' teach
the same, as Vladimir Lossky has shown with reference to Eckhart in
his *Negative Theology and Knowledge of God in Meister Eckhart*.

> When the mind receives the representations of objects it naturally
> copies each of them. When it contemplates them spiritually it
> takes on different forms of being according to the objects of its
> contemplation. When it is in God it dispenses with any shape or
> form whatever.
>
> MAXIMUS THE CONFESSOR *Centuries on Charity*, III, 97 (PG 90,
> 1048)

God's love for the individual, when he accepts it, inflames his
heart and his body. He is held up in the presence of the Wholly
Other in a continuing dialogue. This communion enables the divine
life to take hold of him. And here once again there is not only the
symbol but also the reality of an exalted inebriation that transports
him past all limits, whether of modesty or of death, in the direction
of heaven. 'The inebriation leads us into what I might call the domain
of the uncontrollable, the domain of the divine Power that breaks
all bounds, brings down all barriers, and fills us with the Holy
Spirit' (Quoted from a monk of the Eastern Church, *La Colombe*

et l'Agneau, Chevetogne 1979, p. 61). Meeting and sharing together – they suggest the picture of marriage, of two people madly in love.

> God's love is by its nature warmth. When it lights on someone without any limit, it plunges the soul into ecstasy. That is why the heart of one who has felt it cannot bear to be deprived of it. But he gradually undergoes a strange alteration in proportion to the love that enters into him. These are the signs of that love: his face becomes inflamed with joy and his body is filled with warmth. Fear and shame desert him as if he had gone outside himself . . . he is like a lunatic; a terrible death is a joy to him . . . he no longer has his normal awareness or his natural sight. He no longer knows what he is doing. Although he continues to act he feels nothing, as if his mind were suspended in contemplation. His thought is in continual dialogue with the Other.
>
> ISAAC OF NINEVEH *Ascetic Treatises*, 24 (p. 104)

The world is within for the spiritual person. So are the angels, who are at the same time a personal presence and a translucent degree of universal existence, a universe of music and praise around the Lord. So too is the Trinity itself who comes to take up its abode in him. 'The kingdom of God is within you', Jesus said. A more-than-subjective fulfilment opens the inner person to the most real of realities.

> Purify yourself and you will see heaven in yourself. In yourself you will see angels and their brightness, and you will see their Master with them and in them . . .
> The spiritual homeland of the person whose soul has been purified is within. The sun that shines there is the light of the Trinity. The air breathed by the entering thoughts is the Holy Spirit the Comforter. With the person dwell the angels. Their life, their joy, their cause for celebration is Christ the light of the Father's light. Such a person rejoices every hour in the contemplation of his soul, and marvels at the beauty that appears, a hundred times brighter than the brightness of the sun . . . That is the kingdom of God hidden within us, according to the words of the Lord.
>
> ISAAC OF NINEVEH *Ascetic Treatises*, 43 (p. 176-7)

True knowledge is to be aware of all things in God. This brings such happiness that the heart is consumed in love and the person is

ready to die for the beloved, that is to say for all and for each one
individually.

> Love is sweeter than life.
> Sweeter still, sweeter than honey and the honeycomb
> is the awareness of God whence love is born.
> Love is not loth to accept the hardest of deaths
> for those it loves.
> Love is the child of knowledge . . .
> Lord, fill my heart with eternal life.
>
> Isaac of Nineveh *Ascetic Treatises*, 38 (p. 164)

Mysteries of the divine embrace. The enjoyment of God fills the
spirit, but also the body. It penetrates and awakens the habitually
unconscious depths of bodily existence. Between sleep and wakefulness, when the frontier can be crossed that separates the conscious
from the unconscious, when the body within the body is exposed,
enjoyment seizes hold of the whole personality. This is the joy of the
Kingdom. This is the joy of the eternal marriage feast.

> It happens at certain moments that delight and enjoyment invade
> the whole body. And the fleshly tongue can say no more; to
> such a degree now have earthly objects become but dust and
> ashes. The initial delights, those of the heart, fill us while we
> are awake. The spirit burns at the hour of prayer, at the mo-
> ment of reading, in the course of frequent meditations or long
> contemplations. But the final delights come to us differently, often
> during the night, in the following way: when we are between sleep
> and wakefulness, when we are asleep without being asleep and
> awake without being really awake. These delights invade a person
> and the whole body throbs. It is clear then that this is nothing
> other than the kingdom of heaven.
>
> Isaac of Nineveh *Ascetic Treatises*, 8 (p. 39)

The brightness is sometimes so great that one has to cry out.
This is the ultimate fulfilment of the Song of Songs.

> A hundred times mingling love and fervour this [monk] would
> kiss the cross . . . then return to psalmody. And the thoughts
> that were inflaming him with their heat so burned within him that

he would cry out, giving in to the joy, when he could not bear the brightness of that flame.

Isaac of Nineveh *Ascetic Treatises*, 75 (p. 294)

There are cries, but also abysses of silence, immersion in an ocean of light and of silence. The personality is not dissolved. The longing attacks again; the tenderness is once again embedded in the person.

It is not easy to know how and in what respects spiritual tenderness overwhelms the soul. Often it is by an ineffable joy and by vehement aspirations that its presence is revealed. So much so that the joy is rendered unbearable by its very intensity, and breaks out into cries that carry tidings of your inebriation as far as a neighbouring cell. Sometimes on the contrary the whole soul descends and lies hidden in abysses of silence. The suddenness of the light stupefies it and robs it of speech. All its senses remain withdrawn in its inmost depths or completely suspended. And it is by inarticulate groans that it tells God of its desire. Sometimes, finally, it is so swollen with a sorrowful tenderness that only tears can give it consolation.

John Cassian *Conferences*, IX, 27 (SC 54, p. 63)

God is felt by the 'feeling of the heart'. Others, more succinctly, speak here of the 'feeling of God'. It is a paradox for minds formed by the Greek language and Greek thought to associate the divine with feeling. The whole of a philosophical tradition, in fact, could regard only the mind, the intellect, the power of reasoning as in any way similar to the divine. The fact that it is a question of a 'feeling' or of bringing into play the heart, where all the faculties and all the senses are gathered together, proves that it is a metamorphosis of the whole personality, body and soul, by the divine energy. Diadochus speaks more exactly of this organic unity when he notes that the 'feeling of the heart' becomes a 'feeling of the bones' – the bones, that part of the human being that is the hardest, the most alive, the mineral concentration of life and its source (the connection between the marrow of the bones and the blood is well known). When the divine fire reaches this living stone, it transforms it into precious stone, integrates it into the foundations of the heavenly Jerusalem, which are built of such precious stones. In this way the glorious body is formed.

One who knows God by the feeling of the heart has been known by him: to the extent, in fact, that the person has received God's love into the secret places of the soul, that person has become

God's friend. Therefore such a one from then on lives with a burning desire for the enlightenment of knowledge until it is recognizable by the very feeling in the bones. The person no longer knows himself but has been entirely transformed by God's love ... Without respite from now on the heart is ablaze with the fire of love, united to God by an irresistible longing, since the person has been once and for all torn away from the self by divine love.

DIADOCHUS OF PHOTIKE *Gnostic Chapters*, 14 (SC 5 bis, p. 91)

The body of slavery and death, tied to the 'spirit of heaviness', is dissolved in the waters of baptism, the waters of creation, and now the glorious body is born, not just symbolically but in actual fact. Or, if you prefer, the seed of baptism is now bearing its fruit.

Hence these powerful and meaningful expressions: 'I am dissolved', 'his limbs are melting'.

The disciple of Abba Silvanus, Zachary, went in and found him in ecstasy with his hands stretched up to heaven. Closing the door he went out. He came back at the sixth and the ninth hour and found him in the same state. At the tenth hour he knocked, went in and found him inwardly at peace. So he said to him, 'How have you been today, Father?' Silvanus replied, 'I was carried up to heaven and saw the glory of God. And I stayed there until just now. And now I am dissolved.'

Sayings of the Desert Fathers, Silvanus 3 (PG 65,409)

A different state overtakes us when we are going forward on the path of life ... and from on high the grace is given us to experience the sweetness of the awareness of the Spirit. We receive the certainty that God is watching over us ... and we are full of admiration at the spiritual nature of objects ... It is then that the sweetness of God and the fire of his love enter into us ... This power is felt when all the beings of the created world, all the objects that we meet, are observed with contemplative attention ... As a result of this careful attention we attain to God's love from then on and are inebriated with it as if with wine. Our limbs melt. Our spirit is outside itself. And our heart is carried away after God.

ISAAC OF NINEVEH *Ascetic Treatises*, 40 (p. 169)

It is an experience that is continually attested and renewed, of light, or rather of fire. The heart is the crucible in which the divine fire re-creates the personality. And there are numerous testimonies to show saints transfigured as Christ was transfigured on Tabor; the rays of the divine light penetrated his flesh itself. And it is by sharing in his very flesh through the mysteries of the Church that the glorious body is awoken in us.

> A brother came to Abba Arsenius's cell. He half-opened the door and saw the Abba as it were all on fire.
>
> *Sayings of the Desert Fathers*, Arsenius 27 (PG 65,96)

> Ascesis . . . is setting a log of wood wholly on fire.
>
> *Sayings of Those who are Growing Old in Ascesis*, 32 (SO 1, p. 407)

> One who watches carefully over the heart will quickly see how the heart of its own nature is emitting light. As a coal catches fire, or as the fire lights a candle, so does God set our heart ablaze as it looks in contemplation at him who is dwelling in our heart.
>
> HESYCHIUS OF BATOS *On Vigilance*, 104 (Philokalia I,157)

> Peter and the Sons of Thunder saw Beauty on the mountain, Beauty that was shining brighter than the brilliance of the sun. Thus they were judged worthy to see with their own eyes the pledge of his coming in glory.
>
> BASIL OF CÆSAREA *Homily on Psalm 45*, 5 (PG 29,400)

> Today the divine brightness in its limitless diffusion is shining for the apostles on Mount Tabor . . . The divine light is radiating from an earthly body. The glory of the godhead is emanating from a mortal body . . . The godhead is triumphant and enables the body to share in his own brightness and his own glory.
>
> JOHN OF DAMASCUS *Homily on the Transfiguration of the Lord* (PG 96,545,548)

5. Martyrdom: Death-and-Resurrection

Martyrdom means witness. But to bear witness to Christ to the point of death is to become one who has risen again. Christian martyrdom is a mystical experience, the first attested in the history of the Church. It is recorded right at the beginning by the example of Stephen the 'protomartyr' in the *Acts of the Apostles* thus: '[Stephen], full of the Holy Spirit, gazed into heaven, and saw the glory of God, and Jesus standing at the right hand of God; and he said, "Behold, I see the heavens opened, and the Son of Man standing at the right hand of God" . . . Then they cast him out of the city and they stoned him; . . . And as they were stoning Stephen, he prayed, "Lord Jesus, receive my spirit." And he knelt down and cried with a loud voice, "Lord, do not hold this sin against them." And when he said this, he fell asleep' (Acts 7.55-60). Vision of glory . . . prayer for the executioners . . . when history comes full circle and another witness is put to death, this very death 'opens the heavens' and allows the energies of love to make their entry into the world.

Martyrdom was the first form of sanctity to be venerated in the Church. And when there were no longer any martyrs in blood, martyrs in ascesis, monks, came instead. It was the monks who coined the saying that expresses the meaning of martyrdom: 'Give your blood and receive the Spirit.' Then martyrdom returned.

A martyr can be, at first sight, any man or woman at all. But when they are crushed by the suffering they are identified with the Crucified Christ, and the power of the resurrection takes hold of them. In very direct accounts composed at the time without embellishments, at the beginning of the third century, we see a young Christian woman in prison lamenting the birth of her child (if a pregnant woman was arrested she was not sent to execution till after the birth). The gaoler jeers at her. But Felicity gently explains to him that in the moment of her martyrdom *another* will suffer in her. Her friend Perpetua in fact feels nothing when she is exposed to the wild bulls. She is momentarily spared before coming out of the 'ecstasy of the Spirit', as if awakening from a deep sleep. And the martyrs, before meeting death together, give one another the kiss of peace, as during the eucharistic liturgy.

For the authentic Christian, death does not exist. He casts himself into the risen Christ. In him death is a celebration of life.

> Felicity was eight months pregnant when she was arrested . . . Her labour pains came upon her . . . She was suffering a great deal and groaning. One of the gaolers said to her, 'If you are already crying out like this, what will you do when you are thrown to the wild beasts? . . .' Felicity answered him, 'Then there will be another within me who will suffer for me because it is on his account that I am suffering . . .'
>
> Perpetua was tossed in the air first [by a furious bull]. She fell on her back. As soon as she could sit up . . . she pinned back her hair which had come loose. A martyr cannot die with disshevelled

hair, lest she seem to be in mourning on the day of her glory. Then she got up and noticed Felicity who seemed to have collapsed. She went to her, gave her her hand and helped her to her feet. When they saw both of them standing up, the cruelty of the crowd was subdued. The martyrs were taken out through the gate of the living.

There Perpetua was welcomed by a catechumen, Rusticus, who was very much attached to her. She seemed to awake out of a deep sleep, so long had the ecstasy lasted. She looked around her and asked, 'When shall we be delivered to the bull?' When she was told it had already taken place she could not believe it, and refused to accept the evidence until she saw on her dress and on her body the traces of the ordeal. Then she called her brother and the catechumen. She said to them, 'Remain steadfast in the faith. Love one another. Do not let our sufferings be a subject of scandal for you . . .'

The people demanded that the wounded be brought back into the arena so that they could enjoy the spectacle of the sword piercing the living bodies . . . The martyrs . . . came to the place that the crowd wanted. They gave one another the kiss of peace to consummate their martyrdom, in accordance with the rite of faith. All of them remained motionless to receive the fatal blow.

Martyrdom of Felicity and Perpetua, in the year 203, at Carthage (Knopf-Krüger, p. 35-44)

The blood of the martyrs is identified with that of Golgotha, and so with that of the Eucharist, which imparts the inebriation of eternity. The martyr becomes Eucharist, *becomes Christ*. And that is why the relics of the martyrs, regarded as fragments of the glorified cosmos, of the 'world to come', are enshrined in the altars on which the Eucharist is celebrated.

O blessed martyrs, human grapes of God's vineyard, your wine inebriates the Church . . . When saints made themselves ready for the banquet of suffering they drank the draught pressed out on Golgotha and thus they penetrated into the mysteries of God's house. And so we sing, 'Praise be to Christ who inebriates the martyrs with the blood from his side.'

RABULAS OF EDESSA *Hymn to the Martyrs* (Bickell II, p. 262)

In the following passage from the letter written by Ignatius of Antioch to the Christians of Rome – the bishop of Antioch was being led to the capital of the Empire for solemn execution, at the beginning of the second century – almost all the aspects of this 'death-and-reurrection' are brought together. The martyr crushed by the teeth of wild animals, like grains of wheat in the mill, becomes eucharistic matter; he shares fully in Christ's divinizing flesh; he reproduces, in a quasi-liturgical sense, the Passion of the Crucified, in order to put on the Glorified, and to feel his victorious power. *Victor*, the conqueror, was the name given to every martyr. In Christ the Spirit is, for Ignatius, a stream of living water that leads to the Father.

Here the body of death is no longer dissolved by ascesis and spiritual experience, but all at once by human violence. The martyr hastens the coming to birth of the glorious body.

> I am writing to all the Christians to tell all of them that I am gladly going to die for God ... Let me be the food of beasts thanks to which I shall be able to find God. I am God's wheat and I am being ground by the teeth of wild beasts in order to become Christ's pure bread ... By suffering I shall be a freedman of Jesus Christ and I shall be born again in him, free ... let no being, visible or invisible, prevent me out of jealousy from finding Christ. Let fire and cross, wild animals, torture, disclocation of my bones, mutilation of my limbs, the grinding to pieces of my whole body, the worst assaults of the devil fall on me, provided only that I find Jesus Christ ... My new birth is close at hand. Forgive me, brethren, do not hinder me from living. Let me come into the pure light. When I reach that point I shall be a man. Allow me to reproduce the passion of my God. May anyone who has God in him understand what I desire and take pity on me, knowing what it is that straitens me ... My earthly desires have been crucified. There is no longer in me any fire to love material objects, only living water that murmurs within me, 'Come to the Father' ... It is the bread of God that I desire, which is the flesh of Jesus Christ ... and for drink I desire his blood, which is imperishable love.

IGNATIUS OF ANTIOCH *To the Romans*, 4-7 (SC 10, p. 130-7)

In the account of the martydom of Polycarp, bishop of Smyrna, in the same period, one is struck by the affectionate simplicity of the man and the power of his intercession. He welcomes the police officers as neighbours sent to him by God. He does not pray for himself but for all those whom he has met, good or bad, and for the universal Church.

Since his conscience is involved, the martyr deliberately disobeys the authorities. He calmly proclaims before magistrates and crowd that the only 'Lord' is Christ, namely God-made-man, and not the holder of power, not the sacralized might of Rome. Thereby he asserts the transcendence of conscience, of the person made in the image of God. He makes his own the protest of Antigone and Socrates, but in the joy of the resurrection. He radically relativizes political importance.

For all that, the martyr is not a rebel. Like Socrates, he accepts the sentence of the magistrates and prays for the Emperor. By that very fact he is a blessing to the city of men, and without disrupting it he enriches it with an uncompromising freedom.

The end of the passage takes up again the identification of martyrdom with the Eucharist, the witness of victory over death.

> Learning then that the police officers were there, he [Polycarp] went down and talked to them. They were amazed at his age and his calmness and at the trouble that was being taken to arrest a man as old as he. He had served them with as much food and drink as they wished, asking them only for an hour to pray as he desired. They allowed him that, and standing upright he began to pray, so full of God's grace that for two hours he could not stop, and those who heard him were astonished, and many repented of having come to arrest so holy an old man.
>
> In his prayer he remembered all the people he had ever met, illustrious or obscure, and the whole catholic Church spread throughout the world. When he had finished, the hour having come to depart, they mounted him on an ass and took him to the city ... Quickly they piled round him the materials prepared for the pyre. As they were about to nail him to it he said, 'Leave me like this. He who gives me strength to endure the fire will also enable me to remain firm at the stake.' Accordingly they did not nail him to it, but they bound him. With his hands behind his back he looked like a ram chosen for sacrifice from a large flock ...
>
> Raising his eyes to heaven he said:
>
> 'Lord, almighty God, Father of thy well-beloved and blessed Son Jesus Christ through whom we have received the knowledge of thy name, God ... of all creation ... I bless thee for having judged me worthy of this day and of this hour, to share among the number of thy martyrs in the chalice of thy Christ, looking for the resurrection of body and soul in the fullness of the Holy Spirit ... And so for everything I praise thee, I bless thee, I glorify thee, through the eternal heavenly high priest Jesus Christ thy well-beloved Son, through whom be glory to thee with him and

the Holy Spirit, now and for ever. Amen.' . . . In the midst of the
fire he stood, not like burning flesh, but like bread baking.

Martyrdom of St Polycarp, Bishop of Smyrna, 7,2-8,1;14,1-3;15,2
(SC 10, pp. 250,252,260,262,264)

The following dreams, which are visions, show the souls of the
martyrs taking part in the heavenly liturgy as it is described in the
Apocalypse. The gardens of paradise with the leaves of the trees
singing to the breeze of the Spirit, a temple or a palace with walls of
light; at the centre of it all, the Ancient of Days with white hair but
a face radiating youth; the face of Christ in the youthfulness of the
Spirit; the kiss of peace; the mouthful of food offered by the Shepherd;
the ineffable perfume that is as food; so many symbols of the mystical
state of martyrdom similar to the actual experience of the Eucharist.

Perpetua's Vision

Then I went up. I saw an enormous garden. In the middle there was
a tall man dressed as a shepherd. He was engaged in milking sheep.
Around him, in thousands, were men clothed in white. He raised
his head, looked at me and said, 'Welcome, my child.' He called me
and gave me a mouthful of the cheese he was preparing. I received
it with hands joined. I ate it and they all said 'Amen'. At the sound
of the voices I woke up with the taste of a strange sweetness in my
mouth. I related this vision at once to my brother [Saturus] and we
understood that it was martyrdom that awaited us.

Saturus's Vision

Our martyrdom was over. We had left our bodies behind. Four
angels carried us towards the East but their hands did not touch
us . . . When we had gone through the first sphere that encircles
the earth we saw a great light. Then I said to Perpetua who was at
my side, 'This is what the Lord has promised us.' We had reached
a vast open plain that seemed to be a garden with oleanders and
every type of flower. The trees were as tall as cypresses and their
leaves sang without ceasing . . . We arrive at a palace whose walls
seem to be made of light. We go in and hear a choir repeating,
'Holy, Holy, Holy.' In the hall is seated a man clothed in white.
He has a youthful face and his hair shines white as snow. On either
side of him stand four elders . . . We go forward in amazement and
we kiss the Lord who caresses us with his hand. The elders say to

us, 'Stand up!' We obey and exchange the kiss of peace ... We recognized many of the brethren martyrs like us. For food we all had an ineffable perfume that satisfied us wholly.

Martyrdom of Felicity and Perpetua (Knopf-Krüger)

6. Deification

The whole of this transformation of the human being is summed up by the Fathers in the celebrated formula, 'God became man in order that man might become God'. In order, that is, for him to share through grace in the divine nature, as the Second Epistle of the apostle Peter says (1.4).

This formula does not in any way imply the removal of the human element. On the contrary, it foreshadows its fullness in Christ who is true God and true man. The human part is given life by the Spirit. 'God became the bearer of flesh,' says Athanasius, 'in order that man might become bearer of the Spirit' (*On the Incarnation*, 8).

The human being is truly human only in God. The Word, incarnate, crucified, glorified, constitutes the place of resurrection, the Pentecostal place where humanity is raised up towards God.

Because God has become man, man can become God. He rises by divine steps corresponding to those by which God humbled himself out of love for men, taking on himself without any change in himself the worst of our condition.

MAXIMUS THE CONFESSOR *Theological and Economic Chapters* (PG 90,1165)

In Christ the Holy Spirit imparts to human beings a renewed sonship of God. They share in the eternal procreation of the Son. They are introduced into the heart of the Trinity. Deification is identified with this adoption.

'In him [Christ] the whole fullness of deity dwells bodily,' says St Paul (Colossians 2.9). And John the Theologian reveals this sublime mystery to us when he says that the Word dwells among us (John 1.14). For we are all in Christ, and the humanity we all share in him regains its life in him. The Word dwelt amongst us through a single Person in order that, from the one true Son of God, his dignity might pass into all humankind by means of the sanctifying Spirit, and through a single Person the words might be fulfilled, 'I say, "You are gods, sons of the Most High, all of you"' (Psalm 82.6; John 10.34).

CYRIL OF ALEXANDRIA *Commentary on John's Gospel*, 1,14 (PG 73,161)

It is a transformation made possible by the Church, in so far as it is 'mystery' – sacrament in the ontological sense – and unites us with the human nature of the Word, that is full to the brim with divine energies, with the presence and power of the *Pneuma*.

[The body of the Word] in its own nature has been enriched with the Word who is united to it. It has become holy, life-giving, full of the divine energy. And in Christ we too are transfigured.

CYRIL OF ALEXANDRIA *That Christ is One* (PG 75,1269)

[Christ] fills his whole body with the life-giving energy of the Spirit. For henceforward he calls his flesh Spirit without denying that it is flesh . . . It is united in fact to the Word who is life.

CYRIL OF ALEXANDRIA *Commentary on John's Gospel*, 6,64 (PG 73,604)

The Alexandrine Fathers, and especially St Cyril, developed this mysticism of the adoption that deifies. Only the Word is the Son by nature, but in his body, in his Spirit, we become 'sons by participation'. This is an energy-based, spirit-filled Christology in which the humanity is shot through with the brightness of the divinity like iron red-hot in the fire.

Participation in the Holy Spirit gives human beings the grace to be shaped as a complete copy of the divine nature.

CYRIL OF ALEXANDRIA *Treasure*, 13 (PG 75,228)

Anyone who receives the image of the Son, that is the Spirit, possesses thereby in all fullness the Son, and the Father who is in him.

CYRIL OF ALEXANDRIA *Treasure*, 33 (PG 75,572)

To be deified is therefore to become someone living with a life stronger than death, since the Word is life itself and the Spirit is the one who brings life. All human possibilities are brought into play. The structures of thought, feeling, friendship, creativity, while remaining only human structures, receive an infinite capacity for light and joy and love.

> It is not possible to live without life and there is no life except by participation in God. Such participation consists in seeing God and rejoicing in his fullness.
>
> IRENÆUS OF LYONS *Against Heresies*, IV,20,5 (SC 100 bis, p. 642)

> The glory of God is a living person and the life of humanity is the vision of God. If the revelation of God through creation already gives life to all living beings on earth, how much more does the manifestation of the Father through the Son give life to those who see God.
>
> IRENÆUS OF LYONS *Against Heresies*, IV,20,7 (SC 100 bis, p. 648)

> God is himself the life of those who participate in him.
>
> IRENÆUS OF LYONS *Against Heresies*, V,7,1 (SC p. 153,86-8)

Thus holiness is life in its fullness. And there is holiness in each human being who participates vigorously in life. There is holiness not only in the great ascetic but in the creator of beauty, in the seeker after truth who heeds the mystery of creation, both living and inanimate, in the deep love of a man and a woman, in the mother who knows how to console her child and how to bring it to spiritual birth.

> The saints are the living ones: and the living ones are the saints.
>
> ORIGEN *Commentary on John's Gospel*, 2,11 (GCS 4,74)

Let us bear in mind that the virtues are divine-human: they are a sharing in the attributes of God. Through them God becomes human in the human being and makes the human being God.

> The spirit that is united to God by prayer and by love acquires wisdom, goodness, power, beneficence, generosity ... in a word, that person bears the attributes of God.
>
> MAXIMUS THE CONFESSOR *Centuries on Charity*, III,52 (PG 90, 1001)

In the deified person is reconstituted the single sense that brings together intellect, emotions and vigour, and transfigures them into the divine light. 'Your youth is renewed like the eagle's,' says the psalm (Psalm 103.5).

> Spiritual awareness teaches us that the soul has only one natural sense . . . shattered in consequence of Adam's disobedience. But it is restored to unity by the Holy Spirit . . . In those who are detached from the lusts of life, the spirit, because it is thus freed, acquires its full vigour, and can experience in an ineffable manner the divine fullness. It then imparts its joy to the body itself . . . 'In him,' says the psalmist, 'my flesh has blossomed afresh'.
>
> DIADOCHUS OF PHOTIKE *Gnostic Chapters*, 25 (SC 5 bis, p. 96-7)

Already here below, the human being becomes one who is 'risen again'. This is the 'little resurrection' of which Evagrius speaks. It anticipates the definitive victory over death and the transfiguration of the cosmos that will happen at the moment of the Parousia.

Communion with God is, then, a sharing in his very being. By grace, according to the energy, the sharers are identified with him in whom they share. Motion and rest balance and reinforce each other: rest in the identity, motion in the irreducible otherness.

> The aim of faith is the true revelation of its object. And the true revelation of faith's object is ineffable communion, with him, and this communion is the return of believers to their beginning as much as to their end . . . and therefore the satisfaction of desire. And the satisfaction of desire is the stability, eternally in motion, of those who desire, around the object of their desire . . . resulting in eternal enjoyment of it without any separation . . . the sharing in the things of God. And this sharing in the things of God is the similarity between the sharers and him in whom they share. And this similarity, thanks to the energy, becomes identity of the sharers with him in whom they share . . . This identity is deification.
>
> MAXIMUS THE CONFESSOR *Questions to Thalassius*, 59 (PG 90,202)

Only apparent contradiction can convey the meaning of deification. The human being while remaining completely human is completely enlightened by glory.

> *The deified person, while remaining completely human in nature, both in body and soul, becomes wholly God in both body and

soul, through grace and the divine brightness of the beatifying glory that permeates the whole person.

MAXIMUS THE CONFESSOR *Ambigua* (PG 91,1088)

God envelops in his fullness the person whom he deifies. And that person by the clinging power of love is united wholly to the divine energy. From now on there is only one energy of God and the saints: God is 'all in all', 'everything in everything'.

The creature, having by deification become God, no longer displays any energy other than the divine, so that in everything from now on there is only one energy belonging to God and to his elect, or rather, henceforward there is only God, because the whole of his being, as is proper to love, enters into the whole of the being of his elect.

MAXIMUS THE CONFESSOR *Ambigua*, 7 (PG 91,1076)

Everything, however, remains pointing towards the transfiguration of the cosmos. Everything is still caught up in the dynamism of the communion of saints and, through it, in the power of the general resurrection.

The communion of saints delineates little by little the face of Christ who is coming. It gives birth to the Logos in history and in the universe, or rather, it gives birth to history and the universe in the Logos. The light of Mount Tabor which is the light of Easter is gradually spreading. It already shines brightly in holiness. It will set everything ablaze at the Parousia.

The Word comes to dwell in the saints by imprinting on them in advance, in a mystery, the form of his future advent, as an icon.

MAXIMUS THE CONFESSOR *Gnostic Centuries* II,28 (PG 90,1092)

There, in peace, we shall see that it is he who is God ... we who were unfaithful to this God, who would have made us gods if ingratitude had not banished us from communion with him ... Created anew in him and made perfect in a more plentiful grace, we shall see in that eternal rest that it is he who is God, he with whom we shall be filled, because he will be all in all ... that day will be our Sabbath and it will have no evening, but it will end in an eternal Sunday. That Sunday will be the revelation of the resurrection of Christ, who offers to all of us perpetual fullness, not only of the soul but of the body. There we shall be in peace and we shall see. We shall see and we shall love. We shall love and we shall worship.

AUGUSTINE OF HIPPO *The City of God*, XXII,30,4 (PL 41,803)

Just as the body of the Lord was glorified on the mountain when it was transfigured in the glory of God and in infinite light, so the bodies of the saints will be glorified and shine like lightning ... 'The glory which thou hast given me I have given to them' (John 17.22). As countless candles are lighted from a single flame, so the bodies of all Christ's members will be what Christ is ... Our human nature is transformed into the fullness of God; it becomes wholly fire and light.

PSEUDO-MACARIUS *Fifteenth Homily*, 38 (PG 34,602)

The fire that is hidden and as it were smothered under the ashes of this world ... will blaze out and with its divinity burn up the husk of death.

GREGORY OF NYSSA *Against Eunomius*, 5 (PG 45,708)

What is hidden within will cover up completely what is seen on the outside.

GREGORY OF NYSSA *Homilies on the Beatitudes*, 7 (PG 44,1289)

Resurrection begins already here below. For the early Church a deeply spiritual man is one who is already 'risen again'. The truest moments of our life, those lived in the invisible, have a resurrection flavour. Resurrection begins every time that a person, breaking free from conditionings, transfigures them. Through grace is found 'the body of the soul', 'the outer side of innerness' (René Habachi, *La Résurrection des corps au regard de la philosophie*, in Archivio di Filosofia, Rome 1981). Resurrection begins every time that a person plunges this world's opaque, divisive, death-riddled modality into its Christ-centred modality, into that 'ineffable and marvellous fire hidden in the essence of things, as in the Burning Bush' (Maximus the Confessor, *Ambigua*, PG 91,1148). Teilhard de Chardin, at the end of a questionable theory of evolution, rediscovered this lofty vision of the Greek Fathers: 'Like a flash of lightning darting from one pole to the other, the presence of Christ, which has silently grown up in created objects, will all of a sudden reveal itself ... Like a thunderbolt, like a conflagration, like a flood, all the swirling elements of the universe will be seized by the attractive power of the

Son of Man, to be brought into unity or subjected to his body' (*Le Milieu Divin*, Paris 1957, p. 196).

The saints are seeds of resurrection. Only they can steer the blind sufferings of history towards resurrection.

4

The Difficult Love

While [the abbot] is preoccupied with exterior matters he must not lessen his solicitude for the interior. Nor when he is preoccupied with the interior may he relax his watch on the exterior. Otherwise, by giving himself up to pressing duties from outside, he would experience an interior collapse; or by keeping himself busy solely on interior matters, he would be neglecting his external duties towards his neighbour.

GREGORY THE GREAT *Pastoral Rule*, 1,7 (PL 77,38)

Amid the tumult of outward cares, inwardly a great peace and calm is reigning, in love.

GREGORY THE GREAT *Commentary on the Book of Job*, 18,43,70 (PL 76,79)

1. *The Foundations of Love*

Spiritual progress has no other test in the end, nor any better expression, than our ability to love. It has to be unselfish love founded on respect, a service, a disinterested affection that does not ask to be paid in return, a 'sympathy', indeed an 'empathy' that takes us out of ourselves enabling us to 'feel with' the other person and indeed to 'feel in' him or her. It gives us the ability to discover in the other person an inward nature as mysterious and deep as our own, but different and willed to be so by God.

In this fallen world the unity of human beings has been broken, everything is a 'rat race', and I try to free myself from the anguish that torments me by projecting it on to another, the scapegoat of my tragic finiteness. The other person is always my enemy and I need him to be so. In Christ, however, death has been defeated, my inner hell transformed into the Church, I no longer need to have enemies, no one is separated from anyone. The criterion of the depth of one's spiritual growth is therefore love for one's enemies, in accordance with the paradoxical commandment of the Gospel that takes its meaning solely from the cross – Christ's cross and ours – and from the resurrection – again Christ's and our own.

> One day I saw three monks insulted and humiliated in the same way at the same moment. The first felt he had been cruelly hurt; he was distressed but managed not to say anything. The second was happy for himself but grieved for the one who had insulted him. The third thought only of the harm suffered by his neighbour, and wept with the most ardent compassion. The first was prompted by fear; the second was urged on by the hope of reward; the third was moved by love.
>
> JOHN CLIMACUS *The Ladder of Divine Perfection*, 8th step, 29(34) (p. 73)

The true miracle, the most difficult achievement, is therefore the example and the practice of love in the spiritual sense of that word (and here the Gospel speaks of *agape*, the Latin *caritas*). To enter into God is to let oneself be caught up in the immense movement of the love of the Trinity which reveals the other person to us as 'neighbour' or (and this is better) which enables each one of us to become the 'neighbour' of others. And to become a 'neighbour' is to side with Christ, since he identifies himself with every human being who is suffering, or rejected, or imprisoned, or ignored. We need only call to mind the Last Judgement scene in the Gospel according to St Matthew: "I was hungry and you gave me food, I was thirsty and you gave me drink, I was a stranger and you welcomed me, I was naked and you clothed me, I was sick and you visited me, I was in prison and came to me" . . . "Lord, when did we see thee hungry and feed thee, or thirsty and give thee drink? And when did we see thee a stranger and welcome thee, or naked and clothe thee? And when did we see thee sick or in prison visit thee?" And the King will answer them, "Truly I say to you, as you did it to of the least of these my brethren, you did to me"' (Matthew 25.35-40).

The love which is *agape* discovers that each individual, and especially each one who is suffering, is a sacrament of Christ, 'another Christ' as St John Chrysostom says. The human being is a creature in relationship, after the likeness of the Triune God.

> After having given us these seeds which he cast into our hearts, the Lord comes to look for the fruits and says, 'A new commandment I give to you, that you love one another' (John 13.34). Although he wished to stir up our souls to keep this commandment, the Lord did not require prodigies or unprecedented miracles of his disciples, as proof of their fidelity – although he had given them, in the Spirit, the power to perform them. But what did he say to them? 'By this all will know that you are my disciples, if you have love for one another' (John 13.35). He combines these two commandments in such a way as to assign to himself the benefits we confer on our neighbour. 'For I was hungry,' he says, 'and you gave me food.' And he adds, 'As you did it to one of the least of these my brethren, you did it to me' (Matthew 25.35). Thus by means of the first commandment it is possible to keep the second, and by the second commandment to go back to the first; by loving the Lord to love also our neighbour, for, 'He who loves me,' says the Lord, 'will keep my commandments,' and 'My commandmentment is that you should love one another as I have loved you'.
>
> BASIL OF CÆSAREA *Longer Rules*, 3, 1 & 2 (PG 30,340)

Take the analogy of the circle, or better still of its radii. The radii are separate. But at the centre they meet. To approach the centre, which is God, is to have the revelation of one's neighbour. For only by revelation does one know another person as a person, with a knowledge that is also unknowing. Love is poverty, *kenosis*. Knowing one's neighbour is inseparable from an attitude of non-possession.

> This is the nature of love: to the extent that we distance ourselves from the centre [of the circle] and do not love God, we distance ourselves from our neighbour; but if we love God, then the nearer we draw to him in love, the more we are united with our neighbour in love.
>
> DOROTHEUS OF GAZA *Instructions* (SC 92, p. 286)

Mystery and splendour of the body of Christ: members of Christ, we are all, as Paul writes, 'members one of another'. This is to see the whole of humanity as consubstantial, one person only, in the most realistic of senses. In this spacious body love circulates as divine-human blood.

> An elder said, 'I have spent twenty years fighting to see all human beings as only one.'
> *Sayings of Those who Grow Old in Ascesis* (SO 1, p. 407)

This unity through Christ finds expression in the Holy Spirit whom the whole of Tradition, from St Paul and St John onwards, designates the spirit of *communion*. This is nothing other than the translation into the human situation of the majestic unity of the Trinity.

> When perfect love has driven out fear, or fear has been transformed into love, then everything that has been saved will be a unity growing together through the one and only Fullness, and everyone will be, in one another, a unity in the perfect Dove, the Holy Spirit . . . In this way, encircled by the unity of the Holy Spirit as the bond of peace, all will be one body and one spirit . . . But it would be better to quote the very words of the Gospel literally: 'That they may all be one; even as thou, Father, art in me and I in thee, that they also may be in us' (John 17.21). Now the bond of this unity is glory. And that this glory is the Holy Spirit, anyone familiar with Scripture will agree if he is attentive to the word of the Lord: 'The glory which thou hast given me, I have given to them' (John 17.22). He has indeed really given them such glory when he said: 'Receive the Holy Spirit' (John 20.22).
> GREGORY OF NYSSA *Homilies on the Song of Songs*, 15 (PG 44, 1116)

The sanctified person is someone no longer separated. And he is only sanctified to the extent that he understands in practice that he is no longer separated from anyone or anything. He bears humanity in himself, all human beings in their passion and their resurrection. He is identified, in Christ, with the 'whole Adam'. His own 'self' no longer interests him. He includes in his prayer and in his love all humanity, without judging or condemning anyone, except himself, the last of all. He is infinitely vulnerable to the horror of the world, to the tragedies of history being constantly renewed. But he is crushed

with Christ and rises again with him, with everyone. He knows that
resurrection has the last word. Deeper than horror is the Joy.

> Those who have been judged worthy to become children of God
> and to be born from on high of the Holy Spirit . . . not infrequently
> weep and distress themselves for the whole human race; they pray
> for the 'whole Adam' with tears, inflamed as they are with spiritual
> love for all humanity. At times also their spirit is kindled with
> such joy and such love that, if it were possible, they would take
> every human being into their heart without distinguishing between
> good and bad. Sometimes too in humility of spirit they so humble
> themselves before every human being that they consider themselves
> to be the last and least important of all. After which the Spirit makes
> them live afresh in ineffable joy.
>
> PSEUDO-MACARIUS *Eighteenth Homily*, 8 (PG 34,79)

Our spiritual life and death are at stake in our relations with
others. We are reminded of St John of the Cross: 'On the last day
we shall be judged by our love'.

> Abba Anthony said again, 'Life and death depend on our neighbour.
> If we gain our brother we gain God. But if we scandalize our brother
> we are sinning against Christ.'
>
> *Sayings of the Desert Fathers*, Anthony, 9 (PG 65,77)

To find *parrhesia*, trusting friendship with God, there is no other
way but compassion, or in Greek, 'sympathy', the ability as we said
to suffer with, to feel with. For the person without compassion the
suffering of humanity is an obstacle to knowing God.

> Abba Theodore of Pherme asked Abba Pambo, 'Give me a word to
> live by.' And with great reluctance he said to him, 'Go, Theodore,
> and have compassion on all. Compassion allows us to speak freely
> to God.'
>
> *Sayings of the Desert Fathers*, Pambo, 14 (PG 65,371)

For, in fact, compassion comes in the end to be united with the
same compassion that God feels for the world. Gregory of Nyssa
speaks of the 'pathos', the passion of God for human beings, of the
'suffering God', the God of feeling. And Pascal wrote: 'Jesus will be
in agony until the end of the world.'

Brother, I recommend this to you: 'Let the weight of compassion in you weigh the scales down until you feel in your heart the same compassion that God has for the world.'

ISAAC OF NINEVEH *Ascetic Treatises*, 34 (Spanos p. 151)

To love humanity is in the last resort to be ready to renounce one's own salvation, provided that they are saved, as Moses and St Paul prayed.

To love humanity is to share, even to death, the *kenosis* of God's love itself which is given in his only-begotten Son.

This is the sign by which to recognize those who have arrived at perfection: even if they were to throw themselves into the fire ten times a day for the sake of humanity, they would not be satisfied. That is what Moses says to God: 'Now, if thou wilt, forgive their sin – and if not, blot me, I pray thee, out of thy book which thou hast written' (Exodus 32.32). That is also what the blessed apostle Paul says: 'I could wish that I myself were accursed and cut off from Christ for the sake of my brethren' (Romans 9.3).

And above all God himself, in his love for creation, delivered his own Son to the death of the cross. 'God so loved the world that he gave his only Son to death for the world's sake' (cf. John 3.16) ... So too the saints ... like God, pour out the superabundance of their love upon all.

ISAAC OF NINEVEH *Ascetic Treatises*, 81 (p. 307)

The truly spiritual person draws apart from everyone for the 'one to one' alone with God, but going more deeply and anonymously into God, finds the self afresh in Christ, in the great movement of Trinitarian love, no longer separated but united with everyone.

Blessed is he who thinks of himself as the sweepings of all.
Blessed is he who considers the salvation and progress of all as his own, in fullness of joy.
Blessed is he who regards every human being as God, after God ... who is separate from everyone and united with everyone.

EVAGRIUS OF PONTUS *On Prayer*, 123,122, 121, 124 (Philokalia I, 187)

2. *The Demands of Love*

Ardent meditation on the cross, that is, on God's unbounded love for us, banishes all our rancour, resentment and hatred. In the presence of the immensity of God's forgiveness, the Gospel says, how can we do other than forgive others? And how can we receive God's forgiveness if we do not forgive one another?

'Forgive us our trespasses as (to the extent that) we forgive those who trespass against us,' we pray in the Lord's Prayer.

> The remembrance of Christ's sufferings cures the soul of rancour, so confused is it by the example of Christ's love.
>
> JOHN CLIMACUS *The Ladder of Divine Ascent*, 9th Step, 12 (14) (p. 75)

On this point, Maximus the Confessor indicates some attitudes that make it possible to triumph over hatred: realizing that every refusal to forgive deprives us of Christ; preventing aggressive impulses from expressing themselves in words – in argument, in self-justification, in the sort of psychological analysis that on the pretext of objectivity or lucidity reduces the mystery of the other person and becomes a subtle means of destroying him, a shrewd form of malice – also: not avoiding what annoys or threatens us, but trying humbly and gently to clear up the misunderstanding and, if that is not possible, taking the other person into one's prayer, keeping silent, absolutely refusing to speak evil of him.

Only so can crucified love, secretly victorious, triumph over the depth of hatred in us that we need to recognize, fight against, reduce and transform by grace.

> Has your brother been an occasion of trial for you? Has your annoyance led you to hatred? Do not let yourself be defeated, but triumph over hatred by love. This is the way to do it: by praying to God sincerely for him; by accepting the excuses others make for him or by constituting yourself his defender; by taking responsibility for your trial on yourself and bearing it with courage until the cloud has lifted.
>
> Be careful, if you were praising the goodness and proclaiming the virtue of someone yesterday, not to disparage him today as wicked and perverse, just because your affection has turned to aversion. Do not seek by blaming your brother to justify your culpable aversion, but continue faithfully praising him, even if

you are overcome with annoyance, and you will soon return to a wholesome charity.

Never wound your brother with ambiguous words lest he pay you back in your own coin, and both of you depart from sentiments of charity. But with the frankness of friendship go and reprimand him, and with the causes of trouble removed, you will both be delivered from distress and bitterness.

A soul that nourishes hatred against anyone cannot be at peace with God ... 'If you do not forgive people their trespasses,' he says, 'neither will your Father forgive your trespassess' (Matthew 6.14). If the other will not make peace with you, you at least for your part must guard yourself from hating him, and pray for him sincerely without speaking ill of him to anyone.

The whole purpose of our Lord's commandments is to rescue the spirit from chaos and hatred and lead it to love of him and love of one's neighbour. From this springs forth, like a flash of lightning, holy knowledge.

MAXIMUS THE CONFESSOR *Centuries on Charity*, IV,22,27,32,35,56 (PG 90,1052,1053,1056,1060,1061)

The Gospel requires us to be reconciled with our neighbour before bringing our gift to the altar. Accordingly we have to forgive him, in order to dare to offer a little true love to Christ.

If you want to preserve love as God has asked, do not let your brother go to bed at night with a feeling of bitterness towards you. Do not, for your part, retire to rest with a feeling of bitterness towards him but go and be reconciled with your brother and then you will come to offer to Christ, with a pure conscience and in fervent prayer, the gift of love.

MAXIMUS THE CONFESSOR *Centuries on Charity*, I,53 (PG 90,972)

The following hymn to charity by St Isaac of Nineveh calls to mind what the apostle Paul wrote in his First Epistle to the Corinthians: 'Love is patient and kind; love is not jealous or boastful; it is not arrogant or rude. Love does not insist on its own way; it is not irritable or resentful; it does not rejoice at wrong, but rejoices in the right. Love bears all things, believes all things, hopes all things, endures all things' (1 Corinthians 13.4-7).

What is wrong is destructive suffering inflicted on others. Wrong must not be returned for wrong. The only thing that counts is shared sympathy, based, as in Evagrius, on private solitude with God. As for the sins of others, hide them, and if possible take them on yourself.

> Let yourself be persecuted but do not persecute others.
> Let yourself be crucified but do not crucify others.
> Let yourself be insulted but do not insult others.
> Let yourself be slandered but do not slander others . . .
> Rejoice with those who rejoice and weep with those who weep.
> Such is the sign of purity.
> Suffer with the sick. Be afflicted with sinners.
> Exult with those who repent. Be the friend of all.
> But in your spirit remain alone . . .
> Spread your cloak over anyone who falls into sin and shield him.
> And if you cannot take his fault on yourself and accept punishment in his place, do not destroy his character.
>
> ISAAC OF NINEVEH *Ascetic Treatises*, 58 (p. 238)

True friendship remains faithful even when the friend is severely tried or seems to be in the wrong, even and especially when he is despised or ostracised.

> Interior freedom is not yet possessed by anyone who cannot close his eyes to the fault of a friend, whether real or apparent.
>
> 'There is nothing so precious as a faithful friend' (Ecclesiasticus 6.15), for he makes his own the misfortunes of his friend and endures them, suffering with him, even to death. Friends are legion in time of prosperity. But in the hour of trial scarcely one will be found.
>
> Only those who keep the commandments carefully, and those admitted to the secrets of God's judgments, do not forsake their friends when their friends, by God's permission, are put to the test.
>
> MAXIMUS THE CONFESSOR *Centuries on Charity*, IV,92,93,94,97 (PG 90,1069-72)

'Agapeic' love is not a sentimental whim or a physical attraction, both of which are doomed to fade away quickly, and anyway do not come at will. No. It is the awareness of God's love for another person. Only God can enable us to understand our neighbour according to the 'feeling', the intuition of the 'Spirit'. Then we perceive in him an irreducible personal existence beyond limitations and errors, beyond even the disappointment we may have felt for a moment. The other is in the image of God, not of us.

> When we begin to feel in its fullness the love of God, we begin also to love our neighbour in the experience of the Spirit. That is the love of which the Scriptures speak. For friendship according to the flesh breaks down too easily on the slightest pretext. The reason is that it lacks the bond of the Spirit. Therefore even if a certain irritation takes hold of the soul on which God is acting, that does not break the bond of love. For if it has been set ablaze again by the fire of divine love, it seeks with great joy to love its neighbour, even if in return it should have to undergo wrongs or insults. In fact, the bitterness of the quarrel is entirely consumed in the sweetness of God.
>
> DIADOCHUS OF PHOTIKE *Gnostic Chapters*, 15 (SC 5 bis, p. 92)

Consider two people who are friends according to the intuition that is a gift of the Spirit. Despite their peculiarities they will not be able to quarrel because 'mine' and 'yours' have no meaning between them. Their friendship is a greater thing than possessions.

> Two elders who were living together in a cell had never had any disagreement. So one day one of them said to the other, 'Come on, let us have at least one quarrel, like other people.' The other answered, 'I don't know how to begin.' The first replied, 'I am going to put this brick between us, then I shall say, "It is mine." Then you have to say, "No, it belongs to me." That is what leads to strife and arguments.'
> So they placed the brick between them. One said, 'It is mine.' And the other, 'No. I am sure it belongs to me.' The first replied, 'It is not yours. It is mine.' Then the other cried, 'All right. If it belongs to you, take it!' And they did not succeed in quarrelling.
>
> *Sayings of the Desert Fathers*, Anonymous series, 221 (SO 1, P. 398)

Love of neighbour is more important than prayer.

> It can happen that when we are at prayer some brothers come to see us. Then we have to choose, either to interrupt our prayer or to sadden our brother by refusing to answer him. But love is greater than prayer. Prayer is one virtue amongst others, whereas love contains them all.
>
> JOHN CLIMACUS *The Ladder of Divine Ascent*, 26th Step 43(52) (p. 131)

Practical service of others, with the detachment from self, the patience, and the true affection that it implies is worth more than all mortification.

> A brother said to one of the elders, 'Here are two brothers. One never leaves his cell where he prays, fasts for six days at a time, and gives himself up to all sorts of mortification. The other looks after the sick. Which of the two lives a life more pleasing to God?'
> The elder replied, 'The brother who fasts for six days on end would not be the equal of the one who looks after the sick, not even if he hanged himself by the nose.'
> *Sayings of the Desert Fathers*, Anonymous series, 224 (SO 1, p. 339)

Even the book of the Gospels would be better sold if there were no other means of feeding the hungry. The gift of life is worth more than the holiest of books. Especially when the book is the price of life.

> A brother had as his only possession a book of the Gospels. He sold it and spent the proceeds on food for the starving. And he added these memorable words: 'What I sold was the very book that tells me: "Sell what you have and give to the poor".'
> EVAGRIUS OF PONTUS *Practicus*, 97 (SC 171, p. 704)

Love desires, and accomplishes as far as it can, an exchange of lives, when the other person's existence is a slow destruction of the body and ruthless social ostracism. The importance in the mystical tradition of the 'leper's kiss' is well known.

> Abba Agathon said, 'If I could meet a leper, give him my body and take his, I should be very happy.' That is true love indeed.
> *Sayings of the Desert Fathers*, Agathon 26 (PG 65,115)

3. *A Paradoxical Morality*

> ... Those who humbly choose what is folly in the eyes of the world clearly contemplate the wisdom of God himself ... What could be more foolish in the eyes of the world ... than to abandon one's possessions to thieves? To return no wrong for the wrongs one has suffered? ... By virtue of this wise folly, one catches a

glimpse of God's wisdom, not indeed in all its completeness but already in the light of contemplation.

GREGORY THE GREAT *Commentary on the Book of Job*, 27,46,79 (PL 76,444-6)

Beyond an ethic of law (certainly not within it as far as the Christian is concerned) we are called, as we gradually deepen our faith, to invent a paradoxical morality, that of creative love. This morality gives precedence to the person, the mystery of the person's nature and destiny, over social ideas of right and justice. So Jesus, faced with the woman taken in adultery, reminds her would-be executioners of their own state of separation from God and of their spiritual adultery. 'Let whichever is without sin among you be the first to throw a stone at her.' And to the woman he said, 'Neither do I condemn you; go, and do not sin again' (John 8.1-11).

For the person who has begun to tread the spiritual path, nothing is more important than the Gospel command: 'Do not judge'. Greed and vanity are passions that belong to those who are novices on the way or who have only just begun to advance along it. But for the more advanced, the breakdown always comes from judgement pronounced on others. Then all their ascesis is affected by spiritual Pharisaism, in the sense given that word in the Gospel.

Ascesis has no value if it does not help to deepen humility – humility as the capacity for disinterested love. That is why, according to spiritual teachers, the whole of virtue is comprised in the refusal to depise.

> The failures of beginners result almost always from greed.
>
> In those who are making progress the failures come also from too high an opinion of themselves.
>
> In those nearing perfection they come solely from judging their neighbour.

JOHN CLIMACUS *The Ladder of Divine Ascent*, 25th step, 16, (18) (p. 87)

Abba Theodore of Pherme said, 'There is no other virtue than that of not despising anyone.'

Sayings of the Desert Fathers, Theodore of Pherme, 13 (PG 65,189)

The fundamental temptation is admirably depicted in Genesis in the dialogue that takes place after the Fall, between God and the first human couple. 'The man said, "The woman whom thou gavest to be

with me, she gave me fruit of the tree, and I ate." ... The woman
said, "The serpent beguiled me, and I ate."' (Genesis 3.12-13). It was
the serpent's fault, it was the woman's fault, it was God's fault, who
'gave this woman to be with me'.

To justify ourselves by condemning others is our permanent
tendency, in private as in public life. True nobility is to take responsibility oneself. True humility and true love, in the spiritual
order, consist in knowing ourselves to be guilty 'in everything and
for everyone'.

> Abba John said, 'We have rejected the light burden of condemning
> ourselves, and we have chosen to carry the heavy one of justifying
> ourselves and condemning others.'
>
> *Sayings of the Desert Fathers*, John Colobos, 21 (PG 65,212)

How can we judge another person without imprisoning that
person in his past acts? Without shackling him to one moment
of his development? A change of heart is always possible, even
'between the stirrup and the ground' in a fatal fall from a horse, to
quote the English proverb beloved of Graham Greene. Magistrates
must certainly judge actions to maintain the social order, or at least
to lessen the disorder. But the Gospel limits their power and helps
them to find a balance between the common good and the mystery
of a personal destiny. In particular, if Christians must reject the death
penalty, it is not from an idolatrous sacralization of biological life,
but in order to leave a person the opportunity of repentance.

> Remember this, and you will no longer judge: Judas was an apostle,
> and the thief crucified at Christ's right hand was a murderer. What
> a transformation in an instant!
>
> John Climacus *The Ladder of Divine Ascent*, 10th step, 4(5)
> (p. 76)

The heart must purify itself in order to see God. 'Blessed are the
pure in heart, for they shall see God' (Matthew 5.8). The criterion of
that purification is the clear and loving look that is able to discern
in each human being the person whom God calls, and for whom, as
Pascal says, he shed on the cross that particular drop of blood ...
Then human criteria of pure and impure vanish, and even those of
right and wrong. Each person is basically good, having been created
by God, in the image of God, with the desire for God. And the fact
that this desire has gone wildly astray means that it does exist. It is
great sinners who 'soften up' best when touched by grace, according

to Péguy, and the Church has a special veneration for the good thief and the repentant prostitute, or for St Mary of Egypt, the woman who had been prodigal with her body but was suddenly carried off by the call of the desert. All of us are the people who put Christ to death, the daily executioners of love. And Christ loves us and, when put to death by us, offers us resurrection.

> Question: When is a person sure of having arrived at purity?
> Answer: When he considers all human beings are good, and no created thing appears impure or defiled to him. Then he is truly pure in heart.
> ISAAC OF NINEVEH *Ascetic Treatises*, 85 (p. 3401)

In this regard all human beings are equal, not with an equality that is jealously measured, but because each one, being an image of the Absolute, is himself an absolute. Existences which converge on the infinite are equal in dignity.

Rejecting taboos and prohibitions, Jesus took his meals with tax collectors and prostitutes, the better to express his love for them. To love one whom others despise is to demonstrate God's love for that person, for one who is more precious than the whole world. It is perhaps to save that person from self-hatred.

We remember the great Western mystics who bestowed their love on the most criminal or the most hopeless: Thérèse of Lisieux, who begins her spiritual life by praying like a loving mother – young girl as she is – for a murderer, and ends it by taking her seat voluntarily 'at the table of sinners', undergoing the terrible experience of contemporary nihilism, of the 'night of nothingness'; or Catherine of Siena assisting Nicholas Toldo on the scaffold, a political prisoner condemned to death whom she had visited in prison: 'I suddenly saw the God-Man as one sees the brightness of the sun. His side was open and he was receiving the blood of the executed man. In that blood there was the fire of the holy desire that grace had given him and hidden in his soul.'

We remember the highest (and also popular) spirituality of the Russians. Think of Dostoyevsky, Sonia's regard for Raskolnikov, the ministry of the 'Siberian missionary' among the convicts, the respect that the people showed for criminals . . .

> When you give, give generously, your face lit up with joy. And give more than you were asked for . . . Make no distinction between rich and poor. Do not try to find out who is worthy and

who is not. Let all people be equal in your eyes. Thus you will be able to influence even the unworthy for good ... The Lord ate at the table of the tax collectors and harlots. He did not keep the unworthy at a distance. He wanted thus to draw all humankind to himself. Therefore consider that all human beings, even if infidels or murderers, are equal in worth and honour, and that each one of them in virtue of his nature is your brother, even if, all unknowingly, he has strayed far from the truth.

Isaac of Nineveh *Ascetic Treatises*, 23 (p. 99)

The spiritual person hides the faults of others, as God protects the world, as Christ washes our sins in his blood, as the Mother of God stretches the veil of her tears over the human race ...

It was said of Abba Macarius the Great that he became, according to the writings, a god on earth, because in the way God protects the world, so Abba Macarius would hide the faults he saw as though he had not seen them, and the faults he heard about as though he had not heard of them.

Sayings of the Desert Fathers, Macarius the Egyptian 32 (PG 65, 273)

How could anyone who judges himself – and discovers thereby the cross as 'judgment of judgment' – dare to judge others? He will rather go to join the condemned and ostracised sinner, as Christ came to seek humankind even in hell.

It happened that one of the brothers at Scete committed a serious sin. The elders held a meeting and asked Abba Moses to join them.

He however refused to come. The priest sent him a message in the following terms: 'Come, the community are waiting for you.' So then he arose and started the journey, carrying an old basket with a hole in it. He filled it with sand and dragged it behind him.

The elders went to meet him and asked him, 'Father, what does this mean?' The old man answered, 'It is my sins running out behind me and I do not notice them. That is how I am coming today to judge the sins of another.'

Upon hearing this they said nothing to the brother and pardoned him.

Sayings of the Desert Fathers, Moses, 2 (PG 65,281-3)

A brother who had sinned was expelled from the church by the priest. Whereupon Abba Bessarion rose and went with him, saying 'I too am a sinner.'

Sayings of the Desert Fathers, Bessarion 7 (PG 65,141)

And now two stories full of humour, the humour of the desert, about thieves. Here non-violence, as Gandhi had understood, does not only express a radical detachment, it is also practical, paradoxical love that overwhelms the guilty man, awakens the person in him, and makes him attentive to his true destinty.

Abba Anastasius had copied on very fine parchment, worth eighteen gold pieces, the whole of the Old and New Testaments. One day a brother came to see him and, noticing the book, took it away with him. That same day, when Abba Anastasius wanted to read the book, he noticed that it had disappeared and he realized that the brother had taken it. But he did not send anyone to question him for fear he might add a lie to his theft.

Now that brother went to the neighbouring town to sell the book, for which he asked sixteen gold pieces. The buyer said to him, 'Let me have it to see if it is worth that price.' And the buyer took it to St Anastasius, saying to him, 'Father, have a look at this book, and tell me whether you think I ought to give sixteen gold pieces for it. Is that its value?' Abba Anastasius replied, 'Yes, it is a fine book. It is worth that price.' The buyer went back to find the brother and said to him, 'Here is your money. I showed the book to Abba Anastasius who considered it a fine book and judges it to be worth at least sixteen gold pieces.' The brother asked, 'Is that all he said? Did he not make any other remarks?' 'No,' replied the buyer, 'not a word.' 'Well, I have changed my mind,' said the brother. 'I no longer want to sell this book.' Then he hurried back to Abba Anastasius and begged him with tears to take back his own book. But the Abba refused, saying, 'Go in peace, brother, I make you a present of it.' But the brother answered, 'If you do not take it back I shall never have any peace any more.' And the brother stayed with Abba Anastasius for the rest of his life.

Sayings of the Desert Fathers (in T. Merton, p. 49-50)

One day some thieves said to an elder, 'We have come to take away everything in your cell.' He replied, 'My sons, take everything you want.' Then they took all that they could from the cell except

for a little bag that was hidden and went away. But the elder followed them, shouting, 'My sons, take this bag that you forgot.'

Abashed at the attitude of the elder, they brought back what
they had taken, and did penance, saying, 'That elder is truly a man
of God.'

Sayings of the Desert Fathers, Anonymous series 206 (SO 1, p. 392)

It is better to tell a lie to save a person than, by telling the truth,
to hand him over, to surrender him, even if it is not a bandit who is
pursuing him, as in Kant's celebrated example, but a police officer,
who is seeking him in order that justice may be done. The spiritual
person, in a radical departure from Kantian principles, tells a lie and
lets the criminal go free, for the grace of God.

> Abba Agathon one day questioned Abba Alonius, saying, 'How can
> I control my tongue so as to tell no more lies?' And Abba Alonius
> said to him, 'If you do not tell a lie, you are set to commit many
> sins.' 'How is that?' he asked. And the old man replied, 'Suppose
> a man has committed a murder before your eyes and fled into
> your cell. The police officer looking for the man asks you, "Has
> a murder been committed in your sight?" If you do not tell a lie,
> you are delivering that man to death. It is better that you should
> hand him over to God unbound, for God knows all things.'
>
> *Sayings of the Desert Fathers*, Alonius, 4 (PG 65,133)

4. *In the world but not of it*

Consider the witness that is given by a Church that is full of joy,
though persecuted. It is persecuted but deeply faithful, as is the
case today in several countries.

The attitude of these Christians displays neither aggression nor
compliance, neither the temptation to lose their identity in the world
by following its fashions, nor the opposite temptation to set themselves apart by making themselves externally distinct. Christians
conform to the law so long as it does not contradict their conscience.
In the latter instance – and we have seen this in the case of the
martyrs – they disobey, but accept the sanctions of the law. Their
basic requirement is not to overturn the law but to rise above it.
Their behaviour is by way of example and intercession. In a society
governed by Roman law which accords an absolute and indisputable
value to private property, they practise mutual assistance and, with

a free originality, a certain sharing of possessions. In a society that takes eroticism for granted and where utterly heedless cruelty holds sway in regard to the embryo and the new born child, Christians bear their witness to the chastity of conjugal love and they oppose abortion and the desertion of infants. Their communities engender fellowship. They try to return good for evil and to serve humanity even if the State now and then unleashes public opinion against them. In times of widespread anguish and of depressing scepticism they give thanks for life and are able to lead others to give thanks for it. Nourished by the joy of the resurrection, to which the luminous and free art of the catacombs testifies, this Church of the second century is a 'spiritual republic' that discreetly but radically transforms human relationships.

At the same time, it feels itself to be a community of prophets, priests and kings, 'set apart' not only for its own salvation but also to work for the salvation of the world. The presence of Christians in society and in the universe is that of the soul in the body, a life-giving presence. It is life-giving through the grace of the cross, and by a witness that is challenged, vilified, with martyrdom on the horizon. The Church's worship opens up the world to the infinite. It allows it to breathe beyond its own confines. The prayer and the goodness of Christians are for society both protection and creative inspiration. It is here that humiliation becomes *humus*.

Thus Christians appear as the righteous few who were not found in Sodom, as 'the light of the world' and the 'salt of the earth' – to use the expressions of the Gospel. Clement of Alexandria thought of the most spiritually aware Christians (already the tendency is discernible to transfer to monks alone this role of 'soul of the world') as 'seed, image and likeness of God, his true son and heir, sent here below on a mission in pursuance of the Father's majestic design. It was for them that all beings were created ... As long as this seed remains here below everything is preserved, but as soon as it is harvested everything will be dissolved' (*What Rich Man can be Saved?* 36,3). The Church is the mystical foundation of the world. It is in the Church that the trees grow, the constellations revolve, history unfolds and is steered towards its fulfilment. The 'dissolution' of the world, when the 'seed' has been harvested, will also be its transfiguration.

If Christians remain faithful to the message of the resurrection and become truly eucharistic people, they are in society like a forest in the middle of cultivated lands – an unlimited reserve of silence, peace and authentic life that makes possible all the good and lasting creations of history.

Christians are not distinguished from others by country or language
or the way they dress. They do not live in cities reserved to themselves,
they do not speak a different language, there is nothing peculiar
about their way of life ... They are distributed among Greek and
non-Greek cities, according to the lot of each of them. They conform
to local usage in their dress, their diet, and in their way of life, while
exhibiting the extraordinary and truly paradoxical attitudes of their
spiritual republic. They live each in his own native country, but they
are like resident aliens. They discharge their duties as citizens and
submit themselves to every burden. Every foreign country is home
to them, and every home country is foreign territory.

They marry like everyone else. They have children, but they
never abandon them at birth. They share the same table, but not
the same bed. They are in the world, but they do not live according
to the world's ways. They spend their time on earth, but they
are citizens of heaven. They obey the established laws but their
way of life trancends those laws by far. They love their fellows,
but they are persecuted. They are misunderstood and condemned.
They are killed, and in this way they win life. They are poor,
and make many rich. They lack everything, and abound in all
things. They are despised, and in this contempt they find their
glory ... They are slandered, and they are in the right. They are
insulted, and they give a blessing.

In a word, what the soul is in the body, Christians are in
the world. The soul is spread over all the limbs of the body, as
Christians are spread over all the cities of the world. The soul
inhabits the body, as Christians inhabit the world without being
of the world. Although it is invisible, the soul is housed in a visible
body. So too with the Christians. They are clearly seen to be in the
world, but the worship they offer to God remains invisible ... The
soul is shut up in the body, yet it is the soul that maintains the body.
Christians are as it were imprisoned in the world, yet it is they who
maintain it ... The soul becomes better by purifying itself through
hunger and thirst: when Christians are persecuted, their numbers
increase day by day. So noble is the post assigned to them by God,
that they are not allowed to desert it.

Letter to Diognetus, 5,1-10 (SC 33, p. 62 & 64)

The 'last of the righteous' are enough to save the world. This
conception is common to early Christianity and Judaism. According
to the Talmud, this universal intercession is ensured by the thirty
six righteous men who 'daily welcome the *Shekinah* [the divine

presence]'. At the heart of Islam, in Sufism, a similar idea is to be found, one beloved of Louis Massignon: 'apotropaic saints'.

> Someone again asked [of St Epiphanius], 'Is a single righteous person enough to make peace with God?' He answered, 'Yes, because he himself has said, "Look for one who lives righteously and I will forgive the whole people".'
> *Sayings of the Desert Fathers*, St Epiphanius, 14 (PG 65,165)

'In my Father's house,' says Jesus, 'are many rooms' (John 14.2). St Paul emphasizes the complexity of the gifts of the Spirit, that should be understood as so many compelling and distinct personal vocations. (The Old Testament knows of the spiritual gift of a king, of a wise man, of a scholar, an artist or a craftsman.) It is good, in the texts which follow, that these legitimate differences should have been recalled by some great monks, at a time when monasticism tended to consider itself as the only Christian way. Those first monks lived in humility in anticipation of the Kingdom at the heart of the Church.

In these texts Elijah symbolizes solitary contemplation, Abraham a broad, noble, hospitable humanity, David a poetic talent and a humble and firm exercise of power. Or again, some people radiate interior peace; others, even living apart from society because of disease, make themselves transparent to the divine light; others again serve their fellows in all domains of culture and society. All these ways meet in one and the same love for God and for one's neighbour. For it is impossible to serve one's neighbour unselfishly unless one is a person of prayer, unless one discerns through prayer the image of God in one's neighbour. Nor can one go deep into contemplation without interceding for all human beings and making oneself their servant.

> A brother asked one of the elders, 'What good can I do to have eternal life?' He answered, 'Only God knows what is good. However, I have heard it said that when someone put this question to Abba Nistheros the Great, who was a friend of St Anthony, he replied, "Not all good works are alike. For Scripture relates that Abraham practised hospitality and God was with him; that Elijah loved to pray on his own and God was with him; that David was humble and God was with him. Therefore do all that your soul longs to accomplish in accordance with the will of God and your soul will be saved."'
> *Sayings of the Desert Fathers*, Nistheros, 2 (PG 65,305-7)

Abba Poimen said, 'If three people meet and one of them is keeping inner peace, the second is giving thanks to God in sickness, the third is serving others from an unselfish motive, those three are performing the same work.'

Sayings of the Desert Fathers, Poimen, 29 (PG 65,329)

In the very beautiful poem which follows, Gregory Nazianzen celebrates human love and shows how the ennobling of *eros* makes possible all the positive developments of civilized life. Marriage, far from alienating the married from God, is the sacrament of his love. The making of *eros* into a sacrament is achieved in the Church. The fellowship of the Trinity which Christ imparts to humanity from then on upholds, sustains and renews the relationship of man and wife.

But 'virginity', or rather monastic celibacy, is just as indispensable. It alone can bear radical witness to the transcendence of the person who is seeking God. Only this monastic witness proves that marriage is not merely a regular and necessary function of the species but the meeting of two persons. It alone can mark the boundaries of social and political life and enable the conscience to be free, beyond all conditioning. The monk is a happy Antigone, an Antigone who dies only to rise again.

By fulfilling this law and the union of love
we help one another, and though born of the earth
we are following the law of the earth that is also God's law.
See then what profit wise marriage brings to the human race.
Who has taught wisdom? . . .
Who has explored all there is on earth, in the sea, under the
    heavens?
Who then gave laws to cities and, before laws,
who filled the market place, the houses, the wrestling schools . . .
the tables for feasts?
Who gathered together the choirs that sing in the temples?
Who subdued the ferocity of wild life, cultivated the earth,
crossed the seas, and joined in one what was separate,
unless it was marriage? But here is something better still . . .
We are each other's hand, ear and foot
through the blessing of marriage which doubles our strength and
    gladdens our friends . . .
Anxiety shared sweetens our trials,
joys are the sweeter for being in common.
Marriage is the seal of an affection that nothing can break . . .

Those who are joined in the flesh form a single soul
and, by their mutual love, together they sharpen the spur of their
    faith,
for marriage does not distance them from God,
rather it draws them all the nearer to him, since he himself is the
    instigator of it.
To which virginity replies:
What this life is worth I leave to others to decide.
But for me there is only one law, one purpose:
that, filled with the love of God,
I may depart from here to the God who reigns in heaven,
who is the Creator of the light . . .
To him alone have I bound myself by love.

GREGORY NAZIANZEN *On Virginity*, Dogmatic Poems (PG 37,
537-55)

But on the subject of marriage it is essential to quote the testimony of an author who despite his rigorism belongs, nevertheless, to
the pre-monastic period and regards human love, with the support
of the ecclesial community, as a spiritual way in its own right. For
Tertullian, this love ought to be unique, so he advised against a second
marriage after widowhood. (Even today, in the Eastern churches
that have preserved the original tradition of a married priesthood,
a widower who has married again cannot become a priest.)

How sweet the yoke that joins two of the faithful in the same hope,
the same law, the same service! Both are brethren in the service of
the same Lord. They are truly two in one and the same flesh. And
where the flesh is one, the spirit is one. Together they pray . . .
instructing, encouraging and supporting each other in turn. They
are equal in the Church of God, equal at God's banquet, they share
equally troubles, persecutions, and consolations. They hide nothing
from each other, they never avoid each other's company, they never
cause each other pain . . . Christ rejoices to see such a couple and
he gives them his peace. Where they are, there he is himself.

TERTULLIAN *To his Wife*, II, 9 (PL 1,1302)

And always the last word belongs to compassion, in the strongest
sense of the word. 'He who says he is in the light and hates his brother
is in the darkness still' (1 John 2.9).

Better to be one living in the world and devoting himself to the service of a sick brother than to be a hermit who has no pity for his neighbour.

EVAGRIUS OF PONTUS *Mirror of Monks*, 34 (Gressman, p. 156)

The certainty that the monks acquired of the transcendence of the person enabled the theologians and spiritual writers of early Christianity to assert, in opposition to the patriarchal attitude of the Mediterranean world, the complete equality of man and woman.

Woman has the same spiritual dignity as man. Both of them have the same God, the same Teacher, the same Church. They breathe, see, hear, know, hope and love in the same way. Beings who have the same life, grace and salvation are called . . . to the same manner of being.

CLEMENT OF ALEXANDRIA *Tutor*, 1,4 (PG 8,260)

Sacred Scripture does not set men and women in opposition to one another in respect to sex. Sex does not constitute any difference in the sight of God.

ORIGEN *Homilies on Joshua*, 9 (GCS 8,356)

Woman is a person in the image of God, just as man is. Gregory of Nyssa vigorously emphasizes this assertion of Basil's – which unfortunately is not as clear in St Augustine and his Western followers.

Woman is in the image of God equally with man. The sexes are of equal worth. Their virtues are equal, their struggles are equal. . . Would a man be able to compete with a woman who lives her life to the full?

GREGORY OF NYSSA *Let us make Man in our Image and Likeness*, 2nd discourse (PG 44, 276)

St Basil in the preface to his *Ascetica* shows how the martial symbolism that Paul applies to the Christian life is equally valid for women, and recalls the important part played by women among Christ's disciples. 'Apostles of the apostles' the Byzantine liturgy calls the women who brought spices to the tomb and were the first witnesses of the resurrection.

These words [of the Apostle] apply not only to men, for women also belong to Christ's army by the strength of their souls ... Many women have distinguished themselves no less than men in the spiritual warfare, and some of them more ... It was not only men but also women who followed Jesus, and he accepted help from women as much as from men.

BASIL OF CÆSAREA *Shorter Rules*, 3 (PG 31,624)

The martyr Julitta sealed the assertion of this equality with the sacrifice of herself.

[To the women surrounding her who were commiserating with her:] 'We are made of the same dough as men. Just like them we were created in the image of God ... Are we not their equals in everything? ... To form woman God did not only take flesh but also bone from the other bones, so that we women like men are indebted to the Lord for firmness, strength and endurance.' So saying, she leapt into the furnace.

BASIL OF CÆSAREA *Homily on the martyr Julitta*, 2 (PG 31,240)

What Julitta suggests in the language of martyrdom is clarified by a profound Jewish exegesis: to create woman, God would have taken, not a rib but a side, a half of the human being, *ha adam*, which was created both masculine and feminine.

And if the ordination to the priesthood because of a whole liturgical symbolism (which is also psychological) is reserved to men, Christian antiquity was acquainted with charismatic *Ammas*, spiritual Mothers, who, equally with the Fathers, *Abbas*, practised the discernment of spirits and penetrating insight into souls.

The Church, after all, has never ceased saying that humanity reaches its highest fulfilment in a woman, Mary, 'mother in all truth, of all those who live according to the Gospel' (Evagrius, Pseudo-Nilus, *Letter 1*). Only the Virgin's assent made the incarnation possible. And Nicholas Cabasilas went so far as to say that God created humanity in order to find a mother. There exists a mysterious correspondence between femininity and the most fundamental gifts of the Holy Spirit. 'You shall honour the deaconesses', the *Didascalia* recommends, 'because they hold the position of the Holy Spirit.' Like the Spirit, or Breath, who in certain respects is motherly (*ruach* in Hebrew is also feminine), woman is able to give life.

During the first three centuries, actions of mutual help were performed even in the course of the liturgy, in a sacramental context. When the Emperors were converted and the Church was brought to assume some responsibility for history, the Fathers never ceased recalling both the dignity of the person and the need for justice, in order to give a social content to the communion of persons. Enthusiastically, and sometimes with violence, they took for their own the appeals of the great Jewish prophets, giving them extra depth by reaffirming that the poor man is 'another Christ', as is shown by the judgement scene in the twenty-fifth chapter of St Matthew. For them, the earth and all its riches belong only to God, while human beings receive no more than the benefit of their use, provided that they accept a fair distribution of resources so as to banish hunger and misery. 'To possess more than is needed,' St Basil says, 'is to defraud the poor, to rob them.' And close by his episcopal city he built a large hospital and guest house to accommodate the sick and the starving.

The Fathers have no ready solutions to offer. They reject both the conception of private property in Roman law and the systematic and levelling communism of certain Gnostic sects. But they consider that when social inequalities reduce individuals – or countries – to a degrading state of poverty, they are the outcome of the fall, and the weight of the fall must be countered by God's original plan, namely the equal dignity of all human beings. This is admirably exemplified by the original Church of Jerusalem, which practised the voluntary sharing of possessions. There is a constant need to rediscover 'almsgiving', which then meant voluntary sharing, and thus to endure the oppressions of history. The Fathers are not in the least opposed to what Paul Ricoeur calls the 'short methods' and the 'long methods' of charity, namely mutual help given by one individual to another, and essential reforms in general. St John Chrysostom, who laid special emphasis on the sacrament of the brother, multiplied hospitals and put forward vast plans for social reorganization. It would be anachronistic to speak of 'socialism' in the Fathers, but the word *socius* to define man's attitude to society would certainly have suited them well. 'You are to love your neighbour as yourself,' and 'the sabbath was made for man, not man for the sabbath,' was at the root of their inspiration, if by 'sabbath' you mean, as Petru Dumitriu suggests in his commentary on St Mark's Gospel, not only ritual directives but also economic and social obligations.

And everything is seen from an ascetic and mystical point of view. It is Christ himself who has to be fed, welcomed, honoured, by transforming people into *socii*, investing them with enough dignity, and according them sufficient equality for friendship to be possible. 'You are putting God on the same footing as your slaves,' thundered St John Chrysostom. 'Set Christ free, free from hunger, from need, from prison, from nakedness.' And this effort at sharing is connected, for the rich, with an ascesis of voluntary limitation, of fasting in the whole sense of the term. Today, the approach of the Fathers would be to invite well-fed societies to a collective ascesis that would make possible a better distribution of the world's resources, and prevent the gap between the rich and the poor of the planet from growing constantly wider. It would be to learn to exercise self-restraint for love of others, as Solzhenitsyn invites us to do.

> Brethren, let us not be bad managers of the goods that have been entrusted to us, unless we want to hear Peter's sharp condemnation: 'Shame on you who hold back the possessions of others. Imitate God's liberality and there will be no more poor' (*Apostolic Constitutions*). Let us not kill ourselves heaping up money when our brothers are dying of hunger ... Let us imitate God's law of creation. He makes the rain fall on the righteous and the wicked and makes his sun rise upon all human beings without distinction. He gives to all the creatures living on earth vast spaces, springs, rivers, forests ... and his gifts ought not to be appropriated by the mighty nor by governments. Everything is common, everything is in abundance ... He honours natural equality by the equal distribution of his gifts ...
>
> Human beings have accumulated in their coffers gold and silver, clothes more sumptuous than useful, diamonds and other such objects that are evidence of war and tyranny; then a foolish arrogance hardens their hearts; for their brothers in distress, no pity. What utter blindness! They do not realize that poverty and riches, social contrasts and other such distinctions were late arrivals among human beings. They spread like epidemics. They were inventions of sin. But in the beginning 'it was not so' (Matthew 19.8) ... Hold fast then to that primitive equality, forget subsequent divisions. Attend not to the law of the strong but to the law of the Creator. Help nature to the best of your ability, honour the freedom of creation, protect your species from dishonour, come to its aid in sickness, rescue it from poverty ... Seek to distinguish yourself from others only by your generosity. Be like gods for the poor, imitating God's mercy. Humanity has nothing so much in common with God as the ability to do good ...
>
> You who are Christ's servants, his brethren and fellow-heirs,

while it is still not too late, help Christ, feed Christ, clothe Christ, welcome Christ, honour Christ . . .

GREGORY NAZIANZEN *On Love of the Poor*, 24-27,40 (PG 35,274-7,285)

Why do we fast? To commemorate the Passion of the Lamb who, before he was nailed to the cross, underwent insults and brutalities . . . Isaiah teaches us the rules for a pure and sincere fast: 'To loose the bonds of wickedness, to undo the thongs of the yoke, to let the oppressed go free, and to break every yoke . . . to share your bread with the hungry, and bring the homeless poor into your house' (Isaiah 58.6) . . .

Do not despise the poor. Ask yourself who they are and you will discover their greatness. They have the face of our Saviour . . . the poor are the stewards of our hope, the guardians of the Kingdom. It is they who open the door to the righteous, and close it to the wicked and self-centred. They are frightening accusers, powerful plaintiffs . . .

Compassion and sharing are things that God loves. They deify the one in whom they dwell . . . they make him the image of the primordial Being, eternal, surpassing all understanding.

GREGORY OF NYSSA *On Love of the Poor*, 1 (PG 46,247)

5. *Hell and the Communion of Saints*

For the early Church salvation is not at all reserved to the baptized. We repeat: those who receive baptism undertake to work for the salvation of all. The Word has never ceased and never will cease to be present to humanity in all cultures, all religions, and all irreligions. The incarnation and the resurrection are not exclusive but inclusive of the manifold forms of this presence.

Christ is the first-born of God, his Logos, in whom all people share. That is what we have learned and what we bear witness to . . . All who have lived in accordance with the Logos are Christians, even if they have been reckoned atheists, as amongst the Greeks Socrates, Heraclitus and the like.

JUSTIN *Apology*, 1,46 (PG 6,397)

It is certainly for Christians to make people understand that Christ comes for all, since he combines the maximum of humanity with the maximum of divinity. But when they fail in this, Christ himself appears to those who are dying. This, for the first Christians, is one of the fundamental dimensons of the descent of Jesus into hell. A descent and a proclamation mysteriously coextensive with all times and all places.

> There has never been a time when the saints did not have the gift of a spiritual salvation pointed towards Christ.
> The Word became man at the final hour; he became Jesus Christ. But before this visible coming in the flesh, he was already, without being man, mediator for humanity.
> ORIGEN *Commentary on John's Gospel*, 20,12 (GCS 4,342) and a fragment of the *Epistle to the Colossians* (PG 14,1297)

> There is only one and the same God the Father, and his Word has been present to humanity from all time, although by diverse dispositions and manifold operations he has from the beginning been saving those who are saved, that is, those who love God and follow his Word, each in his own age.
> IRENÆUS OF LYONS *Against Heresies*, IV,28,2 (SC 100 bis, p. 758)

> Christ did not come only for those who, since the time of the Emperor Tiberius, have believed in him, nor has the Father exercised his providence only in favour of people now living, but in favour of all without exception, right from the beginning, who have feared God and loved him and practised justice and kindness towards their neighbours and desired to see Christ and hear his voice, in accordance with their abilities and the age in which they were living.
> IRENÆUS OF LYONS *Against Heresies*, IV,22,2 (SC 100 bis, p. 688)

> And therefore 'he descended into the lower parts of the earth' (Ephesians 4.9), the infernal regions, to take to all the dead the good news of his coming, for he is the remission of sins for those who believe in him.
> IRENÆUS OF LYONS *Against Heresies*, IV,27,2 (SC 100 bis, p. 738)

Does the matter stand otherwise today for unbelievers? Christ is close to them and they are often following him without realizing it, 'practising justice and kindness towards their neighbours', gaining a foretaste of the mystery through love and beauty. Christ reveals himself fully to them at the moment of their death, flooding them with sweetness and splendour. Doubtless he has to wait about through years of hardening and spiritual insensitivity before he can rediscover the vulnerable and astonished child.

The hell of the fallen condition is abolished in Christ. Everything now depends not on merits, but on faith and love, on the relationship of each individual with Christ and with the neighbour. The early Church with its gaze fixed wholly on the Parousia had no conception either of the present existence of souls definitely damned, nor of an already consummated beatitude for the saints (or even for Christ, according to Origen), nor again of a 'purgatory' in the strictest sense of the word, meaning penal 'satisfaction' of a juridical nature, such as developed in the mediaeval West. What we find rather in the Fathers is the idea of a progressive purification and healing. After death the soul crosses either a 'sea of fire' or spiritual 'frontier', where the powers of evil wrest from it what belongs to them and leave it stripped, ready to embark on a life of peace and silence (the 'abodes', one above another, of which St Ambrose speaks here suggest a progressive perfecting). Thus the 'sleep' of death appears as a contemplative state. Death, undoing the tangles of idolatry and sin, offers the soul that peace, *quies, hesychia*, which spiritual persons know already here below, a blissful visitation of Christ who is always present in hell. For since Holy Saturday and the Ascension he is the fulfilment of all things. The Church does not forget that for the dead, fixed on their ignorance or greed or pride, there are states in which the peace, the silence, the light, and the glimpse of the Physician's presence are experienced as torments. But the Church with all her love and all her power of intercession – that intercession for the damned to which Péguy's Joan of Arc summoned the saints – prays for all the dead, including those who are in transitory 'hells'. That is so especially in the Byzantine rite during the 'prayers of genuflexion' at the Vespers of Pentecost. The love of God, multiplied by the prayers of the faithful, works from within upon the individual in order that, since no one is alone, each may, with a personal effort, become opened up to the ontological unity of the Body of Christ.

As for the communion of the angels and the saints, they keep watch over the slow and painful exodus of humanity towards the Kingdom. As discarnate souls, the saints after their death, which is for them a very simple passing over 'to the other side of things', also keep watch in the light for the ultimate transfiguration of the cosmos and therewith of their bodies. They await the fulfilment of the illimitable human and divine communion when God shall be manifestly 'all in all'.

One day a soldier asked an elder whether God grants pardon to
sinners. The elder answered, 'Tell me, my good friend, if your cloak
is torn, do you throw it away?' The soldier replied, 'No. I mend it
and continue to use it.' The elder concluded, 'If you take good care
of your cloak, will not God be merciful to his own image?'

Sayings of the Desert Fathers (In T. Merton, p. 113)

God in his love punishes, not to take revenge, far from it. He
seeks the restoration of his own image and does not prolong his
anger.

ISAAC OF NINEVEH *Ascetic Treatises*, 73 (p. 285)

In their waiting and preparing for the Parousia, spiritual people
are impelled to pray for the salvation of all by their sense of universal
fellowship in Christ, and by their conviction that the only way to be
saved is to accept responsibility for all. Dionysius the Areopagite
powerfully reminds us that we ourselves cannot condemn or damn
anyone at all, and that our zeal to 'avenge God' in fact shuts us into
the hell of our own vindictiveness. It is true that thunderbolts were
needed to protect the Hebrew people, that amazing laboratory of
humanity, from idolatry. But the coming of Christ was the coming of
a fellowship without limits. Jesus refused to let the Samaritans who
would not receive him be consumed by fire (Luke 9.53). He prayed
for his executioners, he remains close to those who reject him and
makes himself their advocate. In Jesus, God is not one who hurls
thunderbolts but one who lets himself be crucified.

Is it not true that Christ draws near with love to those who turn
away from him? That he struggles with them, begs them not to
scorn his love, and if they show only aversion and remain deaf to
his appeals, becomes himself their advocate?

DIONYSIUS THE AREOPAGITE *Letter 8*, To Demophilus (PG 3,1085)

For those who have behaved wickedly towards him, Jesus during
his Passion implores the Father's forgiveness. But he reproaches
his disciples who thought it right to punish mercilessly the hy-
pocrisy of his Samaritan persecutors (Luke 9.53). Now, what
you have the audacity to repeat thousands of times in your letter
is that you have not been seeking personal revenge but venge-
ance on God's behalf. Tell me then truly, is it with evil that one
avenges him who is Goodness itself?

'We have not a high priest who is unable to sympathize with our weaknesses' (Hebrews 4.15). On the contrary he knows nothing of wickedness and has compassion on us. 'He will not wrangle or cry aloud' (Matthew 12.19), for 'He is gentle' (ibid. 11.29) and 'He is the expiation for our sins' (I John 2.2). Therefore we cannot tolerate outbursts of anger. They do not bear witness to true zeal, not even if you were to invoke a thousand times the examples of Phineas (Numbers 25.1) and Elijah (1 Kings 18.40). When those of his disciples who did not at all share the spirit of gentleness and kindness invoked those precedents, Jesus was not in the least impressed by them (Luke 9.54). So it is that our divine Master instructs with benevolence those who set them-selves against the divine teaching. For the ignorant need to be instructed, not punished. You do not strike a blind man; you take him by the hand to lead him.

DIONYSIUS THE AREOPAGITE *Letter 8*, To Demophilus (PG 3,1096)

Dionysius relates the vision of a holy man whose indignation which he considered righteous had led him to pray for the damnation of a blasphemer, and for one of the faithful whom he had expelled from the Church. Carpus's vision convinces him that to wish to damn anyone is to attack Christ himself, to annul his Passion and so to compel him to undergo it again; similarly it is to throw oneself, by one's own action, into the abyss.

One day I was in Crete. The holy man Carpus welcomed me to his home. If there exists anyone predisposed to contemplation by the purity of his mind, it is he ... yet he told me that one day he was exasperated by the infidelity of a man. The cause of his bitterness was that this infidel had turned away from faith in God one of the members of his church, at a time when he was still celebrating the solemnity of his baptism. Carpus in his goodness should have been duty bound to pray for both of them ... to try tirelessly to regain them until the day when their objections had been cleared up ... Instead, Carpus for the first time in his life felt grieved and indignant. It was in this state of mind that he went to bed and fell asleep. In the middle of the night, at the hour when he was in the habit of waking of his own accord to sing the praises of God, he arose, still prey to unspiritual irritation, saying to himself that it was not right to let someone live ... and he begged God to hurl his inexorable thunderbolt to put an end at a single stroke to the life of two unbelievers. At that moment, he said, the house where he was suddenly seemed to rock this way and that, then to split in two from the roof down the middle. A vivid flame appeared which came down on him; the sky was rent; Jesus revealed himself in the midst of a multitude of angels . . .

Carpus lifted his eyes and stood astonished at what he saw. Looking down, he told me, he watched the ground itself opening to make a black yawning abyss, and in front of him on the edge of the abyss the two men he had cursed, trembling and gradually losing their foothold. From the bottom of the abyss he saw snakes crawling up and wrapping themselves round the men's feet trying their utmost to drag them down. The men seemed to be on the point of succumbing, partly despite themselves, partly quite willingly, since they were being assaulted and at same time seduced by the Evil One. Carpus was overjoyed, he told me, as he contemplated the spectacle beneath him. Forgetting the vision above, he was growing impatient and indignant that the unbelievers had not yet succumbed. Several times he joined his efforts to those of the snakes . . .

In the end he lifted his eyes and saw again in the sky the same vision as shortly before. But this time Jesus, moved with compassion, came down to the unbelievers and stretched out a hand to help them . . . then he said to Carpus, 'Your hand is already raised. It is I whom you should strike, for here I am to suffer again for the salvation of humanity . . . moreover you should consider whether you yourself should not stay in the abyss with the snakes, rather than live with God . . .'

That was Carpus' story, and I believe it.

DIONYSIUS THE AREOPAGITE *Letter 8*, To Demophilus (PG 3, 1097-100)

Certainly the Church has rejected Origen's theory that finally, after going through a multitude of spiritual states, all human beings and even the fallen angels would be reconciled and restored to their original condition. Such a conviction actually conflicts with Christ's warnings so emphatically formulated in the synoptic Gospels. It also belittles the irreducible nature of our freedom. To admit with Origen that evil will come to an end by exhaustion, whereas God alone is infinite and therefore alone able to satisfy the inexhaustible desires of human nature, is to forget the absolute character that belongs to personal freedom precisely because it is in the image of God.

That said, it remains spiritually impossible to talk of hell for others. The theme of hell can only be broached in the language of

I and Thou. The threats in the Gospel concern *me*; they form the serious tragic element in *my* spiritual destiny; they prompt *me* to humility and repentance, because I recognize them as the diagnosis of *my* state. But for *you*, the numberless *you* of my neighbour, I can only serve, bear witness, and pray that you will experience the Risen Christ, and that you and everyone will be saved.

In *My Missions in Siberia*, a book published in 1917, the archimandrite Spiridon quotes the words of a peasant, the 'holy man Simeon': 'For me, sufferings are not an object of fear. What does make me afraid is that God might deprive sinners of his grace . . . I am ready to pray to God not only for all Christians but also for those who have not been baptized. On all of them I have such pity! . . . on those who have been hanged and on those who have committed suicide . . . on all who have died I take pity, and finally even on the devil I take pity. That is what I feel in my heart, O servant of God. Whether it is right or not I do not know. But my heart is like that. St Isaac of Nineveh used to pray 'even for serpents', 'even for demons' (*Ascetic Treatises*, 81).

> St Anthony had prayed to the Lord to be shown to whom he was equal. God had given him to understand that he had not yet reached the level of a certain cobbler in Alexandria. Anthony left the desert, went to the cobbler and asked him how he lived. His answer was that he gave a third of his income to the Church, another third to the poor, and kept the rest for himself. This did not seem a task out of the ordinary to Anthony who himself had given up all his possessions and lived in the desert in total poverty. So that was not where the other man's superiority lay. Anthony said to him, 'It is the Lord who has sent me to see how you live.' The humble tradesman, who venerated Anthony, then told him his soul's secret: 'I do not do anything special. Only, as I work I look at all the passers-by and say, 'So that they may be saved, I, only I, will perish.'
>
> Quoted by the staretz Silvanus (in Archimandrite Sophrony, *Staretz Silouane* (i.e. Silvanus), Paris Sisteron 1973, p. 203).

> Abba Poimen said, 'As far as I am concerned, I reckon I have been thrown into the place where Satan has been thrown.'
>
> *Sayings of the Desert Fathers*, Poimen, 184 (SO 1, p. 252)

These astonishing words of Abba Poimen are a prelude to what Christ was to say in our century to staretz Silvanus of Mount Athos: 'Keep your spirit in hell and despair not.'

There remains the problem of the 'second death' of which the Apocalypse speaks (Revelation 20.14), the problem of the 'eternal' hell after the Parousia.

For the highest spirituality (and theology) of the first centuries, God will be 'all in all'. Certain Fathers granted that God would turn away from those who turned away from him. This is what Western Scholasticism was to term *poena damni*, the penalty of damnation. Such a fundamentalist reading of the Gospels (which leads to speculation on the nature of the 'worm' and the 'fire' that will torment the damned) was denounced not only as external but as 'absurd' by the greatest representatives of the earliest Christianity, for example by St Ambrose of Milan and John Cassian in the West, and in the East, quite apart from strict Origenism, by Gregory of Nyssa, John Climacus, Maximus the Confessor, and Isaac of Nineveh.

For this last author, whose development of the doctrine of hell is undoubtedly the most important contribution to this subject in the whole of Christian theology, it is unthinkable and contrary to the very spirit of the Christian revelation that God should abandon anyone. God, in Christ, gives to everyone the fullness of his love. But this love can be experienced as torment by those who reject it. In its light they discover how much they have sinned against it. The fire of hell is the fire of love that gives remorse a terrible clarity.

> As for me, I say that those who are tormented in hell are tormented by the invasion of love. What is there more bitter and more violent that the pains of love? Those who feel that they have sinned against love bear in themselves a damnation much heavier than the most dreaded punishments. The suffering with which sinning against love afflicts the heart is more keenly felt than any other torment. It is absurd to suppose that sinners in hell are deprived of God's love. Love . . . is offered impartially. But by its very power it acts in two ways. It torments sinners, as happens here on earth when we are tormented by the presence of a friend to whom we have been unfaithful. And it gives joy to those who have been faithful. That is what the torment of hell is in my opinion – remorse.

ISAAC OF NINEVEH *Ascetic Treatises*, 84 (p. 326)

We must pray, however, that the fire of judgement – which is the fire of God's love – will not consume the wicked, but only that part in each one which is evil. The division into 'sheep' and 'goats' of which the Last Judgement scene speaks would thus be made, not between two crowds of human beings, but between two kinds of character within each individual. In practice, other parables of a similar kind like that of the 'good seed' and the 'tares' cannot be interpreted in any other way. Jesus explains that the 'good seed means the sons of the Kingdom; the weeds are the sons of the evil one', and that at the end these latter will be cast into the blazing furnace (Matthew 13.36). Only Gnostics and Manicheans can hold that it is a question here of people. All human beings are creatures of God. What is 'sown by the devil' is destructive suggestions, the seeds of idolatry and folly. Good seed and tares are human dispositions. To destroy the thoughts sown by the evil one is not to destroy the person but to cauterize him. What Gregory of Nyssa suggests is precisely this divine surgery.

> The body is subject to various sorts of illness. Some are easy to treat, others are not, and for the latter recourse is had to incisions, cauterization, bitter medicine ... We are told something of the same sort about the judgement in the next world, the healing of the soul's infirmities. If we are superficial people, that amounts to a threat and a process of severe correction, so that the fear of a painful expiation may lead us to fly from wrongdoing and become wiser people. But the faith of deeper minds regards it as a process of healing and a therapy applied by God in such a way as to bring back the being he created to its original grace.
>
> In fact those who by incisions or cauterization remove boils or warts that have formed contrary to nature on the surface of the body, do not bring about the healing without pain; but it is not to do harm to the patient that they carry out the incision. It is the same with the 'warts' that have formed on our souls ... at the moment of judgment they are cut out and removed by the ineffable wisdom and power of him who is, as the Gospel says, the physician of the sick.
>
> GREGORY OF NYSSA *Great Catechetical Oration,* 8 (PG 45,36-7)

Certainly one cannot put limits to our terrible freedom as human beings (God himself had his hands bound on the cross). Nor, however, can one limit the prayer and the hope of the saints.

> That all should attain to complete detachment is impossible. But it is not impossible that all should be saved and reconciled to God.
>
> JOHN CLIMACUS *The Ladder of Divine Ascent,* 26th step, 54(65), (p. 133)

The same individual is at the same time saved and condemned.
AMBROSE OF MILAN *Commentary on Psalm 118*, 20,58 (PL 15,1238)

And what does he need in order to be saved, except to know himself condemned and not to despair? Deeper than hell is Christ the conqueror of hell.

Prayer then has the last word.

We do not speculate about hell.

Neither need we formulate a doctrine of universal salvation.

We pray that all may be saved.

'One does not save oneself on one's own,' wrote Péguy. 'One does not return alone to the Father's house. One gives a hand to others. The sinner holds the hand of the saint and the saint holds the hand of Jesus.'

The third of the sons' petitions is this, 'Thy will be done on earth as in heaven' . . . this petition can be understood to mean that it is God's will that all should be saved, in accordance with St Paul's well-known words: 'God wills that all should be saved and come to the knowledge of the truth' (1 Timothy 2.4) . . . Therefore when we say, 'Thy will be done on earth as it is in heaven,' we are praying: 'Like those who are in heaven, may all those who are on earth be saved, Father, by the knowledge of thy name.'

JOHN CASSIAN *Conferences*, IX,20 (SC 54, p. 58)

St Isaac of Nineveh, in writings inspired by perfect adoration, designs and paints an icon of God's crazy love for humankind, an icon as beautiful and disturbing as the fresco of the descent into hell at Chora. No, the Lord's compassion will not be defeated. For it must indeed be said 'God is not just', not as atheists say, who only see the earth and do not notice on it the cross or the empty tomb, but on the basis of the cross, the tomb and Easter. This contradicts many theologians who are petrified in their own human idea of justice, and seek to impose it on God. Many indications in the evolution of Jewish thought suggested, and still do suggest, that the essence of biblical justice is Love. An evening prayer of the synagogue says: 'Almighty Lord, King of heaven and earth, I give thee thanks for the gift of the Law by which I can impress on my flesh my love for thee.' The Law is already an exchange of Love. The 'Lord-Love', the 'Love without limits', in the words of a 'Monk of the Eastern

Church' (*Amour sans Limites*, Chevetogne 1971, p. 18) completes
his self-revelation on the cross. God is not just. He is infinitely more
than just. He is the foolishness of love that never ceases coming
down into our hell to raise us up again. Each one of us is the
labourer of the eleventh hour of whom nothing else is asked but
a cry of trust and hope. The only sin, in fact, is 'not to understand the grace of the resurrection'. 'If I had committed all possible
crimes, I should feel that this multitude of offences would be like
a drop of water in a blazing furnace', said St Thérèse of the Child
Jesus, taking up, without being aware of it, almost word for word
the expressions of St Isaac. That is why the Christian message,
today more than ever among so much scepticism, can only be the
proclamation and witness of Christ's victory over death and hell.

> As is a grain of sand weighed against a large amount of gold,
> so, in God, is the demand for equitable judgment weighed against
> his compassion. As a handful of sand in the boundless ocean, so
> are the sins of the flesh in comparison with God's providence
> and mercy. As a copious spring could not be stopped up with a
> handful of dust, so the Creator's compassion cannot be conquered
> by the wickedness of creatures.

ISAAC OF NINEVEH *Ascetic Treatises*, 58 (p. 235-6)

> Do not say that God is just . . . David may call him just and fair,
> but God's own Son has revealed to us that he is before all things
> good and kind. He is kind to the ungrateful and the wicked (Luke
> 6.35). How can you call God just when you read the parable of
> the labourers in the vineyard and their wages? 'Friend, I am doing
> you no wrong . . . I choose to give to this last as I give to you . . .
> do you begrudge my generosity?' (Matthew 20.13). Likewise how
> can you call God just when you read the parable of the prodigal
> son who squanders his father's wealth in riotous living, and the
> moment he displays some nostalgia his father runs to him, throws
> his arms round his neck and gives him complete power over all his
> riches? It is not someone else who has told us this about God, so
> that we might have doubts. It is his own Son himself. He bore this
> witness to God. Where is God's justice? Here, in the fact that we
> were sinners and Christ died for us . . .
>   O the wonder of the grace of our Creator! O the unfathomable
> goodness with which he has invested the existence of us sinners
> in order to create it afresh! . . . Anyone who has offended and
> blasphemed him he raises up again . . . Sin is to fail to understand

the grace of the resurrection. Where is the hell that could afflict us? Where is the damnation that could make us afraid to the extent of overwhelming the joy of God's love? What is hell, face to face with the grace of the resurrection when he will rescue us from damnation, enable this corruptible body to put on incorruption and raise up fallen humanity from hell to glory? ... Who will appreciate the wonder of our Creator's grace as it deserves? ... In place of what sinners justly deserve, he gives them resurrection. In place of the bodies that have profaned his law, he clothes them anew in glory ... See, Lord, I can no longer keep silent before the ocean of thy grace. I no longer have any idea how to express the gratitude that I owe to thee ... Glory be to thee in both the worlds that thou hast created for our growth and delight, guiding us by the path of thy majestic works to the knowledge of thy glory!

ISAAC OF NINEVEH *Ascetic Treatises*, 60 (p. 245-6)

The spirituality that I have tried to present in this book is a spirituality of resurrection. And resurrection begins here and now. It is life in its fullness, life able finally to absorb, reverse and pass beyond death. Zhivago, to the question, 'Are there things in the world that claim our fidelity?' answers, 'Very few. We ought, I think, to be faithful to immortality, which is another name, a richer name, for life. We should be faithful to immortality, faithful to Christ.' Why to Christ? Because once upon a time there was 'a maiden who in silence and in secret gave life to a child and gave the world life, the miracle of life, the life of all things, "Him who is life" as he was to be called later.' (Boris Pasternak, *Doctor Zhivago*.)

Christ is risen from the dead,
Trampling down death by death,
And upon those in the tombs bestowing life.
Troparion, refrain, in the Easter Liturgy of the Byzantine rite.

BIOGRAPHICAL NOTES

Ambrose of Milan (c.334 – 397)

Of all the Latin Fathers, Ambrose is without doubt the one whose thought is most harmoniously balanced. He combined the virtues of a Roman statesman with a deep faith, and a knowledge of Greek theology with the pastoral and moral sense of Latin Christianity.

Born at Trier into a patrician family (his father who died at an early age was Praetorian Prefect for Gaul), Ambrose studied law and rhetoric at Rome and then became Governor of Liguria and Emilia, with his seat at Milan. After the death of that city's bishop, while he himself was only a catechumen, he went to the cathedral to mediate between Arians and the upholders of the dogma of Nicaea (see note on Arianism. The Council of Nicaea was held in 325 A.D. and defined the relation between Christ and the Father as 'consubstantial'). All of them thereupon agreed in acclaiming him bishop. He fled. But he was brought back and was baptized and consecrated bishop (7 December 374). He distributed his fortune to the poor, whose defender he became thenceforward. He deepened his philosophical and theological knowledge, and preached indefatigably. (The part he played in the conversion of St Augustine is well known.) He asserted the spiritual independence of the Church against the State – 'the Emperor is in the Church and not above it' – he frustrated an attempt at pagan restoration at Rome; he contributed peacefully to the disappearance of Arianism on both coasts of the Adriatic; he counselled princes; and in 390 he obliged the Emperor Theodosius to do public penance for having suppressed a riot at Thessalonica by a massacre.

Very conscious of his responsibility as a privileged witness to the faith, Ambrose, from the time that he was consecrated, gave himself to study under the direction of a learned priest, Simplicius, who was to be his successor. He read Philo and Plotinus, and also the Greek Fathers of his own century, Athanasius, the Cappadocians, and Cyril of Jerusalem; and he received much, though not without exercising the requisite discernment, from the spiritual exegesis of Alexandria, that of Origen and Didymus. His spirituality is deeply ecclesial, as is shown by the two studies that he consecrated to the 'mysteries'. The marriage of the soul to Christ takes place within that between Christ and his Church; the Church is 'virgin in her sacraments, mother of her people'. Like the Greek Fathers, under the influence of the contemporary monastic movement, he valued spiritual virginity very highly, but he is able to speak of ascesis with delicacy, humanity, and evangelical freedom and moderation. He is concerned with the formation of clerics able to teach the laity elementary practical wisdom. Poet and composer, he is the true creator of hymn-singing in the Latin Church, singing that allowed all the people to join in the celebration.

On the Sacraments SC 25 bis; *On Penance* SC 179; *On Virginity* PL 16,272; *Commentary on Psalm 118* PL 15,1224; *On Elijah and Fasting* PL 14,698

ANTHONY THE GREAT (251 – 356)

The most celebrated of the first monks. His life, written by Athanasius of Alexandria who knew him personally, shows his spiritual journey to be the synthesis and the model of monasticism's essential qualities. He was born near Memphis in Egypt into an already Christian family of well-to-do farmers and he was profoundly affected at the age of eighteen by the Gospel injunction that he heard read in Church: 'If you would be perfect, go, sell what you possess and give to the poor ... and follow me' (Matthew 19.21).

So he distributed all his possessions and established himself near his village in a hut, under the direction of an experienced 'elder'. His life was interwoven with prayer nourished on Holy Scripture, with a sober ascesis, with fasts and sleeping rough, and manual work to help the poor. This was an almost cenobitic stage (a community life of sorts). Later he retired, all alone, to the Egyptian desert, finding shelter in a tomb dug out of the rock, then barricading himself into a disused fort. This was the anchorite stage (withdrawal into solitude) in which he confronted, in Christ, death and the demoniacal powers that haunt our unconscious, all of them things of which the desert appeared to be the site and the symbol. Thus he passed through the trial of spiritual abandonment and a long experience of death and resurrection, of descent into hell and of Easter. At the end of twenty years he emerged from his solitude totally imbued with the light and the peace and the strength of the Holy Spirit. From then on he exercised a far-reaching spiritual fatherhood by the 'word of life' and by 'power' (namely, discernment, prophecy, and healing). He died at the age of 105, 'his face radiant with joy', on 17 January 356.

The Life of Saint Anthony by St Athanasius is in PG 26,835-976

APOSTOLIC CONSTITUTIONS: RULES OF THE APOSTLES

The *Apostolic Constitutions* are an enormous canonical and liturgical composition attributed to the Apostles but probably worked out in Syria about the end of the fourth century. Inserted in it, with modifications, are the *Didascalia*, likewise said to be 'of the Apostles' and composed in Syria at the beginning of the third century, the *Didache*, and in the eighth book the *Apostolic Tradition* of Hippolytus of Rome, containing the oldest text of the liturgy known to us.

The 85 *Rules of the Apostles*, concerned with the clergy and the organization of the Church, are found at the end of the *Apostolic Constitutions*, whose provisions they summarize. These also were drawn up about the end of the fourth century in the form of conciliar rules, often like those of the Councils of Antioch (341) and Laodicea (between 343 and 381).

The text is found in E.X. Funk, *Didascalia et Constitutiones Apostolorum*, vol. 1, Paderborn 1905.

ATHANASIUS OF ALEXANDRIA (295 – 373)

Formed not by the apprenticeship of ancient literature and philosophy but by the Christian milieu in the period of the persecutions, this Egyptian who spoke and wrote Coptic as well as Greek was the unremitting defender of the Church's independence from the Empire. He became a Christian but he was continually tempted to support Arianism (see separate Note) which denied the divinity of Christ. Athanasius, then a deacon, accompanied his bishop to the Council of Nicaea which in 325 proclaimed Christ *homoousios*, that is, 'consubstantial', in essence identical with the Father, the 'source' of the Godhead. In 328 he became archbishop of Alexandria and all Egypt. Confronted by the Arian reaction he made himself the staunch defender of the *homoousion* and received the unreserved help of his people and of the monastic movement that was then developing in Egypt. For Athanasius, to say that Christ is fully God is to make possible the deification of humanity. ('What is not assumed is not saved.') All his thought revolves around the bold assertion: 'God became man in order that man might become God.' In Christ all humanity is 'worded' (in the Logos) and human beings become capable of receiving the Spirit . . . As the Arians relied on those texts of the Old Testament which might suggest that the Wisdom of God was something created, Athanasius developed a whole 'sophiology' (from *sophia*, wisdom) to show the connection of the Logos, uncreated Wisdom, with created wisdom, the revelation of the divine activity in creatures and the whole cosmos.

Athanasius's attitude of resistance earned him two periods of exile in the West (at Trier 335-337; at Rome and Aquileia 339-346) where he busied himself in consolidating the dogma of Nicaea. From the fifties when the tension became too great he 'went underground' of his own accord in the Egyptian desert with some monks (356-361 and 362-363) and especially with St Anthony whose *Life* he was to write. His work opened the way to the triumph of the *homoousion*, the foundation of the Christian concept of the person. In his *Twelfth Provincial Letter* Pascal wrote, referring to Athanasius: 'All the efforts of violence to weaken the truth serve only to make it stand out the more clearly'.

Letters to Serapion on the Holy Spirit PG 26, 529-676; *On the Incarnation and Against the Arians* SC 199; *On Virginity* PG 28, 251-282

AUGUSTINE OF HIPPO (354 – 430)

Augustine is the Father of the Church who more than any other has influenced the Church in the West, for better or for worse, and it is important today to reinsert his voice into the patristic symphony from which his work was isolated by the barbarian invasions.

His seeking, his suffering, the stages of his conversion have been admirably recounted in his *Confessions* and are astonishingly modern. Augustine was born at Thagaste (the modern Souk-Akhras in Algeria) into one of those families of small landowners who were oppressed by taxation yet made a point of giving their children a classical education. So Augustine studied in the great classical tradition in which he later became a teacher of oratory. But he did not learn Greek and his knowledge of philosophy was self-taught, though brilliantly so. His temperament was passionate and sensual and he rejected the Christianity of his mother, Monica, in favour of Manicheism. This presented itself as a *gnosis*, a science of the invisible, professing a metaphysical (and dietary) distinction between light and dark beings. At Milan he discovered, through a Latin translation, Plotinus and the deep inner experiences in which a human being could be identified with the Absolute. The influence of Ambrose who was then bishop of Milan, the influence of Monica, his reading of the *Life of St Anthony*, the epistles of St Paul that he opened unexpectedly at the unsought suggestion of a child humming, '*Tolle, lege*' (Take and read) and St Paul bidding him to 'put on Christ', all contributed to his conversion in the summer of 386. Augustine received baptism at the hands of Ambrose during the Easter Vigil in 387.

Back in Africa he was soon, against his will, chosen by the people to help the bishop of Hippo (today Anaba in Algeria) first as priest, then as coadjutor bishop. On the bishop's death Augustine succeeded him. Henceforward the 'episcopal burden' was his – a people to teach and protect, and the African Church to defend from heresy. Augustine had to face the twilight of a civilization. The barbarians sacked Rome in 410 and then invaded North Africa, and were besieging Hippo when Augustine died there. In his *City of God* he elaborated a theology of history that shows the irreducible tension there is between the earthly city and the heavenly city. He laid the foundations of a Christian culture.

His work is enormous, ranging far and wide, often written in response to the demand of polemics. He asserts the fundamental goodness of all that exists, against the Manicheans (for whom 'good' and 'evil', 'light' and 'darkness', are two separate opposed principles). In the face of the Donatists he maintains that the Church is the whole Christ. (The Donatists began by taking up an intransigent attitude towards those Christians who during the persecutions had renounced the faith and later repented. They then founded a Counter-Church in North Africa, administering a second baptism.) Against the Pelagians Augustine proclaims the sovereignty of grace. For them the human being is the cause of his own salvation through ascesis and moral discipline. Augustine shaped the Western approach to the mystery of God, seeing images of the Trinity everywhere, but chiefly in human nature with its facilities of memory, knowledge-intellect and love-will. He declares that the Spirit is the joint gift of the Father and the Son, though proceeding *principaliter* (primarily) from the Father, and identifies him – for nothing in God can be impersonal – with the love that unites the Father and the Son. His experience – a song of love – is that of the overwhelming irruption of the grace that alone can set freedom free. But the emphasis is shifted from the transfiguration of the universe to the tragedy of the human condition. In particular, in the course of controversy with the Pelagians, who taught that salvation is won solely by human effort, he so hardened his systematization as to produce an unacceptable version of the concept of predestination, where sovereign grace is in the last resort arbitrary, rescuing the elect from the *massa damnata*, the *massa perditionis*. It is because Augustine's thought has devastated Western Christianity in these last points, and given rise to the atheism of, for example, Camus, that it is important to bring Augustine into dialogue with patristic thought as a whole.

However, the essential point of his work, from the spiritual point of view, is to be found not only in the *Confessions* but also in his commentaries on the Psalms and on St John. There are dramatic descriptions of desire and of grace, of the insatiable heart that can find its rest only in God, the theme of 'God and my soul', representations of a fallen age as saved 'in the present moment', the sketch of an almost Dostoyevskian concept of salvation through love. His is an expression of the Tradition that is also very biblical – 'because each one of us is singing this song of praise, we are a unity in Christ, and the singer is a single person.'

Commentary on Psalm 41, PL 36,464-76; *Commentary on Psalm 121*, PL 36,1618-29; *Sermon* 23, PL 38,155-62; *Sermon 261*, PL 38,1202-7; *Sermon 346*, PL 38,1522-4; *Confessions* English translations abound.

BALAI (died 460)

A Syrian religious poet, probably a chorepiscopus (i.e. bishop of a rural district, from *chora*, country), of Beroea, the modern Aleppo. Many of his poems are lost. Those that have survived have found a place in the Syriac liturgy. They are characterized by a very Semitic wealth of imagery in which all 'linear' logic disappears amid an arabesque of symbols.

Hymn for the Consecration of a New Church is in Bickell I, pp. 77-82

BARSANUPHIUS (died c. 540)

The sixth century was marked in the Christian East by the condemnation of Origenism that mixed with Christianity the elements of a Hellenistic gnosis. This return to biblical anthropology, to the theme of the spiritual 'heart' open to the divine *agape*, this more virile and realistic teaching is contained in St Barsanuphius' witness and correspondence. Of this 'great elder' who is inseparable from his friend John 'the Prophet' nothing is known except that he was a recluse in the monastery of Seridos in the desert of Gaza, and that he exercised his spiritual fatherhood through his letters – a fact that enables us to receive his teaching just as it was given. He himself, it seems, was endowed with the gifts of prophecy, discernment of spirits and, although he was not a priest, the 'power to remit sins', even at a distance. Emphasis is laid on humility acquired through obedience; it makes possible the approach to inner freedom, 'freedom from care and concern' (*amerimnia*). Profound peace and joy (*hesychia*), if it is not to become delusion and pride, must find its expression in compassion. For those living in the world, humble invocation is always possible – 'for us, the weak, it remains only to take refuge in the Name of Jesus' (Letter 301). It gives an awareness of the presence of God: 'To keep the mind in the presence of God and speak to him' (Letter 78). And always the 'fountain of knowledge' must lead to that 'of love' (Letter 119).

The Greek text of the *Correspondence* was published, edited by St Nicodemus the Hagiorite, at Venice in 1816, and again, with improvements, at Volo in 1960. A translation into French made from more complete Greek and Georgian manuscripts is available in *Barsanuphe et Jean de Gaza, Correspondence*, Solesmes, 1972.

BASIL OF CÆSAREA or BASIL THE GREAT (c.329 – 379)

St Basil, his brother Gregory of Nyssa, and his friend Gregory Nazianzen are known as the 'Cappadocian Fathers' from the name of a province in Asia Minor then strongly Hellenized. They completed the dogma of Nicaea (the *homoousion*), by elaborating the great Trinitarian antinomy of the one Essence and the three Persons (the 'hypostases').

Basil was born into a Christian family which numbered martyrs among its members. Several of them while he was young were drawn to the contemplative life. None the less the young man, the son of a famous orator, attended the best schools including the university of Athens, where he became a friend of Gregory Nazianzen. He drew on the scientific knowledge of his time in his *Hexameron*, studies on the creation of the world. He also wrote a small treatise, *To Young People, on how to profit from pagan literature*. And so, without denying the culture he had gained, he was attracted, about 356, by the immense monastic movement of those days and he travelled in quest of exemplars and spiritual masters in the 'deserts' of Syria, Mesopotamia and Egypt. On his return to Cappadocia he settled in solitude, and with his friend Gregory wrote his first *Philokalia*, an anthology of spiritual texts from Origen. In 364 he began to draw up the monastic rules on which he never ceased to work. They treat less of ascetic feats and charismatic exaltation than of a return to the apostolic life of the first Christian community – a common life of true 'Christians' with no other designation, founded on charity, attention to others, work, social service, prayer and meditation on Scripture. From 362 onwards the Church imposed unforeseen responsibilities on Basil. He was made priest, his bishop's auxiliary, then himself bishop of Caesarea, and in 370 metropolitan of Cappadocia.

He had to deal with a twofold crisis, social and spiritual, which led him to confront the civil authorities with consummate firmness. A more or less totalitarian state was crushing a society in which contrasts were exacerbated. In his speeches and his various interventions, Basil insisted on the equal dignity of all people and on the limits of private property. Near Caesarea he organized a complete city of social service run by monks. The people gave it the name 'Basiliad'. It contained a guest house, a hospice, a hospital, and there were free meals and lodging for the poorest workers. At the same time he increased the number of monastic communities as centres of fellowship. He developed liturgical life – the Eucharistic liturgy 'of St Basil' is still in use today in the Orthodox Church – and his spiritual texts, beneath a Stoic dress, are deeply evangelical and Pauline: 'It is not you who by your virtue have laid hold of Christ, but Christ who has laid hold of you by his coming' (Homily 2). And all the ascesis has as its magnetic attraction the beauty of Christ. 'Ineffable is the beauty of the Word . . . the form of God in his appearance. Blessed are those who with all their longing contemplate the true beauty!' (Homily on Psalm 44).

St Basil contributed powerfully to overcoming the Arian crisis. He attacked the Eunomians vigorously for pretending that human reason can know God completely. Basil emphasized that God is ineffable, inaccessible, knowable only in his 'energies'. On the other hand he showed himself tolerant towards those who baulked at the *homoousion*, without calling into question the divinity of Christ. He admitted them to communion and gradually won them over. When the *Pneumatomachi* denied the divinity of the Spirit, he showed its necessity without explicitly asserting it in his Treatise on the Holy Spirit. He was delicate in health, worn out by ascesis and hardship, and died prematurely in his fifties. But he had opened the way for the Second Ecumenical Council that in 381 proclaimed the divinity of the Spirit 'the Giver of Life'.

On the Holy Spirit SC 17 bis; *Longer Rules* PG 31,889-1052; *Short Ascetic Instruction* PG 31,620-5

BENEDICT OF NURSIA (480 – 547)

The life of St Benedict is known from the *Dialogues of St Gregory*, written about forty years after Benedict's death and based, for all their abundance of miracles, on the memories of actual witnesses.

Benedict was born in 480 near Nursia in Central Italy into a family of the lesser nobility. He was sent to Rome to study rhetoric and law, but took flight without warning to the 'desert' of Subiaco, where he lived for a long time in complete solitude. Disciples then came to him and prevailed upon him to found a dozen small monasteries of the Pachomian type, each with its own superior, Benedict reserving to himself the formation of the novices. Twenty years passed in this way. Then opposition on the part of the local clergy, perhaps also of his monks, caused Benedict to withdraw once again. He founded accordingly a completely communitarian monastery on the top of Monte Cassino. He evangelized the surrounding countryside, and directed a community of nuns that was governed by his sister, Scholastica. In Gregory's account of him he appears as endowed with the spiritual gift of healing and as a mystic who had a vision of the whole universe gathered together in a ray of divine light. He died about 547, after having completed his *Rule*, which was adopted during the sixth century by all the West and was to make him the father of the monks of the Latin Church.

St Benedict's *Rule* or 'Rule for Monasteries' draws its inspiration from an anonymous text received from tradition, the 'Rule of the Master'. Benedict, having practised this Rule at Subiaco, reduced and remodelled it, transforming a diffuse text into a sober and balanced document of great spiritual toughness and flexibility.

The monastery is a 'school of the Lord's service' entirely directed towards the coming of the Kingdom. The monks, who are committed to a lifelong 'stability', owe obedience to the abbot whom they have elected for life. The abbot, who is at once administrator and spiritual director, has to adapt the ascetical training to each person's vocation in accordance with a love that includes 'discretion'. The monastery, where relationships between the brethren strictly follow the grades of the hierarchy, forms a more or less self-contained society that is organized for sharing and welcome. Manual work, the recitation of the Divine Office, and times of solitude and silence in which prayerful meditation on Scripture (the *lectio divina*) holds a prominent place, make up the monk's life. There is a large measure of continuity with Eastern sources of monasticism, either directly quoted (from St Basil) or transmitted by Cassian, whose *Conferences* and *Institutes* are mentioned at the end of St Benedict's Rule. The opening of one's heart to the abbot, the control of one's thoughts, the registering of spiritual progress by the degrees of humility, the fundamental theme of 'peace', resembling Eastern *hesychia*, all these are marks of fidelity to the spiritual Orient, and make Benedictine monasteries still today places of the undivided Church. Moreover, the *Rule*, in its conclusion, defines itself as a 'beginning' and makes reference to the great witness of the original sources.

English translations of the *Rule* abound.

CLEMENT OF ALEXANDRIA (140 – c.220)

He was Christianity's first religious philosopher. Titus Flavius Clemens, born to pagan parents, travelled far and wide in search of wisdom. He visited Greece, Sicily where he became a Christian, Asia Minor, and finally Egypt, where the teaching of the gnostic Pantaenus induced him to settle in Alexandria. He became a spiritual teacher himself, opening his school to pagans as well as Christians. It seems that he was ordained priest. About 210 or 215 he put himself at the service of the bishop of Jerusalem, and died a few years later. Clement considers that Christianity is *the* thought and *the* knowledge par excellence, since the Logos who became incarnate in Christ is he who creates and structures the world, the Great Reason that enlightens every human reason. Consequently it is the duty of Christianity to make its own all the religious traditions of mankind, all its philosophical and scientific searchings. Therefore Clement, whose store of Greek culture was enormous, and who was well acquainted also with Jewish and Judaeo-Christian exegetical traditions, worked out a huge synthesis intended as an appropriate introduction to the study of them all.

In the *Protrepticus* (Exhortation) he addresses himself to the pagans, to convert them to the new Orpheus, the plenary revelation of the cosmic and historical Logos. In the *Paedagogus* (Tutor) he offers the new converts a moral teaching, the aim of which is purification of the mind. It is a transfiguration of Stoic ethics, a Christian humanism that is pacific, serene, moderate in its austerity, not a break with the world but freedom for the soul. In the *Stromateis* (miscellanies, many-coloured tapestries) his exegesis introduces the reader to the mystery of the cosmos and then to the mystery of God. The gnosis of love is an infinite progression in this life and the next through the angelic abodes: God in giving himself 'continually withdraws to a distance from one who seeks him' (*Stromateis* I, II, 5,4).

Paedagogus SC 70, 108, 158; *Stromateis* I, SC 30; II, SC 38; V, SC 278; *What Rich Man can be Saved?* PG 9,603. The Greek of all the books is in PG 8 & 9.

CYPRIAN OF CARTHAGE (c.200 – 258)

He is the principal authority of the Latin Church before St Augustine. He is an important witness to Tradition in regard to the nature and life of the Church, although his thought on the boundaries of the Church and salvation is, under the influence of Tertullian, abrupt and restrictive.

Thascius (Caecilius) Cyprianus was born at the beginning of the third century, presumably at Carthage, into a rich and cultured pagan family. He was a famous but agonized orator, and 'he became a Christian under the influence of the priest Caecilius from whom he received his second name. He gave all his fortune to the poor' (St Jerome, *Illustrious Men*, 67). He was soon elected 'by the voice of the people' to be bishop of Carthage, in 248. A year later the Decian persecution broke out. Cyprian chose to go underground but to keep in touch with his people. On his return to Carthage he had to cope with the schisms that had been brought about, in Africa as in Rome, by the problem of how to deal with the *lapsi*, Christians who had denied their faith during the persecution and later asked to be received back into the Church. Cyprian imposed a severe penance on them. During the plague of 252-254 persecution threatened afresh, many holding those 'atheists', the Christians, responsible for the disaster. But Cyprian appeased the people by his heroic organization of relief.

From 255 Cyprian came into conflict with the Bishop of Rome, Stephen, on the question of baptism administered by heretics. Stephen admitted its validity. Cyprian denied it, and his point of view was confirmed by the councils that met under his presidency at Carthage in 255-256. But soon persecution broke out again and first Stephen and then Cyprian in 258 suffered martyrdom.

Apart from his apologetic and moral writings, Cyprian's most important works – his 81 *Letters* and his treatise *On the Unity of the Church* – are concerned with ecclesiology. Ecclesial communion demonstrates Trinitarian love. Fundamentally the Church is the local eucharistic community around its bishop. The unity of the universal Church remains to be defined. For Cyprian, all the bishops together – *in solidum* – sit on the 'chair of Peter'. Each bishop therefore, to the extent of his communion with the others, is the successor of Peter. The Bishop of Rome is the sign of the unity of the episcopate but he has no jurisdiction over his peers.

The *Letters* have been recently edited, in an English translation by G.W. Clarke, in the Ancient Christian Writers series (4 vols.).

CYRIL OF ALEXANDRIA (c.376 – 444)

This 'pope' of Alexandria, a veritable 'pharaoh' of Christian Egypt by family tradition (he was the nephew of his predecessor Theophilus), presents two different faces to posterity. On the one hand he is a powerful this-worldly ruler, who controls the supply of provisions to the capital of the Empire, Constantinople; who owns vast landed estates; who mobilizes the roughest of the Coptic monks for riots and pogroms; who buys the necessary complicity of members of the Emperor's entourage. Relentless in imposing the superiority of his see on the East, his reputation was permanently blemished by the 'Synod of the Oak' in 403 to which he accompanied his uncle. On that occasion Theophilus brought about the deposition of John Chrysostom, who was doubly his enemy, as an Antiochene and as Archbishop of Constantinople. Cyril himself harshly manipulated the

Council of Ephesus in 431, in his turn bringing about the deposition of Nestorius, the capital's archbishop, not allowing him to defend himself, and without waiting for the Antiochenes to arrive. He was a traditionalist who put the principle of authority in first place (at least in his own Alexandrian tradition). He detested change. He persecuted Jews and heretics and drove them out of Alexandria. He allowed a fanatical mob to massacre the beautiful virgin Hypatia who was a great mathematician and a neo-Platonist philosopher.

Cyril's other face, however, is that of a profound theologian, Johannine in his inspiration; and this phenomenon is understandable in an ideology the kernel of which was not political but spiritual. He laid the emphasis on the unity of the divine and human in Christ, to the extent of speaking of 'a single incarnate nature of the divine Logos', an ambiguous formula which he believed was that of Athanasius but which was in fact that of Apollinaris (for whom the Logos in Christ takes the place of the human soul) and was used by the Monophysites (a sect that asserted that there was only one nature in Christ – the divine, which absorbed or utilized his human faculties). None the less Cyril confesses the full humanity of Christ, but insists on the fact that the subject of this humanity is a divine Person. Therefore Mary is not only the mother of Christ the man, as Nestorius would have it, but she is truly the 'mother of God', *Theotokos*. And it is this expression, and this theology, that were confirmed while Nestorius was condemned, by the strange Council of Ephesus (431), later recognized by the mind of the Church as the Third Ecumenical Council. It is in conformity with this therefore that, according to Cyril, it can be said that on the cross God suffered death in the flesh – the whole mystery of the crucified God.

Cyril develops in this way an 'energetic' theology, a sacramental conception of the humanity of Christ being made divine by the fire of the godhead, and as a result really making us divine.

In 433 this intransigent theologian accepted reconciliation with John of Antioch in an approach in which the unity of Christ's person and the duality of his natures are nicely balanced. It is indeed a preliminary to the grand dogma of Chalcedon (451) on the divine humanity of Jesus.

That Christ is One SC 97, p.302-515; *Dialogue on the Trinity* SC 231, 237, 246; *Commentary on St John* PG 73 & 74; *Thesaurus (Treasure)* PG 75,9-656. The *Homilies on Luke* are extant only in a Syriac version.

CYRIL OF JERUSALEM (c.315 – 387)

Hardly anything is known of Cyril's origins and formation but he was destined for the priesthood, and his priestly ministry consisted chiefly of catechism and preaching. He became bishop of Jerusalem about 350. Persecuted by the Arians whom he steadfastly opposed, he was three times ejected from his see. However, like many Eastern bishops, while admitting Christ's perfect divinity, he avoids the *homoousion*. He was caught up in the great movement of reconciliation that culminated in the Council of Constantinople in 381, a Council that definitively rehabilitated him: 'He was canonically elected and fought against the Arians'. Fighter and peacemaker, he was a foe to all magic forms of sacramentalism and he did not hesitate in a time of famine to sell materials consecrated to sacred uses, which the devout were scandalized to see subsequently being worn by an actress.

Cyril of Jerusalem is essentially a catechist. His 25 *Baptismal Catecheses*, the last five of which, known as 'Mystagogical', are perhaps the work of his successor John, follow the rhythm of Christian initiation: the history of salvation, entirely biblical, during Lent; and access to the mysteries, baptism, confirmation and the Eucharist (which because they are mysteries are explained in the 'mystagogical' catecheses), during the Easter vigil.

These texts are precious for enabling us to understand the meaning which the early Church gave to the principal sacraments, and its practice in administering them. Cyril's sensitivity has something Semitic about it – he looks upon life and the body and creation with the eyes of one who blesses them.

Mystagogical Catecheses SC 126

CYRILLONAS (second half of the 4th century)

A Syrian poet and hymn-writer. Almost nothing is known of his life save that he came from Mesopotamia and was a deacon, perhaps a bishop. Six of his compositions survive, some of them *memre*, narratives, others *madrashe*, hymns. They are as beautiful and spiritually profound as those of St Ephraim. In one of them he alludes to the invasion of the Huns (and of locusts – a cosmic calamity rather than historical!) in 396, the only chronological indication connected with his name.

Supplication to God, for the Feast of All Saints, in the year 396, on the occasion of the invasion of locusts and other misfortunes, chiefly the war against the Huns. Text and translation in G. Bickell I, pp.24-26

DIADOCHUS OF PHOTIKE (5th century)

He is one of the principal spiritual authorities of the Christian East, and one of the first witnesses to the 'Jesus prayer'.

Little is known of his life. He was bishop of Photike in Epirus and connected with the whole monastic movement of the region at the time of the Council of Chalcedon (451). He criticized Monophysitism (the doctrine of a single nature in Christ) which that Council rejected. H.I. Marrou advances the hypothesis that he had been carried off in a Vandal raid on Epirus (Procopius mentions the raid) and taken captive to Carthage. This would account for the fact that the influence of this initiator of Byzantine tradition is found in the treatise *On the Contemplative Life* by Julian of Pomerium who lived in Africa before becoming the teacher of Caesarius of Arles. This might be the origin of Diadochus' uninterrupted influence in the West, right through to Ignatius of Loyola and Teresa of Avila.

Diadochus' spirituality is well balanced: austere, certainly, but with allusions to secular life and art that testify, as his style does, to a profound humanist culture.

Diadochus fought against the amoral (and anti-cultural) quietism of the Messalians. (This Gnostic sect appeared in the fourth century in Asia Minor. The Messalians endeavoured to pray without ceasing by continuously reciting the Lord's Prayer – hence their name, which comes from the Syriac word for prayer. When once the demon that dwelt deep within the soul had been driven out, the 'spiritual' person, whatever he might do, could no longer sin. Like all the Gnostics, the Messalians held the material world to be fundamentally evil, so they rejected the Old Testament, that is, God as Creator, and the sacraments of the Church. They occupy an important place in the complex genealogy of medieval Catharism.) Diadochus criticised the idea of an *apatheia* that once it was acquired would dispense one from ethical endeavour. He showed himself more than reserved in regard to visions. He emphasized that the devil is exterior to the heart of a baptized person, and he stressed the 'educative desolation' by which God leads a person to humility. Steeped in the thought of

Evagrius, he reorganized those ideas into a more biblical, warmer tradition, that of the 'heart' as the organ of loving awareness that brings the whole personality into action. His predominant intuition is that of the 'experience of God', an experience of the 'heart' and also of the 'mind'. He expresses it in a language that is paradoxical, for a Greek, yet it aptly conveys the transfiguration of the whole being, including the body, starting from the organ that is its true centre.

This 'feeling of the heart' that was shattered by the fall is re-unified by grace and it brings a person certainty and *plerophoria* (plenitude). 'Mindfulness of God' is obtained by the 'invocation of the Lord Jesus' and by 'meditation on his holy and glorious Name.' Diadochus is therefore one of the first witnesses to the *monologistos* prayer consisting of one word only: the Name of Jesus.

A Hundred Gnostic Chapters on Spiritual Perfection SC 5 bis; *Catecheses* SC 5 bis

DIDACHE or TEACHING OF THE TWELVE APOSTLES (c.100)

This small book, the exact title of which is *Instruction from the Lord through the Twelve Apostles to the Pagans*, was discovered at Constantinople in 1875 and gives us a better understanding of the life of the first Christians. It was regarded in the Church of Egypt as an inspired book by the end of the fourth century and found a place in canonical and liturgical compilations accredited to the Apostles.

It is meant probably as a sort of manual, a collection of instructions put together by a missionary (an 'apostle') for the use of his communities. It doubtless constitutes – for there is a 'riddle of the *Didache*' – the specifically Christian or Judaeo-Christian development of a Jewish catechism, *The Two Ways*, that is akin to the Rule of Qumran. Thus the *Didache* can be dated to the end of the first century, and assigned to the first Christian communities of Palestine and Syria.

It comprises three parts. The first presents a general view of Christian existence, the way of life opposed to the way of death. The second, liturgical, part treats of baptism 'in the Name of the Father, the Son and the Holy Spirit', in running water if possible; of fasting, on Wednesdays and Fridays; of the eucharistic 'breaking of bread' preceded by a collective confession of sins and the looking for Christ's return. The third part is concerned with the organization of the communities. Their local leaders are called 'bishops' and 'deacons', but the part played by itinerant charismatics – 'prophets' and 'apostles' – is still considerable. The text concludes on a note of eschatological vigilance.

SC 248 prints a critical text.

The Epistle to DIOGNETUS (c. 200)

This short treatise, written in a limpid style and profound in its thought, was composed in Egypt about 200 by an unknown person (Marrou suggests Pantaenus, the teacher of Clement of Alexandria). It is dedicated to a noble and cultured pagan, Diognetus, who is also unknown, but perhaps was the tutor of Marcus Aurelius.

The text gives a most remarkable description of the Christian vocation and way of life at a time when the Church was weak and in a minority, in a pagan society that was often contemptuous and hostile. The horizon for a Christian was martyrdom. The function of example and intercession was ensured by the whole body of the faithful who formed a 'spiritual republic'. There was no institutionalized Christianity as yet, but there was not a ghetto either. Christians lived among other people without anything external to distinguish them, yet bearing the witness of mutual love, of service, of sharing, of conjugal chastity and respect for the new-born child (so often in those days abandoned or killed). By their prayer, by their example, by the mere fact of their presence they are 'the soul of the world', a priestly people set apart not for their own salvation but to protect and save all humankind.

The silence of the ages of Christendom in regard to this text is understandable, as, also, is its relevance to contemporary issues.

Text SC 33

DIONYSIUS THE AREOPAGITE (c. 500)

When St Paul preached before the Areopagus at Athens and proclaimed the resurrection, almost all the hearers scoffed at him or moved away. 'Some men, however, joined him and became believers, including Dionysius, a member of the Council of the Areopagus' (Acts 17.34). Greek tradition regarded him as the first bishop of Athens, Latin tradition as the martyr bishop of Paris.

It was under the name of Dionysius, claiming his authority, that an unknown writer at a considerably later date published a corpus comprising four treatises: the *Divine Names*, the *Mystical Theology*, the *Celestial Hierarchy*, together with about ten *Letters*.

To judge by the theological and liturgical references, by the quotations also from Proclus, the last great Neo-Platonist philosopher, the Dionysian corpus is to be dated to the beginning of the sixth century. However, if the real Dionysius was a Greek thinker converted to Christianity, the texts ascribed to his authorship may be said truly to convey his spirit. They constitute in fact not a Hellenization of Christianity but the brilliant Christianization of the highest thought of expiring Hellenism, perhaps even of the loftiest Indo-European mysticism.

For Dionysius (as we shall call the author of the mysterious texts) the human being is not identified with God, but is made divine in an inexhaustible communion. And God is not the One of the Neo-Platonists. As a result of the encounter of negative theology with revelation, he is seen as 'super-Unity', a unity so productive that it is at the same time Trinity.

Dionysius gives further precision to the distinction, sketched out chiefly by the Cappadocians, between God's inaccessible 'super-essence' and his 'theophanies', the revelations of his energies, his *dynameis*. God is at once 'super-Unity' beyond all naming, and the one to whom all beings give a name. The *dynameis* are not emanations coming down into the material world, as with the Neo-Platonists. They denote an entire presence of the godhead in which each created being participates in accordance with its 'paradigm', its 'predefinition', those 'divine good wills that produce beings and establish them within their limits'. (*Divine Names*, V,8). The universe is thus ordered in three-fold hierarchies – here Proclus can be recognized – traversed by a double movement: that of the 'descent' of the *dynameis*, God 'multiplying himself without losing his Unity' and of the 're-ascent' of creatures towards their origin, becoming as a result divine: and this is the specifically Christian touch, the presupposition of our freedom.

This diversification and unification of created beings expresses a Trinitarian rhythm. The two theological ways, the positive and the negative, correspond to these movements. The negative way, the re-ascent, is therefore superior. Even in symbolic knowledge

Dionysius prefers 'dissimilar' symbols whose poetic violence involves negation – God as rock, fire, sun. The incarnation does not weaken but rather emphasizes, very strongly, the irreducible character of the mystery. Deification transfigures not only the intellect but also the whole person who has become a 'son of the resurrection', caught up into Christ's 'visible theophany'. But deification culminates in 'unknowing', in darkness, where the human person transcends even his intellect to unite himself with the living God.

If Dionysius' ecclesial ideas represent the development of liturgy in the direction of sacred spectacle, where the clergy appear as a hierarchy of the initiated initiating others, it would be impossible to exaggerate the importance of his mystical and symbolic theology, introduced into the main stream of Tradition by the commentaries of John of Scythopolis in the sixth century and completed by Maximus the Confessor in the seventh.

Divine Names PG 3,585-984; *Mystical Theology* PG 3,997-1048; *Celestial Hierarchy* SC 58; *Letters* PG 3,1065-1120

DOROTHEUS OF GAZA (6th century)

Belonging to a well-to-do family, very cultured, so devoted to reading that he took his library with him when he became a religious, Dorotheus as a young man entered the abbot Seridos' monastery near Gaza and became the spiritual son of Barsanuphius and John. These 'great elders' moderated his longing for contemplation and persuaded him to build a hospital for the monks so that he could serve them there. He gradually gave up his possessions, his books, his rich clothes. His correspondence with Barsanuphius is famous for the 'contract' which the latter concluded with him. Barsanuphius took Dorotheus' sins upon himself (Dorotheus was tormented by a sexuality that he had not brought fully under control) on condition that Dorotheus kept himself from pride, scandal-mongering and idle talk, and forced himself to keep God's mercy in mind. It was a case of starting with the most essential things.

After the death of the 'elders', about 540, Dorotheus left his monastery and some distance away founded another community to which he delivered the *Instructions* that have come down to us. His realistic spirituality, full of a serene spirit of renunciation, is resolutely cenobitic; the community forms a veritable ecclesial body, each member of which has his own function to perform. Dorotheus added to the wisdom of the desert a large amount of pagan common sense. He emphasized conscience, the divine spark in everyone, and he defined virtue in the same way as Aristotle, as the 'mean between excess and default'.

Dorotheus puts the accent on 'keeping the commandments' which alone can apply baptismal grace to the root of evil; on 'opening of the heart' to a spiritual father, to whom he recommends discretion; and very particularly on respect for others. He denounces pride among monks and places humility at the summit of spiritual development.

His influence was great on Theodore of Studium, and through him on Eastern monasticism up to the present day.

Instructions SC 92

Ephraim of Syria (c. 306 – 373)

Syriac Christians call Ephraim their 'prophet', the 'doctor of the universe', the 'pillar of the Church', the 'harp of the Holy Spirit'. His hymns have been incorporated into Syriac liturgies. He has been translated, interpolated and imitated in Greek, Armenian, Coptic, Arabic, and Ethiopic. The rhythms of his *memre* – catenae of equisyllabic verses, rather discursive – and of his *madrashe* – unequal strophes sung by a soloist with a refrain taken up by a choir – inspired Byzantine hymn-writing, especially that of Romanus the Melodist.

Ephraim was born in Semitic Mesopotamia, at Nisibis, into a Christian family. He was lastingly influenced by the bishop of that city, James, a great ascetic and a great intellectual who fostered the development of a specifically Syriac theology. He became a 'monk living at home', a vocation common at that time, with brief spells as an anchorite. He was ordained deacon, but always refused the priesthood and the episcopate, going so far, according to Sozomenes, as to feign madness. Under James' successor, Vologesis, (346-361) whom he admired just as much, Ephraim appears as a recognized master of the spiritual life. On several occasions when the Persians were threatening the city, he gave effective advice to his fellow-citizens. In 363 the Roman Empire ceded Nisibis to the Sassanids. Ephraim, with the greater part of the Christian population, took refuge in Roman territory at Edessa, where he founded the famous 'school of the Persians'. He kept in touch with the solitaries of the mountains and often spent a period of retirement among them.

As a deacon, both at Nisibis and at Edessa, Ephraim directed the performance in church of his own compositions, accompanying choirs of children and nuns on the harp.

His enormous literary output is at times autobiographical, as in his Songs of Nisibis in which he mourns the tragedy of his native city and celebrates the two bishops who were his teachers. Most often, however, his treatises are exegetical and his hymns are devoted to faith, to the principal aspects of salvation, and to ascesis. He expresses himself in quite a different cultural universe from that of the Greek Fathers, whose precise and complex elaborations are entirely foreign to him. Ephraim's thought in fact is wholly Semitic, lyrical, biblical, full of images. His images have to be opposed to one another in order to suggest the ineffable character of mystery. In this process it is faith itself that stands out as knowledge and participation in the divine life.

Two main themes run through his thinking: the importance of the Holy Spirit and an existential dualism.

To convey some idea of the Trinity Ephraim speaks of the sun, its rays and its warmth. The Spirit is 'breath and fire'. The incarnation is the work of the Spirit. The body of Christ is white hot with the fire of the Spirit. The same thing is true of his sacramental body, and the Eucharist, especially, appears as 'fire and Spirit'. Deification also is a pneumatization, a being incorporated into the Spirit – sacramental prophecy.

On the other hand Ephraim writes well on Syriac spirituality. He is less sensitive to the cosmic order than the Greeks are, but he pays much more attention to anguish. It is true that he opposed the ontological dualism of the Manichees, but he himself asserted a vigorous existential dualism. The real world is Paradise where God and the angels dwell. We have lost it through the fall, but it has been re-opened to us in the mystical profundity of the Church. The fallen world is that of the beasts that devour one another, and of human beings who are beasts too, damned and damning others, doomed to hell unless they repent. It is essential to flee the world to regain the state of Paradise in which the body is swallowed up by the soul and the soul by the Spirit. Fasting and vigils prepare for this metamorphosis. But the important thing is to break radically with violence and sex, since death and sexuality, those twins, stamp the world with the seal of bestiality. The angel and the Incarnate One are virgin.

This sensitivity to anguish, this passionate desire to escape from the world, this existential dualism, through Syrian authors and also through renewed forms of Manichaeism (Paulicians, Bogomils) passed into the Balkans and Russia. We see them rising up again today with *The Angel* by Jambet and Lardreau, a pitiless interiorization of the revolution, and with *The Power of Horror* by Julia Kristeva, the well known Bulgarian writer.

Sancti Ephraem Syri Hymni et Sermones, T.J. Lamy 4 vols., Malines 1882-1902; *On Faith, Hymns* CSCO 154 & 155 Syriac Text and German Translation

EUTHYMIUS ZIGABENUS (c. 1100)

Euthymius was a Byzantine theologian who at the request of the Emperor Alexis I Commenus (1081-1116) composed a *Dogmatic Panoply*, a vast compilation studying the various heresies without great originality but furnishing much information.

Dogmatic Panoply PG 130

EVAGRIUS OF PONTUS (346 – 399)

One of the most important teachers of ascesis and mysticism, Evagrius was born on the shores of the Black Sea (Pontus), at Ibora. He received his early formation from the Cappadocian Fathers, St Basil who ordained him reader, and especially St Gregory Nazianzen who conferred the diaconate on him and whom he accompanied to Constantinople. In the capital Evagrius, handsome, cultured, and an outstanding orator, distinguished himself in the struggle against Arianism and embarked on a high ecclesiastical career. However, being swept off his feet by an overwhelming love, he fled to Jerusalem where he fell in with the Origenist circle (Melania, Rufinus) and was permanently influenced by it. About 383 he withdrew to the Egyptian desert, became a monk, and frequented the greatest of the solitaries, especially Macarius of Egypt, earning his living as a copyist. But he stood out from the rest, first as an intellectual, and then because he belonged to the small 'confraternity' of Origenist monks. He died shortly before persecution descended on the group.

In the wake of Origen, and to some extent also of Gregory of Nyssa, Evagrius developed an imposing gnosis. To begin with there was an immense spiritual unity of 'pure intellects' open to the divine light and to one another. But either through over-exposure or inadvertence they became separated from God, their unity was broken and they were distinguishable from one another by the different degrees of openness they had lost. Then God, or more precisely Christ, the only intellect to remain faithful, preserved by a second creation the souls that had become so darkened, by giving to each of them the frame and the milieu that suited its state and enabled it to make progress. In this way there appears a multitude of 'aeons', angelic, human, and diabolical. All spiritual evolution in this life and the next comes about by the transition from one 'aeon' to another, from a certain state of 'corporeity' to a different one. In the end all will be brought together again in their original unity and equality, and they will become 'Christs' with Christ who has made himself their way.

At the same time Evagrius formulated monastic experience systematically. The spiritual life is divided into two stages:

1. *The 'practical' life,* the struggle against the passions by which the person who thinks he is improving himself is dragged down. The devils seduce seculars and even cenobites with this-worldly objects; they seduce solitaries with 'thoughts' and these are eight in number: greed, impurity, love of money, depression, anger, aversion ('accidie'), vainglory, pride. 'Thoughts' are neutralized and the soul is made one again with the intellect for the pursuit of the virtues: faith, fear of God, self-control, patience, hope. At the end comes *apatheia* (literally the state of absence of passion), that which makes love possible.

2. *The gnostic life*

(a) contemplation of nature, i.e. of 'second nature', that is, of the spiritual essence of things, their *logoi*, and of 'first nature', a participation in angelic knowledge, the traversing of the higher 'aeons' in which the intellect, coming to know God's providence and judgment, strips itself increasingly.

(b) knowledge of God, i.e. a reabsorption of the human being into the original 'bare intellect', the 'place of God', the interior heaven filled with a 'light without form', which is not only that of the intellect but 'the light of the Blessed Trinity'.

The Church had to exercise discernment, conscious or instinctive, in regard to this admirable but ambiguous work. The Fifth Ecumenical Council in 553 condemned Evagrius' metaphysical system along with that of Origen, from which it is derived and which it made more rigid. The *Gnostic Chapters*, a basic text, disappeared from Greek tradition. The ascetic works on the other hand never ceased being read whether under the name of Evagrius (the *Practicus*) or under that of St Nilus (the fine treatise *On Prayer*). The Syrian Church subsequently translated and venerated the whole of Evagrius' work, which enabled Antoine Guillaumont to reconstitute the *Kephalaia Gnostica*, emending the text and interpreting it with commentary.

Evagrius' influence was great in the East, and also, chiefly through Cassian, in the West. But it was counterbalanced by a more biblical current that put the theme of the 'heart' at the centre, with the transfiguration of the body. This current was swollen by the strong Gospel emphasis of the first monks. The principal expression of it in the early Church is to be found in the homilies of Pseudo-Macarius.

Centuries PO 28,1; *Practicus* SC 170 & 171; *Mirror of Nuns and Mirror of Monks*, Gressmann 39,4 pp. 146-151 & 152-165; *Pareneticus, Letters*, Frankenberg Berlin 1912; *On the Eight Spirits of Evil* (attributed to St Nilus of Ancyra); *On Prayer* (ascribed to Nilus) PG 79,1145-1200; cf. also *Les Kephalaia Gnostica d'Evagre le Pontique* A. Guillaumont Paris 1962

FELICITY AND PERPETUA (martyred 203)

The Martyrdom of Perpetua and Felicity, who were put to death at Carthage on 7 March 203, was written shortly after the event, the anonymous author reproducing an autobiography of Perpetua and some notes by Saturus, these texts concerning in particular their visions. It seems that the author – contrary to the traditional view – was not Tertullian, except perhaps for the introduction and the conclusion.

Vibia Perpetua was twenty two years old. She was accompanied by her slave Felicity who gave birth to a child during her imprisonment. Both received baptism in prison. The narrative describes also the martyrdom of three catechumens and of Saturus who had evangelized the whole group.

This unadorned text, coming in part from the future martyrs themselves, enables us to understand the meaning of martyrdom as a mystical experience, as identification with the Crucified and Risen Christ.

The Passion has come down to us in two texts, one Greek, the other Latin, the latter without doubt the original. Knopf-Krüger, Ausgewählte Märtyrakten, Tübingen 1929.

GREGORY THE GREAT (540 – 604)

In an Italy ravaged by the invasions, Gregory sensed the tragedy of the end of a world, which he took for the end of the whole world (as in the East a century later Maximus the Confessor was to do). But the expectation of the Kingdom increased in him his pastoral zeal for strengthening the faith of the humble and evangelizing the barbarians. Accordingly he gave fresh expression to the spiritual interpretation of the Bible, to the intuitions of the Fathers, and to monastic experience. He did this in the profound and familiar language of a wisdom – and also in the development of a liturgy – in which eschatological disquiet is calmed and transfigured because 'already the glory of the Kingdom on high is communicated to it, by anticipation'. (*Homilies on the Gospels*, 2). In this way without seeking to do so, almost as a superfluous extra, Gregory fertilized the spirituality of the Latin world at least up to the Cistercian twelfth century, and probably laid the foundations of a popular Christian culture.

Gregory was born at Rome into a patrician family that had been faithful to Christianity for a long time and had already produced a Pope and several saints. He received a sound classical education, but without becoming unduly attached to it, as he felt that the old culture was dying. His career was at first administrative, as the ruined city was being included in the Empire again after Justinian's reconquest, and Gregory, in spite of his lively Italian patriotism, always considered himself a subject of the Empire. He became 'Prefect of the City' and quickly made himself conversant with the affairs of the world, in the service of the common good. But quite soon the anguish of the period spurred him on to 'the one thing necessary': he renounced everything and converted his house on the Coelian Hill into a monastery. There followed years of prayer and study, on which he would always look back with nostalgia. He steeped himself in Scripture and the Fathers. He elaborated a balanced synthesis between Augustine's passionate theology and Cassian's calm ascesis. But once again, much against his will, the time to serve came. (He himself later, when Pope in an Italy where men of culture and depth had become rare, often entrusted ecclesiastical responsibilities and missions to monks.) In 579 Pope Pelagius II ordained him deacon and sent him as his representative (*apocrisarius*) to Constantinople. There he spent six years, influenced more than he was aware no doubt by Greek theology, especially Origen and Dionysius. He returned to Rome about 585. In 590 a plague ravaged the city. Pelagius died and Gregory was elected Pope by the clergy and people. Taken aback, he asked the Emperor not to confirm his election. In vain. So, courageously, he accepted his charge as *consul Dei*.

In Italy the political and cultural decadence was so great that with ruin everywhere, in cities as in people, he could only protect what was left and avoid anything worse. He ensured the victualling of Rome by consolidating in Sicily the 'patrimony of Peter'. He reduced the extent of schism, and had to take the place himself of defaulting Byzantines in 592 to negotiate a truce with the Lombards. As Pope of Rome, first bishop of the Christian world, he overcame the temptation hinted at by some of his predecessors, that of consolidating by juridical power an authority that was chiefly moral. He made himself – the title originates with him – 'servant of the servants of God'. He refused the title of 'universal bishop'; that would infringe, he said, the prerogatives of local churches whose communion he wished only to augment. A missionary, he bought some young English slaves, had them brought up in monasteries, and in 596 sent a group of monks educated in this way to the English.

Gregory's spirituality is a monastic spirituality of the traditional type, with emphasis on the 'heart', on 'pure prayer', a humble and serious experience of light, and on peace (the equivalent of the Greek *hesychia*). But this spirituality was made dramatic by the unrest proceeding from a gigantic crisis of civilization, from Augustinian influence, and from the difficult alternations of a troubled career between the urgent demands of service and a taste for the interior life. It was all resolved for him in the immense patience of Job, with the certainty that Job is a figure of Christ, and that therefore the trial leads to resurrection. (The *Commentary on the Book of Job* is one of Gregory's masterpieces.) He did not have to struggle against heresies – intellectual thought in the West was too feeble by that time to give rise to any – so his basic aim was teaching the faith. He was anxious to make available to all, monks, pastors and also laity, the wisdom of Scripture in Tradition. Hence his homilies on the Gospel and on Ezekiel, his *Pastoral Rule* for the use of clerics and particularly preachers, his endeavour to combine rather than separate the active and the contemplative life, his recourse to outstanding examples both biblical and contemporary, since God never ceases revealing himself. (It is through this that we know of St Benedict, from the second book of Gregory's Dialogues.) He developed the use of singing in Church, so that it was to him that 'Gregorian' chant was ascribed, although it is, in fact, much later in date. But legend often uncovers the deep meaning of history.

Commentary on the Book of Job (35 books) PL 75,509-1126 & 76,9-782; SC 32 bis, 212,221; *Homilies on the Gospels*, PL 75,1075-1312; *Homilies on Ezekiel*, PL 76,785-1092

GREGORY NAZIANZEN (c.330 – 390)

Cultured, too cultured; and probably the most profound among the Greek Fathers; known as the 'Christian Demosthenes' for his mastery of the art of rhetoric, and 'The Theologian', that is, the celebrant of the Trinity, whose own life and human words to describe it are 'theology' par excellence.

Like all the great Cappadocians, Gregory belonged to a circle of great landowners who might also with a touch of humour be called 'gentlemen farmers', men of a broad cultured humanity, fervent Christians in that time of transition between martyrdom and monasticism. His mother had converted his father who later became bishop of Nazianzus. Gregory, a child of their old age, 'offered to the Lord' from his birth, received a sound religious education but absorbed the cultural heritage of Hellenism in the best schools: at Caesarea in Palestine, at Alexandria, and especially at Athens where he formed a friendship with Basil of Caesarea. On his return to Cappadocia he became an orator destined for the highest civil appointments. But his soul was divided, somewhat romantic, with a nostalgia for solitude, speculation and contemplation, though eager also for admiration and affection, a melancholy and unreliable temperament, at once desirous of responsibilities and quickly dismayed by them. Involved against his inclination in the service of the Church he let himself be saddled with commitments which he soon afterwards refused to honour. His father ordained him priest, and he disappeared for several months into a 'desert' peopled with intellectuals, in order later to take up his ministry and ardently to defend the poor. About 371, to counter the imperial power, Basil increased the number of dioceses and put his own supporters in them. He consecrated Gregory bishop of Sasimus but

Gregory refused to occupy his see which was a dusty and noisy stopping place for caravans. At the death of his father, the faithful of Nazianzus demanded him as their bishop. He ran away into solitude and study for four years. However in 379 this delicate, complex, awkward intellectual outdid himself: he agreed to leave for Constantinople where the Arians were in possesssion of all the churches and were turning the inhabitants into fanatics. In a private house, under the sign of the resurrection (*Anastasis*) he opened a chapel. His preaching, and in particular his five *Theological Sermons* on the Trinity attracted the people. It was in vain that trouble-makers were sent to insult and stone him. In 381 the Emperor Theodosius, a Spaniard faithful to the Nicene dogma, came into the city. A Council, later to be designated the Second Ecumenical Council, was able to assemble, and in it the teaching worked out by Basil and Gregory triumphed. Gregory was proclaimed Archbishop of Constantinople. But the intrigues and tensions of the Council quickly discouraged him. He resigned, and passed the last years of his life on his estate at Arianzus, writing poems, one of which is an autobiographical Song, the first specimen in Christian literature of the 'secret colloquy', artistically represented, 'of the soul with itself and God'.

In his sermons, which are half way between rhetoric and liturgy, Gregory celebrates above all the mystery of the Trinity which he opposes to the closed monotheism of the Jews and the vague divinities of paganism. The 'hypostases' which, each in its own way, contain and present the divine 'essence' are distinguished from one another by relations of diversity, simple tokens for recognition: the Father by his character of unoriginated origin; the Son by generation; the Spirit by procession. Thus is worked out at a level of Trinitarian theology the metaphysics of the Person who is not a fragment of the whole but contains it in communion. The Absolute is thus permeated with an infinitely personal love.

The controversy with Apollinaris (for whom, in Christ, the Logos takes the place of the human soul) led Gregory to develop a spirituality of deification as Christification: like our body and our soul, our spirit (*nous*) can only be deified by sharing in Jesus' deified human spirit or soul. Many of Gregory's texts that celebrate our death and resurrection in Christ entered into the Byzantine liturgy. 'The cross is the only theologian', the cross alone, death and life, could transform anguish into faith in Gregory's heart.

Sermons PG 35,36 also in SC 247, 250; *Theological Sermons* SC 250; *On Virginity,* in *Poems* II, 1: PG 37,537-55

GREGORY OF NYSSA (c. 330 – c. 395)

Among the great Cappadocians he was the keenest metaphysician, the most profound mystic, and also the most conscious of the nature of suffering.

Gregory was born at Caesarea in Cappadocia and was two years younger than his brother St Basil. He was introduced to the spiritual life by their sister Macrina, who after the death of their father converted the household into a sort of monastery on one of their estates.

Gregory studied only in Cappadocia, but he mastered ancient philosophy and radically transformed its concepts, both Stoic and Platonic, in the crucible of revelation. He became an orator, and married Theosevia, a woman of great culture and strong faith, but that did not prevent him from becoming bishop of Nyssa in 371 at the compelling request of Basil. Basil was fortifying himself against the imperial power by multiplying the episcopal sees within his metropolitan jurisdiction and entrusting them to men on whom he could rely. In the same year, at the request of Macrina, he wrote an encomium on virginity in which he developed the theme of interior chastity as the unification of the whole being in the likeness of the love of the Trinity. The passion of love in paradise took forms that we cannot imagine. Sexuality, which at once expresses that love and misrepresents it, was created by God in view of the fall. This theme was to pass, in a more radical form, into Syriac spirituality (see St Ephraim of Syria). Theosevia died about 385, 'a true saint and the true wife of a priest', as a neighbouring bishop said.

Gregory was given to speculation and mysticism and had difficulty in adapting himself to his episcopal duties. Indeed his problems as an administrator, already deplored by Basil, enabled the Arians to have him deposed and exiled in 376. Two years later the death of the Emperor Valens, who supported Arianism, made it possible for him to return to his city where the people welcomed him ecstatically. After the death of Basil in 379, Gregory asserted himself and engaged in polemic against the rationalism of Eunomius and the monophysite tendencies of Apollinaris. He shared in the triumph of the Council in 381. He played an important part at court as long as the new Emperor Theodosius resided at Constantinople. When Theodosius departed for Milan in 386, Gregory withdrew into the country and devoted himself to monastic spirituality (*Homilies on the Song of Songs; Life of Moses;* perhaps also *On the Christian Way of Life*), as if he wanted to give mystical content to the communities organized by Basil.

Gregory broke up and 'allegorized' Greek concepts to put them at the service of mystery. Against Eunomius, who claimed that reason can cope with all that is real, he declared the unlimited character and therefore the unknowability of the divine essence, and the mystery present in the humblest objects. But that essence is not impersonal; it is love and a love that knows suffering, which leads the inaccessible God to become the 'suffering God'. His 'unlimited character' derives precisely from the fact that the Person cannot be made an object and from the infinite unity of the divine Persons.

Humanity is in the image of God, and therefore as undefinable as God is, beyond all knowledge and all power that might claim to explain or condition it. The likeness is expressed in freedom, an ability given to the person to transcend his nature in the act of communion. In the image of a God who is not a monad but a Trinity there is a 'single person' in a multiplicity of persons, an original unity broken by the fall and restored in Christ. Each individual accordingly bears in himself the whole of the human race. As the perceptible world exists only in the encounter of the divine with the human consciousness, several more or less 'miraculous' degrees of materiality may appear, according to a person's openness to God or otherwise. In Christ's humanity the world is transfigured, and this seed of resurrection is communicated to us by the 'mysteries' of the Church.

The spiritual life consists in purifying in oneself the image of God so that it should become a faithful mirror, according to a likeness-sharing. It consists of three stages: the ethical, the transformation of the passions, of which the biblical equivalent is found in the Book of Proverbs; the physical, when the sensible world is rejected as an illusion and reinterpreted symbolically as a manifestation of God (Ecclesiastes); and the metaphysical, in which the soul expands in the divine sphere (the Song of Songs).

The knowledge of God is an unknowing in which the person soars above and beyond the perceptible and the intelligible. It is a rhythm of enstasis and ecstasis, of light and darkness, in which the more the soul is filled with the divine presence, the more it reaches out towards the Other that is always beyond its reach. Participation increases desire; God is the more unknown the more he is known; humanity advances from marvelling to marvelling, in a dynamism in which otherness is never separation nor unity confusion. The same thing happens in our relationship with our neighbour, in the fullness of the 'single person'. The metaphysics of communion is indeed remarkable.

In the history of human thought Gregory appears as the one who broke the cycles of ancient thought (still traceable in Origenism), who rehabilitated becoming, who gave time a positive value as the apprenticeship of love, and supremely the one who showed that human beings have no other definition than to be undefinable, because they are made by God's infinitude and created for it.

Dialogue with Macrina on the Soul and the Resurrection PG 46,11-160; *On the Creation of Man* PG 44,125-256, *Life of Moses* SC 1 bis; *On Love of the Poor* PG 46,454-469; *Homilies on the Song of Songs* PG 44,755-1120; *Against Eunomius* PG 45,237-1122, *Catechetical Oration* PG 45,9; *Against Apollinaris* PG 45,1123-1270. Recent critical edition of Greek text of all works by W. Jaeger.

HERMAS *(The Shepherd of Hermas)* (2nd century)

An apocryphal apocalypse, written by an unknown author in the second century, doubtless in Roman circles making use perhaps of earlier documents, marked by Judaizing tendencies, in the Essene tradition (the theme of the 'two ways'). The angel regarded as having imparted this revelation is a shepherd: hence its title. This is a text affording important information on ecclesiology and the sensitivity of the first Christian communities. The Church, pre-existent in the divine mind, was created before all things and constitutes the mystical foundation of the universe and of history. It is symbolized, now by a woman who is both old and young, now by a tower in construction, made of living stones, founded on the rock of Christ, surrounded by the water of baptism. When it is completed, the end will come. The human being must choose between the two ways, between the two angels (of righteousness and evil), between the 'evil spirits' and the 'holy spirits' that are the *'dynameis* of the Son of God'. The root of sin is therefore *dipsychia*, compromise, ambivalence, duplicity. Consequently *metanoia*, the turning back by the spirit, repentance, is indispensable – it is not certain whether the Shepherd envisages an ecclesiastical penance that would be possible only once after baptism. A Christian is characterized by the simplicity of his harmonized being, by spontaneous joy, and a deep-seated cheerfulness. Here the frescoes of the catacombs come to mind.

Critical Text SC 53 bis

Hesychius of Batos or Sinai

All that is known of him is that he lived after John Climacus and Maximus the Confessor, between the end of the seventh and the tenth centuries. He was the superior of the monastery of Batos on Sinai. Whilst effecting a synthesis of Evagrius, Diadochus, and Climacus, he lays the emphasis on 'watchfulness' (*nepsis*) and victory over 'thoughts' by the 'Jesus prayer', the invocation of the Name of Jesus in time with one's breathing. His originality consists in this very personal and trustful relationship with Christ. For him it is a matter of 'breathing Jesus'.

On Vigilance and Virtue PG 93,1479-1544 & Philokalia I,141-173

Hilary of Poitiers (315 – 367)

Hilary is the most important Father of Roman Gaul, the 'Athanasius of the West' as the defender of the 'consubstantial', and also a connecting link between Greek and Latin theology.

He was born at Poitiers, into a cultured pagan setting, that of the landowners and magistrates of Aquitaine, by then the most Romanized of the provinces of Gaul. For a long time he was a searcher after God. He moved from hedonism to stoicism, he tried out sects and esoteric cults, he discovered Judaism, and in the end was converted to Christ by the reading of St John's Gospel. Shortly after his baptism he was elected bishop of Poitiers by the people, about 350. It was then that he composed his *Commentary on St Matthew's Gospel*, in which his teaching about the Trinity remains in the tradition of Tertullian, without much trace of the Arian dispute. But the Emperor Constantius in the hour of victory sought to impose Arianism on the West. Some bishops in Gaul yielded, at the Synod of Beziers in 356. Hilary then assumed the leadership of the resistance in Gaul. He was exiled to Asia Minor. It was a fruitful but stormy exile. Hilary deepened his knowledge of the Greek language and Greek theology, entered into the confused controversies over the *homoousion*, and tried in vain to win over those for whom Christ was *homoiousios*, 'similar in nature', to the Father but who baulked at the dogma of Nicaea. It was in Phrygia that he wrote his great doctrinal work, inaccurately called *On the Trinity*. When the Arians gained a lasting superiority they sent him back to the West as he was a nuisance to them.

Back in Gaul he took advantage of political events (the accession of Julian) to procure the triumph of the doctrine of 'consubstantiality' – at the Synod of Paris in 360 – and he restored peace, allowing repentant bishops to retain their sees.

Having failed in his attempt to root out Arianism in Milan (360), Hilary gave up polemic and devoted himself to the interpretation of Scripture. He wrote an introduction to spiritual exegesis, the *Treatise on the Mysteries*, and commentaries on the Psalms and Job, all in the spirit of Origen, whose symbolism and typology he spread in the Latin world.

In an ample and difficult style Hilary, for the first time in the West, clearly asserted the eternity of the generation of the Word. The Father is infinite in his creativity, the Son is in his image, namely Beauty, the Spirit is his grace, that is, Joy. The Infinite, which nothing can circumscribe, for the sake of our joy takes the form of Beauty. At the heart of Hilary's thought is the mystery of the Word made flesh, of the form of the slave become that of Beauty. He emphasizes the glory of the transfigured Christ, but maintains, against Origen, the solid reality of created being. The eschatological fullness that we attain to in Christ transforms matter itself, and through the 'eye of the heart' the 'eternal light' reaches the body also. In this way the principal themes of Eastern spirituality came over by way of Hilary into a West more accustomed to a moral approach to Christianity.

On the Trinity PL 10, 25-472

HIPPOLYTUS OF ROME (170 – 235)

Hippolytus was a member of the presbyterium at Rome at the beginning of the second century. Nothing is known of his origins that were perhaps Oriental. He was very conservative and wrote in Greek at a time when Latin was coming to prevail in the Christian community at Rome. He was the author of erudite essays, among the first in Christian literature, and of long denunciations of heresies, especially Gnostic ones. His *Apostolic Tradition* is a sort of code of regulations for structures and disciplines in the Church. Into this collection Hippolytus inserted eucharistic prayers which are the oldest known for the Roman community – and from these comes the Second Eucharistic Prayer in the Canon of the Mass used by the Catholic Church since the liturgical reform. In 217 Hippolytus refused to recognize the election of Callistus as bishop of Rome and had himself elected in opposition to him by a group of the faithful who were few in number but influential, thus bringing about a schism. Socially conservative, he reproached Callistus for having authorized the marriage of Roman ladies of the upper class to men of inferior rank. He was a rigorist and accused others of undue indulgence towards sinners. As a denouncer of heresies, he saw a tendency to Sabellianism (which regards the Father, the Son and the Spirit as temporally successive aspects of God) in his own environment. But he himself connected the generation of the Son with the creation of the world – a tendency to a certain subordinationism common enough then, especially at Alexandria. In 235 in the persecution by Maximinus the two rivals were sentenced to penal servitude in Sardinia. They both died there, confessors of the faith, Hippolytus having first asked his faithful to renounce their schism.

Apostolic Tradition SC 11 bis

HOMILY FOR EASTER (anonymous: 4th century)

For a long time it was attributed either to Hippolytus of Rome or to an unknown editor inspired by a treatise on Easter by Hippolytus now lost. Today these hypotheses have, in fact, been abandoned since critical internal evidence shows that this writer is familiar with Arianism and rejects it (Christ is called God), but it is prior to the condemnation of Apollinarianism (in which the Spirit of Christ is identified with his divinity: is it 'spirit' with a capital letter or not? – an ambiguity not possible at the end of the fourth century). This homily is therefore later than 325 and earlier than 380.

Critical text in *Homélies pascales* I SC 27

IGNATIUS OF ANTIOCH (martyred between 110 & 117)

Ignatius, a converted pagan, was apparently the first bishop of Antioch (according to Eusebius of Caesarea the author of an *Ecclesiastical History* written at the beginning of the fourth century that gives us unique information about the Christianity of the first three centuries) after the apostle Peter stayed in that city where the disciples of Jesus were first called Christians. During a persecution in the reign of Trajan he was condemned to death and sent to Rome for execution. It was a slow journey, partly by sea, under military escort, a tragic exodus that became a sort of triumphal progress as they crossed Asia Minor, where Christians were increasing in number. At each stage Ignatius was surrounded by the local Church while more distant communities sent delegations. Before setting sail over the Aegean, Ignatius wrote six letters to the Churches that had so welcomed him, and an eloquent plea to the Christians of Rome not to intervene on his behalf to prevent his martyrdom for which he was spiritually prepared. Irenaeus and Origen attest to his being thrown to the beasts.

Ignatius's *Letters* constitute the basic text, after the New Testament, for the understanding of the first Christians' outlook on the world. Everything is centred on the mystery of Christ, a mystery of which the paradox and the greatness are defended by the bishop of Antioch against those who see in Jesus only an appearance of human nature (the Docetists) or the possessor of a secret knowledge reserved for the chosen few (the Gnostics). 'God's *gnosis* is Jesus Christ' who is the Word 'come forth from silence' to take flesh and to raise it up again. By his flesh that suffers death and by his Spirit that raises it up again, Christ is our life, a 'pneumatic' (spiritual) fullness to which we have access through the Eucharist – Ignatius gives this word its openly sacramental meaning. The Church, which is called 'Catholic' for the first time by him, meaning 'according to the whole' of truth and life, is manifested fully in the local eucharistic community around its bishop, who is designated now 'image of God', now 'image of Christ'. Ignatius is thus the first witness to the universalization of the episcopate after the disappearance of the apostles. All local churches form a single identity in the same faith and the same chalice. Rome, the Church of Peter and Paul, 'presides over charity', and Ignatius asks the Romans to be the bishops (*episkopoi*, 'overseers') of his own community that is temporarily without its own bishop.

The expectation of an almost immediate Parousia has been replaced by the awareness of a difficult transition, a slow metamorphosis through the death and resurrection in Christ of his true 'disciples'. The 'disciple' par excellence is the martyr, a living Eucharist, being humbly and lovingly identified with the suffering and victorious Christ.

Letters SC 10

IRENÆUS OF LYONS (c. 130 – c. 208)

In contact with both East and West, Irenaeus worked out the first and largest and soundest synthesis of Christian thought. It was solidly based on the ancient traditions of the Churches of Asia, securely founded by St John the Apostle.

A native of Asia Minor, Irenaeus made the acquaintance at Smyrna of its aged bishop Polycarp, himself a disciple of St John. Irenaeus came to Gaul where Eastern trading settlements were multiplying in the Rhone valley, bringing Christianity with them. In this way the communities of Lyons and Vienne developed at the beginning of the second century, speaking both Greek and Latin. In 177 while Irenaeus, already a priest, was on a mission to Rome, the persecution by Marcus Aurelius deprived these young Churches of their leaders. The aged bishop Pothinus, Blandina and many others suffered martyrdom. Upon his return Irenaeus was elected bishop of Lyons and Vienne. He evangelized the villages and countryside of the Saone, and intervened, around 190, between the bishop of Rome, Victor, and the communities of Asia, on which Rome wished to impose its reckoning of the date of Easter. As a result diversity was allowed to remain without breaking unity. In addition he had to cope with an upsurge of Gnosticism. The Gnostics were appealing to secret apostolic traditions. They rejected matter and the body as evil, and the Old Testament too because it speaks of the Creator of matter and the body, whom they saw as a God of evil. They also claimed to be concerned with the 'perfect', the 'pneumatic' (spiritual), who need only to be made aware of their divine identity. Against them Irenaeus wrote *Pseudo-Gnosis Unmasked and Refuted*, more commonly known as *Against Heresies*.

For Irenaeus, Tradition is preserved in each local Church by the succession of bishops who have received from the Apostles the 'rule of truth'. There is a living Tradition, the life of the Holy Spirit in the sacramental and consequently ecclesial Body of Christ. This is attested by the 'charism of truth' of the bishops. Some of these, in Churches founded by Apostles, are privileged sources of witness. The only such example in the West is Rome.

Most importantly, Irenaeus developed a vigorous theology emphasizing the reality of the incarnation (and therefore of the flesh), the unity of the two Testaments, and the positive nature of history. The Word and the Holy Spirit are the 'two hands of the Father'. With them he creates, directs, attracts and fulfils humanity. History appears thus as an immense procession of incarnation. Time is an *experimentum*, an apprenticeship in communion, for God wishes to deify human beings but without destroying their freedom. Time enables 'man to grow used to receiving God and God to grow used to dwelling in man'. Irenaeus does not dramatize the fall. Man, still a foolish child, easily allowed himself to be deceived. He needs to undergo the experience of death in order to become aware of his own finiteness, and to open himself voluntarily to God who alone can give life. Everything is a dimension of incarnation. The Word never ceases coming down to humanity in history, to fashion his own Body. The covenants are specific; those with Adam and Noah are cosmic; those with Abraham and Moses are historical; both are equally concerns of the Word. And everything is 'recapitulated' in Christ who is the definitive, pan-human Adam, as Mary is the new Eve. Henceforward Christ, the 'head', imparts to all his members the power of the life-giving Spirit who is at work in the Church. And the Church witnesses and intercedes for the salvation of all human beings. Through trials and persecutions, beneath the sun which is Christ, the harvest of history ripens. And first there will be the 'thousand years' reign' of which the Apocalypse speaks, an actual transfiguration of the earth, of which the miracle at Cana constitutes the 'sign and epitome'.

Against Heresies SC 263 & 264 for Book I, 210 & 211 for Book III, 100, 2 vols., for Book IV, 152 & 153 for Book V; *Demonstration of the Apostolic Teaching* PO,12-731

Isaac of Nineveh or Isaac the Syrian (7th century)

One of the greatest spiritual figures of the Christian East where his influence has never ceased to make itself felt, not only in the Syriac world from Lebanon to South India, but also in the other pre–Chalcedonian Churches from Armenia to Ethiopia, and especially in the Graeco-Slav sphere through the Greek translation of his writings made in the ninth century by two monks of St Sabas in Palestine. The influence of St Isaac is particularly noticeable in Russian spirituality, religious philosophy and literature of the nineteenth and twentieth centuries, especially in Dostoevsky. It is emphasized today at Mount Athos and is spreading to the West.

Isaac was born at Beth-Katrage, the modern Qatar, on the shores of the Persian Gulf. Already a monk and recognized as a spiritual master, he was consecrated bishop of Nineveh in the Nestorian Syriac Church between 660 and 680. But at the end of five months he fled to the mountains. For a long time he lived in solitude, then settled at the monastery of Rabdan Shabbur where, having become blind through much reading and austerity, he dictated his works to some disciples who were impressed by his humility and gentleness.

His thought, collected in his *Ascetic Treatises*, effects a synthesis of the spiritual currents of early Christianity: Evagrius, who speaks of the intellect; Pseudo-Macarius, who lays the emphasis on the 'heart'; and Origen, with his nostalgia for universal salvation.

St Isaac who is profoundly Syriac in his sensitivity combines a particularly sharp sense of the need to break with this world of anguish with an unlimited tenderness for all creatures crushed by suffering. At the 'bodily' stage the body has to be pitilessly purged of its 'carnal rottenness' by fasting, vigils, continence and obedience; and must be rescued from 'the world' which for Isaac is a collective name for the passions, a monstrous tangle of possession, power and sex, all of them masks of death. Ascesis necessarily appears then as 'constraint'. The 'psychic' stage has to free the soul from 'thoughts' that are foreign to its deepest nature; it has to enable it to discern, in movements coming from the unconscious, between the 'source of light' that calms and 'softens' even to tears, and the 'source of darkness' that hardens and makes agitated and cold at the same time. At the 'spiritual' stage the heart 'is broken and renewed', it ascends 'from contemplation to contemplation' 'until it reaches the heights of love, and joy dwells deep within it'. Then, beyond all utterance, prayer shot through with moments of inebriation and folly becomes a permanent state. Whether the sanctified person is 'eating, drinking, or sleeping, the fragrance of prayer is spontaneously exhaled by his soul'. From then on it is understood that there is no other salvation but love. What are all our sins but a few grains of sand cast into the sea in comparison with God's mercy? The only sin, in the last resort, is not to pay heed to the power of the resurrection. Universal salvation is not the certainty of a metaphysical system as in Origen, but the hope and prayer of the saints, since one can only be saved in complete communion. On love for creatures and objects Isaac speaks with the most moving of accents. The charity of the 'merciful heart' becomes cosmic, its hope without limits, it prays 'even for serpents', 'even for devils'. Amid universal suffering the resurrection of Christ enables it to perceive 'the fire of created things'. Wild beasts, and human beings who are even more wild, are pacified in the presence of the saint.

It is not therefore surprising that the writings of Isaac of Nineveh inspired the sternest, but in the end infinitely loving, monastic ascesis (love is difficult, let us repeat) and also inspired the Russian religious philosophers of the nineteenth and twentieth centuries, who were pre-occupied with elaborating a metaphysic of knowledge in communion and giving to Christianity a real power of transfiguration.

The Syriac text of the *Ascetic Treatises* has been published by P. Bedjan, Paris-Leipzig 1909. English translation from the Syriac by A.K. Wensinck: *Mystic Treatises* by Isaac of Nineveh 1923. A variant Greek text: Spanos, Athens, 1895.

JAMES OF SARUG (c. 449 – 521)

One of the great hymn-writers of the Syriac Church, James was born at Harra on the Euphrates and studied at the school of Edessa. He became chorepiscopus of Harra in 502 and bishop of Batnan the centre of the Sarug region in 518. In spite of the Monophysite environment he remained aloof from Christological controversies and gave expression to a living and traditional faith in numer-ous *memre*, long portions of which were incorporated in different Syriac liturgies. At an early date he was translated into Armenian, Georgian, Arabic, and Ethiopian. His *memre* are rhythmic chants, each from three to four hundred verses long, and they were read during vigils, according to the custom introduced by St Ephraim. His lyricism is Semitic, and his symbols borrowed from nature are founded on 'biblical typology'.

Hymn to the Mother of God; *Paschal Hymn* Bickell I

JEROME (337 – 419/420)

Sophronius Eusebius Hieronymus, patron of the learned and of translators, author of the great Latin translation of the Bible known as the Vulgate.

He was born in Dalmatia into a Christian family, came to Rome in 354 and studied very thoroughly grammar, rhetoric and philosophy there, forming a friendship with Rufinus.

He was baptized about 367. A journey to Trier, where an impor-tant colony of monks had settled, confirmed him in his own vocation as an ascetic. In 373 he felt the irresistible call of the Bible lands, which gave birth to his other vocation, the service of God's Word.

At Antioch he mastered Greek. In the Aleppo desert where he lived as a hermit for three years he learned Hebrew. From then on he was *vir trilinguis*, 'a man of three languages'. At Constantinople before, during and after the Second Ecumenical Council, he struck up a friendship with the great Cappadocians Gregory of Nazianzen and Gregory of Nyssa and became a fervent follower of Origenist exegesis. On his return to Rome in 382, he became the secretary and confidant of the aged Pope Damasus. He revised the Latin text of the New Testament, and that of the Psalms in the Septuagint version (see note at end). At the same time Jerome was directing a spiritual circle of highly born and beautiful ladies, whom he dissuaded from marriage and encouraged to lead ascetic lives. After the death of Damasus in 385 not only was Jerome not elected bishop as he was hoping, the people accused him of having caused the death, on account of her austerities, of a girl of whom everyone thought highly for her goodness and charm. Thereupon he took himself to Palestine, where he was joined by the wealthy Paula and other devout ladies of his acquaintance. When he came back from Egypt where he had gone to visit the monks, Paula settled him in Bethlehem at the head of a monastery of men, while she herself not far from there was in charge of several communities of women. It was she who provided for the building of these houses, as well as hospices for pilgrims and a monastic school, where Jerome from then on was to write his commentaries on Scripture. At this point there began for him an enormous undertaking, the translation into Latin of the entire Old Testament. He worked at first from the Septuagint text, and the Psalter produced from it entered by way of Gaul into the liturgical use of the Latin Church. But from 391 to 400, because the Jewish scholars with whom he was working did not accept the authority of the Septuagint, he translated directly from the Hebrew original, thus producing the great Latin Bible which in the Middle Ages came to be called the Vulgate. It is certain that the Masoretic text (see note at end) which he used is of later date than that which can be reconstituted from the Septuagint and the first Latin translations. It is certain also that on some points the Septuagint represents an advance in revelation. None the less those ancient translations were full of errors and obscurities and recourse to the original was essential.

Simultaneously with this work Jerome took part in the Origenist controversy, becoming as relentless an adversary of Origen as he had been a partisan of his. He quarrelled with Rufinus. He also plunged into the Pelagian controversy with such effect that a group of Pelagius' followers burned his monastery and he himself had a narrow escape from death. He conducted a polemic, vigorous and at times cruel, against those who called in question the superiority of monasticism and virginity. He proved to pagans, with his *De Viris Illustribus*, which goes from Peter to Jerome himself, that Christians counted among their number as many great men as they, and even more. The Huns and the Bedouins came and went and from time to time he had to flee. In 410 the barbarians sacked Rome. But Jerome was well aware of the relativity of history. He continued to give his attention to the writing of polished *Letters*, and countless generations were to pray the Psalms and nourish themselves on the Word of God thanks to him.

Letters: some of the best are found in the Loeb Classical Library, edited by F.A. Wright 1954.

Note on Septuagint: The Septuagint version is the Greek translation of the Bible made at Alexandria in the third century B.C. According to legend the seventy translators working separately arrived at the same text. During the patristic age this version, the only one known to the authors of the New Testament, was considered as the true Bible of the Church, on certain points marking a progressive revelation or testifying to an older state of the text than the Masoretic version. None the less, the Septuagint was not without errors which can be corrected only by recourse to the Hebrew.

Note on Masoretic text: The Masoretic version (from *masorah*, transmission) is the text of the Hebrew Bible as fixed by the Pharisee rabbis at the Synod of Jamnia in 90 – 95 A.D.

JOHN CHRYSOSTOM (344/354 – 407)

John, surnamed in the sixth century 'golden-mouthed' (Chrysostom), was the famous preacher of God as the 'friend of humankind', as the one who in Christ became the brother of the poor. He bore witness, even to death, to an uncompromising ethic of ecclesial and social service. He was the marvellous liturgist who gave form to the celebration of the Eucharist. The 'Liturgy of St John Chrysostom' is still constantly in use in the Orthodox Church today.

He was born at Antioch into an aristocratic family. At a very early age he was left an orphan by the death of his father. Through the psychological effects of this, as quite often happens in the case of churchmen, he was profoundly influenced for good by the faith of his mother, who when John reached the age of eighteen wanted to keep him near her at home as a 'house monk'. He studied Scripture under the direction of teachers of the school of Antioch who emphasized the actual human nature of Christ.

But he also studied pagan rhetoric, the procedures of which he was to use in his sermons, while retaining an ambivalent attitude towards Hellenism: sometimes he violently denounced it, sometimes he sought consolation from it, even from Stoic detachment in the trials that beset the end of his life. He quite soon tore himself away from his mother and retreated to the mountains where he threw himself into a fierce unrelenting monasticism, animated by a total contempt for human society. Then came a terrible crisis of conscience. Was not monasticism a 'holy deviation' anyway? Was it right to keep oneself 'pure' on the 'heights' while leaving one's brethren to perish? He came to the decision that, since the world was now nominally Christian, what was needed was to Christianize the world.

Back in Antioch he was ordained a deacon in 380 and a priest in 386, not without hesitation. In his *Treatise on the Priesthood* he brings out the sacrificial meaning of that service. He preached indefatigably, sometimes for two hours at a time, amidst acclamation and applause from the people. He wrote commentaries on Scripture, in particular the *Epistle to the Romans*: everything is grace, therefore 'if we will we can'. Since the world, including the Emperor, was Christian, he preached against the reactionary minorities that exercised a corrupting influence, against the Jews especially as for ever accursed – these are basic texts for a Christian anti-semitism – and he denounced above all superstitions, profane festivals, and the theatre. (The 'Christianization' of the theatre is often on the short view just moralization; but allowance must be made for the transition from a 'theatrical' to a 'liturgical' civilization). Against the lust and idleness of the rich, he praised the communion of goods, work and the liberation of slaves, issuing a summons to individual and collective sharing – he outlined a plan for eliminating poverty from Antioch – for 'mine and thine are empty words'; what counts is use that is common to all. For John Chrysostom the social element is sacramental in virtue of the twenty fifth chapter of St Matthew; the poor man like the priest is 'another Christ'; the 'sacrament of the altar' must be carried out 'into the street' by the 'sacrament of the brother'. At the same time, this man who for so long had been a fierce ascetic and doubtless dreamt of transforming society into a vast monastery, this glorifier of virginity, gradually came to affirm that marriage is the 'sacrament of love', the family a 'little church' and true virginity is a spiritual chastity that can co-exist with human love.

In 397, much against his inclination, John was chosen as Archbishop of Constantinople, because of his reputation as an orator. In the capital he won the people's hearts, he increased the number of hospitals and centres of reception, he evangelized the countryside, including the Goths who were settling in the Empire. He waged a relentless war against heretics, but he refused the support of the secular arm. He concluded his admirable homilies *On the Incomprehensibility of God* with the words: 'The Inaccessible comes down to us by love: the Son, the invisible image of God, makes himself visible through the incarnation. To see God is to meet Christ and one's neighbour.' John adds precision to the vocabulary of prayer and of *nepsis*, a 'fasting of the spirit'.

But here, in confrontation with power, we see him above all as the purifying apostle. He resists Eutropius, the all-powerful minister, when he wishes to abolish the right of asylum, yet protects him against a riotous mob when he falls from power and takes refuge in the basilica. John sought to reform the higher clergy and to prevent the bishop of Alexandria from persecuting Origenist monks. He sought also to improve the moral tone of the court and especially of the Empress, that 'modern Herodias'. His enemies combined against him. His illegal deposition in 403 proved only momentary. But in 404 he was exiled to Lower Armenia and remained there for three years, free, but under surveillance. He learned the patience of Job and the primacy of charity. He found that hell matters less than losing the presence of the Kingdom. He discovered that the cross was public and the resurrection secret, yet the true glory is identified with the cross. His correspondence, however, in particular with an old friend the deaconess Olympias, together with the influx of visitors, many of them from Antioch, alarmed the civil power, which decided to deport him to the shores of the Black Sea on the eastern border of the Empire. It was a long and exhausting journey, on foot. At Comana he prepared himself for death. He clothed himself in white, received Holy Communion, prayed for those present, and breathed his last, saying: 'Glory be to God for everything.'

On the Priesthood SC 272; *On the Incomprehensibility of God* SC 28; Homilies: *On Ozias* PG 56; *On Matthew* PG 57-8; *On John* PG

59; *On I Corinthians* PG 61; *On Hebrews* PG 63; *On Compunction*
PG 47; *On the Treason of Judas* PG 49

JOHN CASSIAN (c.350 – c.435)

John Cassian was probably a 'Scythian', born in Dobruja which
today is part of Rumania. He was equally conversant with Latin and
Greek and was an important link uniting the Eastern and Western
parts of the Christian world. When still very young he became a
monk in Palestine and soon gave himself to *xeniteia*, the spiritual
wandering of one who is 'a stranger and pilgrim on earth'. About
385 he went to Egypt, where he spent around fifteen years visiting
monasteries and hermitages. About 400 he arrived in Constantinople
and became a disciple of St John Chrysostom who ordained him
deacon. When John Chrysostom was persecuted by the imperial
power, he charged Cassian with the task of taking to Rome the
protest of the clergy who remained faithful to him. At Rome, where
he came to know Leo the Great, Cassian was ordained priest. In
415 he was called to Provence as a witness to monasticism. At
Marseilles he founded two monasteries, St Victor's for men and
St Saviour's for women. In 417, for the bishop of Apt, he drew
up his *Cenobitic Institutions*, in which he describes the Egyptian
communities from which the bishop wanted to draw inspiration for
his own foundations. Cassian then wrote, for the bishop of Fréjus
and particularly for Honoratus the abbot of Lérins and subsequently
bishop of Arles, his very important *Conferences*.

Cassian considerably modified St Augustine's most cherished
theses on freedom and grace. In particular he transmitted to the West,
with great discernment, the experience of Egyptian and Palestinian
monasticism and the best of the spirituality of Origen and Evagrius.
He put forward a wise combination of community life and the life
of a solitary. He put ascesis at the service of love. His mysticism
is a mysticism of light and of the divine light pervading the whole
person, including the subconscious mind. The praying of the psalms,
meditation, the repetition of a short formula to still the intellect, all
this culminates and is surpassed in the 'prayer of fire', which is a true
sharing in the eternal nativity of the Son.

It was essentially through St John Cassian that continuity was
achieved between the original monasticism, particularly that of Egypt,
and the monasticism of the West. The Rule of St Benedict quotes

Cassian at length, and his Conferences have been read every evening from generation to generation in Western monasteries.

Conferences SC 42, 54, 64

JOHN CLIMACUS (7th century)

John of Sinai came to be called 'of the Ladder' (*klimakos* in Greek) from the name of his principal work. It seems that he lived at the end of the sixth century and in the first half of the seventh. He gave systematic form to three centuries of monastic tradition in an ascetic synthesis resembling the doctrinal synthesis elaborated in the same period by Maximus the Confessor. In both cases it was a decisive transition from the patristic to the properly Byzantine period.

After having received a sound education John, at the age of sixteen, entered the monastery of Mount Sinai where he put himself under the instruction of an 'elder' Abba Martyrios. He became a monk at the age of twenty. After the death of his teacher he made a lengthy trial of *anachoresis* (life as a solitary) interrupted presumably by a journey to Egypt, where he visited the tragic 'monastery of the penitents' of which he speaks in *The Ladder*. This solitude made him a recognized spiritual master. He was then elected superior of the monastery of Sinai. As a very old man, this new Moses wrote *The Ladder of Divine Ascent* at the request of the superior of a neighbouring monastery, John of Raithu, who later was to write his life.

The Ladder is made up of thirty short treatises (*logoi*) subsequently called 'steps'. Each of them is a group of sayings or narratives of which the discontinuity, as the rigorous poetic and enigmatic style, is an encouragement to meditation. First of all the break with the world is described in all its unavoidable violence. Then follow the basic attitudes of purification: obedience, repentance, 'mindfulness of death', *penthos* (spiritual mourning, with the gift of tears). They make possible the fight against the passions, those forms of idolatry: anger, resentment, idle or lying talk, discouragement, gluttony, impurity, avarice, insensibility, sloth, vainglory, pride, blasphemous thoughts. They also make possible the corresponding virtues and this correspondence denotes a metamorphosis: for example, gentleness, silence, chastity, detachment from possessions, vigilance. *Praxis* culminates in simplicity, humility and discernment. The last four *logoi* are devoted to union with God: *hesychia* (peace, silence, contentment), pure prayer, impassibility (a sign of resurrection), and love.

Climacus insists on a permanent correspondence between *metanoia* (repentance) and illumination, similar to the union of the human and divine in Christ. *Metanoia*, in the ontological sense, denotes an awareness of our separation from God. Ascesis in this perspective rehabilitates the body by rescuing it from the manifold forms of death. St John Climacus attaches great importance to invocation of the Name of Jesus 'in the rhythm of the breathing'.

This work of his, at once very traditional and very personal, continually brings one back to fundamentals and by its irony masks any monastic presumptions or reliance on mechanical techniques. It marks out a path that leads through the imitation of Christ who has died and is risen to resemblance to God and participation in him, in fact to the burning bush, to the mystery of Sinai.

The Ladder of Divine Ascent PG 88 (revised 1883, 1970). There are two English translations: by Archimandrite Lazarus Moore, London 1959; by Colm Luibheid and Norman Russell, SPCK London 1982.

JOHN OF DAMASCUS or JOHN DAMASCENE (c. 650 – c. 750)

St John Damascene gave systematic form, with power and clarity, to the theology and the ascetic teaching of the Fathers, and particularly to the 'energetic' post-Chalcedonian Christology, in its origins Alexandrian. But his intervention in the controversy over icons led him at the same time to emphasize, like the older Antiochenes, the actual individuality of Christ. It is obviously an important synthesis.

John was a Christian Arab, in a Near East recently conquered by Islam (his name was Mansur, the same as that of his grandfather who had signed the surrender of Damascus to the Muslims). It was a situation of *dhimma*, a tolerated and controlled autonomy that none the less enabled John to oppose, without any risk to himself, the Caesaro-Papist pretensions of the iconoclastic Emperors of Byzantium. Born at Damascus about 650, bilingual, he became responsible for local finances, the Caliph having kept the organization of the Byzantine state and retained the Christian families who made it work. This high official, the defender of his co-religionists, was also a learned theologian. He regarded Islam as a Christian heresy and did not hesitate, in a Muslim society, to assume the defence of sacred images, and to compose Trinitarian hymns. It is true that he had played with the Caliph when they were both children.

Soon, however, a new Caliph embarked on the wholesale Islamization of state officials. John, probably in disgrace, retired to the monastery of St Sabas near Jerusalem, where he died at the age of over a hundred after having written a considerable amount.

His basic work is the *Source of Knowledge* which includes, in its first part, a remarkable semantic clarification inspired by Aristotle, and culminates in its third part in an exposition of the orthodox faith. *On the Orthodox Faith* is a sort of *Summa* composed from the standpoint of a theology of celebration – John also translated it into hymn form – rather than from the angle of scholastic theology. John adds precision to the Trinitarian antinomy and to the mystery of the *hypostasis* (the person) as the 'source of existence'. In this ontology of the person and of participation, being always appears as 'enhypostasy'. The Son 'enhypostasizes' the whole of humanity, imparts glory to it and thereby unites himself to each of us in an ineffable participation. In this regard the Damascene takes up again the phrase of Maximus the Confessor: 'In his wholeness and entirety he unites himself to me in my wholeness and entirety'.

In his *Homily on the Transfiguration* John emphasizes that humanity is called to an integral deification by participation in the transfigured Christ, whose 'earthly body radiates the divine splendour.' This transfiguration expresses itself in sanctity, supremely in that of the Mother of God – who becomes, for John, the model of the contemplative – but it can already be experienced in the celebration of the liturgy. The icon forms an integral part of the liturgy and John wrote three treatises in its defence. The icon of icons, that of Christ, finds its justification in the incarnation, which causes the divine energies to radiate even from matter: 'I do not venerate matter, but I venerate the Creator of matter who for my sake became matter.' And while Christ assumed humanity whole and entire, he is also an actual individual and therefore can be represented. Here, as we have said, the thinking of Antioch meets that of Alexandria.

Today the question arises whether the theology of icons, in so far as it is the theology of the divine energies present in matter, could not shed some light on culture in a Christian sense.

On the Orthodox Faith PG 94,784 – 1228; *Homily on the Transfiguration* PG 96,545 – 576; *On the Virtues and Vices* PG 95,85-97; *The Eight Spirits of Evil* PG 95,80 – 84

JOHN OF SCYTHOPOLIS (c.475 – c.550)

John of Scythopolis (Beisan, in Galilee) was one of the theologians
who at the beginning of the sixth century defended the dogma
of Chalcedon and interpreted it in accordance with the 'energetic'
Christology of Cyril of Alexandria. He posits a real transfiguration of humanity in Christ through the energies of the divinity.
About 532 John wrote a commentary on the works of the Pseudo-
Dionysius, *scholia*, which for a long time were ascribed to Maximus
the Confessor. They bring Dionysian theology into the mainstream
of Tradition.

On the Divine Names of Dionysius PG 4,14-576

JUSTIN (died c.165)

Justin is the most important of the apologists of the second century.
He was born in Palestine, at Flavia Neapolis, the ancient Sychem,
not far from Jacob's Well where Jesus told the Samaritan woman
about worshipping 'in spirit and in truth'. He belonged to a family
of well-to-do farmers, no doubt Latin in origin, though he himself
wrote in Greek.

This upright man, a transparent and ardent soul, embarked on
the quest of the true 'philosophy', a word that in the second century
denoted an art of living, a wisdom, an approach to the Absolute. He
travelled, investigated, progressed from Stoicism to the disciples of
Aristotle, of Pythagoras, of Plato, until the day when a mysterious
old man whom he met on the sea-shore drew his attention to the
'prophets'. The Bible led him to Christ. He was baptized, at Ephesus
for certain. From now on he in his turn could wear the *pallium*, the
philosopher's cloak, but in order to teach what in his eyes constituted
'the philosophy' par excellence, Christianity. So he founded a school
of Christian wisdom at Rome. A Cynic philosopher, jealous of his
success and publicly convicted by him of ignorance, denounced him
to the imperial police. (Christians were not sought out, but if they
were reported they were sentenced.) Justin was executed, probably
in 165, with six of his pupils. We have two *Apologies* from him
addressed to the Emperor Antoninus Pius, and the *Dialogue with
Trypho*, the account of a debate with a learned rabbi at Ephesus.

Justin emphasizes the universal presence of the Logos, the bridge
between the ineffable God and the world. The Logos manifests

himself in pagan wisdom and more overtly in the Bible, where Justin excels in discovering 'types' and 'images' of Christ. But this germination of the Logos in all humanity, that is completed in the incarnation, is continually being thwarted by the powers of darkness, transforming prefigurations into idolatry and then persecuting Christians. However, it is the vision of the divine-human convergence that prevails.

Justin also presents a predominantly unitary conception of humanity. The soul is inseparable from the body, because the image of God makes them a unique unity.

Apologies PG 6; *Dialogue with Trypho* PG 6; English Translation in the Ante-Nicene Christian Library, vol II, 1867

MACARIUS THE EGYPTIAN or OF SCETE or THE GREAT (c.300 – c.390)

One of the spiritual masters of the Egyptian desert in the fourth century, the organizer of the monastic life at Scete, a disciple of Anthony and teacher of Evagrius. They gave him the nickname of 'child-elder' perhaps on account of the extraordinary gift of discernment that he had manifested from a very early age.

His prestige caused some *Spiritual Homilies* to be ascribed to him that are in fact of later date and of a different origin. The Coptic cycle of *Sayings* concerning him reproduces for the most part the Greek alphabetical collection, but also contains some surprising texts, the oldest known if authentic, on invocation of the Name of Jesus combined with the breathing.

Coptic Apophthegms, in *Histoire des Monastères de basse Egypte*, (Paris 1894)

MACARIUS (PSEUDO-MACARIUS) (c. 400)

This is the real but unknown author of the *Spiritual Homilies* and the *Great Letter* long ascribed to Macarius the Egyptian. He probably lived in Mesopotamia, moving to Asia Minor during the last third of the fourth century. He is not in the least a 'Messalian', as has been suggested. (The 'Messalians' were Quietists who took little account of the sacraments and of morality while attaching the utmost importance to a state of prayer; they sought a more or less physical experience of the Holy Spirit). There are definite connections between the thought of Pseudo-Macarius and that of St Basil and St Gregory of Nyssa who, the last especially, began to make peace with the Messalian tendency and to bring it into harmony with the life of the Church. But it is impossible to decide whether the *Great Letter* precedes or follows the *De Instituto Christiano*, the attribution of which to Gregory of Nyssa remains debatable anyway.

The Macarian *corpus* is essentially a resolute return to the sources of the biblical and evangelical sensitivity that characterizes the earliest monasticism. The primacy of charity, the experience of light and fire, an anthropology centred on the theme of the 'heart' that means at the same time the unconscious (the supra- and the sub- conscious) and the centre of integration of the whole personality. The emphasis is laid, precisely in opposition to Messalian quietism, on the spiritual combat always having to be taken up afresh, and on the genuinely evangelical and Pauline ambivalence of the 'heart', that battlefield of the forces of life and death. Even after baptism the struggle goes on in the depths of the human being between grace and evil. Freedom is the freedom to call for help, to 'cry out' from the utmost despair. Total dispossession – 'counting oneself nothing' – enables the grace of the Spirit to convert despair into faith. Neither observances nor virtues have any meaning, save in and for this humble relationship with God, this brief repeated prayer – 'I beseech thee, Lord, I beseech thee' – that needs to sink deep into our souls. Then the fire of the Spirit consumes the forces of evil, burning prayer makes possible the irruption of the divine light, the very gentle fire of grace, starting from the heart, imparts itself to the whole human being, to the body also, giving the soul an extraordinary feeling of 'fullness' ('plenitude') and 'joy'. The monk who becomes a man of prayer, that is to say one who practises perpetual prayer, ought to be freed from any kind of work. The Spirit who plays a principal part in this spirituality gives, as an extra so to speak, certain charisms – of speech, discernment, prophecy, healing. The essential thing remains the becoming slowly aware through patience and hope of 'baptism with fire and the Holy Spirit'. This leads in the end, eschatologically, to the body no longer containing the soul, but the 'pneumatic' (spirit-filled) soul containing the body. It becomes a *pneuma sarkophoron*, a 'spirit that bears the body'.

The Macarian way, even more than the mystical work of the Cappadocians, made it possible to integrate into the Church the Messalians' exaggerated cult of charisms, a cult divorced from its roots. It combined with the Evagrian current of thought to issue, when the close of antiquity brought a well-balanced spirituality, in the 'union of heart and intellect' that makes it possible to reconstitute the 'heart-mind', the true 'place of God'.

Spiritual Homilies PG 34,449 – 622. There is an English translation by A.F. Mason, *Fifty Spiritual Homilies of St Macarius the Egyptian*, SPCK London 1921; *The Great Letter*, W. Jaeger, *Two rediscovered Works of Ancient Christian Literature: Gregory of Nyssa and Macarius*, Leiden 1954 pp. 281-351

MAXIMUS THE CONFESSOR (580 – 662)

Maximus completed the synthesis of the Patristic age in the East, but in close union with the Latin West. He was able to keep the Eastern sense of the unity of Christ in balance with the Western sense of his duality. He laid a theological foundation for the mystery of human freedom. The Sixth Ecumenical Council in proclaiming the existence in Christ not only of the divine will but also of a human will is the outcome of his reflection, prayer, and martyrdom.

The publication in 1973 of a Syriac *Life of Maximus* makes it possible to rectify the statements of a later hagiography. Maximus, we now learn, was not born in the capital city of a noble family, but in a village of the Golan. He was left an orphan at the age of nine and entrusted to a Palestinian monastery, a centre of Evagrian thought, where he was introduced to the Evagrian tradition. In 614 he fled from the Persian invasion and resumed monastic life near the capital at Chrysopolis. But in 626 the Persians threatened Constantinople itself. Like so many other refugees, Maximus wandered about the Mediterranean until he finally settled at Carthage. There he became the spiritual son of a great Palestinian monk, Sophronius, who was to be the Patriarch of Jerusalem when the city fell into Muslim hands. In the middle of this enormous tragedy, a veritable apocalypse within history, Evagrian serenity and the Dionysian return of all things to God no longer corresponded to reality. Sophronius acquainted Maximus with the spirituality of Macarius, with the conversion of despair into faith and with the primacy of love. The *kenosis* of God and the corresponding *kenosis* of the Christian acquire more precise lineaments in the thought of Maximus, who seems to have written most of his spiritual works at Carthage.

From 638 onwards the Empire was making desperate efforts to achieve reconciliation with the Monophysites (see separate note on Monophysitism) who were prepared to open their gates to all invaders. Doctrinal compromises were necessary: 'monoenergism' then 'monothelitism' (a single divine operation or will in Christ). Maximus, whose eminence as a teacher was now recognized, threw himself into the theological battle, insisted on the importance of the human will in Christ, and thereby appeared as a rebel jeopardizing the unity and strength of the Empire. He sought support from the See of Rome and prompted the Lateran Council of 649 which asserted that there were two wills in Christ, for 'He willed and effected our salvation both divinely and humanly at the same time.' This definition was to be sealed by the double martyrdom of the Pope and the theologian. Pope Martin and Maximus were arrested by imperial troops in 653 and taken to Constantinople. Pope Martin was condemned to deportation and died of exhaustion in the Crimea in 655 – the last Pope to die as a martyr, the last Pope also to have opposed the temporal power simply by martyrdom. Maximus was exiled to Thrace, refusing any compromise. In 658 he was taken back to Constantinople to face complete isolation. The episcopate, the Patriarch and even Pope Vitalian had accepted the imperial decrees of silence on the problems causing controversy. Maximus as a lone prophet was content to reply: 'When the God of the universe declared Peter blessed for having confessed him in the correct terms, he showed that the Catholic Church is the right and saving confession of God's own nature'. The Church at that moment of history was Maximus. After four years of harsh exile he was condemned in 662 by a Monothelite synod. He died on 13 August 662, in the fortress to which he had been banished in the Caucasus.

Maximus' work has the dimensions of a *Summa Theologica*. He makes free use, as well, of Aristotelian categories. But the form and the spirit are those of a mystic.

The world was created by successive divisions and humanity is invited to effect the corresponding syntheses. It is possible to respond to that vocation through Christ, who in himself recapitulates the universe and history. Christ makes available again to humanity its function as mediator until the End when the communion of saints clearly exhibits the features of the Christ who comes. Humanity, the personal image of the Logos, has to discover and present the *logoi* of objects, their spiritual essences. Human rationality is thus offered boundless fertility in unifying and transfiguring the universe.

Humanity is freedom. But its properly personal freedom, thwarted by *philautia* (self-centredness), invests in the 'passions' the deep impulses of spontaneity or 'natural freedom' that actually can be fulfilled only in God. Christ by his loving sacrificial life restores that natural freedom and tries to re-direct our personal freedom by his *kenosis* on the cross – the proof of his 'mad love'. By faith and charity we conform ourselves to his mode of existence. Thereby in this encounter we share in the compenetration of the divine and human energies brought about in his 'composite *hypostasis*'. Desire then finds its true meaning in the divine-human reality of the virtues that are unified in love. Human existence becomes a liturgy, an interiorization and a cosmic extension of the 'mysteries'. It becomes a 'mystagogy' of deification.

The Christian West was to lay the emphasis on our moral communion with Christ, on the imitation by humanity of Christ's filial mode of existence. The Christian East for its part was to insist on humanity's ontological participation in the divine energies. Maximus' theology is an admirable synthesis of these two approaches. And therein lies its relevance.

Centuries on Charity PG 90,959-1080 also SC 9; *Ascetic Dialogue* PG 90,912-1080 cf. Ancient Christian Writers Vol. XXI for English translations; *Commentary on the Lord's Prayer* PG 90,872-908; *A Hundred Theological and Economical Chapters* PG 90,1083-1124; *Mystagogia* PG 91,657-717; *Quaestiones ad Thalassium* PG 90,244-773; *Letter on Charity* (Letter 2) PG 91,391-408; *Ambigua* PG 91,1032-1417; *Gnostic Centuries* S.L. Epifanovitch, Kiev, 1917; *On the Divine Names* PG 4,14-576 (Most of this text is by John of Scythopolis.)

MELITO OF SARDIS (2nd century)

Melito, bishop of Sardis in Lydia, was one of the 'great luminaries' of Christian Asia Minor in the second half of the second century. About 170, he addressed to Marcus Aurelius an *Apology* (of which only fragments remain), in which he is one of the first to express the wish for an alliance between Church and Empire, whereby Christianity should be a source of prosperity and blessing for the Empire. Of his considerable output the only item that has come down to us intact, having recently been discovered among some papyri, is a remarkable Easter Homily, vibrant with the original meaning of the descent into hell and the resurrection.

Homily on Easter SC 123

ODES OF SOLOMON (early 2nd century)

This collection of 42 hymns was discovered in 1905 in a Syriac manuscript. Before this only five of the hymns were known, in a Coptic translation. The *Odes* date probably from the first half of the second century. They were undoubtedly written in Greek for the Christian communities of Syria. The attribution to Solomon was an everyday procedure in the Jewish and Judaeo-Christian circles in which apocrypha using famous authors' names abounded. The *Odes of Solomon* is not an interpolated text either Gnostic or Jewish, as some have supposed, but evidence of a Christian mysticism quite close to the inspiration found in the Gospel and the Epistles of St John.

The Odes and Psalms of Solomon J.R. Harris-A. Mingana, 2 vols. Manchester 1916-1920

ORIGEN (185 – 254)

Origen was the most powerful mind of early Christianity. His work inspired Christian spirituality and exegesis both in the East and in the West. But his philosophical hypotheses, which were organized into a system by his disciples who abused his name, demanded of the Church a painful process of discerning of spirits.

Origen was born at Alexandria into a particularly fervent Christian family. His father was a confessor of the faith and introduced him while still very young to the knowledge of the Scriptures. His family's property was confiscated for the crime of being Christian, so he earned a livelihood for his family by teaching. He was scarcely eighteen years old when the Bishop of Alexandria entrusted him with the catechetical instruction of candidates for baptism. He was formed, in the footsteps of Pantaenus and Clement, at the school of Ammonius Saccas, who was perhaps a Christian and was the founder of Neo-Platonism and the future teacher of Plotinus. But there was in him a thirst for martyrdom which he turned in on himself, as he did with his erotic tendencies, by a relentless ascesis, making himself in the most literal sense 'voluntarily a eunuch for the Kingdom of God'.

His classes, open to all, aroused the interest of the pagans and he was called upon to expound his teaching both to the Governor of Arabia and to the mother of the Emperor. Difficulties with his bishop led him to settle in 231 at Caesarea in Palestine where, in spite of the canons declaring a mutilated person ineligible, he was ordained priest. He continued his teaching there. But martyrdom that had been near him in childhood and in his work pursued him. During the Decian persecution he was cruelly tortured and died shortly afterwards.

Origen created almost all the approaches indispensable to Christian thinking – religious philosophy, theology, ascetical and mystical doctrine, preaching, but above all unflagging study of the Bible, from large-scale commentaries to notes on points of detail, from philosophy to popular sermons. His exegetical work no doubt presents at first sight an academic appearance. He practised rabbinic and Judaeao-Christian exegesis and edited the text of the Old Testament in six columns (the *Hexapla*): the Hebrew text, its transcription into Greek letters, and four ancient Greek translations, including the Septuagint, with a whole system of critical signs to mark passages added by the Septuagint or needing to be added to it from the Hebrew. But it is all undergirded with spiritual dynamism, seeing that the understanding of Scripture demands ascesis and contemplation. Scripture embodies the mystery of Christ in order to feed the soul with it. Scripture reveals to the soul, in proportion to its progress, new aspects and new names of the Word. The Platonizing tendency that keeps cropping up at Alexandria from the time of Philo seeks to turn history into myth. But it is balanced, in Origen, by the sense of the drama of salvation and by the mystery of the cross that is victory over the power of the devil. Origen distinguishes, most often, three kinds of meaning: the 'literal meaning' that corresponds to the body; the 'moral meaning' that corresponds to the soul; and the 'spiritual meaning' corresponding to the spirit. But the moral meaning often extends beyond the ethical domain; it is derived from the mystical meaning and expresses the life of the divine Word in the soul.

At the same time, in his treatise *On Principles*, Origen outlines a vast philosophical and theological synthesis. After having recalled the foundations accepted by everyone, he embarks on a series of explanatory hypotheses in a hazardous attempt to reach understanding of the faith. Spirits that were created equal and transparent – a sort of collective Adam – abandoned God and separated from one another because they were sated or because they wanted to experiment with their freedom. This 'cooling down' of souls gave rise to materiality, the consequence, not the cause, of the fall. In a system in which many of the elements are alien to biblical revelation this cosmic range of freedom is profoundly Christian. God by a second creation fixed the worlds that had appeared in this way. For humanity he stabilized the perceptible universe in which the incarnation reopens to embodied souls the way to freedom. Except for the saints – and they also with Christ himself are awaiting and preparing for the final reintegration – souls after death pass through manifold 'aeons', states of universal existence which are expressed in corresponding spiritual states. Each soul is driven by a thirst for the absolute which only God can satisfy. Gradually all creatures having come to appreciate evil for what it is and being fundamentally dissatisfied will turn to God and regain, consciously now, their original fullness: this will be the *apokatastasis*, the 're-establishment' of all things.

Finally Origen is a mystic and we find in him almost all the themes that will be developed by later spirituality: imitation of Christ that becomes a sharing in his life; the liberation of freedom lost through the passions; knowledge of God in the purified mirror of his image; the necessity of 'discernment'; the alternation of 'refreshment' and 'bitterness'; the interplay of presence and absence; the change from the words of the Logos (the Old Testament) to his face (the New Testament); *apatheia* making *agape* possible; the marriage of the Logos with the soul within the marriage of Christ with the Church, described in symbol in the Song of Songs; the pilgrimage in the Spirit through the Logos to the Father; and most fundamental of all, perhaps, the 'sharing in the godhead' through 'friendship with God and communion with him'.

A certain number of Origenist theses were condemned by the Fifth Ecumenical Council in 553: the pre-existence of souls; boredom as the cause of the fall; the denial of proper reality to the material world; and universal salvation as the inevitable outcome of a system. These are condemnations, not so much of Origen's intuitions and hypotheses as of their systematization by Evagrius. The highest spirituality of the Christian East took up the theme of universal salvation not as a doctrine but as a hope and a prayer.

Against Celsus SC 132,136,147,150,227, English translation by H. Chadwick, Cambridge 1953; *De Principiis* SC 252,253,268,269, English translation by G.W. Butterworth, SPCK 1936; *On Prayer* GCS 3, 297 – 403, English translation by J.T. O'Meara, ACW 19,

1953; *Letter to Gregory Thaurmaturgus* PG 11, 88-92; Homilies: *On Genesis, On Leviticus and Numbers* GCS 29; *On Isaiah and Ezekiel* GCS 33; *On Jeremiah* SC 232, 238; *On the Song of Songs* SC 37 bis, English translation by R.P. Lawson in ACW 26, 1957; *Commentary on the Gospel of Matthew* SC 162; *Commentary on the Gospel of John* SC 120, 157, 222; *Fragments on the Psalms, Proverbs, Ephesians, Colossians* GCS 6

PACHOMIUS (287 – 347)

The founder of communitarian and hierarchically organized monasticism, called 'cenobitic'.

Pachomius was born in Upper Egypt into a pagan family. At the age of twenty he was sent, with others, under a strong escort to a recruiting centre for the army. The Christians at Thebes were the only people who gave any welcome or assistance to the exhausted recruits. Their behaviour came as a revelation to Pachomius and he resolved to imitate them. On his release he settled in a Christian village, received instruction and was baptized. For seven years he underwent an apprenticeship of ascesis and prayer with an old hermit. One night an interior voice reminded Pachomius of his vow to serve others. He built a few shelters with an enclosing fence around them. Brothers came whom he served in the best way that he could. But for lack of discipline disorder soon broke out. Then Pachomius imposed a strict discipline on his monks in the form of a Rule, written in Coptic and dictated, it was said, by angels. A Pachomian monastery looked like a village surrounding its church, and the monks who were mostly laymen were grouped according to trades. Each 'house' had its own superior and all the superiors obeyed Pachomius. Soon a cenobitic monastery for nuns was organized near by, with his sister in charge.

Thus side by side with a purely charismatic monasticism, that of solitaries, there appeared a communitarian monasticism in which the basic aims were obedience and mutual service. St Basil was to make it clear that such a monasticism bears witness primarily to apostolic love on the model of the first Christian community, that of Jerusalem. Communitarian monasticism is often regarded as a school in which preparation is made for the perpetual prayer of solitude.

Sources in *Pachomian Koinonia* by A. Veilleux 1980

PHILOTHEUS OF SINAI

He was the Superior, at an unknown date, of the monastery of Batos in Mount Sinai. In the spiritual succession of St John Climacus he lays the emphasis on the 'keeping of the commandments' and he attests an already established use of the 'Jesus Prayer'.

Forty Texts on Watchfulness in the Philokalia, translated and edited G.E.H. Palmer, P. Sherrard, Kallistos Ware, Vol 3,1984; *On Sobriety, Philocalie des pères neptiques,* Astir, Athens, pp. 274-286

POLYCARP OF SMYRNA

According to the statements of Irenaeus, Polycarp sat at the feet of the apostles themselves and they consecrated him bishop of Smyrna. Ignatius of Antioch addressed one of his letters to him. In 155 he went to Rome to discuss the date of Easter with the bishop of that city. They reached no conclusion, but their talks were held in amity and mutual esteem. Shortly after his return he was arrested. He refused to curse Christ – 'For eighty six years I have been serving him ... How could I blaspheme my King and Saviour?' – and he was burnt at the stake. We possess a description of that event written by an eye-witness in the form of a letter from the faithful of his church to another church of Asia Minor. It is a narrative that shows us this bishop's profound tranquillity, his 'love for his enemies', his determination to imitate Christ in total simplicity, and to be united with him in his sacrifice.

The Martyrdom of Polycarp SC 10, 242 with the *Letters* of Ignatius of Antioch.

RABULAS OF EDESSA

A Syrian theologian and hymn-writer, perhaps the author of the translation of the New Testament into Syriac. He was a pagan, converted about 400, and in 412 he became bishop of Edessa. At the Council of Edessa he joined the 'orientals' led by John of Antioch but soon rallied to Cyril of Alexandria. He played a part in the negotiations that ended in the agreement of 433. He fought the Nestorians who were influential in the school at Edessa. The authenticity of his hymns is contested.

Hymn to the Martyrs Bickell II, p. 262-263

RUFINUS OF AQUILEIA

He is one of the men who made the main works of Greek exegesis and theology known to the Latin world.

Born into a Christian family near Aquileia, Rufinus studied at Rome where he formed a friendship with Jerome, whose career impinged on his own. He withdrew for some years to Aquileia into a monastic community where Jerome also stayed for a short time. The vocation of this peaceful and conciliatory man was to prayer and study. It was at Aquileia that he received baptism. Back in Rome he became the protégé of a rich patrician lady, Melania the Old. Both went together to Egypt to visit the great Abbas in its celebrated deserts. Rufinus who was fluent in Greek studied for six years at Alexandria, under the direction of Didymus the Blind. Didymus introduced him to Greek theology and imbued him with his own fervent admiration for Origen. In 377 Rufinus settled in Jerusalem, in the monastery founded by Melania on the Mount of Olives. As Jerome was pursuing a similar course and had settled at Bethlehem they resumed their friendly relations. But not for long. A traditionalist hunter-out of heresies, Epiphanius of Salamis, questioned Origen's orthodoxy. Rufinus defended him, while Jerome with a complete volte-face attacked him. In 397 Rufinus returned to Italy and translated Origen's *On Principles*, modifying or omitting the risky passages which he believed (it seems) had been added by enemies of the master. In his Preface he mentions the admiration that Jerome had long professed for Origen. Jerome, angered, published a complete translation of the same book to bring out its heretical character. Pamphlets were exchanged, utter confusion reigned, and it became incumbent on Rufinus to justify his position, with difficulty, before Pope Anastasius. In disgust he withdrew from the controversy and settled in silence at Aquileia where he undertook an enormous series of translations. He was aware that knowledge of Greek was dying out in the West, and he wanted to transmit to the Latin world texts that seemed fundamental to him, the exegetical works of Origen, the treatises of the great Cappadocians, witnesses to monastic spirituality. Many works lost in the original are known to us now only through

Rufinus' translations. It was the right moment. The Visigoths invaded Italy. Rufinus, caught up in the general exodus, fled southwards, and died at Messina in 410 at the time that Rome was being sacked.

History of the Monks in Egypt PL 21,387 – 462: either Rufinus' original work or the adaptation of a Greek narrative. Some young monks visit Egyptian Abbas, about 395. Cf. *The Lives of the Desert Fathers*, translated by N. Russell, London, 1981.

Sayings (Apophthegms) of the Desert Fathers

This is an anonymous collection of 'words' and 'works' of the great solitaries of Egyptian desert, the first Abbas (Fathers). There is no doubt that they are based on a coptic oral tradition, and that, in the fifth and sixth centuries, this was translated into Greek, with the names arranged in alphabetical order, from Abba Anthony to Abba Or (whose name begins with omega, the last letter in the Greek alphabet).

There is not yet a critical edition in SC; in the meantime, the Greek collections of the apophthegms are scattered, PG 65,71-440; *Revue de l'Orient chrétien*, years 1907, 1908, 1912 & 1913; PO 8,164-183. A sixth century Latin translation from the Greek is extant, but it does not correspond exactly to the Greek collections: *Verba Seniorum* PL 73-4.

SYNESIUS OF CYRENE (c.370 – 413/414)

In an age when disagreement and antitheses were more in evidence, Synesius unexpectedly and probably prematurely, expounded the virtues of synthesis. He was eager for the interior life but also for literature and for political involvement. He was a Platonist, but one who, in complete continuity through a deepening of his spirituality, became a sincere Christian. Though he was a Christian, he always remained faithful to Hypatia whom an Alexandrian mob, stirred to fanaticism by some clerics, were to slaughter, without any protest from Cyril the Archbishop. Synesius was a bishop who demanded to remain married at a time when treatises on virginity were being multiplied.

Synesius was born at Cyrene in Libya and studied at Alexandria where Hypatia introduced him to Neoplatonism and the sciences. He remained in correspondence with her throughout his life. A country gentleman, keen on hunting and literature in both of which he excelled, he accepted political responsibilities and became a member of the provincial council. From 399 to 402 he stayed at Constantinople and successfully negotiated financial concessions for his province – and of course for himself. (It is common knowledge that the burden of taxation had become crushing under the Late Empire.) Synesius delivered, courageously, a speech *On Kingship* before the young Emperor Arcadius, in which he painted a Platonic portrait of the ideal prince, and protested in the name of his class against the proliferation of barbarians in imperial administration. On his return he married a Christian wife at Alexandria, and resumed in Cyrenaica his life as a gentleman farmer. But when in 405 the imperial troops abandoned the frontier, he organized a local militia and repulsed the nomads. In 410 the clergy and the faithful of Ptolemais elected him bishop. He was taken aback and stated frankly to the patriarch certain philosophical objections, but the six months that elapsed before his consecration enabled him to think more deeply: 'not a collapse of philosophy but a fresh step forward in it.' He obtained the right to remain married, which was traditionally permissible but less and less usual under the influence of the monastic movement. He declared that he loved his wife and wanted more children. He was an excellent bishop, struggling against the Arians, against injustices and abuses in administration. He was a man of peace.

Hymns 5 PG 66,1587-1616

TERTULLIAN (c.155 – c.225)

The first of the great Latin-speaking theologians and moralists. Tertullian was born at Carthage into a pagan family. He studied law and rhetoric at Rome where he made a reputation for himself as a lawyer. Impressed by the witness of the martyrs, he was converted about 193. He settled at Carthage in the service of the Christian community. It is not certain whether he was a priest. In that great city where all the currents of the 'new religions' met and mingled, where Christianity itself was still fluid, Tertullian attempted to delineate its features more precisely in opposition to pagans, Jews, heretics amd Gnostics. But his own tendency to extremes led him about 207 to espouse Montanism, a charismatic movement that claimed to be inaugurating the age of the Spirit and professed the utmost rigorism, in a sort of eschatological frenzy. Carried away by the arguments of the sects, Tertullian ended by founding a Church of his own, on the fringe of Montanism.

Tertullian was a man of passionate feeling, full of paradox. He strove relentlessly against error but demanded from the State – which he regarded anyway as evil – freedom of religion. He violently rejected any philosophical approach to Christianity – 'What can Athens have to do with Jerusalem?' – and professed a faith that is irrational by choice. 'The Son of God has died: that imposes itself absolutely on faith because it is absurd.' But at the same time he appealed to the intuition of the soul as the image of God – *anima naturaliter Christiana.*

In his *Adversus Praxeam* in particular he worked out Trinitarian and Christological formulae that anticipated in a surprising way the conciliar definitions of the fourth and fifth centuries. He was the first to use, in regard to God, the words *trinitas, persona, substantia*: 'a single substance in the three together'. He points to two natures in Christ 'in a single person, Jesus, God and man ... so that the property of each nature is preserved.' Like all the early Latin Fathers Tertullian contemplated the divine unity flowing from the Father into the Son and from the Father and the Son into the Spirit: a global *processio* (meaning in this context the movement of the divine consubstantiality of the Father in the Son, and from the Father and the Son in the Holy Spirit) clearly quite different from the Greek *ekporeusis* (which in the Greek theology of the fourth century means the unique relationship by which the Father as the Principle of divinity produces from all eternity the existence of the Spirit). In this *processio* one can see the origins of the *Filioque* – though Tertullian himself prefers to say 'through the Son'.

Tertullian defended the sanctity of marriage and the equality of man and woman, but shows himself increasingly hostile to second marriages for those widowed.

He set out and explained the meaning of fasting which was very strict among the Montanists. This practice, then condemned by the Church, was taken up again by the monastic movement with its interiorization of eschatology. The monastic movement spread it to the whole Church throughout the following century.

To his Wife PG 1,1273-303; *Fasting* CCL 2 (1954) p.1255-77, English Translation by W.P. Le Saint in ACW 13

THEODORE OF MOPSUESTIA (c. 350 – c. 428)

One of the greatest exegetes of the Patristic age, the principal representative of the School of Antioch, Theodore was a fellow disciple and friend of St John Chrysostom. They were both pupils of the creator of Antiochene exegesis, Diodore of Tarsus. Theodore was persuaded by John, in spite of his hesitations, to embrace a monastic life. He was ordained priest at Antioch in 383 and nine years later became bishop of Mopsuestia in Cilicia. He produced a considerable amount of theological and exegetical writing. But he had been the teacher of Nestorius, and when the followers of Cyril became once more in the ascendant in the East, at the beginning of the sixth century, he was denounced as a Nestorian and condemned at the Fifth Ecumenial Council in 553. Like most of the Antiochenes he had laid stress on Christ's actual individual humanity. He was accused of not having clearly confessed the unity of God made man. It may be asked whether he was not the victim of controversies, the significance of which was appreciated only after his death; and whether he was not judged on the basis of an assortment of extracts torn from their context or even interpolated. A large part of his work has disappeared following that negative judgment. What remains of his exegetical writing, in particular on St John (in a Syriac translation) and on St Paul (in a Latin translation) bears witness to a remarkable critical acumen and already perhaps to a certain scholarly objectivity – something not found at all in Origen who never departs from a theological and spiritual meditation on the Bible. In 1932 a Syriac version of Theodore's Catechetical Homilies was discovered. They possess the spiritual quality and historical importance of those of Cyril of Jerusalem or John Chrysostom. One can only deprecate the lack of precision in his Christological vocabulary: but that was common enough in the workings of Christian thought before the clear definition given by the Council of Chalcedon.

Catechetical Homilies Syriac text and French translation, Tonneau-Devresse in *Studi e Testi* 145, Vatican City 1949

THEOPHILUS OF ANTIOCH (2nd century)

One of the defenders of Christianity at the time when the Church, in a minority, was periodically persecuted by the civil power, regarded with mistrust by public opinion and harshly criticized by pagan philosophers and Gnostic teachers.

Theophilus was born on the banks of the Euphrates, of pagan parents. He received a sound Hellenistic education. After a long quest he discovered the Bible (like the other apologists, at the moment when Judaism was concentrating on its *Torah* he laid the emphasis on the prophets). He became a Christian in adult life and later became – according to Eusebius's *Ecclesiastical History* – the sixth bishop of Antioch.

All that is left of his writings is an apology composed shortly before 180 and set out as a dialogue with a pagan friend. Its correct attitude towards the State is remarkable. 'I do not worship the Emperor: I pray for him.' And also the outline of a theology. For the first time in a Christian text in Greek God, is called *trias*, the triad he makes with his *Logos* (his Word) and his *Sophia* (his Wisdom). The Word who was 'brought forth' at the moment of creation is present in God from all eternity. In particular when Theophilus is asked by his interlocutor why God is not visible, Theophilus refers him to man, unable to see until he has 'opened the eyes of his soul' and purified himself so as to become the 'mirror' of God. This is the theme of man as 'image of God', the importance of which was to be immense in Patristic spirituality.

Three Books to Autolycus SC 20 English translation in ANCL vol.3, p. 49 by Marcus Dods. More details of English translations can be found in Johannes Quasten *Patrology* 4 vols. (from 1950); Louis Bouyer *The Spirituality of the New Testament and of the Fathers* 1960; *The Study of Spirituality* ed. Cheslyn Jones, Geoffrey Wainwright and Edward Yarnold S.J., SPCK, London 1986; *Christian Spirituality*, Bernard McGinn, John Meyendorff and John Leclercq, London, 1986 vol 1.

THEOLOGICAL NOTES

Arianism

At the beginning of the fourth century the Church had to confront a heresy which might be called the master heresy, because it is seen to reappear the moment that the sense of mystery is obscured, notably in contemporary forms of Christianity that are seeking a compromise with the world and its ways. For heresy is not just a cultural episode now past. It expresses a permanent temptation of the human mind in its desire to explain the mystery and to reduce its scope. Primitive Arianism was not an abstract and complicated dispute. On the contrary, it was a radical way of simplifying and 'understanding' the incarnation and the Trinity. Arius was a priest of Alexandria who was skilled in subtle discussions, but his work very quickly won a popular following which he took care to foster. With Arianism Christianity became 'easy'. While affirming the pre-eminence of Christ in the order of created reality, Arius confined him to that order, positing a radical difference in nature between him and God. God is God; Christ is the summit of the created world but always a creature. It is a wholly rational approach according to which God remains confined within his own transcendence. At a time when the apparent political victory of Christianity was bringing the masses into the Church, such a conception seemed to make the faith simpler, more readily understandable.

Arianism was to confront Christian reflection with some fundamental problems: how to account for the simultaneous presence in God of the Father as 'first', because he is the source and principle of the godhead, and of the Son of God become Son of Man, who is distinct from the Father and yet declares emphatically: 'I and the Father are one.' Or again, how to reconcile the great biblical affirmation of the unity of God with Jesus's awareness, so clearly defined in the Gospel, of his own divine identity. By its victory over Arianism, the Church was to assert decisively the antinomy in God (and therefore in humanity, his image) of unity and difference.

With Arius the starting point seems to be a conception of God inherited from Greek philosophy, the God of Aristotle rather than the living God of biblical revelation. God is conceived as a perfect essence, enclosed in himself, simple, not admitting any complexity, a reality in the intellectual sphere. The influence of Aristotle makes itself felt also in the method of thought, in the simplistic rigour of logical deduction at the expense of unfathomable and paradoxical mystery – *technologia* not *theologia*, as a Father of the fourth century called it.

God was thus defined, with a fatal play on words, as *agenetos* and *agennetos* – *agenetos* meaning outside all becoming (from *gignomai*, I become, with the alpha privative meaning 'not') and *agennetos* meaning unbegotten (from *gennao* I beget, again with the alpha privative). So not only is God unbegotten, but he could not communicate his essence to another by begetting him, because such a begetting would imply a becoming and therefore in the thought of Greek antiquity a corruption, a division of his essence. The idea of a begotten God, of a God the Son, of a Son who from all eternity would be God, therefore appeared contradictory in itself, the true God being by definition not begotten and not subject to the becoming that characterizes the created. So everything that is distinct from the *agenetos-agennetos* God is necessarily *genetos-gennetos*, created-begotten, created because begotten. Christ is that, first and fundamentally, because being, as Son, begotten, he cannot but be created. The Word is the first, the original creature, brought into being to serve as principle and foundation of the universe. He is not therefore eternal, he has not always existed, he passed from non-being to being, like other creatures. If traditionally he is called God, if allusions to his divinity are to be found in Scripture, that does not mean that he is true God like the Father. It is an image that Scripture uses also for the righteous. Because of his merits, Jesus was adopted by the Father and became the receptacle of the Word, the first creature and the principle of creation. Essentially therefore he is a perfect moral being, and nothing more.

If that is so, there is no mystery of the Trinity nor is there any divine-human being. Humanity is not deified in Christ, and humanity cannot aspire to real union with God. Between God and humanity there can only be moral union, of which Jesus is the model.

It was in order to answer Arianism that the First Ecumenical Council met at Nicaea in 325. The profession of faith, the Creed, was drawn up in the following terms: 'The Son is begotten of the Father, that is to say, he is of the essence (*ousia*) of the Father. He is true God from true God, begotten not created, that is, *gennetos* but not *genetos*, HOMOOUSIOS to the Father.'

The last expression, *homoousios toi Patri* constitutes the incomparable contribution of the Council. This Greek term, which was compromised in the preceding century by the awkward gropings towards a first theology of the Trinity, is now taken up afresh, literally re-created to express an ontology of love. *Homos* denotes identity. *Ousios* refers to ousia which, cleared of the connotation of substance, designates the act of being, not the neuter of a substance but the inexhaustible reality of the Living One, of 'him who is'. To say that the Son is *homoousios*, 'consubstantial to the Father', is to say that they are wholly one, with a unity that is not resemblance but identity. And yet the Son remains the Son, and the Father the Father.

The proclamation of Nicaea framed the mystery of the incarnate Word without any possibility of compromise. The fact that Christ is in essence identical with the Father implies the divinity and eternity of the One who becomes incarnate, as John in his Prologue has declared so emphatically. When the Word becomes incarnate, he integrates himself into the universe and integrates the universe into himself. Now, in virtue of the *homoousion* he has a share in the whole mystery of God. Thus, in Christ, a fundamental relationship is established between God and his creation, between God and humankind. For the first time in so bold a fashion the Church declares that the incarnation, resurrection and glorification of its Lord have integrated humanity with God and through humanity the universe.

The definition of Nicaea, however, was bitterly contested for more than half a century. Many remained Arians or semi-Arians. To the rejection of Christ's divinity some, after 360, added rejection of the Spirit's divinity. These latter were called the *Pneumatomachi*, those who fight against the Spirit. As for the Emperors, for the most part *they supported Arianism*. A transcendent and authoritarian God seemed to them in practice to guarantee their own power more effectively than a God of love, a suffering God, a Father who from all eternity gives his Son all that he has, all that he is, and makes his Spirit rest on him. 'All that the Father has is mine', Jesus said. The Trinitarian revelation is that of a sacrificial and liberating Fatherhood which offers the Spirit and destroys at its very root the relation of master and slave. In our own day a whole process of reflection on power is quickly developing that disparages Christianity by concentrating solely on the authoritarian aspects of 'Christian society', such as were inaugurated by Constantine. That is to forget the phenomena of the confessing Church, the uncompromising prophetic testimony of the monks, the endurance of the great witnesses to the faith such as St Athanasius of Alexandria, so many proofs that the tension between the kingdom of Caesar and the kingdom of God, a space for the freedom of the spirit, has never been able to be relaxed.

To illuminate and complete the dogma of Nicaea, an immense labour of deep theological and spiritual study was carried out by Athanasius himself and, subsequently, by the great bishops who came from Cappadocia, a region of Asia Minor that had long ago been Hellenized. These are the Cappadocian Fathers, Basil of Cæsarea, called 'The Great', his younger brother Gregory of Nyssa, and his friend Gregory Nazianzen. The interpretation of the *homoousion* ran two opposite risks: either of exaggerating the divine unity, depriving the *hypostases* of their individual existences and going back to the previous errors of Sabellius (c. 260) in whose teaching, called 'Sabellianism', the Father, the Son, and the Holy Spirit were regarded as three successive manifestations of the godhead, three 'masks' of God; or, at the other extreme, of separating the divine Persons to the point of approaching tritheism, as if there were 'three Gods'. Athanasius and the Cappadocians gave precise form to the mystery of the living God who is Love, by establishing clearly the antinomy of the unity and the difference: the living God is a single Essence (*Ousia*) in three Persons (*Hypostases*). The Essence designates the infinite unity of the divine Persons, Father, Son, and Holy Spirit. Each of the Persons is neither a substance nor a fragment of the whole, but a way of giving and receiving unity, a 'mode of existence' of the unity. The absolute is identified with Love. The Father, the 'principle' of the godhead, supposes another, his own other, the Son, who is within him and equal to him in infinity; for Love cannot exist alone. 'Thou, Father, art in me and I in thee', Jesus said. But there arises simultaneously a Third, the Spirit, and here the Three, according to St Basil in his *Treatise on the Holy Spirit*, does not signify a number (we are dealing here, he says, with 'meta-mathematics'), rather an infinity that transcends, in the open unity of Love, opposition and confusion equally, so that the love of one for the other is itself a mysterious Person, since nothing can be impersonal in God. Only the Three in One, in an uninterrupted interchange, each one unique and at the same time containing the other two without confusing them, represents the fullness of being, in communion. The communion also reveals itself as the source of being.

At the Second Ecumenical Council that met in Constantinople in 381 the Nicene Creed was completed in terms that proclaim the divinity of the Spirit: 'I believe . . . in the Holy Spirit, the Lord, the Giver of Life, who proceeds from the Father, who with the Father and the Son is worshipped and glorified, who spoke by the prophets.' In addition the Fathers of the Council – all of them from the Eastern Church – in 382 sent to the bishops of the Western Church assembled in Rome a synodical letter in which the antinomy of the one Essence and the three Persons was clearly recalled:

'The Word of Truth . . . teaches us to believe in the name of the Father, the Son, and the Holy Spirit in such a way as to confess a single divinity, power and essence of the Father, the Son, and the Holy Spirit . . . in three perfect Hypostases or in three perfect Persons.'

Early Monasticism

When in the fourth century, with the conversion of the Emperors, the Church ran the risk of too close an accommodation with the secular world, the tension towards the Kingdom 'that is not of this world' was safeguarded by the monastic movement. At the moment when martyrdom seems to have come to an end, the monk internalizes it by ascesis: 'Give your blood and receive the Spirit'. Disregarding the age-old seductions of *eros* and power the anchorite (the word literally means one who withdraws) demonstrates the irreducible character of the human being as image of God. Seeking the personal God who delivers him from all the conditionings of this world, he truly becomes a person and thereby, visibly or invisibly, every one's 'neighbour'.

Monasticism is first of all the reassertion of a need of the human condition in a Christian manner. Monastic life has, in fact, existed in all religions. For 'traditional' societies, the community and the cosmos survive through the openness to the divine of some 'who renounce'. The monk is an explorer of the interior spaces. Whether he is a wise man or a fool, his very existence causes virgin energy to spring forth from the depths. By standing outside the secular world (and the secular world is only made possible by his doing so), he is in league with the angels and the animals, with children and with the old; at once old man and child, he gives birth to himself for eternity.

At the same time Christian monasticism has antecedents that are properly biblical. It spiritually internalizes and expresses afresh externally the Exodus of the Hebrew people through the desert towards the Promised Land. The mystery of monasticism coincides therefore with the mystery of the desert, a place of extremes where nothing can bring salvation but the intervention of the transcendent. The desert is a symbol of death-resurrection. It is there that the divine Bridegroom draws his faithless bride in order to 'speak to her heart' (Hosea 2.16). It is there that God reveals himself to Elijah in a 'still small voice' (I Kings 19.12). The desert is also the site of the great fast of the 'Forty Days' ending with the 'Day of Meeting', the Forty Years of the Exodus, the Forty Days of Moses on Sinai and Elijah on Horeb – these are taken up again by Christ when the Spirit drives him into the desert to confront temptation, constituting already a descent into hell and a paschal dawn. The Church in its turn is in danger of settling down, of becoming insipid, and it is imperative that some of its children should return to the desert and, in Christ, should there become, with him, conquerors over the powers of nothingness and so be prophets of the Kingdom.

Already here below, coming forth in paschal fashion from the death into which he chose to descend, the monk becomes aware of his resurrection in the Risen Christ. The Spirit brings to birth in him the glorified body. 'The whole body is transformed and comes under the power of the Holy Spirit, and something I reckon is already granted to it of that spiritual body it will become at the resurrection of the righteous' (Anthony the Great, *Letter 1,4*). By transfiguration the monk becomes the priest of the world, and the world regains around him its original lucidity and meaning. Miracle reveals this metamorphosis, something that at times rises above the fallen nature of time, space and matter. But it is not miracle that counts for the Christian monk, but love. The monk by making himself wholly one again (the original meaning, it seems, of the word *monachos* is 'unified') is open to the fullness of the Trinity and discovers his own ontological unity with all human beings. He carries in his prayers the whole of humanity. His very presence is protection and peace for the world. In the *Sayings of the Desert Fathers* the principal spiritual gifts of the perfect monk are *rhema kai dynamis*, the 'word' that discerns spirits and the 'power' that heals. This is the very atmosphere of the Gospel, and crowds flock to the monk who has become capable of the love that liberates, just as they flocked to Christ.

Monophysitism

This heresy (the word is derived from *mone physis*, single nature) asserts that there is in Christ a single nature only, obviously 'composite', divine-human but with a preponderance of the divine, an absorption of the human into the divine, so that Christ's humanity seems pure transparency without any solidity of its own. Monophysitism developed chiefly in Egypt and Syria, and often in mitigated forms, it was principally a pretext for asserting the autonomy of those regions over against the Romano-Byzantine domination. More deeply, however, one can discern in monophysitism the temptation to a closed 'divinizing', a re-emergence of the extra-biblical spiritualities of the East, as Vladimir Soloviev correctly observed in his book *La Grande Controversie* (Paris 1953 p. 701). The basic intention of Monophysitism in its origins in Alexandria is to celebrate the transfiguration of all things in Christ. That is true eschatologically, 'in mystery', (and in 'the mysteries', the Church's sacraments). Secretly, the world is already the 'burning bush', everything is in God through Christ's deified flesh, a 'glass torch'. But this sacramental indicative requires an imperative in the ascetic, ethical and historical field. What is offered to us in Christ, in the 'mysteries', we have to realize in our freedom, in the 'newness' of the Spirit. Whereas Monophysitism, which is irresponsible, quietistic, almost magical, is interested only in transfiguration, and that immediately. History is done away with or disqualified. Ecclesial experience becomes a pietistic immersion in the divine. Hence the formulae that made their appearance in extreme Monophysite circles, describing the absorption of human nature in the divine nature as a drop of honey in the limitless sea. (We are not far here from the salt doll that had to be dissolved in the ocean of the godhead, according to an Indian fable.) Others maintained that the Word was 'condensed' into flesh, as water solidifies into ice. They always use these images of condensation and fusion (so important also in Origenism) which rob of all meaning both creation *ex nihilo* and the new creation made by the incarnation of the Word. Emanation takes the place of creation, so that the salvation of the world is only its reabsorption into the divine.

The human destiny was at stake there, just as much as in the Arian crisis. This was particularly so in those mitigated forms of Monophysitism that the Emperors of the seventh century favoured in order to consolidate their hold on the Near East that was threatened by the Persians, and later by Islam. These mitigated forms were *monoenergism* – a single energy or operation in Christ – and

especially *monothelitism* – a single will in Christ, the divine will ab-
sorbing his human will. If Christianity had become Monophysite or
Monothelite, the human dimension of history, humanity's tragic and
creative freedom and the reality proper to the created being would
have had difficulty in asserting themselves and converting themselves into Christian humanism, a 'divine-human reality'. Christianity
would have forgotten the Semitic sense of the body and of history that
were defended in their own way by the great exegetes of Antioch,
not without the risk of falling into the opposite error. It would
have forgotten Job's protest, and the wrestling with the 'angel',
and that admirable balance of the human and divine will in Christ
'without confusion or separation', as defined in 451 by the Council
of Chalcedon and in 681 by the Second Council of Constantinople.